CONTROL OF FOOD QUALITY AND FOOD ANALYSIS

An industry–university co-operation Symposium organised under the auspices of the National College of Food Technology (Department of Food Technology), University of Reading, 22–24 March, 1983

THE SYMPOSIUM COMMITTEE

Mrs A. ALFORD
Tate and Lyle PLC, c/o Thames Refinery, Factory Road, Silvertown, London E16 2EW

GORDON G. BIRCH, B.Sc., Ph.D., D.Sc.(Lond.), F.R.S.C., C.Chem., M.R.S.H.
Reader, National College of Food Technology (Department of Food Technology), Food Studies Building, University of Reading, Whiteknights, Reading, Berks. RG6 2AP

J. A. FORD, B.A.(Oxon)
Assistant Bursar (London Road), University of Reading, Whiteknights House, Whiteknights, Reading, Berks. RG6 2AP

M. KEARSLEY, B.Sc.(Lond), Ph.D.(Reading)
Lecturer, National College of Food Technology (Department of Food Technology), Food Studies Building, University of Reading, Whiteknights, Reading, Berks. RG6 2AP

R. D. KING, B.Sc.(Lond), Ph.D.(Lond)
Lecturer, National College of Food Technology (Department of Food Technology), Food Studies Building, University of Reading, Whiteknights, Reading, Berks. RG6 2AP

K. J. PARKER, M.A., D.Phil(Oxon), F.R.S.C., C.Chem.
'Murrens', Reading Road, Crowmarsh Gifford, Wallingford, Oxon. OX10 8EN

E. J. ROLFE, B.Sc., M.Chem.A., F.R.S.C., C.Chem., F.I.F.S.T.
Principal, National College of Food Technology (Department of Food Technology), Food Studies Building, University of Reading, Whiteknights, Reading, Berks. RG6 2AP

Mrs B. A. SHORE
c/o National College of Food Technology (Department of Food Technology), Food Studies Building, University of Reading, Whiteknights, Reading, Berks. RG6 2AP

CONTROL OF FOOD QUALITY AND FOOD ANALYSIS

Edited by

G. G. BIRCH and K. J. PARKER

ELSEVIER APPLIED SCIENCE PUBLISHERS
LONDON and NEW YORK

ELSEVIER APPLIED SCIENCE PUBLISHERS LTD
Ripple Road, Barking, Essex, England

Sole Distributor in the USA and Canada
ELSEVIER SCIENCE PUBLISHING CO., INC.
52 Vanderbilt Avenue, New York, NY 10017, USA

British Library Cataloguing in Publication Data

Control of food quality and food analysis.
1. Food industry and trade—Quality control—Congresses
I. Birch, G. G. II. Parker, K. J.
664′.07 TP372.5

ISBN 0-85334-239-3

WITH 43 ILLUSTRATIONS AND 48 TABLES

Printed in Great Britain by Galliard (Printers) Ltd, Great Yarmouth

List of Contributors

T. J. COOMES

Food Science Division, Ministry of Agriculture, Fisheries and Food, Great Westminster House, Horseferry Road, London SW1P 2AE, UK.

N. D. P. DANG

Process Analysis and Control Section, Leatherhead Food RA, Randalls Road, Leatherhead, Surrey KT22 7RY, UK.

F. O. FLINT

Procter Department of Food Science, University of Leeds, Leeds LS2 9JT, UK.

P. F. FOX

Department of Dairy and Food Chemistry, University College, Cork, Republic of Ireland.

C. S. GUTTERIDGE

Cadbury Schweppes PLC, Group Research, Lord Zuckerman Research Centre, University of Reading, Whiteknights, Reading RG6 2LA, UK.

R. HARPER

29 Harrow Court, Bath Road, Reading RG1 6JF, UK. Formerly Department of Food Science, Food Studies Building, University of Reading, Whiteknights, Reading RG6 2AP, UK.

J. HAWTHORN

Department of Bioscience and Biotechnology, University of Strathclyde, Food Science Division, James P. Todd Building, 131 Albion Street, Glasgow G1 1SD, UK.

K. I. HILDRUM

Department of Food Technology, Norwegian Food Research Institute, PO Box 50, N-1432 Aas-NLH, Norway.

C. H. S. HITCHCOCK

Unilever Research Laboratory, Colworth House, Sharnbrook, Bedford MK44 1LQ, UK.

M. JUL

Danish Meat Products Laboratory, Ministry of Agriculture, Howitzvej 13, 2000 Copenhagen, Denmark.

W. KEMPF

Federal Research Centre of Grain and Potato Processing, PO Box 23, D-4930 Detmold, Federal Republic of Germany.

G. LISIŃSKA

Agricultural Academy, Institute of Storage & Food Technology, ul. Norwida 25, 50-375 Wroclaw, Poland.

H. MARTENS

Department of Food Technology, Norwegian Food Research Institute, PO Box 50, N-1432 Aas-NLH, Norway.

M. MARTENS

Department of Food Technology, Norwegian Food Research Institute, PO Box 50, N-1432, Aas-NLH, Norway.

P. A. MORRISSEY

Department of Dairy and Food Chemistry, University College, Cork, Republic of Ireland.

D. M. MULVIHILL

Department of Dairy and Food Chemistry, University College, Cork, Republic of Ireland.

R. Sawyer

Laboratory of the Government Chemist, Cornwall House, Stamford Street, London SE1 9NQ, UK.

R. S. Shallenberger

Department of Food Science and Technology, New York State Agricultural Experiment Station, Cornell University, Geneva, New York 14456, USA.

R. H. Skinner

49 Farncombe Hill, Godalming, Surrey GU7 2AU, UK. Formerly National College of Food Technology (Department of Food Technology), Food Studies Building, University of Reading, Whiteknights, Reading RG6 2AP, UK.

R. R. Smith

Process Analysis and Control Section, Leatherhead Food RA, Randalls Road, Leatherhead, Surrey KT22 7RY, UK.

G. Sobkowicz

Agricultural Academy, Institute of Storage & Food Technology, ul. Norwida 25, 50-375 Wroclaw, Poland.

R. Spencer

J. Sainsbury Ltd, Stamford House, Stamford Street, London SE1 9LL, UK.

G. Tegge

Federal Research Centre of Grain and Potato Processing, PO Box 23, D-4930 Detmold, Federal Republic of Germany.

A. F. Walker

Department of Food Science, Food Studies Building, University of Reading, Whiteknights, Reading RG6 2AP, UK.

V. Wilton

Mobile Sensory Testing Services Ltd, Kenley House, Station Road West, Oxted, Surrey RH8 9HT, UK.

Contents

	Page
List of Contributors	v
Paper 1. Control of Food Quality and Food Analysis or the Pursuit of Excellence . . . . J. Hawthorn	1
Paper 2. The Nutritional Quality of Food . . . . . A. F. Walker	13
Paper 3. Food Composition and Analytical Accuracy . . R. Sawyer	39
Paper 4. Research on Analysis of Food Quality . . . . K. I. Hildrum, M. Martens and H. Martens	65
Paper 5. A Scientist Looks at Future Prospects for Legislation T. J. Coomes	81
Paper 6. Market Research as a Support for Quality Control V. Wilton	97
Paper 7. Advances in the Light Microscopy of Foods . . F. O. Flint	103
Paper 8. Immunological Methods . . . . . . C. H. S. Hitchcock	117

Paper 9. Microbiological Quality Control 135
R. Spencer

Paper 10. Rapid Methods for Microbiological Quality Control of Foods 157
C. S. Gutteridge

Paper 11. Sensory Quality Control 181
R. Harper

Paper 12. Potato Storage and Quality 203
G. Lisińska and G. Sobkowicz

Paper 13. Factors Affecting the Quality of Dairy Products 213
P. A. Morrissey, P. F. Fox and D. M. Mulvihill

Paper 14. Meat Quality and its Control 257
M. Jul

Paper 15. The Application of Modelling and Control to Food Processing Operations 279
N. D. P. Dang and R. R. Smith

Paper 16. Control of Quality of Starch and Starch Products 291
W. Kempf and G. Tegge

Paper 17. The Evaluation of Canning Processes from External Temperature History 301
R. H. Skinner

Paper 18. Some Aspects of the Chemical Basis of Fruit and Vegetable Quality 311
R. S. Shallenberger

Index 325

PROCEEDINGS OF PREVIOUS SYMPOSIA

Glucose Syrups and Related Carbohydrates, edited by G. G. Birch, L. F. Green and C. B. Coulson, 1970.

Sweetness and Sweeteners, edited by G. G. Birch, L. F. Green and C. B. Coulson, 1971.

Health and Food, edited by G. G. Birch, L. F. Green and L. G. Plaskett, 1972.

Molecular Structure and Function of Food Carbohydrate, edited by G. G. Birch and L. F. Green, 1973.

Vitamin C, edited by G. G. Birch and K. J. Parker, 1974.

Food from Waste, edited by G. G. Birch, J. T. Worgan and K. J. Parker, 1975.

Intermediate Moisture Foods, edited by R. Davies, G. G. Birch and K. J. Parker, 1976.

Sensory Properties of Foods, edited by G. G. Birch, J. G. Brennan and K. J. Parker, 1977.

Sugar, Science and Technology, edited by G. G. Birch and K. J. Parker, 1978.

Food and Health: Science and Technology, edited by G. G. Birch and K. J. Parker, 1979.

Enzymes and Food Processing, edited by G. G. Birch, N. Blakebrough and K. J. Parker, 1980.

Nutritive Sweeteners, edited by G. G. Birch and K. J. Parker, 1981.

Dietary Fibre, edited by G. G. Birch and K. J. Parker, 1982.

All published by Elsevier Applied Science Publishers.

1

Control of Food Quality and Food Analysis or the Pursuit of Excellence

J. HAWTHORN

*Department of Bioscience and Biotechnology,
University of Strathclyde, Glasgow, UK*

ABSTRACT

About 100 years ago Ralph Waldo Emerson said: 'If a man write a better book, preach a better sermon or make a better mousetrap than his neighbour, tho' he build his house in the woods, the world will make a beaten path to his door'. This homespun truth illuminated the industrial awakening of the USA and many hold that it also made America the great power which she is today. Yet she also invented the slick salesman, and in turn she was to invent the science of marketing to put an apparently healthy skin on what had sometimes been a rotten peach.

Food quality can be considered from the viewpoint of either of these extremes. Historically, the food industry was a rotten peach as recently as 125 years ago. Starting with the first Food and Drugs Act of 1860, successive governments have tightened the legislative noose, despite cries of strangulation from the industry, to the point at which the victim loves the rope, having learned that when everyone is forced to be good, the whole industry and its customers benefit.

Of course all this is an old story and in the past half-century the industry has become ethical in its approach, fighting the cause of honest food at an honest price. Our hurt when the sins of our debauched forebears are thrown at us for poisoning the public with preservatives and giving them allergies with additives is sincere. To be latter-day saints in the service of the community and to be branded as sinners and money grabbers is hard to take. There are those who have an interest in denigrating the industry by making bombs of half-truths.

Attempts to correct the errors attract the Hamlet reaction: 'The lady doth protest too much, methinks'. For two days the nuts and bolts of food quality control will be considered by the saints. For one night, the first night, a sinner seeks leave to whisper sweet heresies, if it be heresy to suggest that 40 years of quality control in our industry has given us powerful weapons to counter the bombs of girning critics.

INTRODUCTION

If we are at our lowest intellectual ebb after supper and before night-caps, it follows that conference organisers, with this evening spot to fill, have the problem of finding a speaker guaranteed to impose no intellectual effort whatsoever on his audience. Having defined the problems thus it was easy to find the right speaker. 'A Professor', wrote the poet W. H. Auden, 'is someone who talks in other people's sleep'. Choose a professor of food science to give an authentic ring to the process, flatter him by describing the slot as a Keynote lecture, and you have the neatest of solutions to an intractable problem.

It was with thoughts such as these that I settled down to the task of preparing this talk. Just over a century ago the American writer and wit Ralph Waldo Emerson gave a lecture in which he is reputed to have said: 'If a man write a better book, preach a better sermon or make a better mousetrap than his neighbour, tho' he build his house in the woods, the world will make a beaten path to his door'. Just a few weeks ago I had a telephone call from a colleague on some technical matter. Now this man, having made several visits to Japan and South East Asia, became interested in the microbiology of soya sauce: so interested that he set a sequence of research students to study the problem. The students were successful, he concluded that the traditional process was very poor, and patented his own scientific technique. With help from others and publicity from local press and television he opened a soya sauce factory which came on stream some months ago. As our telephone call finished I said to him: 'By the way, how goes the factory?'. 'We're making plenty of sauce,' he said, 'but it's not true about the better mousetrap.'

Over the past 20 years I have been involved directly or indirectly with the beginnings of seven small food or food related businesses. The first of these I tried to start myself at the age of 32. I got out without losing any money but I learned a lot that had nothing to do with food science. In the other six cases, which included chocolate confectionery, food preservation, sterilisable pouches, catering, shellfish farming and a whisky liqueur, I was drawn in to help or give advice. In every case, those who started these companies thought that they could produce a better mousetrap. Of the seven, only one has survived. The others failed each for different reasons. Good technology is not enough. Quality is a complex of concepts. Success depends on the understanding of this.

THE PURSUIT OF EXCELLENCE

At a recent BFMIRA lunch I found myself seated beside a stranger with whom I fell into an instant conversation which turned to early retirement. He told me of an acquaintance of his, the former managing director of a large industrial operation, who, forced into retirement as a result of successive take-overs at the age of 56, gave himself two months to recover from the shock. To pass the time he turned to his boyhood hobby of woodcarving. He carved a horse. When he was done, he looked at the three foot high model and wondered what to do with it. It was then he had his great idea. Suppose he were to mount his fine carving as a hobby-horse, get advice about replica leather reins and saddle and try to sell it. When he had finished it was a splendid thing, correct to the last detail and better far than even the best hobby-horse of his childhood. He was offered a price which totally surprised him. 'Now he regards himself as a truly happy man' said my new acquaintance, 'He has more work to do than he can ever finish, every horse he carves is different; he only works when the mood is on him but he enjoys it so much his production keeps rising; he employs no one; has no union troubles; no factory inspectors; no Safety at Work Act; no Security of Employment Act; and he makes a good living to supplement his already-generous pension. For the first time in his life he feels free, and all because he makes the best hobby-horses in the world.'

'Maybe Emerson was right after all', I began to think. Somewhere between the extremes of scientific soya sauce and hand-carved hobby-horses there seemed to be an elusive truth seeking to be grasped. It was associated somehow with the pursuit of excellence, which after all appears to be our mission when we talk of 'Control of Food Quality and Food Analysis'. Or is it?

In the academic world these days 'excellence' is the fashion word which is rapidly replacing the vulgarity of Mr Wilson's 'white-hot technology'. It is even near-equal in competition with the term 'biotechnology', a word which had a clear and useful meaning a decade ago and which now has almost as many meanings as users. If you are a scientific civil servant it usually means the definition given in the Spinks Report; if you are a Member of Parliament it means the scientific miracle which will bring the party again into power; and if you are a working scientist it means patches of lush green grass in an arid desert of research grants. If these confusions give rise to sweet verdure in idiosyncratic locations, this is no concern of mine. However, it helps us to define academic centres of excellence as places of lush vegetation. Please hold that thought in your minds, since we must needs return to it. Meantime I want to discuss two medical problems.

GASTRIC CANCER, CEREBRAL HAEMORRHAGE AND FOOD QUALITY

For 30 years or more, cancer of the stomach has been related to nutritional or dietary factors. Between 20 and 30 different hypotheses have been put forward, some positively and some negatively linked to elements in diet. For example, high-starch and low-protein diets, smoked foods, pickled vegetables, the use of dried and salted fish or meat, and diets low in fresh fruit and vegetables have all been held to be contributory factors by various groups of research workers. Equally, high intakes of fresh fruits and vegetables, high intakes of vitamin C, high fat intakes, the use of milk in the diet, and the presence of selenium as a trace element in food have all been held to be protective factors. Yet while the statistics within any one country might tend to support one of these proposals as against another, comparisons of one country with another showed no consistent pattern. For example, smoked food was considered to be a causal factor in gastric cancer in Iceland but this would not apply in Japan where smoking of food is rare. Yet in both countries the incidence of this illness is high. Milk, in many countries has been held to be a protective factor, and the hypothesis looks good until one considers Finland where milk intakes and gastric cancer rates are both high. After years of such studies there has been a distinct tendency to suggest that cancer of the stomach is a multi-factorial illness.

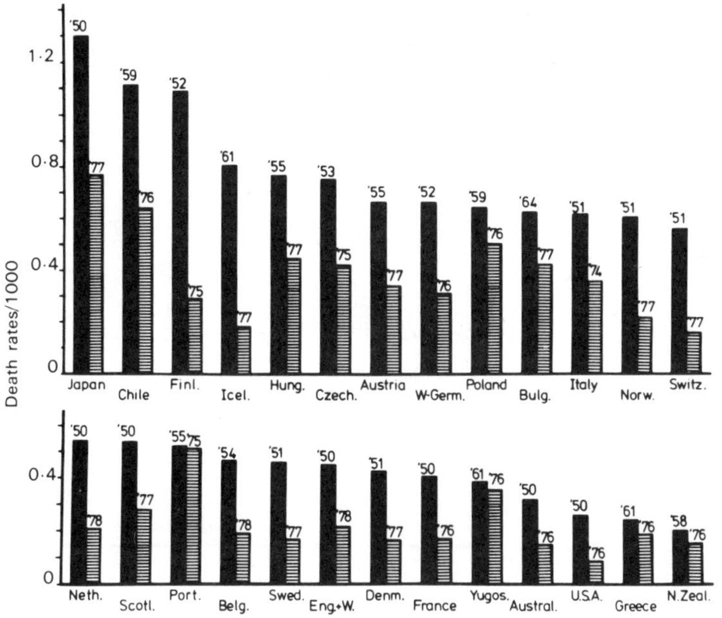

FIG. 1. Time variation and gastric cancer death rates in 26 countries. The numbers at the top of each double column show the first and last available year for the given country.

There is no effective treatment for gastric cancer, and the five-year survival rate after diagnosis is much the same as it was 30 years ago. However, in almost every country studied, the death rate has dropped in recent years (Fig. 1).

Since no effective treatment is available and since the illness is linked with diet, it seems that the falling incidence must be linked to dietary change over the period represented by the figures. Joossens, an epidemiologist working in the public health department of the University of Leuven in Belgium, noticed by chance that there appeared to be a link between cerebrovascular accidents (that is to say, strokes) and gastric cancer. As the years passed, he worked this out in detail for some 12 countries and obtained the results shown in Fig. 2. The link seems so strong and the statistical confidence limits so high that it is reasonable to infer that a common dietary factor is involved in both cases. But the figures start to show a steady but continuing drift from 1972 onwards. Suddenly to Joossens, everything became clear. Salt in diet is known to be a contributory

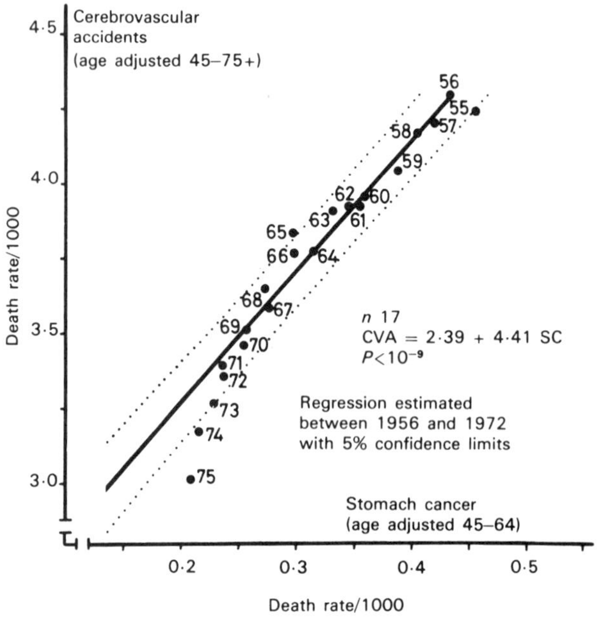

FIG. 2. Gastric cancer and stroke. Each point is the average of 12 countries, between the years 1956 and 1975. (From reference 1.)

factor in essential hypertension, and essential hypertension is the major cause of strokes. But for each country studied, and in any year between the years 1956 and 1975, there was about one death from gastric cancer for every eleven deaths from strokes. And in all 12 countries the incidence of both illnesses was declining. Looking at a broader range of 26 countries there were two in which the decline had been very small, namely Portugal and Yugoslavia. Joossens offers no evidence for Yugoslavia but does show that in Portugal the intake of salt is still very high.

But perhaps his most convincing evidence is from his own country, Belgium. The Belgian Ministry of Health mounted a systematic campaign through the mass media to persuade Belgians to take sensible steps to steadily reduce their salt intakes and the results were monitored between 1966 and 1980 by urine collections from 2493 individuals. From these it can be shown that the campaign led to a drop in average salt intake over the period of just under 40%. Over the same period, the mortality figures for strokes and gastric cancer fell faster in Belgium than in any other Common Market country. There is nothing so convincing in confirming a hypothesis as experiment.[1]

The decline in gastric cancer rates in the USA began as far back as 1930 and perhaps a little earlier. In Japan it did not start until 1960. In Finland the decrease has been dramatic, the mortality in 1975 being rather less than a quarter of that in 1952. In Iceland the figures are even more dramatic. In Sweden, the figures have always been fairly low, but even here, the 1977 figures for mortality are less than half the 1951 figure.

Joossens is quite clear in his conclusions. The incidence of gastric cancer and strokes declines as salt as a preservative is replaced with refrigerated and frozen foods. It is the unique common factor in the dietary patterns of both conditions.[1] He pointed out that the decline in USA began at just about the time that Birdseye introduced the concept of quick freezing, and that the Japanese figures began to decline in 1960 at the commencement of Japan's industrial success. And the argument persists for other countries such as the UK, where the death rates for both these illnesses have more than halved since frozen foods began to become an important item of diet in the early 1950s.

The introduction of frozen foods was a major step forward in improving food quality. But in the decade before it began, other steps had been taken which were also to lead to improvements in food quality.

In the 1920s tuberculosis was the dread in people's minds, and milk was known to carry the organism. In 1929, Dr Norman Wright of the Hannah Institute published figures for the incidence of tuberculosis infection in the milk supplies of Edinburgh, Glasgow and Aberdeen, the percentage of infected samples from each of these cities being 8·5, 2·6 and 5·5. At that time, in the UK, the death rate from tuberculosis was about 2000, with 4000 new cases being reported per annum. Pasteurisation had been developed in the USA by Bitter as early as 1890 as a means of extending the storage life of milk and it was known that, when properly applied, the process destroyed the dangerous tuberculosis bacillus as well as other pathogens likely to find their way into the milk supply. The process involved holding milk at a temperature of between 145 and 150 °F for 30 min after which it had to be cooled. In Scotland there was much opposition, vocal but uninformed, it being held that the process in some way damaged the essential goodness of the milk. The Hannah Research Institute saw the idea of having tuberculin-tested herds as the answer to the problem and in 1929 began an investigation into the feasibility of eradicating the disease in cattle. As a consequence, Ayrshire became the first county in the UK to be free from bovine tuberculosis. The invention of the plate heat exchanger by Richard Seligman in 1923 opened up the possibility of making pasteurisation a semi-continuous or continuous process with heat recovery systems cooling the heated milk with the incoming milk. This greatly reduced fuel costs and made for more compact processing systems better adapted to the needs of large dairy companies. It was soon found that the job could be done better and with less thermal damage to the heat-labile milk constituents by using much higher temperatures with a dwell-time of only a few seconds but the idea, for which the plate heat-exchanger was well suited, was to lie fallow until 1941 when the UK government legislated in favour of high-temperature short-term processes.[2]

At around the same period, Dr John Boyd Orr (as he then was) published his report *Food, Health and Income*,[3] which showed that a substantial section of the UK population were suffering from serious malnutrition as a result of incomes too low to allow them to purchase an adequately balanced diet. It was a follow-up to earlier work by Orr and David Lubbock in which large-scale supplementation of children's diet with school milk led to dramatic improvements in their health. Orr was the son of an Ayrshire family, brought up in the Calvinist tradition of the presbyterian religion. His hatred of needless suffering was kindled by the squalor and misery of the Glasgow slums he encountered during his student days and the tragedy of the lice-ridden, malnourished children he tried to teach when the Glasgow School Board offered him his first job in a slum school. These early experiences launched him from teaching to medicine, then from medicine to nutrition and led, not only to the founding of the Rowett Research Institute, but also to his later advocacy of the cause of the undernourished throughout the world. The Food and Agriculture Organisation of the United Nations was a direct result, its existence proposed and its early structure designed by Orr, and it is by this, his greatest achievement that he will be remembered. But his first major achievement, the Rowett Institute, lives on in Scotland, and continues to influence, not only the prosperity of its farmlands which is its official function, but also the pattern of scientific thought on agriculture, food and nutrition.

I have limited myself to the effects of improvements in food quality leading to dramatic improvements in the incidence of three diseases and to the equally dramatic improvement in the health of children and young people particularly amongst the poorer sections of our community. But I have not exhausted the list. Goitre and rickets are obviously of equal importance but there are others of lesser importance but vital to sufferers from diabetes, coeliac disease, cystic fibrosis, diverticular disease, idiopathic steatorrhoea and some more generalised conditions where the well-being of the patient and his or her quality of life are enhanced by the intake of technically engineered foods designed to restore metabolic imbalances.

This long-term link between food quality and public health is something about which food scientists and technologists have every right to be proud. Fair criticism of the food industry and of food science and technology is to be welcomed. If much has been achieved, much remains to be done, and constructive criticism may help to point the way. However, some of the criticism we receive is unfair, unsound, based on uninformed preconceived ideas and factually incorrect. When criticism is honest, if misinformed, we can equally honestly counter it by the correct information. But often this is too dull to interest the reporter. Scandal has news value but truth is less interesting. We should not fear to be propagandists for the achievements of our subject and our industry because we have much to be proud of. That is why I wished to use this occasion to stress the positive benefits that have been achieved through improvements in food quality. Moreover, I have only chosen to talk about one group of these as they relate to illness. There are others of the kind we shall be discussing over the next two days and I do not need to recapitulate them.

These defences are strong when the attack is honest. When it is dishonest and politically motivated the problem becomes formidable. Let me give an example. The Politics of Health Group have recently published a pamphlet entitled *Food and Profit—It Makes You Sick*.[4] The theme it attaches to the food industry is (page 7): 'Profit comes first, health is incidental', and you can purchase this little gem for a modest 50 p. It is nicely produced, well printed and contains some 14 photographs of food products or food advertisements. It is written with journalistic skill and the early pages discuss obesity, dental caries and life expectancy in a rather slanted but not too unreasonable manner. On the fifth and six pages the attack on the food industry begins with a series of minor misstatements or biased inferences, but as the text progresses these become overt.

Under the heading 'More Than You Bargained For—Food Additives' they open fire by claiming that harmful food additives are added for profit (not a word about the millions of pounds spent on testing under official scrutiny to ensure that additives are safe), and go on to press the attack by claiming that nitrites could be replaced in meat curing by ascorbic acid as a protection against botulism (untrue), nitrites producing nitrosamines which cause cancer. The absurdity of the inferences may not be spotted by the lay reader and he may even be impressed by the paragraph quoted below:

> If it were sold as food, the breast milk of many American mothers would be banned because the level of additives from the mother's diet exceeded the permitted amounts. And the average corpse in the USA contains such highly concentrated additives that it too would be banned. A recent report from the UK undertaking industry revealed that today's corpses keep much longer than they used to because of the preservatives in our diet.

The counter to attacks of this sort is to avoid the Persil syndrome, to make no attempt to prove that the food industry or for that matter, food scientists and technologists are whiter-than-white. We are not. We have similar strengths and weaknesses to any other social grouping. But weaknesses or no, we can rightly claim that modern science applied to foodstuffs has virtually eliminated some ghastly diseases; has contributed to the increase in average life-span which we all enjoy; has provided us with any food at any time of the year in an almost infinite variety of forms and from almost any part of the world at prices we can pay.

It can rightly be said that these fine words only apply to industrialised societies which make up around one quarter of the world's population. Yet food scientists and technologists together with nutritionists are eager and willing and knowledgeable to remedy this unhappy situation. But those who have worked in the field know that the limiting factors are most often poverty (even in the poorest countries, the rich do not starve), lack of economic infrastructure (without transport, a local surplus cannot be taken to a hungry area two or three miles away) or political, for without a stable government capable of enforcing a degree of order there is no framework to ensure an improvement in food supply.

IS EXCELLENCE AN ILLUSION?

In my introduction I described academic centres of excellence as places of lush vegetation in the arid desert of research grants. The word is supposed to describe situations of great merit. But when we unthinkingly try to apply the idea of excellence to a food system we may easily fall into error. Food requirements vary from person to person, and from circumstance to circumstance, and may even vary from country to country. In this field there are no absolutes.

Defining the objectives of food analysis is at least easier than defining those of food quality control. The philosophical objective is the improvement of the human condition by improvement in the quality of the human food supply. It is when we consider what we mean by 'the quality of human food' that we encounter difficulties. In the market place this simply means its sales appeal; in the pages of nutrition journals it means its health appeal; and in the minds of toxicologists it means its safety. But to the majority of our citizens it means value for money.

Because of this diversity, the Mastership of Food Control (MFC), introduced about six years ago as a five-part system of examinations for those who would aspire to the highest ranks of our profession, is of especial significance, because the qualification represents the end-point in an educational process designed to enable the candidate to reconcile these various meanings, and to synthesise a modern approach which integrates them. It is, of course, something new and new ideas attract critics. It seems to me to be inevitable that it, or something closely akin to it, will become a statutory requirement in Europe, but this is many years ahead. In the meantime, it is a Mount Everest, something to be climbed because it is there, but also because those who have climbed it are gradually producing an elite which cannot be ignored.

Food quality has many facets. Their measure is complex. That is why the mastery of this subject requires the searching examination system of the MFC and conferences such as this to amplify selected aspects of the whole.

REFERENCES

1. Joossens, J. V. and Geboers, J. (1981). *Proc. Nutr. Soc.*, **40**, 37.
2. Hawthorn, J. (1978). *Proc. Nutr. Soc.*, **37**, 211.
3. Orr, J. B. (1936). *Food, Health and Income*, Macmillan, London.
4. Politics of Health Group (1981). *Food and Profit—It Makes You Sick*, Politics of Health Group, London.

2

The Nutritional Quality of Food

ANN F. WALKER

Department of Food Science, University of Reading, UK

ABSTRACT

The purpose of good nutrition is to promote health and general well-being. However, the nutritional quality of food is normally measured in terms of its ability to satisfy human nutrient requirements. Even in the richer nations of the world, the diet may not provide some nutrients at adequate levels for certain groups of people.

The nutrient composition of a food depends on the raw material, as well as the effects of processing and storage. Some of these effects may be advantageous and render nutrients more biologically available, while others may have a detrimental effect. Potential losses of nutrients due to processing and storage are well documented for traditional processes. Less is known about nutrient loss for newer techniques such as microwave cooking and irradiation, or within the home or institution. Published data on nutrient loss tend to relate to single food items and rarely to entire diets.

In many countries, such as the UK, health problems caused by lack of nutrient intake are of minor importance compared to those, such as coronary heart disease, which tend to be associated with overconsumption of some major food components. Dietary guidelines and goals have now been published in several countries, in an attempt to reduce the size of the problem. These recommendations suggest that overconsumption is encouraged by food manufacturers, who provide highly palatable food containing too much fat and sugar and not enough dietary fibre. However, the food industry provides foods in accordance with consumer demands, which are determined by a number of factors, of which nutrition is not the most important, although it could become more significant in the future. In the final analysis it is the consumer who determines nutrient intake and not the food manufacturer.

THE NUTRITIONAL ADEQUACY OF THE DIET

To be adequately nourished, in addition to a supply of energy, the human body needs to be supplied with some 40 or so nutrients at specific levels in the diet. Single food items are often judged by their ability to provide all of these nutrients, but in practice they would only be expected to provide part of them in a diet. If the diet provides a nutrient in excess of requirements, then the content of that nutrient in a single food item may be irrelevant. However, if a nutrient is supplied at inadequate or marginal levels in the diet, then care is needed during food processing and storage to ensure its maximum retention.

An assessment of the nutritional adequacy of the diet is normally carried out by comparing the nutrient content of a diet (calculated from data on food intake) with the recommended daily amount (RDA) for specific groups of people. While such comparisons cannot be used as evidence that an individual is undernourished (this can only be confirmed with appropriate clinical examination and biochemical testing), it can be used as an indicator that a population may be marginally nourished or undernourished for that nutrient.

Table 1 shows the nutritional value of household food in the UK as a percentage of the RDA for 1975 and 1980.[1] These data are derived from averaged intakes for different income groups in different parts of the country and are compared with an averaged RDA value taken from Department of Health and Social Security (1969)[2] for 1975 and Department of Health and Social Security (1979)[3] for 1980. Values for energy intake are below the RDA, but these intake figures do not include food consumed outside the home. Of the other nutrients shown in Table 1, only vitamin D is below the RDA in 1975. As this nutrient is also produced in the body, the Department of Health and Social Security (1979)[3] give no dietary recommendation. Iron for both 1975 and 1980 is only marginally provided in the diet. As these are averaged figures, they imply that a large number of people may be underprovided with this nutrient by the diet. Indeed, if households with two or more children are considered, then even averaged values

TABLE 1

THE NUTRITIONAL VALUE OF HOUSEHOLD FOOD IN THE UK AS PERCENTAGE OF RECOMMENDED INTAKE (ADAPTED FROM REFERENCE 1)

	1975	*1980*
Energy	96	99
Protein[a]	185	176
Calcium	186	173
Iron	105	105
Thiamin	122	126
Riboflavin	126	139
Nicotinic acid	185	188
Vitamin C	177	200
Vitamin A	198	193
Vitamin D	82	NA

[a] Minimum requirement.
NA, Not applicable.

for iron from food consumed within the household, are below the RDA.[1]

The National Food Survey data given in Table 1 are based on records of foods entering households in the UK. To obtain further information on the foods that people eat it is necessary to examine data obtained from individual weighed dietary surveys. These have been shown to give good reproducibility when carried out with care.[4] Data from many parts of the Western World show, for certain human groups, that some nutrients are supplied in the diet in inadequate levels with respect to RDA (e.g. reference 5). Table 2 shows the daily intake of some nutrients for 67 British female students, aged 18–22 yr, studying food science at Reading University. Data were calculated using *McCance and Widdowson's The Composition of Foods*[6] from a 6-day weighed dietary survey carried out from 1980 to 1983.

The averaged value for energy intake was below the RDA, although not as far below as Pao and Mickle[5] had found for women of the same age group in the USA. The range of values for individuals in Table 2 was wide, extending from 947 to 2710 kcal. This variation accounts for some of the variation in the other nutrient intakes. Calcium, thiamin, riboflavin and vitamin C showed averaged intake values above the RDA, but the lowest value of the range was well below the RDA. For iron, zinc and folic acid even the mean values

TABLE 2

DAILY INTAKE OF SOME NUTRIENTS FOR 67 BRITISH FEMALE STUDENTS, AGED 18–22 YR AT READING UNIVERSITY FROM A 6-DAY WEIGHED DIETARY SURVEY (DATA COLLECTED 1980–1983, AND NUTRIENTS CALCULATED USING REFERENCE 6)

	RDA[a]	*Intake of nutrient*	
		Mean	*Range*
Energy (kcal)	2 150	1 842	947–2 710
Calcium (mg)	500	826	333–1 310
Iron (mg)	12	11·4	4·7–27·1
Zinc (mg)	15[b]	8·7	3·7–14·9
Thiamin (mg)	0·9	1·1	0·5–2·2
Riboflavin (mg)	1·3	1·7	0·7–5·2
Vitamin C (mg)	30	72	17–208
Folic acid (free, μg)	300[c]	74	25–291

[a] Reference 3.
[b] Reference 7.
[c] Total folate.

were below the RDA. As there is no RDA given for zinc in the UK,[3] the value given in Table 2 is drawn from the RDA for the USA.[7] Interest in zinc nutrition has increased in recent years, following findings of evidence of zinc deficiency in adolescent males in Iran[8] and biochemical evidence of zinc deficiency in children in the USA.[9] In fact, most dietary studies in the Western World have reported zinc levels that do not meet these RDA of 15 mg/head/day, indeed, the current level of zinc intake in the USA is 12·5 mg/head/day.[10]

For folic acid (Table 2), the RDA given by Department of Health and Social Security (1979)[3] is expressed in terms of total folate, while that calculated using *McCance and Widdowson's The Composition of Foods*[6] gives values as free folic acid. In general terms, free folate is approximately half the value of total folate for most foodstuffs.[11] Even taking this into consideration, the mean value of 74 μg/day for the women students is much lower than the RDA, and the extremely low value of 25 μg/day at the bottom of the range for the individual intakes may give cause for concern. Discrepancies between the intake of folate and the RDA have also been noted by Bates *et al.*,[11] who conclude that caution is needed in interpreting these discrepancies until more is known about the nutritional role of the various forms of folate.

Most of the foods we eat are processed in one way or another. In 1980 £23 230 million was spent on food for home consumption in the UK, of which 72 % was spent on processed food.[12] As some nutrients may not be provided in the diet in adequate amounts for some groups of people, it is important that nutrient retention of food is maximised during processing. For some nutrients, such as protein, which are present in our diets in excess, changes brought about by processing, such as the decreased bioavailability of lysine, are not important from

TABLE 3

FACTORS DETERMINING THE SIGNIFICANCE OF NUTRIENT CHANGES DURING PROCESSING

1. The nutrient (the quantity and stability)	
2. The nutritional status of the group:	
Children Pregnant women Elderly Invalids	Iron Folic acid Calcium Vitamin D
Vegetarians	Vitamin D Iron Vitamin B_{12}
Malnourished populations	Energy Protein Vitamin A Iron Iodine

a nutritional point of view. For other nutrients, such as iron and folic acid, which may be inadequately supplied by diet, it is important to offer food processed in the best possible way to preserve these nutrients. Nutrient deficiencies caused, for example, by lack of energy or protein in the diet, are usually associated with poorer countries of the world and are not normally encountered in industrialised countries. Table 3 gives a summary of the possible nutritional significance to specific human groups of nutrient changes brought about by processing.

Effect of Processing on the Nutrient Content of Food

The effects of processing are normally considered in terms of their detrimental effects on the nutrient composition of food. There are, however, some beneficial effects. Foods are processed to improve their sensory qualities, to destroy pathogenic organisms and for preservation purposes. At the same time the nutritional quality may be increased by improved digestibility of (a) starch due to gelatinisation and of (b) protein due to denaturation and destruction of toxic substances.[13] Heat degradation of the cell walls of plant foods may lead to increased availability of nutrients such as carotenoids. Other forms of processing which have beneficial effects on nutritional quality of foods are fermentation which is known to increase the content of the B-complex vitamins, and germination which leads to increased vitamin C content of grains.[14]

The detrimental effects of processing on the nutritional quality of food are summarised in Table 4. Dry matter loss may be considerable

TABLE 4

LOSS OF NUTRITIONAL QUALITY OF FOOD DUE TO PROCESSING

Major components:
Dry matter (milling, peeling etc., leaching)
Dietary fibre (milling, peeling, etc.)
Protein quality (excessive heat treatment)
Sugar (leaching)
Lipids (oxidation → rancidity and loss of acceptability)
Minor components:
Water-soluble vitamins (milling, peeling, etc., leaching, instability)
Fat-soluble vitamins (instability)
Minerals (milling, peeling, etc.)

for some processes, but often these losses are inadequately reported in the literature.[14] Dry matter loss is of considerable importance with respect to cereals, which still provide a large proportion of the diet in the industrialised world (one-third of the total energy of the diet in the UK in 1980[1]). Because of the large quantities eaten, loss of nutrients due to milling of cereals has a large effect on the overall nutrient content of the diet. Besides loss of niacin, thiamin, iron and calcium, which are made up by nutrient restoration in most countries, there is a large loss of dietary fibre, as illustrated by values of 9·6 and 3·0 %, respectively, for dietary fibre contents of whole wheat flour and 72 %

extracted wheat flour.[6] The significance to health of removing dietary fibre from cereal foods has become apparent over recent years (see, for example, reference 15).

Leaching is a process which leads to considerable loss of minerals and water-soluble vitamins. Mabesa and Baldwin[16] found, when comparing microwave cooking with conventional cooking of peas, that there was no advantage with respect to total ascorbic acid retention if the same amount of water was used for both forms of cooking (77 and 78% retention, respectively). However, microwave cooking did show an advantage if the peas were cooked without added water (87% retention).

Karel[17] has summarised the various factors which affect the stability of nutrients in food. As far as heat processing is concerned, the most important chemical changes from a nutritional point of view are those occurring to vitamins. Some vitamins are more heat-labile than others; in particular thiamin is very susceptible in this respect. Loss of vitamin activity may also depend on the amount of oxygen present in the foodstuff (for vitamins A and C) or the amount of exposure to light (for riboflavin and to some extent vitamins A and C). The vitamin C content of fruit and vegetables is often used to monitor the effects of various processes. The combined effects of enzyme degradation and susceptibility to oxidation and leaching, make the vitamin C content of foods particularly susceptible to processing.

Throughout the literature there are many examples showing the effects of processing, especially thermal processing, on the retention of vitamins in foods. Table 5 gives one such example[18] in which a comparison is made between frozen/cooked and canned vegetables for water-soluble vitamins. The canning process leads to greater mean loss of vitamins than freezing and cooking, but for each mean value there is a wide range of values. In recent years, attempts have been made to formulate mathematical relationships to be able to predict and optimise nutrient retention during thermal processing. These are described in reviews, for example, references 19 and 20. So far these mathematical relationships have found little practical use due to a number of factors.

Firstly, there is the wide variability in composition of raw materials.[21] As an example of this, Table 6, taken from Hagen *et al.*[22] shows the variability in vitamin C and A contents of canned Californian tomato juice from 1972 to 1975. While some of this

TABLE 5

COMPARATIVE LOSSES OF VITAMINS FROM VEGETABLES DURING CANNING AND FREEZING (REPRINTED FROM *Food Technol.*, 1977, **31**(12), 32–8. COPYRIGHT © BY INSTITUTE OF FOOD TECHNOLOGISTS)

Processing/ preparation	*No. of vegetables examined*		*Loss of vitamins compared to fresh-cooked (%)*			
			Thiamin	*Riboflavin*	*Niacin*	*Vitamin C*
Frozen, boiled, drained	10	*Mean:*	20	24	24	26
		Range:	0–61	0–45	0–56	0–78
Canned, drained	7	*Mean:*	67	42	49	51
		Range:	56–83	14–50	31–65	28–67

variability, particularly for the vitamin C, may be accounted for by differences in the processing conditions, a large part is due to variability of the composition of tomato juice. This is emphasised by the wide range of values for vitamin A in Table 6, as the levels of vitamin A are not greatly affected by thermal processing.

Secondly, analytical problems may also make prediction of nutrient loss due to processing difficult. While established analytical methods for some vitamins may be relatively straightforward, others, such as that for folacin or vitamin D, were cumbersome in the past. Although vitamin analysis has undergone something of a comeback in recent years, particularly with the introduction of high-pressure

TABLE 6

VARIATION IN VITAMIN C AND A CONTENTS OF CANNED TOMATO JUICE (REPRINTED FROM *Hortscience*, 1979, **14**, 251–6 WITH PERMISSION OF THE PUBLISHERS)

Year	*No. lots*	*Vitamin C (mg/100 g)*		*Vitamin A (IU/100 g)*	
		Mean	*Range*	*Mean*	*Range*
1972	18	12·1	7·9–21·6	400	231–519
1973	23	11·6	4·3–15·5	588	478–679
1974	23	9·5	2·0–18·7	516	374–657
1975	26	9·1	2·0–16·4	497	369–597

liquid chromatography (HPLC) techniques,[23] much research is still needed to make these methods robust and reproducible before they are suitable to be used as routine quality control measures in industry by relatively unskilled technicians. To complicate matters for the analyst, nutrients may be present in foods in a number of chemical forms (Table 7), each having a different nutrient potency.

TABLE 7
SUBSTANCES CONTRIBUTING TO NUTRIENT ACTIVITY

Nutrient	*Substance*
Vitamin C	Ascorbic acid
	Dehydroascorbic acid
Vitamin B_6	Pyridoxine
	Pyridoxal
	Pyridoxamine
Niacin	Niacin
	Tryptophan
Vitamin E	8 {Tocopherols
	Tocotrienols
Vitamin A	Retinol
	β-Carotene
	α-Carotene
	γ-Carotene
Methionine	Methionine
	Cystine (partly)
Phenylalanine	Phenylalanine
	Tyrosine (partly)

Thirdly, nutrients may be degraded by more than one mechanism, each proceeding at a different rate and influenced differently by reaction conditions.[19] If the nutrient is degraded by an enzyme, as ascorbic acid is by ascorbase, then enzyme inactivation must also be considered. Some nutrients may be protected from degradation within specific food products by other components. Thus, folates are often found in combined forms which are biologically active and more stable than the free form.[24]

Although prediction of nutrient loss is not an easy matter, empirical studies have shown that because of the close relationship between the temperature dependence of quality factors such as colour, texture, vitamins and flavour, processes optimised for organoleptic quality attributes are also optimal for nutrient retention. In most industrialised countries, food processing practice is already optimised for organoleptic properties, therefore one would not expect to be able to bring about large improvements in nutritional quality, by changing processing conditions. However, slight improvements can result from modifications based on optimisation techniques as shown with studies to compare nutrient retention in retort pouches with conventional canning. Rizvi and Acton[25] showed that for pouches and cans of equivalent capacity, the retention of thiamin in sweet potato purée (processed to $F_0 = 8{\cdot}0 \pm 0{\cdot}3$ min at 121·1 °C) was 77 and 60 %, respectively, compared with the unprocessed product.

Nutrient loss in recently developed processing methods

While a considerable amount of data exists on the processing losses of nutrients due to well-established commercial practices such as canning and freezing, less information is available on the vitamin losses due to recently developed techniques. These include microwave thawing and cooking, aseptic canning, irradiation, slow cookers, 'boil-in-bag' techniques and various continuous steamers and cookers for large-scale catering. The studies which do exist usually compare the new technique with a more conventional method. As far as microwave cooking is concerned, Klein *et al.*[26] showed (Table 8)

TABLE 8

VITAMIN C AND FOLACIN CONTENT OF SPINACH (REPRINTED FROM *J. Food Sci.*, 1981, **46**, 640–1. COPYRIGHT © BY INSTITUTE OF FOOD TECHNOLOGISTS)

Treatment	*Total vitamin C (mg/g)**	*Total folacin (μg/g)**
None	4·05 a	26·0 NS
Microwave cooked (100 ml water, 6·5 min)	1·83 b	26·6 NS
Conventionally cooked (100 ml water, 7 min)	2·12 b	19·5 NS

* Dry basis.
NS, Not significant.
Values with unlike (a, b) letters are significantly different ($p < 0{\cdot}05$).

that very little folate is lost from spinach cooked either conventionally or in a microwave oven. Hall and Liu[27] showed no advantage of microwave cooking over roasting in a conventional oven at 204 °C for thiamin retention for broiler chicken.

Food irradiated to an average 'dose' of 1 Mrad or less has recently been declared wholesome for human consumption without further testing, by a Joint Expert Committee convened by the World Health Organisation (WHO).[28] In future the use of irradiation may extend to spore decontamination of food ingredients such as spices, prolongation of storage life of certain fruit and fish under refrigerated conditions, disinfestation of grain and inhibition of sprouting of potatoes or growth of mushrooms, with doses ranging from 0·02 to 1·0 Mrad.[29] Thiamin is particularly susceptible to degradation by irradiation as can be seen from Table 9, taken from reference 30.

TABLE 9

EFFECT OF γ-RADIATION (0·6 Mrad) AND COOKING (4 MIN AT 15 lb/in^2) ON SOME B-COMPLEX VITAMINS IN COD (REPRINTED FROM *J. Sci. Fd. Agric.*, 1971, **22**, 146–8 WITH THE PERMISSION OF THE PUBLISHERS)

Vitamin[a]	*Raw/unirradiated control* (µg/g)	*% Vitamin retention*		
		Raw/irradiated	*Cooked/unirradiated*	*Cooked/irradiated*
Nicotinic acid	166	99	96	97
Riboflavin	1·98	94	91	84
Thiamin	2·67	50	90	46

[a] Fat and moisture-free basis.

Data are also presented in Table 9 on the combined effects of γ-radiation on cod, followed by the effect of cooking. The cooking step has a greater effect on the riboflavin content of cod than γ-radiation, while the reverse is true for thiamin for this food substance. In the home, food eaten may have been subjected to a number of processes such as canning and reheating or freezing and stewing. It is rare to find papers, such as that of Kennedy and Ley,[30] in the literature dealing with the effects of more than one process. Where studies of the combined effects of processing have been carried out, they show a greater loss of vitamin C in comparison with the cooked, fresh food.[31]

On the whole, food eaten in the home contains nutrients at predictable levels, as found in a recent survey of 23 healthy elderly people living in their own homes.[32] This study showed that for a large number of foods, including cooked samples, analysed values for vitamin C contents of foods were close to values taken from food tables.[6] The same is not true for institutional catering, as the vitamin C contents of foods taken from the British food tables overestimate the vitamin C content[33] of foods prepared in this way.

Large-scale catering

An increasing proportion of meals are eaten outside the home in the Western World.[34] In 1980 in the UK, 13% of the money spent on food was spent outside the home.[12] The combined effect of various processes on nutrient retention is particularly important in institutional catering, where so many steps are involved. Some of these steps can be seen in Fig. 1. Conventional cooking of food from fresh is still used for catering purposes, with food held warm after cooking, until served. More recently, cook/chill/reheat and cook/freeze/reheat operations have been introduced (for a review of these, see reference 35). Further innovation in large-scale catering has been the buying in of precooked, frozen convenience meals from the food manufacturers, which are ready to reheat.

Ang *et al.*[36] give one example of the effects of large-scale catering

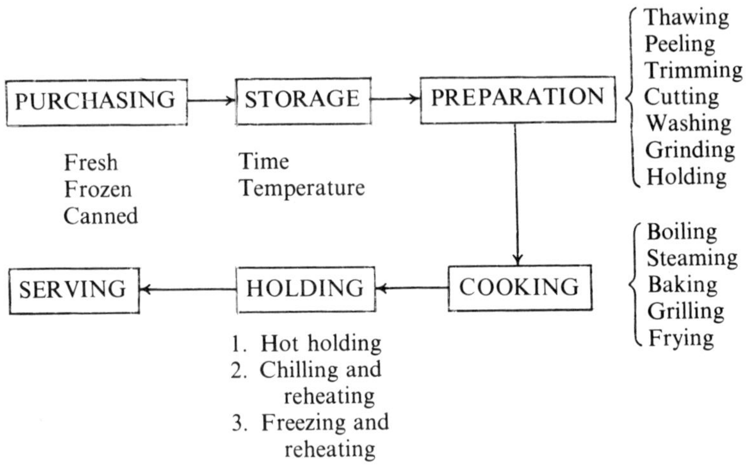

FIG. 1. Main steps in large-scale catering. (Adapted from reference 34.)

on the nutritional quality of food. They showed, for frozen mashed potatoes, that the method of reheating influenced the vitamin C content. Expressed as a percentage of the amount in the freshly prepared product, reheating in an infrared oven, microwave oven, conventional oven and steamer gave 24, 24, 36 and 41% vitamin retention, respectively. Dahl-Sawyer *et al.*[37] identified the steps in food preparation which caused largest nutrient loss in a simulated hospital cook/chill catering system. They monitored the thiamin retention in beef loaf and peas and the ascorbic acid content of potatoes. Largest nutrient losses were found for beef loaf in the precooking step, for peas at reheating and for potatoes in the 24 h chilled storage. These authors showed no effect of the method of reheating.

Even greater losses of nutrients may occur during the delivery of hot meals, especially if considerable delay occurs between preparation and serving. This is exemplified by data from Turner and Glew[38] shown in Table 10, in which food from three services providing 'meals on wheels' in Leeds (UK) were analysed for their vitamin C content. Reductions in vitamin C content of c. 50% (compared with the freshly prepared food) were recorded on average for the last meal served.

TABLE 10

VITAMIN C CONTENT OF 'MEALS ON WHEELS' IN LEEDS (UK) GIVEN IN MICROGRAMS PER MEAL (REPRINTED FROM *Food Technol.*, 1982, **36**(7), 46–50. COPYRIGHT © BY INSTITUTE OF FOOD TECHNOLOGISTS)

Item	*Food service*		
	Social service	*Education*	*Aged persons home*
Reference meal			
No. of samples:	16	7	7
Mean:	15·7	32·3	12·4
First meal			
No. of samples:	19	16	8
Mean:	10·9	14·9	7·6
Last meal			
No. of samples:	19	14	8
Mean:	8·4	16·2	5·2

A number of surveys have shown that even in our highly technological society, a large proportion of the population may be below the RDA for some nutrients. In institutional catering this may be further exacerbated for nutrients such as vitamin C which are susceptible to oxidation during long, heated holding periods. Patients in hospitals often have increased requirements for certain nutrients after surgery to ensure a speedy recovery and these are seldom met in the food provided.[39] Food provided by the food industry in the Western World has never been more wholesome,[40] but there is no room for complacency and we must continue to strive to provide food of as high a standard of nutritional quality as possible.

DIETARY GUIDELINES AND THE NUTRITIONAL QUALITY OF FOOD

Infective disease was a common cause of death at the turn of the century in the Western World. Sanitation and the application of science to medicine have led to the virtual disappearance of these diseases, leading to a change in the pattern of disease. Death is commonly caused by the degenerative diseases, in particular cancer, ischaemic heart disease and cerebrovascular disease. These, together with diabetes mellitus, dental caries, diseases of the large bowel, such as diverticular disease, gall bladder disease, hypertension and obesity have been loosely termed the 'diseases of affluence'. While many of these diseases are multifactorial in origin, with factors such as genetic predisposition, smoking, lack of exercise and stress playing important roles in their aetiology, there has been growing concern over their association with diet composition. This concern has led to the publication of dietary guidelines or goals by a number of countries.[12] Those of Sweden, Norway, the USA, France and the UK are in agreement in the recommendation to reduce intake of energy to avoid obesity, to reduce total fat and sugar and to increase starch and dietary fibre consumption (the latter recommendation in some guidelines or goals may be to increase the intake of cereals, potatoes and vegetables). There is less agreement about the recommendation to reduce the consumption of salt and cholesterol and to increase consumption of polyunsaturated fatty acids. Few of these dietary guidelines or goals give specific figures, but merely recommend

TABLE 11

FIRST EDITION OF DIETARY GOALS FOR THE USA[41]

1. Complex carbohydrates increased to 55–60% of total energy intake (40%).[a]
2. Total fat to be reduced to 30% of total energy intake.
3. Saturated, monounsaturated and polyunsaturated fats each to supply 10% of total energy.
4. Cholesterol to be reduced to 300 mg per day.
5. Sugar to be reduced to provide no more than 15% of total energy intake (refined sugar reduced to 10%).[a]
6. Salt to be reduced to 3 g per day (5 g).[a]

[a] Figures in brackets are from the second edition.[42]

changes in diet composition; however, the dietary goal for the USA[41] (given in Table 11) known as the McGovern report, does give target values. Had the recommendations made in the first edition been adopted they would have led to dramatic changes in food consumption patterns. Pressure from the farming community and some parts of the food industry, whose economic stability was threatened, led to a modified version of the McGovern report being published at the end of 1977.[42] The recommendations made in both the first and second editions of the McGovern report can be seen in Table 11.

Over the last few decades diet in the industrialised countries has changed. Data giving the percentage of total energy in the diet derived from protein, fat and carbohydrate energy for the household food in the UK[43] (Table 12) for the period 1952 to 1980, shows that the trends are towards eating a diet containing more, rather than less,

TABLE 12

PERCENTAGE OF ENERGY DERIVED FROM PROTEIN, FAT AND CARBOHYDRATE CONTENTS OF AVERAGE HOUSEHOLD FOOD CONSUMPTION IN THE UK 1952 TO 1980 (ADAPTED FROM REFERENCE 43)

	Protein (%)	*Fat* (%)	*Carbohydrate* (%)
1952	12·6	34·5	52·9
1960	11·4	39·3	49·3
1970	11·5	41·8	46·5
1980	13·0	42·8	44·4

fat, with decreasing carbohydrate content. Data from the USA show similar trends,[44] with a fat and carbohydrate content of the diet of 32 and 57% in 1933, changing to 42 and 47%, respectively, by 1970. Further analysis of the data from the 6-day weighed dietary survey of women undergraduates from Reading University (for which data, daily intakes of some nutrients are presented in Table 2) shows that most had an intake of fat energy in excess of 30% of total energy intake (see Fig. 2), with correspondingly low total carbohydrate. (The values for total carbohydrate in Fig. 2 include sugar, therefore the complex carbohydrate content of the diet will be even lower.) Figure 3 shows that for these students, there is an inverse relationship between energy in the diet supplied by fat and alcohol. Indeed, those students with a contribution of energy from fat below 30% of total energy of the diet (the level recommended by the McGovern report[41]),

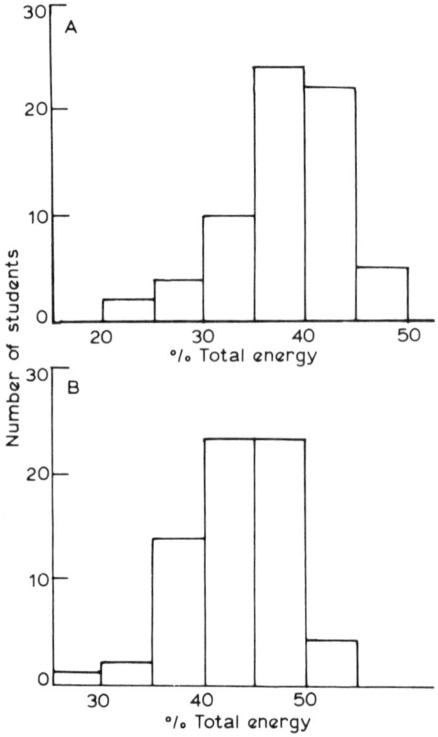

FIG. 2. Intake of fat (A) and carbohydrate (B) of Reading University women undergraduates aged 18–22 yr from a 6-day dietary study.

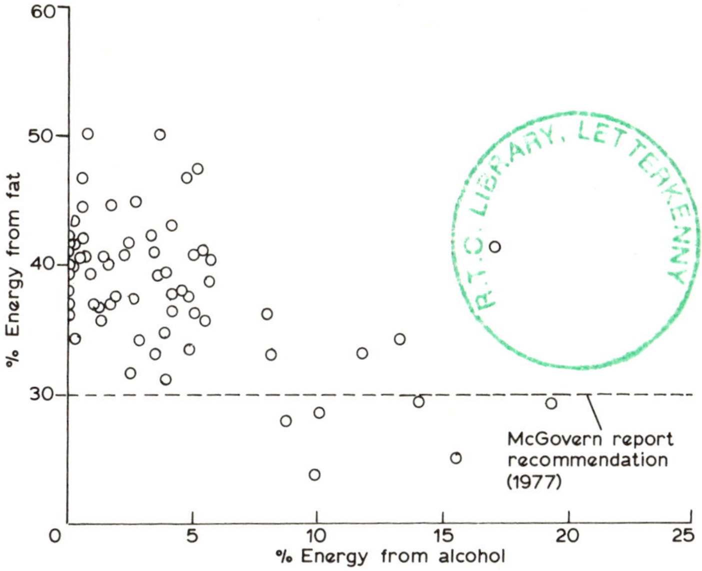

FIG. 3. Relationship between energy from fat and alcohol for women students at Reading University aged 18–22 yr (expressed as percentage of total energy).

obtained a considerable proportion (in excess of 7%) of their total energy from alcohol. Very little information is available in the literature on the influence of alcohol at socially acceptable levels on the composition of the diet. The average contribution of alcohol to the total energy content of the diet was about 7% for the entire population of the UK for 1980.[1] For adults this figure must be higher, as a large proportion of the population such as babies and young children do not drink alcohol. Reduction of the fat content of the diet by increased consumption of alcohol may not be recommended practice, but high alcohol consumption is increasing in countries of the West, especially among adolescents.[45]

Dietary guidelines or goals couched in terms of percentage of total energy supplied from different food components are exceedingly difficult for the general public to interpret. Passmore *et al.*[46] have, in their publication *Prescription for a Better British Diet* interpreted the guidelines for the UK[48] in terms of foods. Based on this publication by Passmore *et al.*,[46] McLaren[47] calculated that in order to bring about the recommended changes, this would mean, on a weight basis, a 15% reduction in meat, oils and fats, and sugar and syrups consumption, with a 20% increase in the consumption of grain products. Even greater changes in consumption of various foods would have to be made on a weight basis to meet the USA dietary goals,[49] with a decreased consumption of 50% for eggs, sugars and sweets, 16% for oils and fats, and 20% for meat, poultry and fish, with an increased consumption of 66% for grain products, 25% for vegetables and fruit, and 12% for skim milk.

Despite these recommendations, figures from 1955 to 1980 for the UK (Fig. 4) show that there is an increase in the consumption of dairy products and fats. Only the trend in the consumption of fruit and vegetables is moving in the right direction to comply with the dietary guidelines.

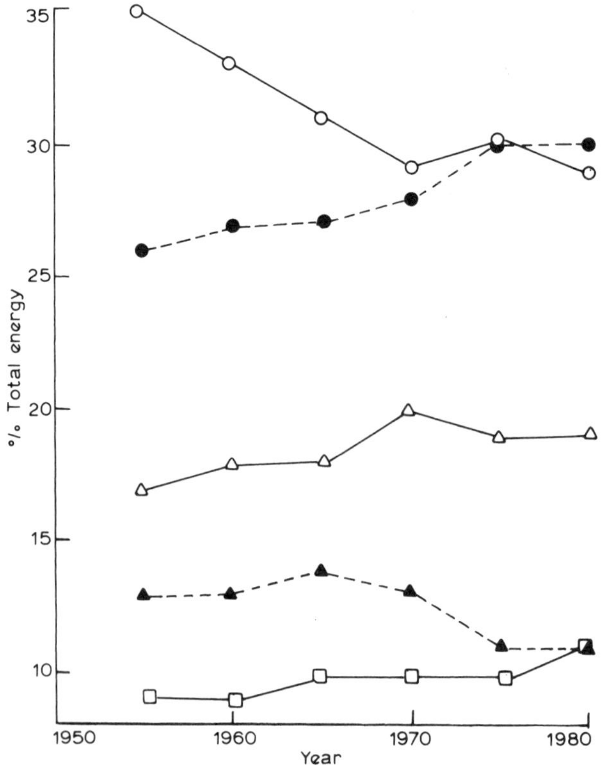

FIG. 4. The contribution of 5 broad groups of foods to total energy value of food consumed within households of the UK. ○, Cereals; ●, dairy products and fats; △, meat, fish and eggs; □, fruit and vegetables; ▲, all other foods. (Adapted from reference 1.)

If dietary guidelines are to be implemented in the Western World, we will need to modify our affluent diet to come more into line with that of a poorer country where the gross domestic product is approximately half of that of the UK. The now well-known representation of Périssé *et al.*[51] (Fig. 5) serves to illustrate this point. This shows, for a rich country, the energy supplied in the diet by fat, starch and sugar to be 40, 32 and 18 % of the total energy of the diet, respectively. Comparative figures for a poor country are 12, 77 and 2 %. If the energy provided by fat in the diet is to be reduced to 30 % of total energy as suggested by the McGovern report,[41,42] then total carbohydrate would contribute 61 % of total energy with 48 % of total energy provided by starch and 13 % by sugar, which is close to the USA dietary goals.

Possible Approaches to the Implementation of Dietary Guidelines

The main approaches to bringing about changes in the overall composition of diet are through:

Institutional catering
Food price control
Consumer education
Food manufacture

Some of these routes are reviewed in detail by Turner and Gray.[12] As institutional catering provides food in some form or another for most of us, through, for example, works canteens, this would seem an ideal medium for changing diet compositions. However, training for personnel in these establishments tends to be traditional and ingrained habits die hard. In some sectors of the catering industry there is still a problem in providing food containing adequate nutrients (see subsection 'Large-scale catering' above), no matter the greater problem of altering the balance of the major dietary components. Caterers are concerned, in the main, with keeping costs down and, at the same time, providing food which is acceptable to the customer. More nutritional education during training of catering staff would help to change attitudes.

If nutritional guidelines are to be supported by governments by way of taxation or subsidy, then changes would affect all industries involved in the food chain. These include agriculture, food and drink processing, hotel and catering and ancillary services like transport, fertiliser manufacture and packaging. The industries of the food

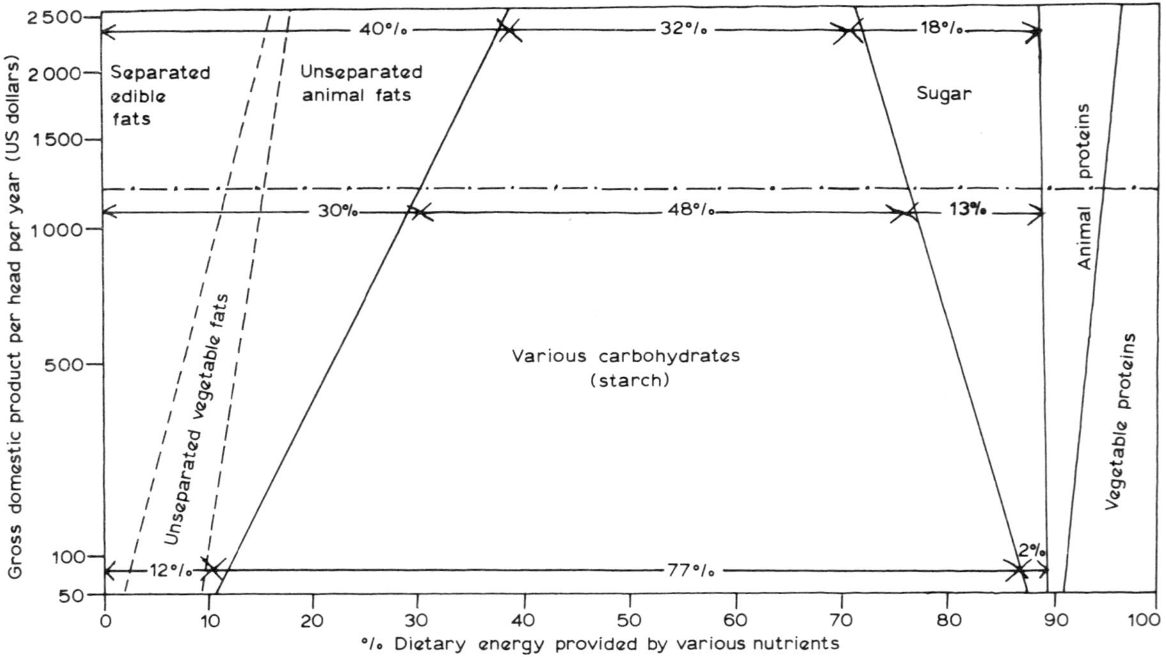

FIG. 5. Energy derived from fats, carbohydrates and proteins as percentage of total energy, according to income of the countries (1962). (Reproduced from reference 51 with the permission of the Food and Agriculture Organization of the United Nations.)

chain provide the livelihood for a great many people and are a major factor in the economy of any nation. Any governmental policy would be aimed at agricultural policy, which, in the case of the UK, is determined by that of the European Economic Community (EEC) of which it is a part. The present agricultural policy of the EEC is based on a number of objectives, which include availability of supplies and market stability. The repercussions of subsidy and taxation on certain foods are likely to be felt in particular in the farming community, who feel especially threatened by dietary guidelines or goals as shown in the USA.[50] Therefore, any government introducing agricultural policy based on dietary guidelines or goals would be subject to heavy political criticism, as the US government was at the time of the publication of the first edition of the McGovern report.[41]

Another way of influencing the composition of the diet is by educating the consumer in the advantages to health of certain patterns of eating. Consumers are, of course, influenced by a number of factors when purchasing a food, including its cost, convenience and sensory qualities.[52] Indeed, nutrition may only have a small part to play in the purchase decision, although there is evidence from the USA[44] that the perceived 'health benefit' may be an increasingly important factor.

Very little nutritional information comes to the consumer from school or the family doctor. A survey by Kraft Foods Ltd[53] showed that 56 % of women and 59 % of men obtained their information from magazines, newspapers and books. There is now considerable information on nutrition, mainly aimed at slimming, in women's magazines or in special slimming magazines, promoting a wide range of different diets. Over the last year, the publication which has greatly increased public awareness of one aspect of healthy eating is the 'F-Plan' by Audrey Eyton,[54] which extols the virtues of foods high in dietary fibre. A popular book such as this can spread nutrition knowledge very rapidly, far more so than the qualified statements of many nutritionists based in academia.

There is no doubt that the public are interested in nutrition and health.[55] However, a major problem in nutrition education is that attitudes towards foods are not based on an understanding of nutritional principles but on ill-founded beliefs. In addition, the public is subjected to considerable misinformation and to changing nutritional information as the nutritional sciences progress. One example of this is that some years ago the public were being advised to cut down on starchy foods to reduce energy intake and avoid obesity. Now they are told that they should increase the starch content of their diet at the expense of fat and that certain whole foods (e.g. potatoes in their jackets and whole grain cereals) can actually help to reduce weight.

So far, at least in the UK, no concerted effort has been made to educate the public in nutritional principles. One of the reasons put forward to explain this is that there is still dispute among nutritionists over the validity and utility of the dietary goals or guidelines. However, despite the lack of consensus, a survey in the USA[50] showed that 78 % of nutrition academics were in agreement with the goals, as were 90 % of government nutritionists. A summary of opportunities for imparting nutrition education can be seen in Fig. 6. Nutrition teaching in schools has been underemphasised in

FIG. 6. Opportunities for imparting nutrition information.

the past in the UK, but there is evidence that this is changing as nutrition is starting to be included as an environmental factor in the teaching of life sciences.[56] Moody[57] discusses possible approaches to nutrition education which might be included in some economics courses in secondary schools. He condemns the use of simplified schemes such as the use of food groups, as he argues that pupils would be ill-equipped to understand diet/health interrelationships in the context of modern eating patterns.

If the approach to nutrition education for the young presents problems, adult education is even more difficult. To keep the attention of adults, entertainment needs to be combined with nutritional information. Holdsworth and Davies[58] discuss this aspect with respect to the elderly. Information to the general public should be unbiased, but at the same time it must have popular appeal. Fullard[59] suggested the use of cartoon characters which would linger in the imagination like 'Mr Jacket Potato', emphasising the high starch and vitamin C contents of potatoes and the dietary fibre in the skin. Recent full-page advertisements by the Health Education Council in the Sun Newspaper[60,61] indicate an increasing concern to improve the nutritional knowledge of the man in the street. These are entitled: 'If you're overweight, try eating more bread and potatoes' and 'Why thin people should be as worried about fatty foods as fat people'.

If change in diet towards greater moderation is to come about through consumer education, then change will be slow. Traditional eating habits are not easily changed, although dietary modification can eventually be achieved even in old age.[58] The acceptance of good dietary practice by people in the Western World is not likely to be adopted without assistance from the food industry. Slow changes towards a more moderate food consumption pattern, brought about by consumer education will leave enough time for food manufacturers to respond. In the past food manufacturers have responded to pressures to implement nutritional principles by (for example) the voluntary fortification of foods with minerals and vitamins and providing low-energy foods for slimmers. The food industry has always been particularly responsive to new toxicological findings, e.g. the reduction in lead content of baby foods. (Toxicological aspects have not been dealt with in this paper for lack of time.)

At the moment the nutritional issues with which the food industry is concerned include the addition of dietary fibre to foods and the provision of a choice of types of dietary fat. For the future, there may be more emphasis on the manufacture of low-fat, low-cholesterol and vegetarian foods. It is likely that there will be increasing understanding of the bioavailability of minerals and vitamins in their different forms. More low-sodium foods may be demanded and food manufacturers may have to pay increasing attention to allergens.

In the USA, the dietary goals have already led to a flurry of research and development activity within the food industry[62] to produce new products. It is likely that this will also happen in the UK. Considerable problems await the food analyst in devising appropriate, rapid methodology suitable for quality control.

CONCLUSION

In the past, the nutritional quality of a food was measured in terms of its vitamin, mineral and protein content. However, foods are not eaten as single items, but as part of a diet. In recent years dietary guidelines and goals have been published in several countries, which have indicated that to maintain health, the diet should be moderate in total energy content and in specific components, in particular in fat, sugar and salt, and contain adequate amounts of starch and dietary fibre. These guidelines or goals pose an enormous challenge to the food industry, as they are not as easy to implement as, for example, nutrient fortification. In the long term, however, it is not the food manufacturer who decides diet composition, but the consumer, through food choice. Any modification to diets in the future will be only slowly introduced, as the best approach to the implementation of the recommendations will be through consumer education. This will leave enough time for the necessary research and development needed for new product development and for devising suitable methods for quality control.

REFERENCES

1. MINISTRY OF AGRICULTURE, FISHERIES AND FOOD. (1982). *Household Food Consumption and Expenditure: 1980*, Annual Report of the National Food Survey Committee, HMSO, London.
2. DEPARTMENT OF HEALTH AND SOCIAL SECURITY. (1969). *Recommended Intakes of Nutrients for the United Kingdom*, Report on Public Health and Medical Subjects No. 120, HMSO, London.
3. DEPARTMENT OF HEALTH AND SOCIAL SECURITY. (1979). *Recommended Daily Amounts of Food Energy and Nutrients for Groups of People in the United Kingdom*, Report on Health and Social Subjects No. 15, HMSO, London.
4. MARR, J. W. (1981). In: *Preventive Nutrition and Society*, Ed. Turner, M. R., Academic Press, London, Chapter 3.
5. PAO, E. M. and MICKLE, S. J. (1981). *Food Technol.*, **35**(9), 58–62, 64, 66–69, 79.
6. PAUL, A. A. and SOUTHGATE, D. A. T. (1978). *McCance and Widdowson's The Composition of Foods*, 4th edition, MRC Special Rep. No. 297, HMSO, London.
7. NATIONAL RESEARCH COUNCIL. (1974). *Recommended Dietary Allowances*, 8th revised edition, National Academy of Sciences, Washington, DC.

8. PRASAD, A. S., HALSTEAD, J. A. and NADIMI, M. (1961). *Am. J. Med.*, **31**, 532–46.
9. HAMBIDGE, K. M., HAMBIDGE, C., JACOBS, M. and BAUM, J. D. (1972). *Prediat. Res.*, **6**, 868–74.
10. WELSH, S. O. and MARSTON, R. M. (1982). *Food Technol.*, **36**(1), 70–6.
11. BATES, C. J., BLACK, A. E., PHILLIPS, D. R., WRIGHTS, A. J. A. and SOUTHGATE, D. A. T. (1982). *Hum. Nutr.: Applied Nutr.*, **36**A, 422–9.
12. TURNER, M. and GRAY, J. (Eds) (1982). *Implementation of Dietary guidelines: Obstacles and Opportunities*, The British Nutrition Foundation, London.
13. BENDER, A. E. (1978). *Food Processing and Nutrition*, Academic Press, London.
14. HSU, D., LEUNG, H. K., FINNEY, P. L. and MORAD, M. M. (1980). *J. Food Sci.*, **45**, 87–92.
15. BIRCH, G. G. and PARKER, K. J. (Eds) (1983). *Dietary Fibre*, Applied Science Publishers, London.
16. MABESA, L. B. and BALDWIN, R. E. (1979). *J. Food Sci.*, **44**, 932–3.
17. KAREL, M. (1979). *Food Technol.*, **33**(2), 36–7.
18. FENNEMA, O. (1977). *Food Technol.*, **31**(12), 32–8.
19. THOMPSON, D. R. (1982). *Food Technol.*, **36**(2), 97–108, 115.
20. KAREL, M. (1979). In: *Nutritional and Safety Aspects of Food Processing*, Ed. Tannenbaum, S. R., Marcel Dekker Inc., New York, Chapter 8.
21. FARROW, R. P., KEMPER, K. and CHIN, H. B. (1979). *Food Technol.*, **33**(2), 52–4.
22. HAGEN, R. E., ELKINS, E. R. and FARROW, R. P. (1979). *Hortscience*, **14**, 251–6.
23. MACRAE, R. (ed.) (1982). *HPLC in Food Analysis*, Academic Press, London.
24. MALIN, J. D. (1975). *Wld. Rev. Nutr. Dietet.*, **21**, 198–223.
25. RIZVI, S. S. H. and ACTON, J. C. (1982). *Food Technol.*, **36**(4), 105–9.
26. KLEIN, B. P., KUO, C. H. Y. and BOYD, G. (1981). *J. Food Sci.*, **46**, 640–1.
27. HALL, N. K. and LIU, C. S. (1981). *J. Food Sci.*, **46**, 1292–3.
28. WORLD HEALTH ORGANISATION (1981). *Wholesomeness of Irradiated Food*, Report of a Joint FAO/IAEA/WHO Expert Committee, Tech. Rep. Ser. No. 659, WHO, Geneva.
29. LEY, F. J. (1983). *BNF Nutr. Bull.*, **8**, 37–45.
30. KENNEDY, T. S. and LEY, F. J. (1971). *J. Sci. Fd Agric.*, **22**, 146–8.
31. ARCHER, M. C. and TANNENBAUM, S. R. (1979). In: *Nutritional and Safety Aspects of Food Processing*, Ed. Tannenbaum, S. R., Marcel Dekker Inc., New York, Chapter 3.
32. BLACK, A. E., ASHBY, D. R., DAY, K. C., BATES, C. J. and PAUL, A. A. (1983). *Hum. Nutr.: Applied Nutr.*, **37A**, 9–22.
33. EVANS, E. and STOCK, A. L. (1971). *Nutr. Metab.*, **13**, 21–35.
34. LIVINGSTON, G. E. and CHANG, C. M. (1979). *Food Technol.*, **33**(3), 32–7, 42.
35. GLEW, G. (1980). *Wld. Rev. Nutr. Dietet.*, **34**, 1–45.

36. Ang, C. Y. W., Chang, C. M., Frey, A. E. and Livingstone, G. E. (1975). *J. Food Sci.*, **40**, 997–1003.
37. Dahl-Sawyer, C. A., Jen, J. J. and Huang, P. D. (1982). *J. Fd. Sci.*, **47**, 1089–95.
38. Turner, M. and Glew, G. (1982). *Food Technol.*, **36**(7), 46–50.
39. Isaksson, B. (1982). *Hum. Nutr.: Applied Nutr.*, **36A**, 367–73.
40. Hegsted, D. M. (1980). *Food Technol.*, **34**(8), 48–50, 113.
41. U.S. Senate Select Committee on Nutrition and Human Needs (1977a). *Dietary Goals for the United States*, US Govt. Printing Office, 81-6050, Washington, DC.
42. U.S. Senate Select Committee on Nutrition and Human Needs (1977b). *Dietary goals for the United States*, US Govt. Printing Office, 052-070-04376-8, Washington, DC.
43. Ministry of Agriculture, Fisheries and Food (1952 onwards). *Household Food Consumption and Expenditure*, Annual Reports of the National Food Survey Committee, HMSO, London.
44. Scala, J. (1978). *Food Technol.*, **32**(9), 77–8.
45. Truswell, A. S. and Darnton-Hill, I. (1981). *Nutr. Rev.*, **39**, 73–88.
46. Passmore, R., Hollingsworth, D. F. and Robertson, J. (1979). *Brit. Med. J.*, **1**, 527–31.
47. McLaren, D. (1981). In: *Dietary Goals for the UK in the 1980's*, Van den Berghs & Jurgens Ltd, West Sussex.
48. Department of Health and Social Security (1978; rev. 1979). *Eating for Health*, HMSO, London.
49. Peterkin, B. B. (1978). *Food Technol.*, **32**(2), 34–42.
50. Austin, J. E. and Quelch, J. A. (1979). *Food Policy*, **4**, 115–28.
51. Périssé, J., Sizaret, F. and Francoise, P. (1969). *FAO Nutrition Newsletter*, **7**(3), 1–9.
52. Richardson, D. P. (1981). *IFST (UK) Proc.*, **14**(2), 87–102.
53. Kraft (1978). *Attitudes to Food and Health—Part 1*, Survey, Kraft Foods Ltd, Cheltenham.
54. Eyton, A. (1982). *The F-Plan*, Penguin Books Ltd, Harmondworth, Middlesex.
55. Richardson, D. P. (1982), *BNF Nutr. Bull.*, **7**, 31–8.
56. Wheeler, E. F. (1982). *Human Nutr.: Applied Nutr.*, **36A**, 11–17.
57. Moody, R. (1982). *Human Nutr.: Applied Nutr.*, **36A**, 18–21.
58. Holdsworth, M. D. and Davies, L. (1982). *Hum. Nutr.: Applied Nutr.*, **36A**, 22–7.
59. Fullard, E. (1981). In: *Dietary Goals for the UK in the 1980's*, Van den Berghs & Jurgens Ltd, West Sussex.
60. Sun Newspaper (1983). February 4th, p. 25, London.
61. Sun Newspaper (1983). March 1st, p. 10, London.
62. Przybyla, A. (1981). *Processed Prepared Fd.*, **150**(5), 84–8.

3

Food Composition and Analytical Accuracy

R. Sawyer

Laboratory of the Government Chemist, London, UK

ABSTRACT

Accurate assessment of composition is a prerequisite feature of the commercial and dietary evaluation of foods and food ingredients. The degree of accuracy required is variable according to detailed considerations, but the attainment may be illusory.

Compositional data may be based on analytical techniques which are well authenticated; other data may be assumed to be sound but evidence of authenticity may be sparse. The introduction of newer analytical techniques into food analysis and the more critical use of collaborative studies have highlighted the inadequacies of some erstwhile acceptable methodology and have pointed to the need for refined definitions of some of the determinants. The statements above are illustrated by examples from current problems in food analysis as they relate to legislative controls and dietary evaluation.

INTRODUCTION

Information on the composition of foods, whether as raw materials or processed products, is needed for a variety of purposes. Broadly, these purposes are separately contained within the General Provisions of the Food and Drugs Act 1955; in particular, Section 2 requires that a food be of the 'nature', 'substance' and 'quality' demanded, Section 4 allows for control of composition, whilst Section 6 prohibits false description.

Establishment of 'nature' is concerned with the proof that the item is consistent with the description given or the claim made. Where it is of a different variety, kind or description then the analysis required may be a relatively simple visual or microscopic examination. However, if the food is a blend of two or more varieties or species then the examination takes on a quantitative (or substantive) aspect according to the circumstances. For example, a substance sold as salad oil may be a blend of appropriate oils of vegetable or animal origin but 'X oil for salads' must be wholly derived from the source 'X'. In the latter case proof of the presence of a second species of oil regardless of origin is sufficient to establish that the food is not of the substance defined although it may have the nature of 'salad oil'. With modern techniques, the analysis required to establish 'nature' and 'substance' may be achieved with relative ease but proof of the authenticity of substance 'X' is dependent not only on the discriminating power of the techniques used but also on the quality of compositional data available for 'X' and oils of similar character.

In general terms, the criteria for establishing 'substance' may be closely related to a compositional standard where a food is subject to a regulation or specification. The difficulties which may arise in the analysis of an individual food will depend on the ease of defining a specific constituent or ingredient in chemical terms. For example, the use of prescribed amounts of ingredients such as salt, sugar, flour, meat, milk or fruit in a recipe presents different levels of difficulty in assessment of the amounts actually used when a finished product is examined. This may be due to changes which occur in the basic ingredients on cooking such as the conversion of sucrose to invert sugar or the dextrinisation of starch. The dependence on the use of accepted average conversion factors for specific components of a recipe is a source of variability between the results obtained from examination of products of similar, but not identical, manufacture. The tendency is to assume that the 'substance' of a food can only be affected by gross changes in constituents; however, as indicated above, there can be no absolute limit since proof of a change of 'substance' may be possible with use of a technique which readily identifies, at a low level, the presence of a similar but foreign material. Similarly, the demonstrable presence of non-permitted additives, contaminants or other materials at relatively low level may be deemed to affect the substance of a food.

The criteria by which a food is judged for quality are wider than those affecting nature and substance. A food may be altered significantly in chemical or physical terms as a food substance without material effect on quality; in some cases the quality (in terms of commercial or nutritive value) may be improved by judicious use of other ingredients. Analytical measurement of quality is thus a more ephemeral concept since it may involve the cumulative assessment of a number of less easily defined parameters. Whilst considerable progress has been made in the identification of chemical constituents of foods by the use of advanced analytical techniques, much remains to be achieved in the identification of the source of raw material and in the replacement of subjective quality assessments by objective test methods.

Many of the older methods of food analysis are empirical and rely for a successful outcome on consistency of application both in terms of analytical operation and in the field of use. Provided they are applied to a homogeneous sample these methods are precise and reproducible and are accurate only by virtue of the definition applied to the determinant. The concept of accuracy may be said to depend on the precision of definition of the determinant in relation to the selectivity of the method and the substrate to which the method is to be applied. Many errors of interpretation are introduced by the misuse of a specific method either by a lack of recognition of its limitations or by use of unsubstantiated modifications. The preparation of a sample for analysis, especially the steps taken to homogenise the material, to effect the separation and concentration of the constituent of interest and to facilitate the removal of interfering components, is likely to contribute substantially to the limitations of use of the method.

As indicated above, the use of modern analytical techniques has served to highlight interpretative problems arising from the use of empirical methods. A typical example is the characterisation of fats by chemical 'constants', such as iodine value and saponification value, as opposed to the use of chromatographic and spectroscopic procedures to establish detailed structure and presence of minor characterising constituents such as sterols. Similarly, the lack of selectivity of traditional chemical methods and the variable contribution of isomers or related chemical compounds to a functional dietary activity and to dietary value has been long known in the field of vitamin analysis. Recent developments in the use of HPLC have allowed direct estimation of the individual isomers in selected foods and thereby have contributed to the improved value of the analyses performed.[1]

As products have become more sophisticated, and with the increased availability of more selective methods, the assessment of food composition is becoming a more complex analytical task. The need for reliable, accurate and reproducible information has become increasingly evident. To meet this need, emphasis has been placed on validation of methods both by collaborative study and by the search by a number of organisations for relevant reference materials with which to test new methods. Regardless of his allegiance, the principal purpose of the food analyst is to ensure that first, the quality of information obtained in any examination is appropriate to the circumstance of its use and that second, due recognition is given to the cost of obtaining the information relative to the benefits which accrue from its procurement. In this context, detailed consideration has been given to the harmonisation of approach to collaborative studies of analytical methods.[2,3]

For 100 years the Association of Official Analytical Chemists (AOAC) has operated a system of regular examination and approval through publication of analytical methods for foods, fertilisers and feeds. Much of the parallel work in other international organisations has not received the same attention to detail in respect of open publication of the results of collaborative studies and in the validation of methods, although as a result of inter-agency collaboration on the harmonisation of the approach to collaborative studies, attention is now being paid to the need to publish the results of work on these studies. Recently a limited attempt has been mounted within the UK both to study and publish data on methods proposed for inclusion in EEC legislation. A series of reports on methods proposed for inclusion in EEC legislation has been published.[4-8] The topics which have been studied are determination of crude fibre in flour, erucic acid in oils and fats, biphenyl and 2-hydroxy biphenyl in citrus fruit, vinyl chloride in foods, and milk fat in cocoa butter. Further reports on insoluble matter in coffee extracts, hydroxyproline in meat products, composition of cocoa and chocolate, soya protein in meat products, and dietary fibre are in preparation. In each study the repeatability and reproducibility of the method or methods has been established and the reports indicate the suitability or otherwise of the methods for inclusion in legislation. Further work has been undertaken on other topics in addition to those studies which have been successfully concluded; a number of these for one reason or another are considered to be unsatisfactory. These latter studies include the compositional analysis of bacon, the estimation of soya protein in meat products by a serological method, determination of specified sugars in chocolate, trace metals in fish, liver, meat and milk powder, and sorbic acid in soft drinks and low fat spreads. In many respects, information on methods which have been shown to perform badly in interlaboratory studies may be regarded as of equal importance to that on successful studies. More emphasis is now being given by the AOAC to encourage the investigation by Associate Referees of unsatisfactory performance by individual laboratories in order to determine the weaknesses in recommended methods.

Parallel work has also been undertaken internationally in Codex Alimentarius with studies on the determination of trace metals in foods, fat in meat and milk based foods, alcohol insoluble solids in quick frozen corn-on-the-cob, and loss of mass on drying of quick frozen French fried potatoes. A trial of a general chromatographic method for identification of preservatives in foods carried out within Codex has been reported;[9] information on the other work carried out in Codex is not readily available but it appears in the reports of the sessions of appropriate Codex Committees.

In the European Community (EC) funding has been made available by the Community Bureau of Reference (BCR) to establish certified food reference materials. A representative range of food products including oils and fats, biscuit, chocolate, processed cheese and a homogenised meat based baby food, have been proposed as suitable materials on which to establish reference data on the major compositional criteria. It has been proposed to prepare each food from a single production batch. A random selection of individual containers is to be analysed to establish the batch characteristic; the principal difficulties to be overcome are homogeneity and stability. It should be noted that statistical analysis of analytical data generally starts with the assumption that the data are obtained from a homogeneous population and that the sample is stable.[10] Initial feasibility studies to establish these factors have been authorised. Similar but more specific projects have been developed by the BCR to study toxic and nutritional elements in cereals and cereal products, organic and total mercury and arsenic in tuna fish, toxic elements in meat, trace elements and nitrate in milk powder, matrix elements in milk powder, and mycotoxins in vulnerable foods. Summary status reports on each project were issued in June, 1982.

The activities summarised above indicate the developing interest, the establishment of methods of proven characteristics and provision of a suite of relevant materials suitable for testing these and any new methods which may be developed. Further consideration is given to selected topics in the sections following.

CALCULATION OF MEAT CONTENT

The long established practice for calculation of meat content of a food is based on the method of Stubbs and More.[11] The original procedure established for the analysis of sausages is based on the use of a factor to convert that amount of the total nitrogen content which is not assigned to other constituents into a value for 'defatted meat'. The 'meat content' is defined as the sum of 'defatted meat' and the 'fat content' as determined by solvent extraction. In the original paper Stubbs and More state: 'It should be noted that the percentage of chemical fat is not the same as that of fatty tissue'.

In their *Report on Sausages*, the Food Standards Committee (FSC)[12] discussed the control of the composition of sausages and recommended a minimum standard for meat content coupled with a maximum for the proportion of fat in the total meat. In consideration of the recommendation, due note was taken of the variable amount of fat in lean meat (1–18 %). In paragraph 31 the report states: 'a statutory limit, which has to be based on fat as revealed by analysis rather than on the proportion of trimmable fat used by the sausage maker, must therefore take account of this variable source of fat. We are informed that good commercial practice in making sausages is to use two parts of trimmed lean meat to one part of fat; if this is so a limit of 50 % would allow a reasonable margin. We therefore recommend that the amount of fat in all sausages should be limited to 50 % of the meat content'.

Following this report and related studies on other meat products[13] the current comprehensive set of Regulations on Meat Products[14,15] was enacted. That the Regulations have inconsistencies in definitions has been long recognised. A critical review[16] highlights the difficulties created: in particular, the control of composition is based on a set of provisions for total meat content coupled with prescribed minimum proportions for lean meat. The definitions of 'meat', 'meat content' and 'lean meat' used in the various regulations differ in respect of their treatment of cured meat and the allowance for the contribution of offal. By this simple departure from the recommendations of the FSC (viz. to control the total meat content with a limit on the proportion of fat) the way to argument on interpretation was opened. The extent of the problem was highlighted[17,18] in two publications in which Pearson developed refinements of the Stubbs and More formula for general application to meat products whether controlled or not. He proposed the use of correction factors to allow for the fat and collagen in lean tissue and for the protein content of fatty tissue. All the calculations were dependent on the use of arbitrary allowances for the relative amounts of these constituents in the primary tissue. The recent *Report on Meat Products*[19] also draws attention to the 'additional allowance' of 10% for fat in lean meat in the interpretation of the control limits; thus, by comparison with the earlier report a pronounced drift in the intent of the 1956 Report has developed and definitions are emerging more complex from the analytical viewpoint than those enunciated by Stubbs and More. A diagrammatic representation of the definitions of meat is given in Fig. 1, which is similar to that presented by Hannan.[20]

The common feature in control of meat products is the use of an appropriate factor to convert the total nitrogen to defatted meat. A series of studies to establish appropriate conversion factors was undertaken by the Analytical Methods Committee (AMC) of the

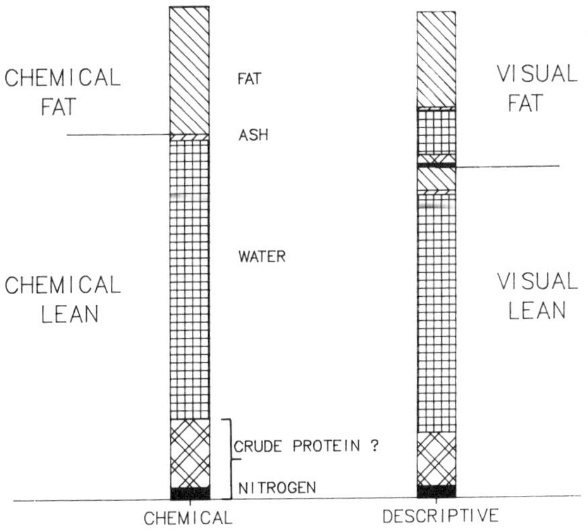

FIG. 1. Chemical and visual description of meat.

TABLE 1

NITROGEN FACTOR (Nf) USED TO CONVERT NITROGEN CONTENT TO 'DEFATTED MEAT'

Variety	*Nitrogen factor*		*Reference in the journal 'Analyst'*
	Mean	*Range*	
Kidney	2·7	2·4–3·0	1966, **91**, 538
Tongue	3·0	2·25–3·59	1967, **92**, 326
Blood	3·2	2·32–3·48	1968, **93**, 478
Veal	3·35	3·04–3·68	1965, **90**, 256
Liver, ox	3·45	3·15–3·90	1964, **89**, 630
Pork, whole sides	3·45	3·18–3·72	1961, **86**, 557
Chicken, leg	3·45	2·70–3·80	1963, **88**, 503
Turkey, dark meat	3·5	3·07–3·67	1965, **90**, 581
Beef	3·55	2·96–4·53	1963, **88**, 422
Chicken, dark meat	3·6	3·20–3·89	1963, **88**, 583
Turkey, whole	3·65	3·37–3·87	1965, **90**, 581
Liver, pig	3·65	3·25–4·00	1964, **89**, 630
Chicken, whole	3·7	3·37–4·38	1963, **88**, 583
Chicken, breast	3·9	3·48–4·35	1963, **88**, 503
Turkey, breast	3·9	3·56–4·21	1965, **90**, 581

Society for Analytical Chemistry (now the Analytical Division of the Royal Society of Chemistry); the recommendations are summarised in Table 1. In all cases the recommended factor is a compromise value which represents the weighted mean of a number of determinations of the nitrogen content (as expressed on a fat-free basis) of the material under study. Studies on individual materials were organised on an *ad hoc* basis and in the various reports there is no evidence of the testing of data according to any statistical method; in some cases there is little evidence of preselection of samples to represent the weight of various market practices of the time. As an example of the latter situation, the 1963 AMC report[21] on nitrogen factors for chicken indicates that equal weight was given to data from a random selection of samples analysed in various laboratories and to that obtained from a study on preselected material treated in a defined way. A study of the descriptions of the carcasses examined reveals that most of the data relates to mature poultry varying in age from 1·5 yr to 4 yr old. Rearing and marketing practices have changed radically in the last 20 years and proposals have been made to reconsider the effects of age and rearing on poultry meat. In contrast, the AMC report[22] on the nitrogen factor for pork reveals that consideration was given to the effect of anatomical cuts and carcass weight on the factor.

Although Bradstreet[23] has shown that the nitrogen content obtained by the Kjeldahl method is related to the conditions of digestion and to the catalyst used, the studies reported by the AMC do not contain substantive evidence of the methods used for any of the relevant determinations. Lee[24] has collected compositional data on a variety of species of meat, fish and poultry. Although source references are given, the data have been reproduced without any attempt to evaluate the quality or validity of the analyses. In many cases evidence of methods used is sparse. Dransfield *et al.*[25] have studied the intralaboratory and interlaboratory variations obtained in the analysis of carcass meat by 8 laboratories. All laboratories analysed subsamples from a common bulk of prepared beef; prescribed analytical methods were used for determination of nitrogen, moisture, fat, ash, collagen and pH.

Estimates of precision were made for all the analytical parameters although in the case of ash content, only one laboratory submitted duplicate results. In the cases where two laboratories submitted complete data for all parameters, the total (moisture + protein + fat + ash) averaged 100·5 (SD 0·3) 'laboratory B' and 100·4 (SD 0·5) 'laboratory C', respectively. The former laboratory analysed each sample once whilst the latter analysed all 16 samples in triplicate. In both cases a comparison of the average total matter found with the theoretical value shows that the calculated value was significantly different from 100 %. A calculation of the apparent factor required to convert nitrogen to protein consistent with a summation of the analyses to 100·0 % showed a value of 6·12 for laboratory B and 6·19 for laboratory C. Taking into account that both laboratories determined free fat by direct extraction and that laboratory B obtained a consistently lower ash content (0·9 %) than laboratory C (1·1 %), which were both lower than the value (1·3 %) found by a third laboratory, the lower apparent nitrogen to protein factor gives some limited support to the criticism of accepted values by Heidelbaugh *et al.*,[26] although the difference is not so substantial as that proposed by de Rhan[27] who suggests 5·7–5·9 for meat on the basis of amino acid analyses. The estimate of Nf for the whole data set (8 laboratories × 16 samples) was 3·52 which compares with the AMC recommended factor of 3·55. Inspection of the data showed significantly different values for *M. semimembranosus* from the

TABLE 2
COMPOSITION OF LEAN BEEF (*M. gracilis* EX GALLOWAY) (AFTER DRANSFIELD *et al.*[25])

	Sum (M + P + F + A)	% Protein fat free	Nf	Water/protein
'B'	100·45	20·92	3·35	3·75
	99·65	21·68	3·47	3·55
	100·68	20·98	3·36	3·76
	100·63	21·53	3·44	3·63
	100·67	20·94	3·55	3·76
	100·70	21·49	3·44	3·64
	100·44	21·04	3·37	3·73
	100·67	21·64	3·46	3·61
Mean	100·49	21·28	3·43	3·68
'C'	99·72	21·33	3·41	3·63
	98·58	20·35	3·26	3·79
	100·15	20·69	3·31	3·79
	101·46	21·69	3·47	3·63
	99·81	21·47	3·44	3·60
	100·74	21·46	3·43	3·64
	103·27	21·06	3·37	3·87
	99·98	21·66	3·47	3·56
Mean	100·46	21·21	3·40	3·69

M, Moisture; P, protein; F, fat; A, ash.

Charolais cross steers and for *M. gracilis* from Galloway steers. The group data for Nf is similar to that reported from laboratories B and C, which is summarised in Tables 2 and 3.

When tested against modern requirements, the evidence for certain conversion factors may be regarded as less than satisfactory, since, as indicated earlier, the problem of control of meat content has been confused by the departure from the simple concept expressed by Stubbs and More.[11] In the current trend towards control by lean meat content,[19] the FSC leaves open the question of an appropriate analytical (chemical) definition for lean meat.

Arbitrary allowances for interstitial fat and connective tissue content which have been proposed can only serve to make the analysis less exact and at the same time to give impetus to the search for direct indicators of lean tissue content. Proposals to use 3-methyl histidine titre have been made by Rangley and Lawrie.[28] This index is

TABLE 3

COMPOSITION OF LEAN BEEF (*M. semimembranosus* EX CHAROLAIS) (AFTER DRANSFIELD *et al.*[25])

	Sum $(M+P+F+A)$	% Protein fat free	Nf	Water/protein
'B'	99·28	23·16	3·71	3·24
	100·77	23·44	3·75	3·26
	100·27	22·75	3·64	3·36
	100·63	23·27	3·72	3·28
	100·54	22·13	3·54	3·50
	100·62	22·92	3·67	3·35
	100·50	21·37	3·42	3·66
	100·23	22·64	3·62	3·39
Mean	100·36	22·71	3·63	3·38
'C'	100·73	23·44	3·75	3·25
	100·71	23·34	3·73	3·27
	100·47	22·73	3·64	3·36
	100·05	22·85	3·66	3·33
	100·79	22·64	3·62	3·40
	100·59	22·77	3·64	3·36
	100·23	22·01	3·52	3·51
	99·31	22·46	3·59	3·39
Mean	100·36	22·78	3·64	3·36

M, Moisture; P, protein; F, fat; A, ash.

finding acceptance in restricted applications but it is subject to variations of a similar magnitude to the nitrogen (Nf) factors. However, the method has the merit of using a selective index rather than a general nitrogen factor.

The proposals to revise the UK Meat Product Regulations foreshadowed by the FSC *Report on Meat Products*[19] have focused attention on the definitions of meat and cured meat and thereby have drawn attention to the need for re-assessment of appropriate factors to be used in particular circumstances.

CURED MEAT

The lack of clear distinction between meat and cured meat has led to arguments on the interpretation of limits for meat content in certain cured products. By common usage the UK enforcement authorities have interpreted all compositional standards in terms of 'raw meat' equivalent on the grounds that any other interpretation gives rise to confusion. The subtleties of interpretation of the meat content of products such as corned beef, which result in a raw meat equivalent in excess of 100 %, are difficult to explain to non-English speakers when the parent definition of meat makes no distinction between raw and cured meat. The problem is even more confused in the classification of canned cured meats in the Common Customs Tariff (CCT) in categories which are expressed in terms of meat content, although the legal definitions used in the UK have no direct force in the interpretation of the CCT. Foreign traders have frequently claimed that the limit for meat content of canned ham imported into the UK relates to 'ham content' rather than 'meat content'. The implications of this suggestion are obvious if the ham in question contains amounts of added water in excess of 15 %.

Currently, the EEC has proposals in hand for the definition of meat content and for the description of a method of analysis for inclusion in a Regulation.

As indicated in the previous section, the method of analysis adopted in the UK for establishing the meat content is based on that of Stubbs and More.[11] Meat content of the product is expressed on a raw meat basis, the calculation thus relies on the use of the factors recommended by the AMC for conversion of nitrogen to fat-free tissue. After allowance for added gelatine and any other nitrogenous constituent plus the fat and salt content, an estimate of added water may be made. Alternative control methods for cured meat products have been recommended for use internationally by Codex Alimentarius; the standards for corned beef and cured pork products contain limits for protein on a fat free basis. By comparison the system currently used in the USA is based on in-plant product inspection and for prime products such as bacon and ham the US Department of Agriculture (USDA) regulations require that the finished product after curing and processing is returned to the raw, uncured weight. In-plant control is effected by check weighings of raw ingredients, including the curing solution, and during the various process stages.

Exceptions to this form of control are allowed in the case of cured and cooked-in-the-can products such as ham, and pork shoulder. Initially the added moisture was limited to 8 % over the raw weight but various sophistications of name and labelling have allowed the incorporation of increasing amounts of curing solution to products of this type. Similar concessions have been applied to products such as ham which is cured but not precooked provided the labelling reflects the amount of water added.

The amount of natural water in the cured product is estimated by first determining the protein content and multiplying by an average factor which is related to the anatomical cut used to prepare the product. The resulting figure is subtracted from the total water content found by analysis and the difference is expressed as 'added water'. The water/protein ratios (W/P) used vary from 3·79 for smoked ham to 4·0 for 'miscellaneous' cuts; prime ham and loin attracts a factor of 3·83. Tolerances are allowed for single sample examination to allow for 'natural variability'. Recent evidence to the USDA Inspector General[29] has shown that for a 10 % water limit the practical single sample limit allowed is 15·8 % added water. The tolerance allowed has been criticised by the Inspector General on the grounds that it is too generous 'since it has been shown that plants can and do operate at the upper levels of established tolerance levels'. In the same report the control methods of analysis for detecting added water were also considered to be 'out-of-date'. By comparison, in the field of Customs surveillance and classification of canned cured pork products, compositional boundaries are set at 80 % and 40 % meat content. In the case of the upper limit, the classification calls for the water/protein ratio to be less than 4·3 for the meat component of meat products. A similar value is used within the EEC for assessment of monetary compensatory amounts (MCA) under the Common Agricultural Policy (CAP). As a result of the criticism voiced within the USA, USDA has proposed a change in the control system to one based on determination of protein on a fat-free basis, together with the use of a prescribed statistical sampling plan.

One of the arguments advanced within the USA for the change is that the proposed system is in line with that adopted by Codex Alimentarius. The major difference between the USDA proposals and Codex is that the former proposal includes a prescribed sampling regime in which the results are tested against a standardised value by a Cusum procedure whilst the Codex Standards utilise a minimum limiting value for fat-free protein. Whilst at first sight the new proposals may appear to be a radical departure from the old system, the two control parameters, water/protein ratio and protein on fat-free basis, are linked mathematically.

The relationships may be represented as follows:

% Fat-free protein (PFF)

$$= \frac{\%\ \text{Protein} \times 100}{(100 - \%\ \text{fat})}$$

$$= \frac{\%\ \text{Protein} \times 100}{\%\ \text{Water} + \%\ \text{Protein} + \%\ \text{Ash}}$$

$$= \frac{\%\ \text{Protein} \times 100}{(\text{Water/Protein}) + (\text{Ash/Protein}) + 1}$$

Similarly, for the Stubbs and More factor Nf, where Nf = % nitrogen in fat-free tissue, and % protein = N × 6·25:

$$\text{Nf} = \frac{16}{(\text{Water/Protein}) + (\text{Ash/Protein}) + 1}$$

in the case of meat with ~1 % ash:

$$\text{for W/P} = 4{\cdot}0,\ \text{Nf} \sim 3{\cdot}2 \qquad (1)$$

$$\text{for W/P} = 3{\cdot}0,\ \text{Nf} \sim 4{\cdot}0 \qquad (2)$$

It may be seen from the above equations that the fat-free protein content, water/protein ratio and the nitrogen factor for chemical lean meat used in the Stubbs and More estimation have interrelated values. Calculations of Nf and water/protein ratio for all meat samples recorded in *McCance and Widdowson's The Composition of Foods* may be shown to fall on a simple curve which passes through the limiting points defined in eqns (1) and (2). Displacement from the theoretical line is observed in the case of cured meats, the amount of displacement being related to the salt (ash) content of the product.

Since the relationships exist, it is appropriate to examine the sensitivity of these indices to addition of water and salt to raw meat. In order to show the effect, two model systems have been studied using analytical data for raw pork from the tables defined by Lee.[24] One sample was selected with a low fat content (5·1 %) and the second with a high fat content (33·4 %). The analytical data were used to calculate, in a closed system model, the effect of adding up to 25 % water without added salt and up to 25 % water with 5 % added salt (to simulate a cured product). The data are presented in Tables 4 and 5. Figure 2 shows the data for Nf against added water and water/protein

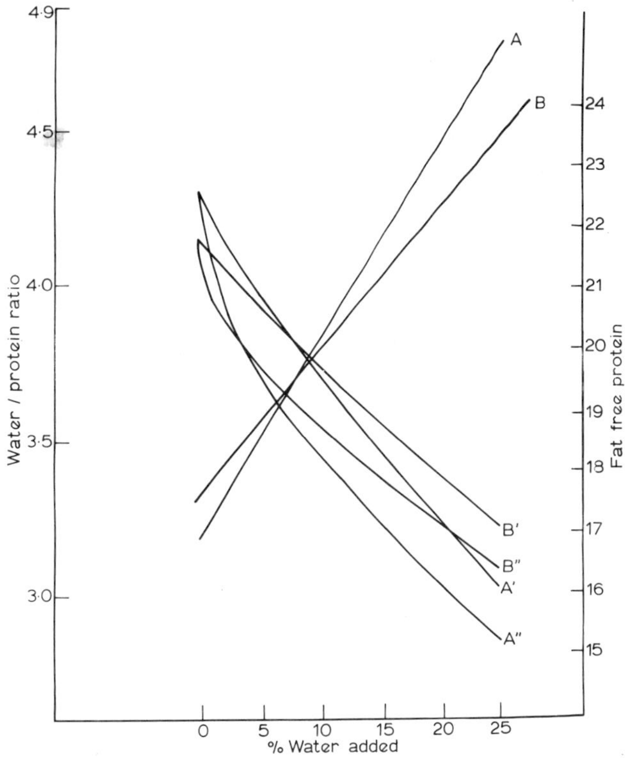

FIG. 2. Effect of salt (5 %) on analysis of raw pork for water/protein ratio (W/P) and fat-free protein (PFF) against water added.

	Fat (%)	*Salt* (%)	
A	33	0 and 5	Water/protein ratio
B	5	0 and 5	
A′	33	0	Fat-free protein
B′	5	0	
A″	33	5	
B″	5	5	

ratio against added water for each of the two systems, the former being without addition of salt.

From the figure it can be seen that a linear relationship exists between added water and the water/protein ratio; for any sample the plot is unaffected by the salt content of the sample but the slope of the line is dependent on fat content (lines A and B). The relationship

TABLE 4

EFFECT OF VARYING AMOUNTS OF ADDED WATER ON ANALYSIS OF RAW PORK (HAM) FOR WATER/PROTEIN RATIO (W/P) AND FAT-FREE PROTEIN (PFF)

	Added water					
	0%	*5%*	*10%*	*15%*	*20%*	*25%*
Sample 1						
Water	50·1	52·48	54·64	56·61	58·42	60·08
Protein	15·7	14·95	14·27	13·65	13·08	12·56
Fat	33·4	31·81	30·36	29·04	27·83	26·72
Ash	0·9	0·86	0·82	0·78	0·75	0·72
W/P	3·19	3·51	3·83	4·15	4·47	4·78
PFF	23·57	21·92	20·49	19·24	18·12	17·14
Nf	3·77	3·51	3·28	3·08	2·90	2·74
W/P + Nf	6·97	7·02	7·11	7·23	7·37	7·52
Sample 2						
Water	72·01	73·34	74·55	75·66	76·68	77·61
Protein	21·67	20·64	19·70	18·84	18·06	17·34
Fat	5·13	4·89	4·66	4·46	4·28	4·10
Ash	1·2	1·14	1·09	1·04	1·00	0·96
W/P	3·32	3·55	3·78	4·02	4·25	4·48
PFF	22·84	21·70	20·66	19·72	18·87	18·08
Nf	3·65	3·47	3·31	3·16	3·02	2·89
W/P + Nf	6·97	7·02	7·09	7·18	7·27	7·37

between protein on a fat-free basis and added water is not linear and the curves for the individual samples are affected both by the fat content and by the added salt. Curve A′ is for the high fat sample with no salt added; curve A″ is for the high fat sample with 5% added salt. Curves B′ and B″ are those for the low fat samples. From these relationships it is evident that the sensitivity of the index fat-free protein to water added (ΔPFF/ΔAW) is highly variable and is significantly reduced as the percentage of added water is increased, whilst the index water/protein ratio to water added (ΔWP/ΔAW) is dependent only on the fat content; for 46 samples the relationship has the form $\Delta WP/\Delta AW = 0{\cdot}048 - 0{\cdot}019\ (\%\ \text{fat}/100) + 0{\cdot}23\ (\%\ \text{fat}/100)$.[2] The data are summarised in Tables 6 and 7.

Thus, it may be seen that the proposal to change the method of control from one using limiting values for water/protein ratio to one based on limits for fat-free protein content is not a fundamental one, and by virtue of the mathematical relationships explored above and

TABLE 5

EFFECT OF SALT (5 %) AND VARYING AMOUNTS OF ADDED WATER ON ANALYSIS OF RAW PORK (HAM) FOR WATER/PROTEIN RATIO (W/P) AND FAT-FREE PROTEIN (PFF)

		Added salt, added water				
		5 %, 5 %	*5 %, 10 %*	*5 %, 15 %*	*5 %, 20 %*	*5 %, 25 %*
Sample 1						
Water	50·1	50·09	52·26	54·25	56·08	57·7
Protein	15·7	14·27	13·65	13·08	12·56	12·08
Fat	33·4	30·36	29·04	27·83	26·72	25·69
Ash	0·9	5·36	5·13	4·92	4·72	4·54
W/P	3·19	3·51	3·83	4·15	4·47	4·78
PFF	23·57	20·49	19·24	18·42	17·14	16·26
Nf	3·77	3·28	3·08	2·90	2·74	2·60
Nf + W/P	6·96	6·79	6·91	7·05	7·21	7·38
Sample 2						
Water	72·01	70·01	71·31	72·51	73·61	74·62
Protein	21·67	19·70	18·84	18·06	17·34	16·67
Fat	5·13	4·66	4·46	4·28	4·10	3·95
Ash	1·2	5·64	5·39	5·17	4·96	4·77
W/P	3·32	3·554	3·785	4·015	4·245	4·476
PFF	22·84	20·662	19·719	18·867	18·081	17·355
Nf	3·65	3·306	3·155	3·019	2·873	2·777
Nf + W/P	6·97	6·860	6·940	7·034	7·138	7·253

TABLE 6

EFFECT OF FAT CONTENT AND SALT CONTENT ON THE SLOPE OF THE PLOT FAT-FREE PROTEIN (PFF) AGAINST ADDED WATER (AW)

Fat (%)	*PFF/AW*				
	0–5 % AW	*5–10 % AW*	*10–15 % AW*	*15–20 % AW*	*20–25 % AW*
2·5	0·232	0·210	0·192	0·176	0·160
5·1	0·228	0·208	0·188	0·170	0·158
18·3	0·248	0·222	0·200	0·176	0·164
33·4	0·333	0·286	0·250	0·224	0·196
42·5	0·382	0·330	0·282	0·242	0·216
5·1 (+5 % salt)	0·436	0·189	0·170	0·157	0·145
33·4 (+5 % salt)	0·616	0·251	0·223	0·197	0·177

TABLE 7

EFFECT OF FAT CONTENT ON THE SLOPE OF THE PLOT WATER/PROTEIN RATIO (WP) AGAINST ADDED WATER (AW)

WP/AW	% *Fat*
0·140	66
0·110	56
0·081	42
0·064	33
0·061	28
0·058	25
0·057	18
0·048	11
0·046	5
0·044	2

lack of sensitivity, the procedure could cause difficulties in enforcement at higher levels of water addition (viz. > 10% for 'new style' products).

The rapidly decreasing sensitivity of the index at higher levels of added water together with the dependence on fat content creates a high degree of uncertainty in the result obtained from the analysis of a single sample (as is the case in Codex and in the UK). The method of control based on water/protein ratio appears to be less vulnerable since it has the merit of linearity over the likely range of added water content and independence from variations of salt content. The dependence of the index on fat content of the input raw material must be taken into account in the assessment of the result of analysis of any product.

WATER CONTENT OF POULTRY

With the exception of its use in CAP control of cured meats, the water/protein ratio is not generally used in the UK as a control measure, however, it has found favour in the EEC not only in assessment of meat products for classification in the Customs Tariff but also for the control of water content of frozen poultry under Regulation 2967/76. A choice of control procedures (detailed as Annex I, II, and III in the EC Regulation) is allowed by the EEC Regulation and by the Statutory Instrument recently enacted in the UK (SI 1982/1602).

The in-factory method is based on check-weighing a random selection of carcasses after evisceration and before the final chill/wash. The carcasses are marked individually and after completing the process of washing and draining each is reweighed. A limit of 5% of the net carcass weight is allowed on average for water retention. The limit defined by the Regulation varies with the method of estimation chosen for use by the regulatory authorities or prescribed by national legislation.

The method of analytical control selected for use in the UK (SI 1982/1602) is that described in Annex III of the EC Regulation; it depends on an agreed figure for the average water/protein ratio for freshly killed poultry. The prescribed limit for extraneous water is expressed in the form of a regression line which is based on a research study carried out by a number of laboratories within the Community.[30] Jonas[31] reported on a study carried out in UK process plants which showed that uptake of water in excess of 12% was found in individual carcasses examined by the direct weighing procedure (Annex I) when the plant was set to operate a 5–6% weight gain. The gross carcass weight was found to be a controlling factor on water uptake whilst other process conditions were held constant. The study of the Annex III method showed that interlaboratory variations in the observed mean protein content resulted in a variation of approximately 5% in calculated physiological water content. This is to be compared with the EEC limit which is calculated on the basis of an average pick up at all weights of 8% water when control by chemical analysis is used.

For each of 6 laboratories and 3 process plants, individual linear correlations of water (W) and protein (P) content, expressed in grammes, were calculated in the form $W = aP + b$. The variability of the constants a and b was studied and it was noted that the regression lines were clustered around, but not parallel to, the proposed EEC control limit. The data were examined to test the probability of failure of one or two groups of seven carcasses, the number required for examination as the official sample. Significant differences between the probability of failure were noted for each of the 3 process plants. The variation in regression constants is summarised as follows:

	Lowest value	*Highest value*	*Mean*
a	3·19	4·01	3·5
b	−12·16	+208·13	120

The studies embraced the effect of variations in carcass weight and the effect due to presence or absence of offal in the packed carcass. The conclusions drawn were that, under commercial conditions, the water pick-up during spray-washing/chilling is inversely related to carcass weight and that offal contains a higher physiological water content than carcasses. Thus, it was shown that under conditions of the trial the risk of failing the prescribed EEC procedure was inversely dependent on the size of the carcass and directly dependent on the inclusion of offal in the pack.

ESTIMATION OF BUTTER FAT IN COMPOSITE PRODUCTS

For many years the identification and estimation of butter fat in food products has depended on the use of the Reichert–Polenske–Kirchner procedure. The method is empirical and requires a skilled analyst and strict attention to detail if reproducible results are to be obtained. Attempts have been made to replace the method by gas chromatographic procedures based on separation and estimation of free butyric acid or of the methyl ester. Phillips and Sanders[32] proposed a method in which the fat is first saponified and the resultant aqueous phase is acidified, filtered and analysed by direct injection onto a column of acid washed Celite loaded with Carbowax/terephthalic acid. These authors reported individual results on a range of 19 butter samples varying from 3·38 to 4·00 % of the total fat.

The mean butyric acid content of the samples examined was found to be 3·62 %; the authors recommended a mean factor of 3·6 for calculation of butter fat in preparations of unknown composition and claimed that results would not be in error by more than 10 %. Since the publication of the original method there has been considerable debate within a number of international organisations on the appropriate procedure for measurement of butyric acid either as free acid or as methyl ester and on the appropriate conditions for GLC.

Recently, the matter has been brought into a sharper focus by the activities of the EC analytical working group in Brussels. The Council Directive EEC 73/241 of 11 December, 1972 prescribes minimum limits for milk fat in milk and cream chocolate products; the Directive made provision for the development of methods of analysis to enforce the compositional standards. Although many European chemists tend to prefer the methyl butyrate procedure, the UK has promoted the simpler direct method for estimation of free butyric acid.

A recent collaborative study of the methyl ester method and two variants of the method of Phillips and Sanders has been undertaken in the UK; the samples examined were composite preparations of milk fat with coconut oil or lard together with cocoa butter. A report on the study by Biltcliffe and Wood[8] has shown that the results from 16 out of 30 laboratories using the specified column and conditions of use were rejected by the Youden Rank Sum Test[10] at the $P < 0{\cdot}05$ level; at $P < 0{\cdot}001$ the results from 6 laboratories were rejected. Recoveries of added milk fat were considered to be generally satisfactory but the value of the 'factor' required to obtain a mean of 100% recovery was assessed at 3·73. The performance reported for the Phillips and Sanders procedure was better than the proposed variation, the results in general indicating that the method as originally described is suitable for estimation of milk fat in chocolate at a concentration approximating to that found in the commercial product (viz. c. 10%). The reproducibility of the method is approximately 1·6 and is not concentration dependent; hence, at lower levels of milk fat content (c. 4–5%) the procedure is regarded as unsatisfactory.

The concluding comment in the report by Wood which indicates the use of a factor of 3·6 for conversion of butyric acid into butter fat content, also suggests that consideration is being given to a factor for inclusion in a Statutory method. Such a proposal is unusual and could be contrasted with the current practice on meat products in which publication of a Statutory factor for conversion of nitrogen to meat has been avoided.

However, in any assessment of the utility of the method the variability of the natural level of butyric acid in milk fat must be taken into account. Egan *et al.*[33] report that typically the butyric acid content of milk fat varies from 2·6 to 3·9%, and that the ratios C_{12}/C_{10} and C_{14}/C_{12} are 1:1 and 3:4, respectively. Several reports on the butyric acid content of butter appear in the literature; two of the more extensive European studies in which GLC methods were used are those due to Hadorn and Zurcher.[34,35] In the former, 39 samples were examined, the range reported was 3·46–4·13 (mean 3·75); in the latter, covering 75 samples chosen to illustrate seasonal variations, the range was 3·55–3·91 (mean 3·72). Comparison of literature values must be approached with some caution since the mode of expression of results used by different workers is not uniform. The variants are butyric acid as a proportion of the total fatty acids, as a proportion of the anhydrous fat, as methyl butyrate in the fat or as the proportion of methyl butyrate in the total methyl esters of fatty acids.

Equally, there is a need to describe clearly the full calibration procedure adopted in gas chromatography; the influence of varying carbon/oxygen ratios on the response factors of fatty acids is occasionally overlooked. This variation is highly significant for the lower molecular weight fatty acids. Care must be taken to ensure that the butyric acid (or methyl butyrate) response is directly related to an appropriate standard. Normalisation against a mixed molecular weight group of fatty acids can lead to a distortion of the results of analysis.

DETERMINATION OF FIBRE

During the last few years much emphasis has been placed on the dietary importance of fibre in maintaining physiological efficiency. Development of a sound understanding of the function of fibre in the diet has been hindered by confusion as to its nature, definition and appropriate methods of estimation. The all embracing definition developed by Trowell *et al.*[36] includes all the polysaccharides and lignin in the diet that are not digested by the enzymes of the digestive tract. Thus, the feature which distinguishes dietary fibre polysaccharides from starch is that the material is resistant to hydrolysis by amylase or disaccharidases. Structurally, the resistant polysaccharides include cellulose, hemicellulose and pectin which constitute the major components of plant cell wall material. Lignin, a complex of branched polymer polyphenols constitutes up to 20% of plant cell wall structure; tannins are also phenolic polymeric compounds which occur in some plant materials. Also included in the definition will be the non-structural, non-digestible carbohydrates which occur naturally or which are used as additives. This latter group includes thickening, emulsifying and bulking aids derived from gums, mucilages, algal polysaccharides, agar, and carrageenans, together with the range of synthetic thickening agents such as modified cellulose.

Early methods which were utilised to determine fibre were those based on acid and alkali treatment used to establish the 'digestibility' or 'crude fibre' in animal feed. The 'crude-fibre' so determined is generally held to be an underestimate of the dietary fibre content since the alkali treatment solubilises hemicellulose and lignin. The neutral detergent fibre (NDF) method, which estimates cellulose and lignin, relies on digestion in sodium lauryl sulphate solution in the presence of buffering and chelating agents; the value obtained by use of the method approximates to the definition of fibre. However, problems occur with high starch foods, and the acid detergent fibre (ADF) method has been developed to cater for the analysis of starch-rich materials.[37,38] A more rigorous chemical method using a mixture of trichloroacetic acid, acetic acid and nitric acid to solubilise protein and starch was developed by van de Kamer and van Girkel.[39] The residue after washing is oxidised with acid dichromate and the unused dichromate is estimated iodometrically.

Enzyme digestion procedures have been developed by a number of workers. The method requires the use of efficient and reproducible enzyme preparations to effect the amylolytic and proteolytic steps; a combination of pepsin and pancreatin treatments most resembles the conditions of human digestion. Alternative methods use a combination of chemical extraction and enzyme treatment: soluble sugars, amino acids and some lipids may be removed by extraction of the sample with ethanol. Enzymic digestion to hydrolyse starch and protein may be used to isolate the insoluble fraction.

The procedure adopted by Southgate *et al.*[40] attempts fractionation of the various carbohydrates (free sugars, hexoses, pentoses) and uronic acid, the residue after fractionation by selective solubilisation and enzyme hydrolysis being weighed as lignin. The insoluble cellulose fraction is hydrolysed and determined as sucrose. Thus, the estimation of fibre is represented as a summation of the component fractions which are selectively isolated and estimated by a number of chemical methods.

Fractionation procedures have been studied collaboratively; in general, the results indicate that the methods require skill and practice to obtain consistent results on 'within laboratory tests' but between laboratory replication is poor.[41] Minor variations in pretreatment of the samples and in the hydrolysis stages contribute substantially to the analytical problem. Workers in different laboratories have reported varying experience in gelatinisation of starch and in the results of enzymolysis. Considerable effort has been spent in the refining of methods to determine the sugar components, uronic acids and the other fractions obtained in the various methods. However, it is apparent from the evidence of collaborative studies that precise definitions of applicability, sample preparation and conditions of treatment through the various stages is of major importance if successful and reproducible assays are to be achieved. In addition, it is necessary to establish in more precise terms the chemical identity of the various fractions which are thought to contribute to the factors which are of importance in the diet.

Player and Wood[4] reported on a collaborative trial in 19 laboratories of three methods for the estimation of fibre in flour. The aim of the study was to assess the analytical enforcement of the prescribed limit of 0·6% (on dry matter) for fibre in wheat meal or brown flour. The FSC (1974) report on bread and flour suggested that the AMC (1943) gravimetric method was the most appropriate for enforcement of the provisions of subsequent legislation. However, within the EC the most favoured method is that of van der Kamer and van Ginkel.[39] The study included both these methods and that of van Soest[37,38] using acid detergent.

Following the normal statistical analysis, the results from one laboratory were excluded from the moisture set and results from two different (in each case) laboratories were excluded from each of the tests of the fibre methods. Repeatability and reproducibility of the results for moisture at the 95% confidence level averaged 0·45 and 1·34, respectively, at a moisture content of 13%. Comparison of the results from the three fibre methods showed that the acid detergent method gave significantly higher values than the two 'crude fibre' methods. The repeatability and reproducibility for the crude fibre methods were similar over the range of fibre values tested (0·2–2·2%), but the acid detergent method gave less satisfactory performance over the range (0·3–3·1%) found by that method on the same samples.

CONCLUSIONS

If progress is to be made at national and international level in the specification and standardisation of foods it is evident that there is no room for ambiguity of definition either in the legal (descriptive) sense or in the technical sense. The cross-section of topics selected and discussed above is by no means exhaustive. It serves to illustrate not only that accurate analysis of food composition is dependent on research to establish in chemical terms a clearer understanding of the nature of the substances being analysed but also that there is a need for the development of thoroughly tested methods of known performance. The problems of obtaining stable, homogeneous and relevant test materials are being tackled in a more comprehensive way than hitherto. Equal prominence is being given to the establishment of agreed, harmonised protocols for testing methods and the methods of testing results.

REFERENCES

1. Jackson, P. A. (1982). *Food Flavourings, Ingredients, Processing, Packaging*, **4**, 12.
2. Egan, H. (1978). *IUPAC Inf. Bull.*, (2), 132.
3. Horwitz, W. (1976). *J. Assoc. Off. Analyt. Chem.*, **59**, 238.
4. Player, R. B. and Wood, R. (1980). *J. Assoc. Publ. Analysts*, **18**, 29.
5. Player, R. B. and Wood, R. (1980). *J. Assoc. Publ. Analysts*, **18**, 77.
6. Player, R. B. and Wood, R. (1980). *J. Assoc. Publ. Analysts*, **18**, 109.
7. Biltcliffe, D. O. and Wood, R. (1982). *J. Assoc. Publ. Analysts*, **20**, 55.
8. Biltcliffe, D. O. and Wood, R. (1982). *J. Assoc. Publ. Analysts*, **20**, 69.
9. Adams, W. S. (1978). *J. Assoc. Off. Analyt. Chem.*, **61**, 354.
10. Youden, W. J. and Steiner, E. H. (1975). *Statistical Manual of the AOAC*, AOAC, Washington, DC.
11. Stubbs, G. and More, A. (1919). *Analyst*, **44**, 125.
12. Food Standards Committee (1980). *Report on Sausages*, FSC, Report 37, HMSO, London.
13. Food Standards Committee (1956). *Report on Canned Meat*, FSC, Report 46, HMSO, London.
14. Statutory Instrument (1967). No. 861 and No. 862, HMSO, London.
15. Statutory Instrument (1968). No. 430, HMSO, London.
16. Hornsey, H. C. (1969). *Food Manuf.*, **44**(1), 48.
17. Pearson, D. (1968). *J. Assoc. Publ. Analysts*, **6**, 129.
18. Pearson, D. (1970). *J. Assoc. Publ. Analysts*, **8**, 22.
19. Food Standards Committee (1980). *Report on Meat Products*, FSC, Report 72, HMSO, London.
20. Hannan, R. S. (1982). SCI Meat Panel Lecture, London.
21. Analytical Methods Committee (1963). *Analyst*, **88**, 583.
22. Analytical Methods Committee (1961), *Analyst*, **86**, 557.
23. Bradstreet, R. B. (1965). *The Kjeldahl Method for Organic Nitrogen*, Academic Press, New York and London.

24. Lee, D. M. (1971). *Scientific and Technical Surveys No. 69*, BFMIRA, Leatherhead.
25. Dransfield, E. *et al.* (1983). *Meat Science*, **8**, 79.
26. Heidelbaugh, G. H., Huber, C. S., Bednarczyk, J. F., Smith, M. C., Rambaut, P. C. and Wheeler, H. O. (1975). *J. Ag. Fd. Chem.*, **23**, 611.
27. de Rhan, O. (1982). *Lebensm,-Wiss. u-Technol.*, **15**, 22.
28. Rangley, W. R. D. and Lawrie, R. A. (1976). *J. Food Technol.*, **11**, 143.
29. US Department of Agriculture (1982). 9 CFR, Parts 317, 318 and 319, USDA, Washington, DC.
30. Commission European Community (1976). *Water Content of Deep Frozen Poultry, Information on Agriculture No. 15*, Office for Official Publications of the European Communities, Brussels.
31. Jonas, D. A. (1981). *J. Food Technol.*, **16**, 683.
32. Phillips, A. R. and Sanders, B. J. (1968). *J. Assoc. Publ. Analysts*, **6**, 89.
33. Egan, H., Kirk, R. S. and Sawyer, R. (1981). *Pearson's Chemical Analysis of Foods*, Churchill Livingstone, Edinburgh and London.
34. Hadorn, H. and Zurcher, K. (1970). *Deutsche Lebensmit.-Rundschau*, **66**, 249.
35. Hadorn, H. and Zurcher, K. (1969). *Mitt. Geb. Lebensmittelunters Hyg.*, **60**, 466.
36. Trowell, H. *et al.* (1976). *Lancet*, **1**, 967.
37. Van Soest, P. J. (1973). *J. Assoc. Off. Analyt. Chem.*, **56**, 781.
38. Van Soest, P. J. (1973). *J. Assoc. Off. Analyt. Chem.*, **56**, 825.
39. Van der Kamer, J. H. and Van Ginkel, L. (1952). *Cer. Chem.*, **29**, 239.
40. Southgate, D. A. T., Hudson, G. J. and Englyst, H. (1978). *J. Sci. Fd. Agric.*, **29**, 1979.
41. James, W. P. T. and Theander, O. (1981). *The Analysis of Dietary Fibre in Food*, Marcel Dekker Inc., New York.
42. Statutory Instrument (1982). *No. 1602, Poultry Meat (Water Content) Regulations*, HMSO, London.

4

Research on Analysis of Food Quality

KJELL IVAR HILDRUM, MAGNI MARTENS and HARALD MARTENS
Norwegian Food Research Institute, Aas, Norway

ABSTRACT

Most foods are made up of complex biological materials, and the precise assessment of food quality is usually a difficult task. Obtaining relevant information at sufficient speed and low cost is an important problem in food research and food production, e.g. in on-line process control, where quality deviations must be corrected quickly.

Quality parameters range from highly relevant ones like consumer acceptance and microbiological shelf-life (the measurements of which are slow or expensive) via, for example, sensory and chemical analysis, to rapid or inexpensive on-line electronic measurements of, for example, spectrometric properties—methods which in themselves give less product-relevant information.

An important question is: how can we use rapid or low-cost methods to get the information that normally has to be obtained by slow and expensive methods? Part of the answer is to develop reliable calibrations, i.e. mathematical relationships between the different types of quality assessments.

Up to recent years, analysis of food quality has been characterised by univariate measurements of single quality parameters, either by direct or indirect methods. The development of the new multivariate instruments has created a new situation, where estimation of several quality features is done simultaneously from large amounts of data.

Examples from the analysis of meat and vegetable products will be presented, which will focus on the new multivariate techniques and their correlations with the more traditional types of food analysis.

When using the multivariate methods, there are several pitfalls to be aware of. Problems with calibration techniques, outlier detection and interferences will be elaborated. Possible further developments in this field will be touched upon.

INTRODUCTION

As a starting point, there is one main question that needs to be reflected upon: do we really need research on analysis of food quality today? In the libraries we find stacks of literature describing numerous methods for analysis of foods. Is there any real need to replace the old proven methods, like Kjeldahl analysis for protein or Soxhlet extraction for fat, with new methods?

Let us leave this question for a while and look at some developments in recent years and some possible future trends in the area. We shall particularly consider research concerning new methods for quality assessment in food—methods that can be used in food research as well as in the food industry and in agricultural science.

We analyse food products because we want to assess their quality. Quality has been defined as fitness for purpose, but is commonly associated with the degree of excellence of a product. The European Organisation for Quality Control defines quality as 'the totality of features and characteristics of a product or service that bear on its ability to satisfy a given need'.[1]

The 'given need of the consumer' in this definition is of crucial importance, and it is highly relevant to try to predict the consumer's response to the product. Industrial approaches nowadays treat quality more in terms of consumer acceptance than expert opinion.[2]

As most foods are made up of complex biological materials, the precise assessment of the important 'features and characteristics' of a food product is a difficult task. Quality features range from highly relevant ones like consumer acceptance and microbiological shelf-life via sensory and chemical properties, to spectral or mechanical properties suitable for on-line instrumental measurements (Fig. 1). The latter methods normally give less consumer relevant information, but are usually inexpensive, precise, reliable and fast. The highly relevant consumer tests in contrast, are often costly, imprecise and slow. Traditional 'wet-chemistry' analysis and sensory laboratory analysis are usually between these two extremes in relevance and speed.

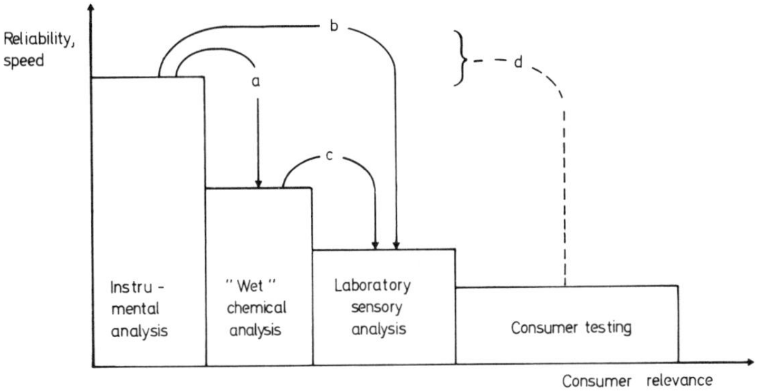

FIG. 1. Relationship between consumer relevance and reliability/speed of different types of analysis. (a) Crop or process optimisation with respect to chemical composition, based on rapid instrumental measurements. (b) Crop or process optimisation with respect to sensory quality, based on rapid instrumental measurements. (c) Research on chemical basis of sensory quality. (d) Prediction of consumer response from sensory, chemical or instrumental measurements.

How can we use rapid or low-cost methods to get relevant quality information that usually has to be obtained by slow and expensive methods? One answer is to interface or bridge the different types of analyses. For this end, we have to develop reliable calibrations, i.e. mathematical relationships between the different types of quality measurements. If such relationships are found, it may be possible to make accurate predictions of consumers' response from sensory and chemical analyses in the laboratory or to optimise industrial processes with respect to sensory or chemical quality from on-line instruments.

DIRECT AND INDIRECT METHODS

An important difference to be discussed here is that between direct and indirect correlation. Most traditional chemical analyses are based on direct correlations, which describe causal, physical relationships between the measurements and the specific properties which are of interest to us. A hypothetical example of a direct correlation is the prediction of bitterness in vegetables by the concentration of the bitter compound coumarin (Table 1).

Correlations may be univariate or multivariate. In multivariate

TABLE 1
BASIC CALIBRATION MODELS ILLUSTRATED HYPOTHETICALLY FOR BITTERNESS IN VEGETABLES

Complexity	*Types of relationship*	
	Direct	*Indirect*
Univariate	Bitterness = function (coumarin)	Bitterness = function (colour)
Multivariate	Bitterness = function (coumarin, phenols, etc.)	Bitterness = function ($colour_1$, $colour_2$, etc.)

direct correlations, two or more known constituents contribute to the property of interest. In our example, if the bitterness of the vegetable was caused both by coumarin, phenols and other known constituents, it could be predicted from measurements of all these constituents.

In indirect correlations, on the other hand, the relationships between the measurements and the properties are empirical rather than causal, but can still be used if they are reliable. We might use the colour of the vegetable as an easy measure of bitterness, provided that the concentration of the colourless, bitter coumarin followed that of the main pigment.

Indirect correlations may also be used in food analysis although with some care. Such calibrations often need to be multivariate, where several measured variables are simultaneously correlated with the property of interest. Thereby one can compensate for possible systematic interferences. In our example, a second pigment, uncorrelated to coumarin concentration and other bitter compounds,

TABLE 2
EXAMPLES OF MEASURING TECHNIQUES WHICH MAY BE (ARE) USED IN MULTIVARIATE, QUANTITATIVE ANALYSIS

Measuring technique	*'Spectrum variable'*
Spectrophotometry	Wavelength
X-radiation	Wavelength/energy
Ultrasonics/sonics	Frequency
Chromatography/electrophoresis	Retention time
Mass spectroscopy	Mass fragmentation pattern
Image analysis	Pixel frequency
Calorimetry	Phase transition temperature

might interfere with the colour measurement that predicts coumarin bitterness. This interference could be compensated for by measuring the colour at two or more wavelengths.

The recently developed multivariate, quantitative instruments are based on multivariate calibrations. The calibration may be used on any instrument producing a 'spectrum' of some kind. Table 2 shows some measuring techniques that can be, or are being used in multivariate quantitative instruments. With the appropriate computer program, the analysis can be done in a short time on more or less intact samples. The multivariate instruments have proven valuable for quantitative analysis ('unscrambling') of individual components in complex mixtures such as agricultural produce.

NIR REFLECTANCE: A RAPID, INDIRECT, MULTIVARIATE TECHNIQUE

Up till now, spectrophotometric measurements have often been used for multivariate analysis, particularly in the near-infrared and infrared regions. Near-infrared (NIR) reflectance spectrophotometers with multivariate computer programs have been available for several years, and are particularly widespread in the cereal industry.[3-6]

Near-infrared measurements with these instruments have to rely on indirect calibration. This is because we are usually unable to measure each component separately, or because an isolated constituent is not representative of that constituent in the mixed sample. The indirect calibration consists of 'teaching' the instrument how to recognise the percentages of the main components as follows:

1. Select a representative set of calibration samples.
2. Measure the desired chemical data in these samples.
3. Measure their NIR light absorbances at different wavelengths.
4. Compute a mathematical relationship between NIR and chemical data.

This mathematical relationship is later used to predict the composition of unknown samples from their NIR spectrum.

Applications of NIR reflectance analysis on meat have been explored in recent years.[7-9] In the following, a study on meat products, done in co-operation with a Norwegian meat processing plant, will be described.

One hundred and sixty-four samples of 3 different product types, which were sampled from processing lines, were homogenised and analysed directly on a NIR instrument with 19 wavelength filters in the region 1400–2600 nm (InfraAlyzer 400®, Technicon). The 3 product groups were raw, cooked and fried comminuted meat products. The calibration was performed with standard software, a downward stepwise Multiple Linear Regression analysis (MLR). Separate calibrations were made for each product group to improve the precision. The chemical composition of the samples was analysed for fat (Foslet), water (drying) and protein (Kjeldahl). The calibrations were tested by predicting the composition of 122 unknown samples, which were afterwards submitted to the standard chemical analysis.[10]

The results are shown in Tables 3 to 5, where the goodness of the calibration and prediction steps is estimated by the standard errors. Between 7 and 11 filters were used in the analysis of each component. SEE is the standard error of estimation, which is the 'average' difference between the predicted concentrations by NIR of the calibration samples and the chemically obtained concentrations. Samples yielding calibration residuals >2 SEE were taken as 'outliers' and deleted before recalibration. The number of samples deleted on this basis is given in the tables. SEP is the standard error of prediction, i.e. the corresponding difference obtained when testing the calibration for new, unknown samples. Both SEE and SEP are given in per cent of wet weight. SEP gives the more realistic description of the precision of the whole analysis.

The protein contents were predicted with the best precision for all 3

TABLE 3
ANALYSIS OF RAW COMMINUTED MEAT BY NIR REFLECTANCE SPECTROMETRY

Component	*Calibration*				*Prediction*	
	No. of samples	*No. of deletes*	*No. of filters*	*SEE*	*No. of samples*	*SEP*
Protein	53	8	9	0·49	20	0·57
Water	53	10	7	0·90	55	1·14
Fat	53	12	9	0·61	55	0·81

TABLE 4
ANALYSIS OF COOKED COMMINUTED MEAT PRODUCTS BY NIR REFLECTANCE SPECTROMETRY

Component	*Calibration*				*Prediction*	
	No. of samples	*No. of deletes*	*No. of filters*	*SEE*	*No. of samples*	*SEP*
Protein	55	4	10	0·45	20	0·60
Water	55	8	9	0·75	38	0·91
Fat	55	7	8	0·60	38	0·85

product groups—SEP ranging from 0·57 % to 0·85 %. The prediction of fat content was also satisfactory, while water content obtained the poorest prediction. No large differences were found between the raw, cooked and fried product groups as for the precision.

A second study included about 200 meat products—raw, cooked, fried, smoked and fermented—from many different manufacturers. The material was randomly divided into subsets, which formed the calibration and prediction sets. The standard errors were found to be substantially higher than in the former study, which points to the fact that multiproduct calibration in NIR is not yet reliable enough.

However, in a process control laboratory where the calibrations are performed individually on a few types of products in which the ingredients are known, the performance of the NIR instrument was satisfactory. Thus, the instrument has been used in routine processing control of meat products for nearly three years in a Norwegian food processing plant, giving rapid fat, water and protein results.

Also, the mid-infrared (MIR) transmission spectrum has found use

TABLE 5
ANALYSIS OF FRIED COMMINUTED MEAT PRODUCTS BY NIR REFLECTANCE SPECTROMETRY

Component	*Calibration*				*Prediction*	
	No. of samples	*No. of deletes*	*No. of filters*	*SEE*	*No. of samples*	*SEP*
Protein	56	7	11	0·58	21	0·85
Water	56	10	9	0·92	29	1·34
Fat	56	6	11	0·52	29	0·68

in multivariate instruments in the analysis of dairy and meat products.[11,12] A comparison of the NIR instruments with a MIR instrument (Super-Scan®, Foss Electric) in the analysis of raw meat samples showed the overall precision of the two methods to be at approximately the same level.[13] For the former method the meat samples were homogenised with an alkaline, aqueous solution of added emulsifiers, and the transmissions were recorded in fundamental IR absorption bands (5730, 6500, 9500 nm). Both instruments gave higher errors at higher fat contents (> 17 %), but MIR was the better device for high fat samples.

The NIR instrument is the faster in operation, but requires a laborious calibration by the user. It is claimed that the MIR instrument needs no 'local calibration', but it was shown that the prediction results of MIR could be considerably improved by optimising the slope and offset of the calibration curve.

RELATING SENSORY QUALITY TO CHEMICAL MEASUREMENTS

Now we will turn to a different type of problem: is it possible to predict sensory variables from chemical/physical data? Here, it is imperative to define which sensory variables are important in describing the quality of a food product. As examples, studies on carrots and peas will be used.

Inner quality of carrots was studied by 12 sensory and 7 chemical variables.[14] A total number of 81 batches, representative for the market with respect to varieties and harvesting times, from three seasons, was included in the study. A profile method was used to describe the sensory quality in an analytical way. Principal Component Analysis (PCA) was used in selecting the main quality attributes. Two principal factors were found to be significant by cross validation. They explained about 70 % of the total variation both in the chemical and sensory data, but PCA could not point to any clear relationship between the two sets of variables. The 5 sensory variables juiciness, crispness, sweetness, fruity taste and bitter taste were found to be important to inner quality of carrots.

To find the ability of the 7 chemical variables to predict the 12 sensory features, a Partial Least Square (PLS-2) regression method was used. Only 23 % of the total variation in the sensory quality data could be explained by the chemical variables. The most useful chemical criteria for predicting the sensory quality of carrots were found to be dry matter, sucrose and soluble solids. However, it was obvious that simple chemical analysis could not replace sensory analysis of carrots.

NIR FOR PREDICTING SENSORY QUALITY?

In a recent study on peas from the 1982 season, it was investigated, on a preliminary basis, whether a NIR reflectance instrument could be used in the prediction of sensory variables. The material consisted of 21 carefully chosen and well characterised batches.

Sensory analysis was carried out by a trained laboratory panel of 12 people. Each batch was judged in 3 replicates with respect to 11 sensory attributes. The same batches were also analysed by a number of standard chemical and rheological methods.

As with carrots, the main tendencies of variation in sensory quality in the material were studied by PCA. The sensory variables are characterised in terms of factor loadings (Fig. 2). Two significant factors were found by crossvalidation. The dominant factor, describing 70% of the variation in the sensory data, is a combined flavour/juiciness factor. A second factor, describing 16% of the remaining variation, is related to texture and appearance.

On the basis of high loadings and assumed relevance for NIR analysis, hardness, mealiness and sweet taste were chosen as sensory

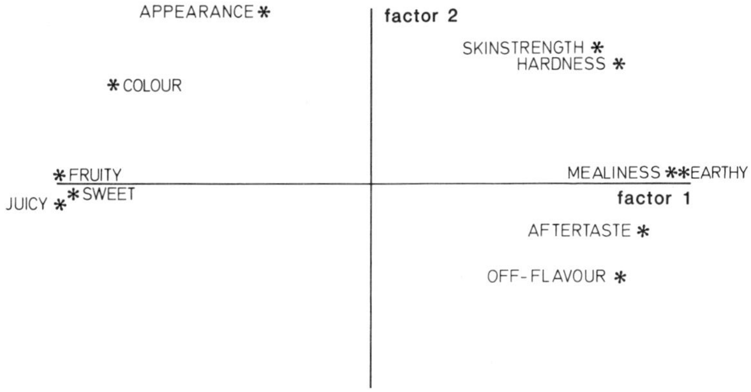

FIG. 2. Principal Component Analysis factor loadings of sensory variables of peas for the first two factors.

variables to be predicted by NIR measurements. A Partial Least Square (PLS-1) regression was used, which can be regarded as a combination of PCA and MLR. PLS-1 is different from conventional stepwise MLR, in that it includes all the 19 NIR filters in the final calibration. Instead it extracts various 'PLS factors' (linear combinations of the 19 NIR filters) and uses them in the prediction.

In Fig. 3 the prediction results for each variable are given. The goodness of prediction of the different variables is given by the noise-corrected Relative Ability of Prediction (RAP), which is the fraction of the total variance correctly predicted by NIR:

$$\mathrm{RAP} = \frac{s_{\mathrm{tot}}^2 - \mathrm{SEP}^2}{s_{\mathrm{tot}}^2 - s_{\mathrm{rnd}}^2}$$

where s_{tot}^2 = total variance of the variable and s_{rnd}^2 = random noise level in the variable estimated by the between-replicates variance. Relative Ability of Prediction was in the range 0·50–0·80 for these sensory variables, where hardness obtained the highest value. The 3 sensory variables, hardness, mealiness and sweetness, could thus be surprisingly well predicted by NIR measurements.

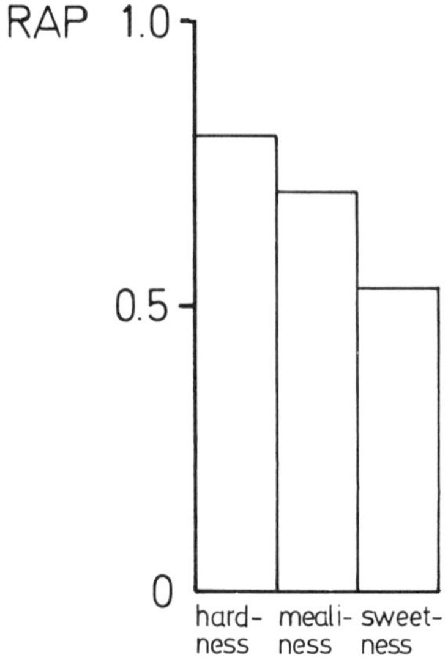

FIG. 3. The NIR measurements Relative Ability of Prediction (RAP) for sensory variables of peas. 1 = Perfect prediction, 0 = no predicting ability.

Figure 4 shows how the PLS calibration was performed in greater detail for hardness. The residual standard errors for the calibration set (SEE) and the prediction set (SEP) are shown as functions of the number of PLS regression factors. The straight dotted line gives the total standard deviation (s_{tot}) and the standard deviation due to random noise (s_{rnd}) level in the hardness data.

As can be seen from the figure, the SEE curve approaches the 'noise' line with increasing numbers of factors. Standard error of prediction for hardness, which indicates how well the 'unknown' samples can be predicted by NIR, has a minimum after 6 factors.

Also, the traditional chemical variables were predicted by NIR data by the same procedure (Fig. 5). Relative Ability of Prediction for the chemical variables, protein, water and alcohol insoluble solids (AIS), were in the range 0·87–0·89. The rheological tenderometer value (TV-hardness value) was also well predicted by NIR.

Since many factors are required to achieve a minimal SEP, it is to

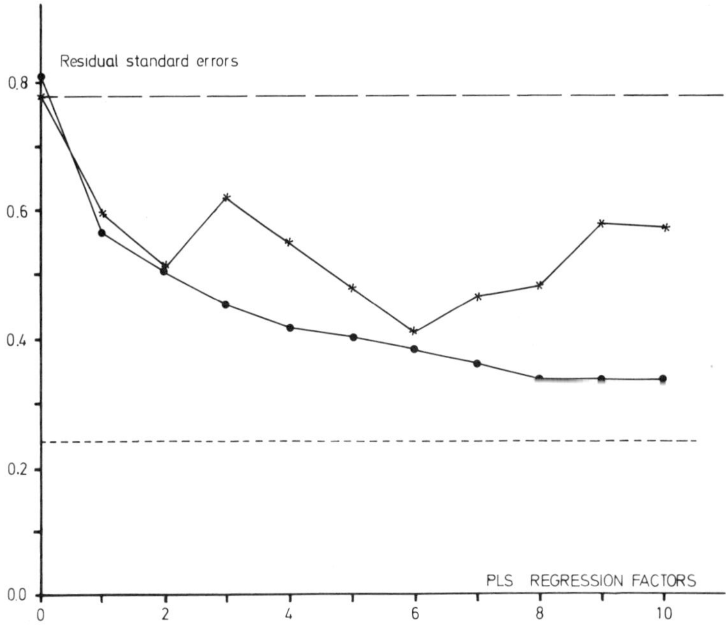

FIG. 4. Residual standard errors for sensory hardness of peas as functions of the number of PLS regression factors. ●, Standard error of calibration (SEE); *, standard error of prediction (SEP); ----, standard deviation due to measurement noise (s_{rnd}); ——, total standard deviation (s_{tot}).

be expected that a univariate calibration will give unsatisfactory results. However, by multivariate calibrations it is possible to overcome disturbances in the analysis like chemical interferences and light scatter.

The pea study indicates that it may be possible to use a fast, multivariate instrument to predict the relevant information of slower quality assessments like sensory analysis, using indirect multivariate calibration. Sensory quality of peas can thus be described by only two

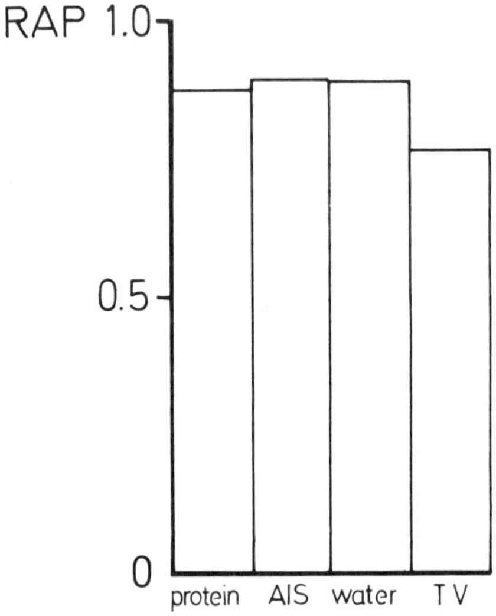

FIG. 5. The NIR measurements Relative Ability of Prediction (RAP) for chemical variables of peas. 1 = Perfect prediction, 0 = no predicting ability. AIS, alcohol insoluble solids; TV, tenderometer value.

main factors. Both chemical and sensory variables were reasonably well predicted by NIR analysis. It is possible that NIR can replace chemical and physical measurements for predicting sensory pea quality. However, the number of samples in the study was low, and the results need to be verified on a larger material.

Work is in progress to improve the NIR calibration by separating light absorbance from light scatter effects in the reflectance data. Also consumer tests (hedonic tests) on peas will be done, and the results will be related to descriptive sensory analysis as well as chemical/physical variables.

CALIBRATION PITFALLS AND PROBLEMS

When using the multivariate quantitative instruments, there are serious pitfalls to be aware of. The indirect calibration techniques used in NIR analysis—stepwise MLR, derivative regression and PLS regression—require that the range of calibration samples must represent all future unknown samples of that type. Also, it is imperative that the calibration and prediction samples should be measured under identical experimental conditions.

In the real world these restrictions are often not fulfilled. In the determination of, for example, protein in meat the calibration range might be exceeded. If proteins like casein, soy protein or collagen are not present as ingredients in the calibration set, the protein analysis will probably be erratic if these proteins are present in the unknown samples. Likewise, the samples to be predicted may contain impurities, be improperly prepared or measured at a different temperature than the calibration samples. An automatic safeguard against these types of errors is strongly needed.

An apparent solution to the problem is of course to include calibration samples that include most of the variability to be expected. This procedure is time-consuming and often means that some precision has to be sacrificed. Another solution is to divide the samples into subgroups as in the meat study, and make separate calibrations for each subgroup. This will maintain a better precision, but introduces a classification problem when unknown samples are to be analysed.

To obtain an automatic warning against such errors, a '2-stage data model' has been proposed[15,16,17] and was used here for the pea data (PLS-1). The first stage is to estimate the error of lack of fit between the NIR data and the NIR model. If the lack of fit exceeds a certain 'normal' level, the sample will be rejected as abnormal. In the second stage the accepted samples will be predicted as for their composition. Using different modifications of PLS calibration will give advantages such as automatic warning, simultaneous calibration of all variables and fewer calibration samples necessary. Also the classification problem mentioned above can be solved in the 2-stage model.

Regular control and adjustments of the calibrations are necessary to keep them reliable and accurate as the time goes by. Care must be taken to incorporate new, representative sample types to the calibration set, which differ from those originally used, and to withdraw samples which are out-dated. Computerised data analysis may be dangerous if the methods are not used correctly. The problem of 'overfitting' is serious, where trivial measurement errors may be presented as important findings of general interest. 'Overfitting' occurs when trying to fit a too complicated mathematical model, or when trying out too many alternative models, on too few independent observations. Another danger is to interpret indirect correlations as casual relationships.

There is also a human tendency to have blind faith in the results generated by computers. As the instruments system become more complex, this danger will be even more serious. It is comforting to know that computerisation also will speed up the incorporation of error-detecting and self-correcting systems into the instruments.

SOME TRENDS IN FOOD QUALITY ANALYSIS

The progress in the field of food analysis is strongly influenced by the developments in analytical chemistry. Therefore, let us have a short look at the trends in analytical chemistry in the last few decades.

Two decades ago analytical chemistry was dominated by traditional 'wet-chemistry' and the emphasis was on the separation of the compound of interest from interfering substances by classical methods, followed by instrumental reading in the final determination step.[18] The overall analysis was time-consuming, and the skill of the analyst was of crucial importance.

The 1970s was the decade of the large surveys of environment contaminants, and the need to rationalise the analysis became urgent. Multicomponent analysis became common, and automatic processing capabilities were introduced into the instruments. The detection limits of the compounds were markedly lowered, which intensified the discussion on the significance of trace amounts of contaminants.

The major trend in the 1980s in analytical chemistry is that the automation of the instruments will continue. Already, many instruments are controlled by computers, which perform data acquisition, data storage and retrieval, data display and library search. Soon the instrument computers will also be programmed for multivariate calibration and pattern recognition, sample selection, and statistical computations as well as data reduction 'on-line'. The role of the traditional analytical chemist will probably be changed. His work will be directed towards supervising and controlling the analytical system, and interpreting the results in co-operation with professionals with other backgrounds. On the instrument side, new sources and detectors will continue to contribute to the capabilities of the methods.

A development towards more complex situations will probably be a major trend in multivariate analysis in the coming years. In the meat study we used the NIR analysis to predict the concentrations of simple chemical components, which is a relatively simple situation. Prediction of sensory properties in peas from similar NIR analysis variables is a more complex problem. Several multivariate measurement techniques may in the future be combined to predict quality properties. An example is NIR, autofluorescence and visible spectrometry measurements combined to predict complex phenomena such as botanical components of plants.[16] A logical final step is to try to predict consumer response from sensory or chemical variables or even from instrumental data—a task of still higher complexity.

A recent editorial in the journal *Analytical Chemistry* goes back 50 years in time and looks at the 'modern trends' in the field at that time.[19] A progress report of 1930 states that 'the application of physical and physicochemical methods had increased rapidly'. Optical, spectroscopic, X-ray and electrical methods occupied important positions. It was noted that the chemists of that time ought to consider themselves very lucky to have such modern materials and equipment as silica ware, Pyrex and electric ovens with automatic control. The editorial makes a point of the fact that half a century later we are still refining and applying many of the same techniques.

So, do we need research on analysis of food quality today? In the years to come the foremost challenge in this research field is to make use of the possibilities that computers and computerised instruments are offering, in combination with advanced instrumental hardware. If we accept that challenge, the opportunities to rationalise food process control and optimise production of wholesome foods are great and should certainly be worth the efforts. On the other hand, if we go on refining and modifying present methods of food analysis for the coming 50 years in a traditional manner, the answer is more uncertain.

ACKNOWLEDGEMENTS

The authors want to thank Ms Ingebjørg Pedersen, Ms Marit K. Hårstad and Ms Sigrid Hurv for technical assistance, Dr Paul Geladi for programming and Ms Ragnhild Norang and Ms Ulla Bråthe for typing and technical drawing, respectively.

REFERENCES

1. Mayrhofer, M. (1982). *EOQC Quality*, **26**(B), 5–7.
2. Sidel, J. L., Stone, H. and Bloomquist, J. (1983). In: *Sensory Quality in Foods and Beverages: Its Measurement and Control*, Eds. Williams, A. A. and Atkins, R. K., Ellis Horwood Ltd, Chichester.
3. Osborne, B. G., Douglas, S. and Fearn, T. (1982). *J. Food Technol.*, **17**(3), 355–63.
4. Allvin, B. (1980). *Kem. Tidskr.*, **92**(1), 24–7.
5. Williams, P. C. (1979). *Cereal Chem.*, **56**(3), 169–72.
6. Hunt, W. H., Fulk, D. W., Elder, B. and Norris, K. (1977). *Cereal Foods World*, **22**(10), 534–6.
7. Kruggel, W. G., Field, R. A., Riley, M. L., Radloff, H. D. and Horton, K. M. (1981). *J. Assoc. Off. Anal. Chem.*, **64**(3), 692–6.
8. Norris, K. (1983). In: *Food Research and Data Analysis*, Eds. Martens, H. and Russwurm, J. H., Proc. IUFoST Symposium, Oslo, September 1982, Applied Science Publishers, London, 95–113.
9. Hauser, E. and Weber, U. (1980). *Die Fleischw.*, **60**(3), 482–5.
10. Martens, H., Bakker, E. A. and Hildrum, K. I. (1981). In: *Proc. 27. Eur. Meet. Meat Res. Work.*, Vienna, August, 1981, 561–4.
11. Arneth, W. (1981). In: *Proc. 27 Eur. Meet. Meat Res. Work.*, Vienna, August, 1981, 557–60.
12. Bjarnö, O. C. (1981). *J. Assoc. Off. Anal. Chem.*, **64**(6), 1392–6.
13. Hildrum, K. I., Valland, M. and Martens, H. (1983). In: *Food Research and Data Analysis*, Eds. Martens, H. and Russwurm, J. H., Proc. IUFoST Symposium, Oslo, September, 1982, Applied Science Publishers. London, 416.
14. Martens, M., Fjeldsenden, B., Russwurm, H. Jr. and Martens, H. (1983). In: *Sensory Quality in Foods and Beverages: Its Definition, Measurement and Control*, Eds. Williams, A. A. and Atkins, R. K., Ellis Horwood Ltd, Chichester.
15. Martens, H. and Jensen, S. Aa. In: *Proc. 7th World Cereal and Bread Congr.*, Prague, June, 1982, Elsevier, Amsterdam (in press).
16. Jensen, S. Aa., Munck, L. and Martens, H. (1982). *Cereal Chem.*, **59**(6), 477–84.
17. Wold, S., Martens, H. and Wold, H. (1983). In: *Matrix Pencils. Lecture Notes in Mathematics*, Springer Verlag, Heidelberg (in press).
18. Tanner, J. T. (1982). *J. Assoc. Off. Anal. Chem.*, **65**(3), 531–4.
19. Morrison, G. H. (ed.) (1981). *Anal. Chem.*, **53**(12), 1729.

5

A Scientist Looks at Future Prospects for Legislation

TREVOR J. COOMES

Food Science Division, Ministry of Agriculture, Fisheries and Food, London, UK

ABSTRACT

An overall consideration of risk evaluation and management as a preliminary to food legislation is presented. National risks are assessed by expert committees following toxicity studies, monitoring and food surveillance, but zero risk is impossible to achieve. The application of surveillance techniques has in many cases allowed risk-management without the need for statutory control. Biotechnological studies, particularly, may radically alter toxicity testing in the 1980s.

In a symposium devoted to the 'Control of Food Quality and Food Analysis' I thought it would be of some interest in this context to look at present strategies for risk-management of chemicals in food, in an attempt to determine whether food quality can be maintained in the future without increasing the demand imposed by legislative control.

As John Hawthorn indicated in his Keynote paper, commencing with the first Adulteration of Food and Drink Act in 1860, through the Keynote Sale of Food and Drugs Act in 1875, the Food and Drugs (Adulteration) Act of 1928, the Food and Drugs Act (1938) which combined food and drugs legislation and all the public health legislation relating to foodstuffs, to the Food and Drugs Act (1955) extant today, successive Governments have tightened the legislative noose around the sale of food to the public. Throughout this process, one of the major driving forces behind the philosophies of control propounded by the various Acts has been the desire to control so-called food chemicals whether they be those whose presence in food is deliberate or those which contaminate the food chain from adventitious sources which themselves may presently be both deliberate as well as fortuitous or accidental. The motivation behind the plethora of controls existing today has been the risk to the health of the human population, and perhaps to their pocket, supposedly, and in earlier times demonstrably, inherent in the uncontrolled sale of food to the population at large. I propose to deal only with risk to health and risk-management techniques which have evolved over the last 20 or so years to accommodate some of the concerns of a population developing both an increasing awareness of exposure to chemicals from all sources, together with a desire to participate in any decision-making process which they consider might affect their health or well-being. In this connection it is pertinent to mention that food analysis, utilising the many present day techniques of high selectivity and sensitivity, has contributed much to the increasing awareness of the population to human exposure to chemicals via the food chain, thus increasing societal demands for effective risk-management techniques.

In 1978 the Royal Society set up a Study Group on the Assessment and Perception of Risks which included people at the height of their professions representing a wide variety of disciplines. At a discussion meeting organised by the Group in order to hear a wide variety of views from within the UK and abroad[1] it was suggested by Lee and Pearce that risk is a two-dimensional entity comprising the probability of an event occurring and the magnitude of that event. In the event, the Study Group[2] chose to regard *risk* as '*the probability that a particular adverse event occurs during a stated period of time, or results from a particular challenge*'.

Acceptance of this particular definition of risk also implies that whoever assesses risk in any particular situation, correctly *perceives* its nature and magnitude. After perception, there follows *risk-assessment* which again the Study Group conveniently subdivided into *risk-estimation* which involves:

1. the identification of the outcomes;
2. the estimation of the magnitude of the associated consequences of these outcomes; and
3. the estimation of the probabilities of these outcomes;

together with *risk-evaluation* which is the complex process of determining the significance or value of the identified hazards and estimated risks to those concerned with or affected by the decision. Finally, *risk-management* is the making of decisions concerning risks and their subsequent implementation.

All of these terms are related to *benefit* which is the gain to a human population, and the expected benefit incorporates an estimate of the probability of achieving the gain. Risk–benefit decisions as we call them today have always been an important duty of Government regulatory activities, and in the field of foodstuffs including additives and contaminants, as I mentioned earlier, the history of regulatory control dates from 1860. The body of regulatory control extant today in relation to food, food additives and contaminants, is suited to the needs of consumers, and hopefully does not over burden either the chemical or the food manufacturing industry with undue costs in the provision of an assurance of safety both for the consumer, and indeed for themselves.

Food chemicals really fall into three fairly distinct groups. These comprise the food constituents themselves, those chemicals we have come to regard as deliberate additives, which include both those with a technological function in food manufacture, together with residues of processing aids and packaging migrants, and chemical compounds whose presence in food is non-deliberate as far as the food manufacturer is concerned. In this area we have the so-called food contaminants such as heavy metals, mycotoxins, nitrosamines and polycyclic aromatic hydrocarbons, together with residues from animal and crop husbandry practices and veterinary treatment such as pesticides, growth promoters, anthelmintics, coccidiostats, hormones, antibiotics and other residues of veterinary practice.

Traditionally the food constituents themselves have always been—to borrow a term from our cousins in the USA—'generally regarded as safe' and indeed, they are of course essential for survival. The tactical need to develop strategies for the risk-management of the deliberate and non-deliberate additives and contaminants in response to public demand has in the past turned our thoughts away from health effects which might involve the diet itself, other than those factors involved with the traditional deficiency diseases. Today, however, we are increasingly aware of the central role played by the diet itself not only in respect of human health and freedom from disease, but also in connection with the laboratory animals which play such an important role in our risk-assessment procedures.

In the case of chemicals in food, or indeed even manufactured foods themselves, we are concerned with the oral exposure of healthy individuals to chemicals, either deliberately or fortuitously, via the so-called food chain, which is often of greater length and indeed more involved than even the highly intelligent consumer realises. If asked, the average man and woman in the population would say that such exposures, which had not been consciously accepted by the individual concerned, should involve 'no-risk', whether or not they had any understanding of the potential effects which might arise from such exposure. This view, which can, upon occasion, be both vociferous and sustained, is the reason for Governmental regulatory activity in these areas, by a variety of mechanisms. Governments clearly recognise that, whilst the man in the street willingly accepts the level of risk involved in personal activities such as driving a motor car, or flying in an aeroplane, he finds the very much lower level of risk involved in the consumption of manufactured foods, in which small amounts of additives have been incorporated, completely unacceptable, unless such chemicals have been subjected to extensive testing and assessment, and their usages subsequently sanctified in law.

Of course the Government as with other regulatory authorities in the world, including our EC partners, have long recognised that it is impossible to give a complete assurance of 'safety' or zero risk. What is done, in the public interest, is designed to avoid risk insofar as this is reasonably possible or practicable in the light of the best scientific data and assessment available at the time. This philosophy places emphasis on good manufacturing practices, observance of hygienic practices and avoidance of obviously dangerous chemicals where these will be ultimately in direct contact with individual members of the public.

Nevertheless, it is still necessary with many chemicals to assess, by suitable tests, the nature of the biological hazards, the exposure which can be tolerated without significant harmful effects, and the actual exposure experienced by the population at risk. Inevitably, since no substance can be evaluated in a free society by using deliberate human exposure as the initial investigational step, laboratory and animal experiments are utilised for the assessment of any likely biological risks which might be involved in human exposure. Indeed, it must be said that it is very difficult to establish by simple observation in man whether continued exposure to a xenobiotic over many years causes adverse health effects. A history of prior exposure of man, even over several centuries, only provides evidence of safety in man if it is in the form of an appropriate epidemiological study. Such studies are few and far between even in today's environment of medical knowledge, partly because they are expensive, partly because the sociological climate outside the medical field tends to believe 'something' must be 'wrong' if participation in such a study is sought, but also because man himself is a 'random' animal whose genetic history may also be regarded as of 'random' construction thus making statistical interpretation of observed effect difficult without many 'assumptions'.

Effective risk-management also requires that the epidemiological studies embrace different population groups, particularly the vulnerable ones such as the young, the old, the sick and the pregnant. Such studies are difficult for ethical reasons, and because parallel controls are not easily identified in a general population.

In general, therefore, animal experimentation and surveillance of human exposure are used as substitutes for epidemiology, and their aims are:

1. To identify and/or characterise chemically the nature of the xenobiotic, the form in which exposure occurs and the form in which its biological effects are mediated (identity, physico-chemical characteristics, specification, biotransformation species, etc.).
2. To establish reliable qualitative and quantitative data describing the biological activities of the xenobiotic in animals (toxicity, metabolism, pharmacokinetics, etc.).
3. To establish reliable exposure or potential exposure data for man, including special groups such as the young, the old, the sick and the pregnant.
4. To identify benefits and disadvantages to man and to the environment of exposure to the xenobiotic.

These four aims enable some *predictions* of risk to be made. However, not all biological effects are predictable from standard biological screening tests. Such unpredictable effects include:

1. Adverse reactions such as hypersensitivity and intolerance where in many circumstances no valid animal models exist, or if they do (e.g. skin tests), extrapolation to man is not always reliable.
2. Antibiotic resistance and transfer of resistance factors to different types of antibiotics to other bacteria.

3. Unexpected transformations in the food chain, such as inorganic mercury to methyl mercury compounds by bacteria in water.
4. Effects of substances of complex composition (e.g. biomass) where the dietary load may be limited by nutritional considerations.

Ancillary data, outside the present day extensive range of toxicological tests in animals, is therefore often needed in order to complete the so-called biological profile of any substance in the food chain, directed particularly towards the identification of some of the less-predictable effects of chemicals in the food chain mentioned above.

Having assembled the data, the extrapolation process from animal to man consists essentially of an interpretation of the biological data, their correlation with other information such as the physical and chemical properties of the chemical, and with estimates of the likely exposure of the population to the chemical from all sources. In certain circumstances members of a given population may be exposed to the substance daily for the whole of their lifetime, and by a variety of pathways, so that the maximum likely exposure from all these sources needs to be considered.

In the UK, the extrapolation process has been and is carried out in respect of food additives and contaminants by a number of advisory committees maintained by Ministers of successive administrations. Thus, the Food Additives and Contaminants Committee advises, as its name suggests on matters referred to it by Ministers in relation to food contaminants, additives and similar substances which are, or may be, present in food or used in its preparation. This committee relies, for advice on the toxic risk to man in respect of food additives and contaminants, on the Department of Health and Social Security Committee on Toxicity of Chemicals in Food, Consumer Products and the Environment, Carcinogenicity and Mutagenicity.

The Advisory Committee on Pesticides advises on the operation of the Pesticides Safety Precautions Scheme, a non-statutory but nevertheless formally negotiated scheme under which every formulation destined to be marketed in the UK is first scrutinised in respect of the safety of the user, potential residues in food and effects on wildlife.

Since 1964, the introduction of the Medicines Act legislation and its subsequent operation has effectively removed drugs from control by the Food and Drugs Act (1955). In respect of veterinary chemicals, the licensing authority then became the Ministry of Agriculture, Fisheries and Food. The Veterinary Products Committee advises the Minister in respect of his responsibility for licensing the production of chemicals destined for veterinary usage deemed to comply with the requirements for efficacy and safety-in-use defined in the Medicines Act (1964).

All of these advisory committees consist of independent experts drawn from appropriate scientific disciplines in the fields of industry, academic life, consultancy and medical/veterinary practice, together with representatives of consumers. These experts are always selected for their experience bearing upon human risk assessment. Their on-going work is subject to peer review within the scientific community, and they are always free to dissent from the collective decisions of any review group to which they belong. The comment has been made by the Royal Society Study Group (loc. cit.) that probably the greatest built-in advantage of such a system is that safeguard which is never discussed in open forum—the naïve truism contained in the observation that the only thing that an 'expert' has to lose is his reputation. This is a powerful self-discipline!

The review system by means of independent advisory committees reporting to Ministers has served the country in respect of both consumers and industry well for the last two or more decades. No doubt the system will continue through the 1980s and beyond. It provides a unique opportunity to utilise the best expertise available at any given time, and ensures that interpretative philosophy develops apace with experimental toxicological research to the benefit of everyone in the field. In this connection, it is often forgotten that industrialists, members of expert advisory committees, toxicologists and even civil servants are consumers of food as well!

All of the expert groups I have referred to whose deliberations have a bearing on food additives and contaminants have issued, at some stage in their history, guidelines for the collection and submission of evidence required to enable risk–benefit decisions to be taken. In the field of direct food chemicals, the *Memorandum on Procedure for Submissions on Food Additives and on Methods of Toxicity Testing*[3] published in 1965 is still the only official guideline in the UK on food additive submissions. The details on toxicity testing contained in this document have now been superseded by the publication of the

Department of Health and Social Security Guidelines on the testing of chemicals for mutagenicity,[4] carcinogenicity[5] and toxicity,[6] all of which are drawn up in a wider context than simply food chemicals. On the other hand the recent Report of the EC Scientific Committee for Food, *Guidelines for the Safety Assessment of Food Additives*,[7] is so restricted.

A revised memorandum on submissions for food additives will certainly appear in the 1980s, and will make reference, *inter alia*, to the guidelines produced by the Department of Health and Social Security for the various safety evaluation areas covered by their expert advisory committees. It will deal largely with that other requirement for a food additive—'need', which I think I can safely say is a concept as important to a food manufacturer as a satisfactory toxicological evaluation. Certainly in terms of timescale and cost the greatest demands of legislative control of food chemicals relate to the establishment of what is known today as the biological profile of the chemical. This provides a good deal of the information enabling risk-management strategies to be recommended by expert advisers. The profiles are established by using the various guidelines available, and I think it is important to remember that these are intended to be exactly that, rather than the mandatory lists of standardised laboratory animal tests to be slavishly followed to completion before any details will be submitted to advisers for assessment.

Thus, today, in general terms, the amount of biological information required is related to the extent, or potential extent of human exposure, so that chemicals likely to be consumed regularly or in large quantities by a substantial proportion of the population will usually require the results of a comprehensive range of biological tests. Conversely, in the case of chemicals present in food in small amounts, for example, a few milligrams per kilogram, or present in only a few food items, less extensive biological information may be acceptable. The importance of metabolic data in the construction of the biological profile of a chemical is illustrated by the fact that if such data demonstrate the chemical to be broken down to constituents of known toxicity, no further testing may be required.

The recent report of the Food Additives and Contaminants Committee, *Report of Enzyme Preparations*,[8] provides a good example of limited demands for biological testing of chemicals used at low levels in the food industry. The Committee on Toxicity considered that, for a Group A classification, they would require as a minimum, the results of a well-conducted 90-day oral feeding study in a rodent, and the results of a general, non-specific biological screening test for the presence of toxins. This is a very reduced requirement in comparison with the full range of toxicity tests which have become almost the norm for a food additive used in significant amounts in food or in a wide range of foods. In this connection also, the Ministry has, within their function of funding food research, initiated a programme which attempts to develop an appropriate non-specific biological screening test for toxins.

During the last 20 years the costs of so-called traditional long-term toxicity studies utilising laboratory test animals have risen exponentially. Much of this increase represents investment in so-called carcinogenicity studies usually involving lifetime feeding studies with more than one species of test animal at several levels in the diet, and utilising sufficient numbers of animals to enable statistically significant conclusions to be drawn from the studies. Superficially, the phenomena of mutagenicity and carcinogenicity are similar, to the extent that both involve heritable changes in cell genotype, and the somatic mutation theory of cancer has received much support in recent years. It is now therefore widely accepted that chemicals capable of inducing mutations should be also suspected of being able to cause cancer, certainly for those chemicals capable, perhaps, following metabolic activation, of alkylating DNA bases.

Short-term tests for mutagenic potential, which are of low cost in comparison with carcinogenicity bioassays have thus become useful screening tests for carcinogens in recent years. Short-term tests are not presently substitutes for carcinogenicity bioassays since the precise relationship between mutagenicity and carcinogenicity has not yet been elucidated. However, the development of activation and mutation systems more closely resembling the *in-vivo* situation may improve the present correlation, and advisers concerned with risk-management may feel able to rely more on mutagenicity tests as screens for potential carcinogens in the future than presently. The adoption of such a philosophy would reduce the investment presently required in carcinogenicity bioassay by several orders of magnitude.

Other *in-vitro* test systems can also be useful in metabolic studies, and can include reactions with gastric or intestinal juices or with liver cells, together with their component enzymes. The latter can allow the identification of possible short-lived reactive metabolites which might cause toxicity under certain circumstances. The importance of such tests, if conducted with both animal and human tissues, resides in the possibilities afforded of direct assessment of risk to man. One such test, presently under extensive study with Ministry research funding, has demonstrated that *in-vitro* cultured rat hepatocytes will respond to treatment with a diverse group of peroxisome proliferators in a manner closely resembling the effects produced by the same compounds *in-vivo*. Such observations lend hope that eventually the evidence from such test systems in relation to both toxicity and carcinogenicity may be accepted in lieu of information currently obtained from tests utilising laboratory animals, with a consequent saving in total costs of clearance by advisers. Whilst it must be emphasised that *in-vitro* tests are not currently a substitute for traditional small animal experimentation, one attractive possibility opened up by such tests is that involving the use of appropriate human cells, thus perhaps enabling some refinement of that perennial problem of risk-management, extrapolation to man.

Another development in the last decade which complements studies in laboratory animals relates to the assembly and examination of data relating to human exposure. Such data is essential to complete any risk–benefit equation and is now made more meaningful utilising modern techniques for assessing dietary intakes, particularly of special groups within the population.[9]

In order to provide a background knowledge about the quality and safety of food in the UK, particularly in relation to the potential contamination of food by certain chemical residues, the Steering Group on Food Surveillance was set up by the Ministry of Agriculture, Fisheries and Food in 1971. Programmes of food monitoring organised by the Steering Group constantly review, assess and where necessary investigate by programmes of monitoring, the contamination of the food chain by certain chemical residues, where these are relevant to the safety and wholesomeness of food.

An essential feature of the work of the Steering Group is to organise food surveillance for those contaminants which:

1. Are present in food in very low amounts.
2. Require specialised analytical techniques for their detection and for which there is little or no information available of their distribution throughout the food chain.

I would particularly emphasise the latter reference to the distribution of a chemical contaminant throughout the food chain because in calculating human exposure from food it is necessary to know the individual contributions to the diet of each of the components containing the contaminant, as well as the amounts of the components of the diet containing the contaminant which are eaten. The Steering Group has adopted a systematic approach to the various problems of surveillance of the food chain along the following lines:

1. To assess the daily intake on average (from food and drink) of the substance in question by the consumer.
2. To determine how much of the substance is contained in the major foods in the human diet in the UK.
3. To determine whether any class of food might present special features with respect to the nature and content of the substance.
4. To identify any local areas of potential contamination or particular circumstances which might affect the amount of the substance in food and make special checks on these.
5. To assess the dietary intake of individuals whose patterns of consumption are atypical or who might be more at risk.

This approach gives a general picture of the position for any substance in food whether a chemical or radioactive substance, additive or nutrient, including residues resulting from environmental factors about which there is little previous history. Where statutory limits are in force for a particular contaminant, the results may also indicate the usefulness of such limits.

In summary, food surveillance studies are aimed primarily at examining the safety and wholesomeness of food supplies. Information from such studies can nevertheless be of use in establishing data-banks on chemical substances in food which ultimately can:

1. Indicate the need to look more closely at the uptake of certain chemicals by plants and animals and at the effects of crop and animal husbandry on such uptake.
2. Identify areas where the technological use of a chemical or where environmental pollution may be causing problems. Trends in pollution can also be identified from such surveillance.
3. Help to ensure that non-tariff barriers to international trade are not set up unreasonably.

Now, the aims of the food surveillance programme in the UK during the last 10 years have been to identify, quantify, evaluate and contain, insofar as is necessary for the protection of human health, contaminants of the total food chain arising from so-called natural processes, from technological processes and from environmental pollution. Our approach has been to use what we term 'the best practicable means' rather than to impose statutory limits for all but one of the recently investigated contaminants of the human food chain. This exception is vinyl chloride in packaging materials for food contact purposes and in food. This, of course, is the subject of a harmonised EC Directive.[10]

I am sure that the generation of appropriate surveillance data will continue during the 1980s to complement the parallel development of toxicological evaluation procedures.

It is now perhaps appropriate to consider briefly some possible areas of activity for the remainder of the 1980s. In the case of food additives we know that today many are manufactured by biotechnological processes. This development can be expected to continue, and with it perhaps a closer look at specifications in the light of alternative methods of manufacture. After all, few chemical products having the same name, but manufactured by different routes, have exactly the same specification or impurities. It is important to ensure that small chemical differences do not represent large differences in biological profile, more particularly because increasingly, modern methods for the development of biologically active chemical species utilise so-called recombinant DNA techniques in which the very basis of the cell itself is restructured.

It will also be important to continue our awareness of any possible effects on the food chain resulting from the introduction of new chemical substances into the ecosystem for whatever purposes, and to continue to utilise the best practicable means to ensure that no untoward contamination of the food chain ensues.

No doubt the pressures to move away from the use of laboratory animals for toxicity testing will continue, and parallel with this, advances in our knowledge of the application of *in-vitro* test systems and their relevance to assessment of effects on human health will occur—slowly!

I have attempted to illustrate, in the area of risk to health from chemicals, how risk-management strategies are developing in parallel with the accumulation of knowledge relating to their effects on biological test systems. Concomitant developments in food surveillance techniques, designed to identify potential new contaminants, quantify both their presence in the food chain and the likely human exposure to them via the diet. These provide an appropriate early-warning system to activate risk-management resources. The application of surveillance techniques has resulted in the containment of exposure problems in many cases without the need for statutory control. In only one instance in the last 10 years have controls been introduced by law, and that relates to vinyl chloride where the statutory limit is 1 mg/kg in poly(vinyl chloride) material destined for food contact purposes and 0·1 mg/kg in food so wrapped. Food surveillance measures conducted at intervals from the time the problem was identified to the present day have shown the way to achieve a reduction of levels both in the plastic material and in food to an order of magnitude below the presently imposed statutory tolerances.

Nevertheless, vinyl chloride is carcinogenic in test animals, and in humans at the same sites. How is it then, that any is allowed in some foodstuffs, even accepting that in a scientific context zero represents the limit of sensitivity of the analytical method used to determine the presence of a contaminant in food. Perhaps the risk-management strategy devolves from the following argument.

First of all poly(vinyl chloride) is a very useful packaging material for certain manufactured or even fresh foods. There is no doubt about its ability to aid the presentation of food at the end of the production, manufacturing, transport, storage and display chain, nor about its ability to aid the maintenance of the packaged food in acceptable condition until this point is reached, or even beyond it, in the home of the consumer. Nevertheless, its parent monomer, vinyl chloride is carcinogenic in humans and in test animals. Some residual monomer, albeit at very low levels is present in the packaging material and some small proportion of this residue migrates into food packaged in poly(vinyl)chloride.

Accepting that in the food area, risk-assessment is basically about dose–response relationships we have to accept, however, that risk evaluation for compounds contaminating food and which are suspected of carcinogenic potential, introduces a further factor into evaluation procedures. The view is generally held that there is no threshold dose for a complete carcinogen or initiator which produces irreversible, self-replicating cellular effects. It is therefore somewhat misleading to refer to a no-effect-level for substances having such properties. In practice, however, a no-effect-level may be observed for such substances in experimental animals as that exposure below which there is no detectable increase in tumour formation as a result of a lifetime's exposure. It must, however, be recognised that this is not an absolute value but rather a probability, which is determined by the design of the experiment, notably the size of the test group of animals. This does not exclude the possibility that clones of precancerous cells exist in the individual animal, with the potential for malignant progression under the influence of appropriate environmental or endogenous stimuli.

In this complex and emotive area it is difficult, if not impossible, to reconcile hypotheses on mechanisms of carcinogenesis with factual observations in laboratory experiments and with the statistical evaluation of the data obtained. Thus biologically, the mean age of cancer onset in exposed populations or treated animal groups is strictly not a function of the dose of a chemical carcinogen, but of its biological mode of action and the genetic predisposition of the exposed individual. However, when this parameter is evaluated statistically, it is largely affected by the longevity of the exposed or treated group. This occurs apparently because, for high doses of exposure, the mean age of cancer onset may be shorter than for very low exposures, when only a very few individuals may develop cancer but at a longer mean age of cancer onset. Although this appears to be a denial of the existence of a no-effect-level for a carcinogen, in practice, it means that the probability of developing cancer from a very low exposure may be almost infinitesimal, unless one happens to be the individual biologically predisposed towards developing cancer. In the latter situation, that individual would develop the cancer after the appropriate biological latent period.

For all practical purposes, and all risk-assessment is about practical situations in a very complex world, it would not be unreasonable to neglect this infinitesimal probability. This is tantamount to considering that a practical no-effect-level exists for a carcinogen, and accepting that a risk-assessment has been made within the limitation of the scientific knowledge of the moment. After all, in this situation death would be much more likely to occur from all other causes than from the characteristic cancer caused by the carcinogen.

Now I would not claim that the foregoing argument is the reason why the UK, the remaining members of the European Economic

Community and indeed many other countries of the world permit the use of poly(vinyl) chloride formulations in food packaging. What I would say is that it is a very practical argument based on observed biological events. Risk-management strategies are about practical things, and in fact the argument extends even further. Risk-management strategies are developed for situations that we recognise. What about those situations which clearly exist, but about which we know little or nothing? Look at history—mycotoxins in 1960, nitrosamines in 1965, packaging monomers in 1978—all with the implications of carcinogenicity. These are the times at which the possibilities of effects on human beings were recognised as a result of the development of scientific knowledge and expertise. Human *exposure* was clearly extant long before these dates.

Is it not possible, that over generations of human exposure to chemical substances having the ability to alkylate DNA bases or to initiate or promote such reactions, a genotype has emerged in which the efficiency of the DNA repair process is such as to negate the effects of very small amounts of such compounds?

REFERENCES

1. Warner, F. and Slater, D. H. (1981). *Proc. Roy. Soc. Lond.*, **A.376**, 1–206.
2. The Royal Society (1983). *Risk Assessment Report of a Royal Study Group*, Royal Society, London.
3. Her Majesty's Stationery Office (1965). *Memorandum on Procedures for Submissions on Food Additives and on Methods of Toxicity Testing*, HMSO, London.
4. Her Majesty's Stationery Office (1981). *Guidelines for the Testing of Chemicals for Mutagenicity*, HMSO, London.
5. Her Majesty's Stationery Office (1982). *Guidelines for the Testing of Chemicals for Carcinogenicity*, HMSO, London.
6. Her Majesty's Stationery Office (1982). *Guidelines for the Testing of Chemicals for Toxicity*, HMSO, London.
7. Office for Official Publications of the European Communities (1980). *Guidelines for the Safety Assessment of Food Additives*, EUR 6892, Office for Official Publications of the European Communities, Luxembourg.
8. Food Additives and Contaminants Committee (1982). *Report of Enzyme Preparations*, FAC/REP/35, HMSO, London.
9. Coomes, T. J., Sherlock, J. C. and Walters, B. (1982). *J. Roy. Soc. Health*, **3**, 631.
10. European Community (1978). *Council Directive No. 78/142/EEC* (OJ No. L44, 15.2.78, 15).

6

Market Research as a Support for Quality Control

Vivien Wilton
Mobile Sensory Testing Services Ltd,
Oxted, Surrey, UK

ABSTRACT

There are many occasions when a company needs *to look to* outside *opinions in order to solve its particular problem. It is not always the opinions of the general public that they are after; it can be the opinions of the trade or suppliers or specialists in any particular field, e.g. doctors, retail outlets, wholesalers, etc. In the majority of cases confidentiality is essential in order to obtain unbiased attitudes and opinions and it is in* this *context that most market research is used. Market research provides the* answers *but only to the questions which are asked; hence it is important to define the problem and be sure of the questions before embarking on a survey of any kind.*

In this paper we will look at just some of the ways in which market research can assist in production and marketing problems.

PROBLEM 1

A company wishes to substitute a cheaper ingredient in a well-established brand—'marketing question': could they do this without losing brand share or sales?

There are two market research questions: (1) can consumers tell the difference between the current product and the new one with the cheaper ingredient?, and (2) if they can detect a difference, which one do they prefer?

Method

Firstly, we need to contact a representative sample of users of the product. Representativeness means that the test sample of consumers matches the profile of the user population in terms of age, sex, social class, region, heavy or light usage, whether they have children in the household, whether they work, etc. For example, there would be no point in interviewing mothers at home if the product is bought mainly by working women.

The size of the sample is determined by how much confidence the manufacturer wants to place on the results. But, more importantly, the main consideration is how much money he has in his budget. Often the sample sizes used in market research are dealing with hundreds of people rather than thousands.

The methodology employed to obtain the answers is then dependent on the type of product being tested. Often, in some cases where the cheaper ingredient is only going to affect taste, then a hall test will suffice. In that instance halls in central locations in the areas to be considered are hired, and teams of trained market research interviewers are used to contact the target population and to invite them into the hall to test the product which has already been prepared ready for tasting.

A standard discrimination test would be used, probably a test where the respondent has to choose the odd one out of the three products he or she is tasting. Another method can be to ask the respondent to pick the two products which are the same out of five being tasted. Yet another method is the report paired comparison test where two products are tasted, preference recorded, the same two products then being retested under different codes and preference recorded again. One then looks for consistency of preference between the two tests.

If the cheaper ingredient is likely to affect the product in other ways, such as *in use* or *in preparation*, then an in-home test would be conducted. This time, interviewers contact the target population at home; they would place the products with the respondent and leave them to be used in the normal way. The interviewer then recalls to obtain the respondent's feelings about the products or preferences.

In-home discrimination testing should only be used when absolutely necessary, as it is very difficult to determine whether the respondents use the products in the same way each time. And this is, of course, fundamental to the theory of discrimination testing.

Results

All the respondents' comments are recorded, coded, then analysed to provide tables of results. These are then inspected and various appropriate statistical tests are applied to calculate the significance of the results. These would then be relayed to the marketing department who will then decide whether to risk the cheaper ingredient or not.

PROBLEM 2

A company has no alternative but to modify its factory and change its production plant. The product produced on the new plant differs noticeably from the original product. Does this matter to the brand overall? What will happen to sales?

The market research question in this instance is: Given that people do notice the difference between the products, which one do they prefer?

A lot depends, of course, on how competitive this market is. For example, consumers may prefer the original product over the new one, but the latter is still better than other products on the market; thus, there might not be any loss in sales. It is therefore important to let the new product stand or fall on its own merits and be judged against the parameters on which the consumer evaluates products in this market.

Having determined whom we should interview and how many, in the same way as for problem 1, we would probably then conduct a sequential monodic test. This means that the tester is given only one product to try at first. This product would be evaluated on the dimensions which are important for products in this market. The respondent's evaluation is thus influenced by his or her product and market experience. The interviewer records these responses, then gives the respondent a second product to try. Obviously, the evaluation of the second product will be influenced by what he/she thought of the first product. Therefore, the order of trial is rotated throughout the sample in order to reduce bias.

The results are analysed and provide a monodic assessment of each product, i.e. how good or bad is it in its own rights? They also provide a forced comparison between the products tested by looking at responses to the products when they are tested second. This has the effect of hot-housing any differences between the products.

Sequential monodic tests can be conducted in home or in a hall, again dependent upon the type of product in question. More often than not they would be tested 'blind', i.e. in completely plain wrappers, unbranded and identified only by codes. This eliminates any effect of the power of branding and advertising.

PROBLEM 3

A company has some new product ideas. Is there a market for the new products? In this case we are looking at desk research and concept work. This is to illustrate that market research is not always concerned with interviewing people in the street.

Desk Research

There are many sources of data available which can provide useful information about markets:

1. Government statistics—national food survey, trade imports/exports, companies house, employment figures.
2. Information services of the *Daily Telegraph* and *Times* newspapers.
3. *Which* Report.
4. Economic Intelligence Unit (retail business).
5. Printel.
6. Independent organisations, e.g. Nielsen and AGB Audits.
7. In-house information, e.g. Company sales, etc.

Concept Work

This is more likely to be of a qualitative nature rather than quantitative.

Qualitative research involves talking to small numbers of people in depth rather than large numbers on just a few points.

Often the respondents are put into a group situation and the researcher will get them to talk for an hour or more on a particular subject. Quite often at this stage products are not even formed and it is the *ideas* which the researcher is evaluating. The ideas are often presented as words and pictures on a board. The respondent has to stretch his imagination in order to be able to discuss the idea. This generates a wealth of information about how each idea can be developed to produce ultimately a branded product.

PROBLEM 4

A company has had problems with its stocking and supply to the trade. Having sorted out the problems at the factory end, the company now wishes to find out to what extent this dispute has affected trade opinion of the company overall.

There are a number of organisations which are set up to monitor sales of products throughout the retail trade. They do this by auditing stores on a regular basis to collect data on which products are stocked and which have been brought in during a specified time period. Regular collection of such data provides sales in and out of the stores and whether a product is in stock or not.

A subsidiary to this is that we can actually interview buyers or managers of stores themselves to get their attitudes towards a company and its products. This will tell the company whether its recent supply problem has had only a short-term effect on sales or whether it has badly damaged its reputation amongst the retail world. Obviously in this instance one talks to tens of respondents rather than hundreds as they are difficult and expensive people to interview. Often one would use a very specialist interviewer force for this type of work.

These are but just a few of the ways that market research is used but they show how considerable savings can be made by either altering a product's construction or avoiding expensive wrong decisions.

7

Advances in the Light Microscopy of Foods

F. Olga Flint

Procter Department of Food Science,
University of Leeds, UK

ABSTRACT

The development of the transmission electron microscope with its increased resolving power and the scanning electron microscope (SEM) with its capacity for producing dramatic three-dimensional images has overshadowed the considerable progress made in optical microscopy since the 1950s. New ways of using light including phase contrast, interference microscopy and fluorescence have become available in forms accessible to the non-specialist, and the fitness for purpose of the light microscope for normal bright field work has been greatly improved. Modern cryostats enable food products to be speedily prepared for the light microscope without the need for fixation or dehydration and the range of one-step staining techniques now available rivals physical techniques in obtaining contrast with the minimum of constituent disturbance. This is important in quantitative microscopy where the retention of section constituents is particularly important. Developments in quantitative microscopy include the histometric analysis of both collagen and soya proteins in meat products and the use of stereology to study the changes undergone by biscuit dough constituents during baking and fatty tissue during meat product processing. Some of this work is now aided by machine image analysis. Accompanying the improvements in the instruments available is a greater appreciation of the theory of microscopic technique. This is important to the food scientist because the histological methods used by biologists have evolved to suit the texture and permeability of native animal and plant tissues. An understanding of staining mechanisms can enable the food microscopist to select and modify techniques, making them suitable for the more processed food tissues with which he deals. For this, histochemically based methods have a special appeal. Based on chemistry rather than texture, histochemical methods are more appropriate for many food products and the number of techniques available for different proteins, carbohydrates and fats is still increasing.

INTRODUCTION

The pioneers of food microscopy Greenish,[1] Winton[2] and Wallis[3] working in the early part of this century had available microscopes whose optics were excellent. The limit of resolution for the light microscope had been reached by 1890, and the elegant drawings we see in the early publications[1,2,3] are proof of the quality of instruments available as well as the undoubted skill with which they were used. From this it might seem that a microscope purchased in the 1950s and used with the techniques then available must encompass all that can be expected of the instrument. If this proves inadequate then the only microscopic solution must lie with the electron microscope. To many food scientists this has meant the scanning electron microscope (SEM) because of the ease with which samples can be prepared for it. Varriano-Marston[4] claims that in the 1970s many cereal scientists abandoned light microscopy techniques altogether in favour of the SEM and she makes a plea for the integration of light and electron microscopy, which is well justified for the research team. For the food analyst or the research worker with little experience in microscopy the modern light microscope has much to offer. The case is well put by Apling[5] who sees the electron microscope as an instrument for the specialist and the optical microscope as the tool more immediately available to any food scientist. The aim of this paper is to look at the modern instrument and the microscopical techniques that have been developed in recent years.

ADVANCES IN MICROSCOPE DESIGN

The Microscope Stand (Fig. 1)

The evolution of the microscope can be seen in the way that the best new features which first appear in expensive research microscopes eventually reach instruments designed for routine work. This is most

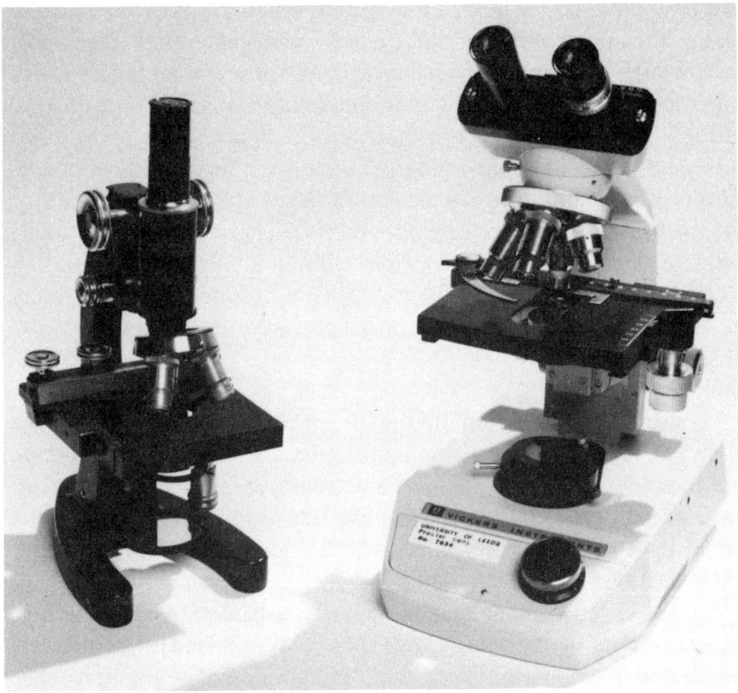

FIG. 1. Routine microscopes: left, 1960; right, 1980.

obvious with the microscope stand itself. The traditional microscope was equipped with a mirror and a separate light source was needed to illuminate the specimen. By the 1960s built-in illumination, then standard for research microscopes, had already spread to some student microscopes. This integral lighting fixed part of the illuminating system so that the microscope was easier to set up as well as being more portable. A concurrent development involved the method of focusing. Instead of the body tube and the nosepiece (which carries the objectives) being moved to focus on a slide, the focus was now varied by movement of the microscope stage. This gave steadier focusing and enabled the focus controls to be brought down to a level which was much more comfortable for the user.

Lenses

Calculations on lens performance and new materials for lenses have both contributed to the improvement of microscope objectives.[6]

We now have larger fields of diameter which are flatter and these make the possession of the newer widefield eyepieces really worthwhile. The modern widefield eyepiece now available on routine microscopes greatly increases the comfort of the microscopist. Instead of looking at a small image situated in the depth of the microscope tube, the widefield eyepiece enables us to see a larger, nearer image. This is because not only can the lens of the eye be regarded as part of the instrument but so can the retina. The wider image angle associated with the widefield eyepiece illuminates more of the retina so that the microscope can be used with a brighter image, enabling more detail to be seen without tiring the eyes.

Illumination

I consider improved illumination to be the most important advance in recent times. More flexible lighting has reached the microscope through the wider interest in colour photography. Transparencies need projection for viewing, and the low voltage bulbs developed primarily for modern projectors reached their peak with the quartz halogen bulb. These small lamps with their intense brightness lend versatility to the instruments to which they are fitted. An intense light source is particularly helpful with those methods of optical contrast where only a small fraction of the illuminating beam finally reaches the eyepiece, e.g. polarisation, dark ground, phase contrast and interference microscopy. With quartz halogen illumination fluorescence microscopy is also possible.[7,8] These lamps also have a constant colour temperature (unlike ordinary tungsten bulbs which yellow on ageing) which makes them particularly suitable for colour photomicrography.

Fibre Optic Lamps (Fig. 2)

The quartz iodine bulb is used to power a useful lighting accessory. The fibre optic lamp consists of a long (300–600 mm) flexible 'swan neck' which carries the bundle of light transmitting glass fibres to a focusing lens. This enables a narrow beam of cool light to be focused on the surface of an unmounted specimen which is then viewed, either by a stereomicroscope, or with the low power objectives ($\times 5$ and $\times 10$) of the standard microscope.

It is particularly useful for powdered foods and solids whose surface detail is of interest. This is relevant for the food scientist studying texture because the low power objectives are able to extend

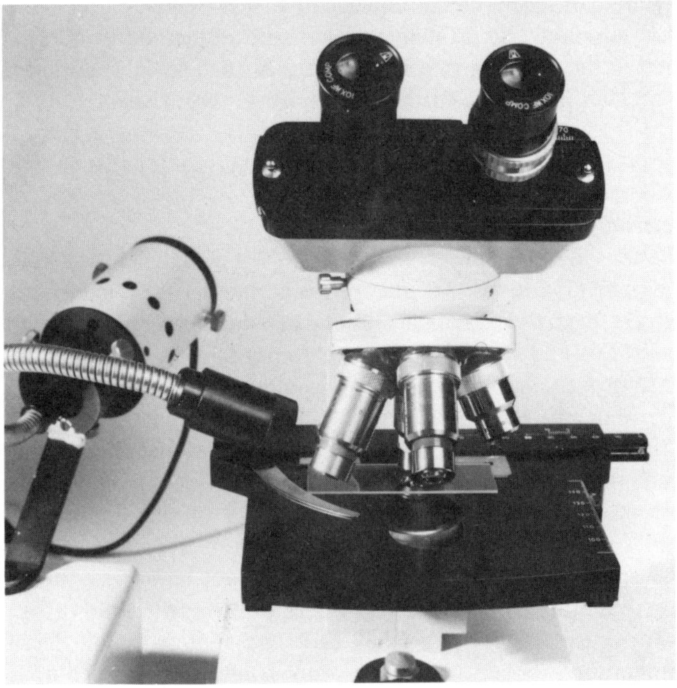

FIG. 2. Use of fibre optics for incident light microscopy.

our vision, enabling us to see features which the unaided eye cannot see, but which the mouth does perceive.

THE LEAST TREATMENT IS THE BEST TREATMENT

The food microscopist dealing with processed foods has a rather different task from the microscopist working with natural tissues. Because of their cellular basis, native plant and animal structures have an inbuilt cohesion which many processed foods lack. Native tissues withstand fixation, wax embedding and lengthy staining procedures. Any one of these stages may so alter a food product that the information that is obtained is totally misleading. It is an important principle in food microscopy that the less done to the specimen the better. But the need for contrast in the microscope image remains. This can be achieved by two strategies, used alone or in combination. One strategy relies on optical methods for obtaining contrast, the other on simple one-stage histochemical staining; both approaches have been further advanced in recent years.

OPTICAL METHODS OF CONTRAST

Polarising Microscopy

Better illumination has been an important factor in the development and use of the physical methods of microscopical contrast. Even the classical technique of using simple polarising filters to view fats and starches is made easier with a modern microscope. The improved illumination allows a polarising filter (the analyser) to be permanently positioned within the body of the instrument without detriment to brightfield work. A circle of Polaroid material which acts as the polariser can then be used below the condenser whenever there is a need to check the birefringence of the specimen. This enables a routine binocular microscope to be used as a qualitative polarising instrument. Provided that it is not homogeneous nearly every material with any structure is birefringent, but often this birefringence is not of a high order so that with low levels of illumination it is missed. A light source that can be turned up when the polars are crossed will, for example, reveal the strain birefringence present in many extruded food products.

Phase Contrast and Interference Microscopy

Both phase contrast and interference microscopy are techniques for viewing transparent material where differences in thickness and reflective index, i.e. optical path differences, are converted into differences of light intensity in the microscope image. This enables detail to be seen without the need for staining. Phase contrast is widely used in biology; it has the advantages of being easy to use and inexpensive, so that it is now fitted routinely to biological student microscopes. It seems surprising that phase contrast has received so little attention from food microscopists. The reason may be that phase images are imperfect, being surrounded by a pronounced halo caused by shortcomings in the optical system, and so food microscopists have turned to other means of obtaining contrast. However, Zernike's work on phase contrast indirectly led to the development of interference microscopy.[9]

Nomarski differential interference contrast

Of the several interference systems available, the Nomarski Differential Interference Contrast (DIC) technique is the choice of those whose interest lies solely in visibility rather than in quantitative measurement of phase change.[10] The Nomarski image is seen to have marked contrast; it appears to have the dramatic raised relief that we associate with the SEM image, but it must be appreciated that this relief is due to differences in refractive index. It is an optical relief rather than a true geometrical relief. This aspect is fully discussed in an excellent article on Nomarski DIC by Padawer.[11] The Nomarski optics can be used with relatively thick preparations because there is minimal degradation of the image by structures which lie above and below the plane of focus. This makes 'optical sectioning' a possibility and the Nomarski system has been used to study living embryos several hundred micrometres thick.[12] The Nomarski microscope uses standard objectives and, being a polarisation instrument, it can be used as a polarised light microscope. With very little manipulation a specimen may be viewed directly, in polarised light, and then when the Nomarski prisms are in place, a range of prism settings gives the DIC method of yielding image contrast.

Fluorescence Microscopy

Although several authors have used quartz halogen illumination successfully for fluorescence microscopy[7,8] the results can be disappointing because the image is not quite bright enough. This has been my own experience especially where colour photography was needed. Undoubtedly the most important advance in the design of equipment for fluorescence microscopy has been the development of epi- (or incident) fluorescent illumination by Ploem.[13] The epi-illuminator is powered by a mercury vapour lamp and dichroic mirrors reflect the exciting band of light through the microscope objective so that it reaches the upper surface of the specimen. From here the rays reflected by the specimen are gathered by the objective and transmitted to the barrier filter and the eyepiece. The ray diagram involved is clearly illustrated in the recent edition of *Hartley's Microscopy*.[14] It can be seen that since the objective is acting as the condenser the alignment of the microscope is always perfect, the act of focusing the specimen automatically focuses the light on to it. Only the field of view is subject to the exciting wavelength so that, if the fluorescence fades, only the area being examined is affected and a new field of view can easily be selected. The epi-illuminator excites only the top surface of the specimen so that fairly thick specimens (even hand sections) can be viewed.

Fluorescence microscopy is important as a technique which subjects the specimen to little or no treatment before viewing. Many food materials and fibres are autofluorescent, i.e. they fluoresce, often quite strongly, without staining. Fluorescence microscopy is not restricted to this primary fluorescence because many dyes are fluorescent and can be used as a source of secondary fluorescence.

Fluorescent reagents have the advantage over the normal brightfield stains of being used at much lower concentrations but still giving an image which is brightly self-luminous.

Recent work with cereals and oil seeds[15–18] shows the potential of Ploem's illuminator. Using both autofluorescence and a range of specific fluorescent markers, Fulcher[17] was able to locate all the major cereal components.

DEVELOPMENTS IN SPECIMEN PREPARATION

Optical methods of contrast enable the microscopist to view specimens without staining, but some preparation is still needed. For incident light work the surface needs to be flat, and for transmitted light the preparation must be sufficiently thin for light to pass through. Thus, the range of foods that can be examined by simple mounting techniques is limited to materials of small particle size, e.g. starches and powders and foods that easily form a thin layer as do emulsions. For composite foods where interest lies in the relative size and position of constituents, there is a need for section cutting. Twenty-five years ago this meant fixation followed by wax or gelatine embedding, a process which took several days to accomplish; during this time tissues shrank and lipids were lost or displaced. The modern cryostat has changed all that. Lipids and soluble materials remain *in situ*, and foods can be prepared for the microscope in a matter of minutes, including the use of simple staining techniques.

Cryostats (Fig. 3)

A cryostat is simply a refrigerated cabinet which houses a microtome. Most sectioning is done at about −20 °C and the sections remain frozen until positioned on a slide or coverslip. The controls

FIG. 3. A modern cryostat.

for setting temperature, section thickness and actually cutting are operated from outside the cabinet. The machines most suitable for food microscopy have a retracting microtome. Sections are cut on the downstroke of the specimen holder which then retracts so that on the upstroke the specimen block cannot be smeared by contact with the back of the knife.

There have been no fundamental changes in cryostat design in recent times but the newer models have features which make them more convenient to use and more versatile in performance. Open top models make access much easier and the lower cabinet temperatures now available (down to $-45\,^{\circ}C$) make the sectioning of sugar-rich foods a possibility. As an alternative to the glass guide plate with its

Sellotape spacers (used to prevent sections curling) there is now a self-aligning perspex anti-roll plate with nylon spacer screws governing the gap between guide plate and knife edge. Models which have hardly changed in the last 20 years are still available, and with experience these will give satisfactory results for a wide range of food materials.

With cryostat microtomy the support medium needed for sectioning comes from the water already present in the food, and it is fortunate that many foods already contain enough moisture to give a sufficiently solid block to permit sectioning. With dry materials minimal hydration, using water-based embedding media, enables sections to be taken without full hydration. This includes many low-moisture foods such as spray-dried powders, mixes and extrusion-cooked products.[19]

HISTOCHEMICAL STAINING

The cryostat section needs only simple mounting and it is then ready for viewing by any of the optical methods for obtaining contrast discussed earlier. Complementing these are staining techniques that involve known chemical mechanisms. These histochemical methods can be relied on to demonstrate classes of compounds because they depend on the chemistry of food materials rather than on their permeability. The periodic acid Schiff reaction for carbohydrates and the hydroxylamine/ferric chloride method for pectin are examples of histochemical methods,[20] but both are lengthy techniques and there is a need for rapid staining to match the speed with which cryostat sections can be cut. A simple stain-mountant is more useful because it can be employed during sectioning to monitor the condition of the sample and as an aid in deciding the optimum cutting thickness. Toluidine blue, when used in an appropriate mountant, is such a tool.

Toluidine Blue Staining

Toluidine blue is a basic dyestuff widely used for staining because of its metachromatic behaviour. Metachromasia is dependent on the fixation of dye polymers by the tissue and, as different materials in a section of foodstuff have different dye binding properties, the resulting colours are an indication of the negative charge density present. This results in a range of colours which enables section constituents to be identified, e.g. muscle cells are coloured a light blue with red–violet nuclei, connective tissue is stained pink, with elastin fibres a turquoise colour, and the anionic carbohydrate materials such as pectins, hemicelluloses, carboxymethyl cellulose, etc., are coloured a deep pink shade. One version of the toluidine blue stain-mountant[21] contains 0·2% toluidine blue. At this strength an aqueous solution of the dyestuff contains metachromatic polymers and used alone it tends to give an overall purple staining. The addition of glycerol and phenol gives a stain-mountant which is distinctly blue in colour but which colours some features blue and others in metachromatic shades of purple and pink. This differential staining is achieved within a minute or so of mounting.

Vapour Staining for Starch and Lipids

Ranking with stain-mountants as non-disruptive techniques are two vapour staining methods.[19]

Starch demonstration using iodine vapour

The classical method for identifying starch involves the use of aqueous iodine/potassium iodide solution. This is satisfactory as a test for the presence of starch but the method has its limitations when used to study the condition of starch granules in foods. Many food products contain starch in a swollen gelatinised state and the addition of water may disrupt these already fragile granules, even intact starch present in sections may be detached during aqueous staining. Now, whilst the iodide ion is necessary for the iodine staining of starch, added iodide ions are not. In the presence of moisture, iodine itself will provide sufficient ions to allow staining and this is the basis of iodine vapour staining.[22] The amount of moisture needed is quite small and can be obtained by storing slides at −20 °C and then bringing them into ambient conditions, the resulting film of moisture is sufficient to allow staining by the iodine vapour formed in a closed staining dish containing elemental iodine.

Demonstration of lipids with osmium tetroxide vapour

The standard method for staining lipids in foods uses an alcoholic solution of an oil soluble dye such as Oil Red 0 or the various Sudan colourants. In many cases the technique is satisfactory but there is always the risk of loss or movement of lipid material and in the staining of emulsions any solvent is undesirable.

Aqueous osmium tetroxide, widely used as a fixative, is a sensitive fat stain but it is also a very toxic material, partly because of its volatility. This volatility suggested its use as a vapour stain for fats, making it suitable for sections which are sensitive to water. The amount needed is very small, 5 ml of a 2% solution of osmium tetroxide being adequate for staining up to 10 slides, but this must be handled carefully with appropriate safety precautions.[19]

QUANTITATIVE MICROSCOPY—STEREOLOGY

Though the strength of the light microscope lies in its ability to provide information of a qualitative nature rapidly, image analysis makes possible the quantitative estimation of any constituent which can be demonstrated by the microscope. By assessing the area occupied by a constituent in a number of two-dimensional images, the volume the constituent occupies in the material as a whole may be deduced. One example of a stereological method is direct point counting at the microscope using a graticule with a fixed number of points. This has been applied to the estimation of the amount of texturised soya protein in meat–soya mixes using toluidine blue as the stain to distinguish soya and meat proteins in cryostat sections.[23] Recently Burt has used the projected photomicrographic image for point counting in a study of biscuit microstructure.[24] Cryostat sections were stained for protein and lipid, and polarised light microscopy was used to show the fraction of starch still intact after cooking. Both these applications used manual point counting but Hildebrandt and co-workers[25] have employed machine assisted image analysis in the form of the Zeiss Micro Videomat. This television computer combination was used to assess the collagen content of comminuted meat products as an alternative to the method of estimating collagen by hydroxyproline content.

CONCLUSION

In this paper I have looked at only some of the advances in the instrumentation and techniques of light microscopy which have been developed in recent years. The choice of topics has been a subjective one and there are gaps, some in important areas like immunofluorescence, autoradiography and image analysis. This stems from a decision to dwell mainly on those aspects of food microscopy I was able to describe from experience and which were felt to be most relevant to food analysts and those concerned with the control of food quality.

REFERENCES

1. Greenish, H. G. (1903). *The Microscopical Examination of Food and Drugs*, 1st edition, J. & A. Churchill, Edinburgh.
2. Winton, A. L. (1916). *Microscopy of Vegetable Foods*, Wiley & Sons, New York.
3. Wallis, T. E. (1923). *Analytical Microscopy: Its Aims and Methods*, 1st edition, J. & A. Churchill, Edinburgh.
4. Varriano-Marston, E. (1982). *Cereal Foods World*, **26**, 558–61.
5. Apling, E. C. (1980). In: *Developments in Food Analysis Techniques—2*, Ed. King, R. D., Applied Science Publishers, London, 151–85.
6. Haselmann, H. (1982). *Proceedings RMS*, **17**, 48–57.
7. Young, M. R. and Armstrong, J. A. (1967). *Nature*, **213**, 649–50.
8. Lovelock, D. W. and Davies, A. (1967). *J. Roy. Mic. Soc.*, **87**, 35–8.
9. Turner, G. L'E. (1982). *Proceedings RMS*, **17**, 100–1.
10. Hartley, W. G. (1979). *Hartley's Microscopy*, 2nd edition, Senecio Publishing Co., Charlbury, UK, 159.
11. Padawer, J. (1968). *J. Roy. Mic. Soc.*, **88**, 305–49.
12. Everingham, J. W. (1967). *Anatomical Record*, **157**, 243.
13. Ploem, J. S. (1967). *Z. wiss Mikrosk*, **68**, 129–42.
14. Hartley, W. G. (1979). *Hartley's Microscopy*, 2nd edition, Senecio Publishing Co., Charlbury, UK, 200.
15. Fulcher, R. G. and Wong, S. I. (1980). In: *Cereals for Food and Beverages: Recent Progress in Cereal Chemistry and Technology*, Eds. Inglett, G. E. and Munck, L., Academic Press, New York, London, 1–26.
16. Fulcher, R. G., O'Brien, T. P. and Wong, S. I. (1981). *Cereal Chem.*, **58**, 130–5.
17. Fulcher, R. G. (1982). *Food Microstructure*, **1**, 167–75.
18. Yiu, S. H., Poon, H., Fulcher, R. G. and Altosaar, I. (1982). *Food Microstructure*, **1**, 135–43.
19. Flint, F. O. (1982). *Food Microstructure*, **1**, 145–50.
20. Jensen, W. A. (1962). *Botanical Histochemistry*, W. H. Freeman and Co., San Francisco and London.
21. Flint, F. O. and Firth, B. M. (1981). *Analyst*, **106**, 1242–3.
22. Little, R. R. (1957). *Stain Technol.*, **32**, 7–9.
23. Flint, F. O. and Meech, M. V. (1978). *Analyst*, **103**, 252–8.
24. Burt, D. J. (1982). *Proceedings RMS*, **17** (Micro 82 Supplement), S29.
25. Hildebrandt, G., Königsmann, T. R. and Kretschmer, F. J. (1977). *Fleischwirtschaft*, **57**, 689–97.

8

Immunological Methods

C. H. S. Hitchcock
Unilever Research Laboratory, Bedford, UK

ABSTRACT

A brief outline of the principles of immunology introduces a mini-review of the methods available for the detection and determination of antigens, based on the corresponding antibodies used as specific analytical reagents. The required analyte itself (or a derivative) can be used to immunise an experimental animal to raise suitable antibodies, but commercially available antisera are often satisfactory. The analytical procedures range from classical precipitation techniques, such as qualitative immunodiffusion, to more recently developed immunoassays, such as quantitative enzyme-linked immunosorbent assay (ELISA). Those techniques more relevant to food analysis are indicated and their application illustrated by reference to the specific determination of food proteins. It is concluded that immunoassay (and ELISA in particular) can provide the food analyst with a powerful technique whose potential is only beginning to be exploited. Already established for clinical analyses, it offers the direct determination of any chosen antigenic analyte in a crude sample in situ *without preliminary separation; it is cheap, rapid, reliable and sensitive as well as being suitable for high sample throughput and semi-automation.*

INTRODUCTION

Food Analysis

The analysis of food is traditionally based on rapid classical methods for its major constituents: water, protein (nitrogen), fat and ash; total carbohydrate is then calculated by difference. Other components of interest, ranging from individual vitamins, sugars, minerals or fatty acids to trace amounts of adventitious materials, require special methods which have often been developed by biochemists studying them in living tissue. As food products become more sophisticated, the analytical problems they raise become more difficult and the necessary methods more expensive. Food analysts often apply powerful chromatographic procedures, particularly GLC and HPLC, to resolve complex mixtures and provide convenient multiple analyses. This approach relies on the effective isolation of each analyte or its derivative, followed by its determination using methods which need not be specific. Indeed, if the final determination were specific for the analyte under test, its separation from other components of the mixture might not be necessary; however, physical parameters and chemical reactions are not normally specific enough to allow the direct determination of a unique analyte in biological samples. Nevertheless, the chemical reactions and physical interactions which occur *in vivo* suggest that such specificity can occur: for instance, enzyme-catalysed reactions are much more specific than the corresponding chemical reaction. Indeed, enzymes are useful in the assay of their substrates in a limited number of cases where the appropriate enzyme is available.

The specificity of immunochemical interactions is a more general phenomenon, and immunoassay represents for the food analyst a powerful method for the determination of a particular analyte (antigen) by means of a specific reagent (antibody) prepared by established immunological methods for the analyte itself. Provided some way is found to monitor the antibody–antigen interaction, the antigen can often be specifically determined without isolation. Immunoassays using labels have been recently developed and are already well established in clinical biochemistry, so that procedures, reagents, apparatus and automated instruments are already available; ready-to-use kits for individual assays of some analytes are already on the market. Food analysts stand to benefit as much from the application of immunochemical techniques in the future as they have done from chromatographic techniques in the past.

Immunological Principles

The analyst needs only a rough outline of immunological principles to understand the basis of immunoassays; readers requiring a deeper treatment are referred to standard textbooks of immunology.

Antibodies are proteins which are biosynthesised and secreted into the bloodstream of animals only when challenged with a chemical ('immunogen') which is significantly different from the animal's own constituents and which may therefore pose a threat to it. The function of the antibody in the serum ('antiserum') of an immunised animal is to bind to the immunogen in order to facilitate its neutralisation; a single antibody molecule recognises and interacts with a particular molecular site ('determinant' or 'epitope') on the immunogen. An antigen (Ag) is then defined as any molecule which interacts with the corresponding antibody (Ab); this will include the immunogen and any similar material which displays an appropriate determinant. If the immunogen is a macromolecule, such as soya protein, it carries many determinants and a mixture of antibodies ('polyclonal') results.

Antigens having a molecular size too small to elicit an immune response (e.g. nitrophenol) can still bind to the appropriate antibodies; these are called 'haptens', and may be made immunogenic by attaching them chemically to an immunologically inert carrier macromolecule such as serum albumin. Antibodies therefore represent an analytical reagent which possesses useful binding properties defined by the immunogen used, and highly specific for a particular antigen.

Antibodies raised in a particular animal are proteins (globulins) which can themselves also act as immunogens in a different species, which therefore yield 'antiglobulins' (antiantibodies). Such antiglobulins can interact with the corresponding antibody whether or not the latter antibody is already bound to its original antigen.

The crude antiserum contains the antibodies required as well as many other proteins, some with unwanted immunochemical activity. It is often used without further treatment, but can be purified (particularly conveniently by affinity chromatography) if necessary. Moreover, antibodies with more highly defined and specific properties can be prepared by the monoclonal technique: this involves the establishment of an immortal line of hybridised cultured cells from one isolated cell secreting a strictly monospecific antibody which recognises only one determinant.

In addition to its specificity, the ideal antibody preparation should have high concentration (titre) and high binding constants (avidity), though it is often difficult to control these parameters during the production of antisera. However, crude, purified and modified antibody preparations are increasingly available, and many are offered as commercial reagents.

The following sections describe the way in which analysts can design an immunoassay based on such preparations, but its success and applicability in any particular case will depend to a large extent on the detailed properties of the antibodies used. Problems in food analysis are largely concerned with the specific detection and determination of individual antigens in food samples, and the procedures are discussed in this form; however, it should be remembered that immunoassays can equally be designed to examine antibody levels.

DESIGN OF IMMUNOASSAY

Immunological methods of investigation have been applied to foods for many years; these classical techniques are important but limited. Recent interest is based on labelled immunoassays whose potential scope suggests widespread application.

Classical Techniques

The major observable bulk change when solutions of antibody and antigen interact is the appearance, under certain conditions, of a precipitated complex. This precipitate is caused when a divalent antibody and polyvalent macromolecular antigen polymerise in such concentration to become insoluble; it seldom appears when either is in excess. However, near the equivalence point unlimited polymerisation is possible, and some food analysts still use the simple precipitin test for qualitative detection of blood serum proteins from different animals. As usually carried out, this consists of layering antiserum onto a solution of the sample and examining the interface for a characteristic precipitate. While this procedure is rapid, it is not easy to observe traces of solid at the junction, nor to distinguish between a true antibody–antigen complex and any non-specific precipitate formed; moreover, like other classical precipitation methods, it requires a plentiful supply of characterised antisera. More convenient for the food analyst are the many forms of immunodiffusion techniques in which antibody and antigen diffuse into each other through a gel matrix: precipitation at the junction gives rise to an immobilised band of the complex polymer. This can be observed directly or stained *in situ*.

A most useful simple technique is provided by two-dimensional immunodiffusion (Ouchterlony), where antibody and antigen diffuse towards each other from wells cut in a slab of appropriate gel (e.g. agarose). A popular procedure is to cast the gel (e.g. on a microscope slide) as a layer about 1 mm thick, and to cut into it an array of wells about 3 mm diameter and 10 mm apart. The pattern often consists of a central well for the antiserum, surrounded by 6 or 8 equidistant wells for the standard and sample antigens. After equilibrium (e.g. overnight) the slide is examined for precipitin lines, which can be interpreted to indicate the presence or absence of antigen in the sample. Moreover, examination of the junction between lines arising from two neighbouring antigen wells can give useful information about the identity or otherwise of the two antigens (Fig. 1): lines which coalesce imply identity. Two different antigens diffuse through each other until they meet corresponding antibodies from the polyvalent antiserum; this results in the formation of characteristic 'spurs'. Non-specific precipitates sometimes appear; these may be significantly blurred and their recognition may be checked by a saline wash in which they are often soluble. Such a wash is necessary if the gel is to be stained to increase visibility of the lines; however, staining is seldom imperative. The simplicity of this qualitative technique recommends it for use in factory laboratories where screening techniques are required.

Single radial immunodiffusion (Mancini) is a well-established quantitative technique exploiting the precipitation principle; here the antigen diffuses from a single central well through a gel which already contains antiserum. Precipitation and immobilisation of the advancing antigen occurs with the neutralisation of the antiserum until the antigen is itself exhausted; the size of the resulting circular complex-loaded gel is a measure of the amount of antigen originally loaded into the well.

Other classical techniques, while important for biochemical investigation of biological tissue, are of less relevance to food analysis. Many of these involve the preliminary separation of antigens or antibodies by electrophoresis in a gel before application of diffusion procedures such as those already described. The detailed examination of protein mixtures for instance can be carried out by traditional gel electrophoresis followed by diffusion of antisera from

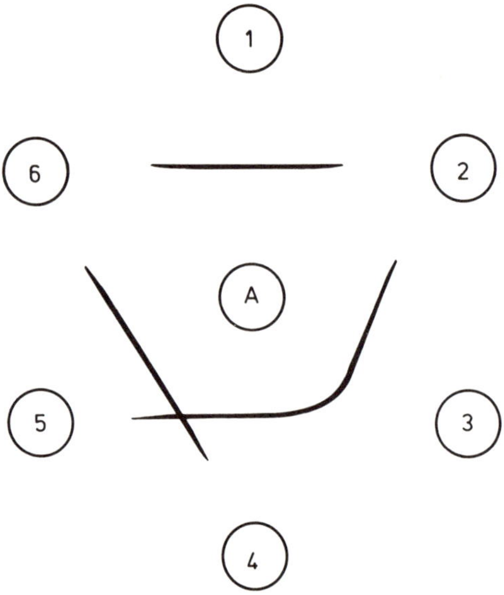

FIG. 1. Immunodiffusion: characteristic patterns of precipitation. The circles represent wells (about 3 mm diameter) cut into a slab of agarose gel (about 3 mm thick). The central well A contains antiserum; the sample in well 1 contains antigen(s) which slowly diffuse outwards to meet antibodies migrating from A. The line of precipitated antibody–antigen complex demonstrates the presence of corresponding antigen in sample 1; the absence of any line between wells A and 2 indicates that sample 2 contains no such antigen. Similarly, wells 3 and 4 contain antigen; moreover, the antigenic properties of samples 3 and 4 are evidently identical since the precipitin lines coalesce to give a smooth curve. Conversely, sample 5 is antigenic but the antigens present are different from those in sample 4: the samples have diffused independently through each other before meeting corresponding antibodies to give characteristic 'spurs', which can only be formed when the crude antiserum from A contains antibodies to both antigens. Sample 6 is a blank. The precipitin lines can be observed directly or after staining with a protein dye.

one or two slots cut parallel to, but well separated from, the band of separated antigens. Electrophoresis can also be used to speed up the process of diffusion: quantitative determination of antigens can be usefully carried out by the 'rocket' procedure (Laurell). Samples and standards are loaded into a row of wells cut into a thin slab of antiserum-loaded gel; traditional electrophoresis designed to move the antigen in one direction through the gel results in the rapid appearance of areas of precipitated complex whose elongated shape is reminiscent of a rocket and whose length is a measure of antigen level. More sophisticated assays involve electrophoresis in one direction followed by rocket electrophoresis at right angles.

Other classical techniques not involving precipitation arise from the phenomenon of hemagglutination, characteristic of blood when challenged with antibodies of another blood group. Here the antigen which characterises each of the blood groups is attached to the outside of the red blood cell; the soluble polyvalent antibodies from a foreign blood may interact, causing visible clumping of the cells. Such interaction is more obvious than precipitation of a complex from a solution of antibody and antigen; the approach can be extended by substituting a convenient plastic bead for the cell and attaching to it any antigen (or antibody) of interest. The effect of interaction between such sensitised particles and appropriate samples can be followed by eye, by optical instrumentation or by cell-sorting/cell-counting techniques.

Classical techniques represent a powerful method supporting reserach into immunochemical properties of macromolecules, but analytical chemists found their use limited by several factors: it was difficult to obtain appropriate antisera, and then to maintain supply for more than occasional determinations; the properties of antisera were variable; quantification involved lengthy procedures; interference from non-specific interactions was possible; and modifications were necessary to investigate antigens which did not precipitate with the corresponding antibody. Whether or not these objections were reasonable, doubtless analysts felt inhibited by the mystique of immunology.

Labelled Immunoassays

The introduction of labelled techniques has opened exciting new possibilities: this is particularly because precipitation is not involved. The interaction can be followed at such great dilution that minute quantities of antisera are sufficient and rapid multiple qualitative and quantitative analysis becomes possible. Moreover, the techniques have been already developed by and for clinical and pharmaceutical biochemists whose problems are similar to those of food scientists. Indeed, at this stage there is a bewildering multiplicity of different approaches to modern immunoassays which can only be outlined here. Many of these established procedures could doubtless be usefully applied more or less directly to a particular analytical problem once a small volume of suitable antiserum has been obtained and tested. In general, the methods involve the use of an antibody or antigen which carried a label such as a radioactive isotope (radioimmunoassay (RIA)), a fluorescent molecule (fluorescence immunoassay (FIA)) or an enzyme (enzyme immunoassay (EIA)). The interaction between antibody reagent and antigen in the sample or standard is followed via the activity of the label, which is chosen to be measurable at high dilution. The recent development of EIA is particularly attractive to the food analyst since the determination of enzyme activity (for instance, by simple colorimetry) is compatible with his existing commitments. Although RIA provides a convenient way to develop and test immunoassays, and is well established in clinical laboratories, it will be unattractive to analysts who are not licensed, equipped nor familiar with radioactive techniques. On the other hand, FIA has not yet realised its full potential and it is perhaps too early to expect many applications to the food area. At this stage, the most useful design will be one which requires reagents which are commercially available or easy to prepare.

Homogeneous assays

If the label is affected significantly by the interaction of the antibody or antigen, then the determination of the label is a direct measure of the degree of interaction; this is the foundation of homogeneous assays in which reagents and sample solutions are simply mixed and examined. While no visible precipitation takes place, the change in label activity can be conveniently measured and the system can often be easily automated. It will be obvious that radioactivity will not be affected, and is therefore not a suitable label in this case. An established example of homogeneous EIA is the 'enzyme multiplied immunoassay technique' (EMIT) in which the enzyme label is attached to the antibody in such a way that it is affected (e.g. by steric hindrance) when the antigen binds. Homogeneous FIA includes procedures relying on fluorescence enhancement, quenching or polarisation.

Homogeneous assays represent a special case of labelled immunoassay where much effort must be invested in the design and preparation of labelled reagents in individual cases. This will be cost-effective only if the simplicity of each assay is valuable, as with some clinical diagnostic problems where the sample throughput is potentially high. In practice, the sensitivity of such assays can be limited by the endogenous optical absorbance or fluorescence of the sample itself.

Heterogeneous assays

In a widely used design of RIA, an antigenic analyte Ag may be determined by mixing it with the identical labelled antigen Ag* and allowing the mixture (in excess) to interact with the corresponding antibody Ab:

$$Ag + Ag^* + Ab \rightarrow AbAg + AbAg^*$$

Under standardised conditions, at (or even before) equilibrium, the level of bound label AgAg* represents an inverse measure of the level of analyte Ag. The level of AbAg* cannot be measured directly without first separating it from Ag*; this leads to a 'heterogeneous' assay. If Ag* is a radioactive hapten, it can often be removed by physical adsorption or conversely AbAg complex can be removed after treatment with protein precipitants. A more general procedure involves the use of antigen Ag or the same antibody Ab or a different antibody Ab_2 immobilised to an inert support: such an 'immunosorbent' can distinguish effectively between the AbAg* complex and its constituents, and remove the unwanted species from very dilute solutions. The use of an immunosorbent is particularly suitable when the label is an enzyme because both the label and the antibody are then proteinaceous, making the physical characteristics of Ag* and AbAg* rather similar. Since enzyme labels are preferred by food analysts, this design of EIA, known as 'enzyme-labelled immunosorbent assay' (ELISA), is of particular interest.[1] One of the most convenient forms of immunosorbent is the inside surface of the vessel in which the assay is carried out; this often takes the form of a plastic microtitre plate with typically 96 identical wells, each about 0·3 ml volume and presensitised with antigen or antibody. Beads, pegs and membranes have also been used as immunosorbent supports. The general procedure involves sequential incubations to allow antibody–antigen interaction, followed by washing to remove any species not immobilised onto the plastic, thus purifying the captured species.

The heterogeneous assay described above allows Ag and Ag* to compete for the limited Ab available; this 'competitive' type of RIA is widely used, but when the label is an enzyme it suffers from two disadvantages: not only may a suitable labelled antigen be difficult to prepare, but the design requires that the enzyme and the crude test

TABLE 1

VARIANTS OF ELISA PROCEDURES FOR DETERMINATION OF ANTIGEN

Mode of ELISA[a]	*Labelled species*	*Initial immobilised species*	*Species in excess*	*Number of incubations*[b]	*Activity: analyte relationship*[c]	*Scheme*[d]
1. Competitive	Ag	Ab	Ag + Ag*	1	Inverse	S.Ab } S.AbAg Ag + Ag* } S.AbAg*
2. Sandwich	Ab_2	Ab_1	S.Ab_1 Ab_2*	2[e]	Direct	S.Ab_1 } S.Ab_1Ag Ag } S.Ab_1Ag } S.Ab_1AgAb_2* Ab_2* }
3. Sandwich/ antiglobulin	(AAb_2)	Ab_1	S.Ab_1 Ab_2 (AAb_2)*	3[e]	Direct	S.Ab_1 } S.Ab_1Ag Ag } S.Ab_1Ag } S.Ab_1AgAb_2 Ab_2 } S.Ab_1AgAb_2 } S.$Ab_1AgAb_2(AAb_2)$* (AAb_2)* }
4. Inhibition/ antiglobulin	(AAb)	Ag	Ab S.Ag (AAb)*	3	Inverse	Ag } AbAg Ab } Ab S.Ag } S.AgAb (AAb)* } S.AgAb(AAb)*

[a] In the competitive mode, analyte Ag and added labelled Ag* compete for immobilised Ab. In the sandwich mode, analyte Ag is quantitatively captured by excess immobilised Ab_1 and quantified with a second (labelled) Ab_2* or with a second Ab_2 followed by labelled antiglobulin. In the inhibition mode, analyte Ag is incubated with excess Ab, followed by a separate determination of uninhibited Ab using immobilised Ag.
[b] Number of incubations excluding initial incubation with Ab or Ag to prepare sensitised plates and final incubation with substrate to assay the immobilised label.
[c] Relationship between measured enzyme activity and level of analyte (antigen).
[d] S, Surface; Ab, antibody; Ag, antigen; AAb, antiantibody (antiglobulin); *, enzyme label; a brace represents an incubation and washing step.
[e] If Ab_1 and Ab_2 are monoclonal and specific for two different epitopes, they may be incubated simultaneously with the Ag to form S.Ab_1AgAb_2, thus eliminating one incubation period.

sample are incubated together, with possible interference. The scheme for a competitive ELISA is outlined in Table 1 (Mode 1). Many other modes of ELISA can be designed for the qualitative detection and quantitative determination of antigens; the variants can be distinguished by characteristic features, such as which of the antibody or antigen carries the label, which is initially immobilised, which is added in excess, whether a direct competitive or inhibition mode is employed, whether two antibodies 'sandwich' the antigen and whether unlabelled antibody (globulin) is monitored using labelled antiglobulin. Of these, three have been selected as illustrations because they seem to be particularly suitable for food analysis: these are the sandwich, the sandwich/antiglobulin and the inhibition/antiglobulin modes. The schemes, outlined in Table 1, demonstrate that all ELISA variants involve the sensitisation of a surface **S** to provide the immunosorbent, followed by the build-up of captured layers of reagents by sequential addition, incubation and washing. Finally the captured enzyme is determined by incubation with a convenient substrate. In very general terms, such assays can determine 1 μg protein or 10 ng steroid per litre of sample; coefficients of variation should be 5–10% (within assay) and 7–15% (between assay). Samples (as well as antibody reagents) are therefore usually highly diluted before assay.

APPLICATION OF IMMUNOASSAYS TO FOOD ANALYSIS

Although immunoassays are widely used in clinical laboratories, relatively few reports have appeared which describe procedures designed for food analysis.

Scope of Application

The potential range of analytes which can be investigated by immunoassay is enormous, since in principle it covers anything to which a suitable antibody can be raised. This range includes macromolecules (especially proteins) and even insoluble material such as viruses or microorganisms which carry accessible determinants. Small molecules which can act as haptens (e.g. steroids) are also suitable analytes, but the determination of smaller molecules and ubiquitous metabolites like glucose cannot be expected. When a particular analytical problem arises, the main factor in considering the application of an immunoassay is the availability of a suitable antibody preparation. Progress in many cases will doubtless be limited by restriction to commercially available antisera; however, development of a new method can be planned on the basis of suitable antiserum from a single animal if this can be secured. It must be remembered that the titre and avidity of antisera are notoriously variable, and different batches will need checking, using the immunoassay as a standardisation procedure.

Sample Preparation

Immunoassays have been established particularly for the convenient analysis of clinical samples of blood and urine. In applying such procedures to tissue samples, for instance those obtained by biopsy or post-mortem, the analyte must normally be transferred to a clear aqueous solution. Lipoidal antigens may first be partitioned into organic solvents, while water-soluble analytes are extracted with buffer and the insoluble residue removed. This is usually straightforward unless small quantities are found to bind to the tissue, leading to inefficient extraction. Raw food can be pretreated in the same way, and the corresponding extract analysed. However, processed food needs special consideration, partly because heating may change the immunochemical properties of an antigen and partly because it is often more difficult to extract antigen from heated food. Neither of these factors is critical if the analyte is a small heat-stable molecule which does not interact with other components during the process. On the other hand, macromolecules may well alter conformation on heating; in particular, proteins suffer denaturation with consequent insolubility and alteration of the nature of exposed determinants. Antibodies raised against native protein interact only weakly (if at all) with the same heat-denatured protein; moreover, it is difficult to solubilise proteins from heated food. The use of antibodies against heated protein is helpful, though these cannot be purchased so readily; the choice of a heat-stable protein alleviates the problem, if such a protein is relevant. If aqueous extraction of a proteinaceous analyte from a heated sample fails, an important general approach is the dissolution of the proteins with detergent or urea: such chaotropic reagents cause proteins to assume individually 'random coil' conformations by suppressing intermolecular and intramolecular interactions. Such a solution has no immunochemical properties because antibody–antigen interactions are similarly destroyed. However, if the chaotropic reagent is removed (e.g. by dialysis), the proteins refold to a 'renatured' (but not necessarily native) state with restored (but not necessarily identical) immunochemical properties.[2] In practice, the simple dilution necessary before immunoassay can reduce the effect of the chaotropic reagent sufficiently to allow direct immunoassay of the diluted renatured protein solution.[3] Ideally the antisera used should be raised against renatured protein; however, antibodies against the heat-denatured or even the native protein may be satisfactory.

Immunoassays for Proteinaceous Components of Foods

For many years, classical immunological methods have been used in food laboratories for the qualitative recognition of fresh meat species. Direct application of the immunodiffusion method (Ouchterlony), using commercial antibodies against the serum proteins of different species, allows the corresponding meats to be easily recognised from patterns such as those illustrated in Fig. 1. Such characterisation is based on the serum albumin[4] extracted from the blood in each sample which interacts with corresponding antibodies in the crude antisera. While useful, such tests need a plentiful supply of concentrated antisera which must be standardised checked and sometimes purified to avoid cross-reactions. The ELISA procedure requires only traces of diluted antibody preparation, allowing its cost-effective use for large numbers of samples; successful identification of species origin of fresh meat by ELISA has indeed been demonstrated,[5,6,7] but it must be emphasised that this is still a blood test and cannot be used to determine the levels of meat itself.

The quantitative determination of a particular protein or of proteins from a particular source is best illustrated by the examination of meat products for soya protein. This example typifies the general problem of distinguishing between proteins in mixed food products; analysts have tested many approaches including classical immunoassay, histology, electrophoresis, peptide analysis and various indirect methods;[8,9] while a few of these have been applied with limited success, ELISA displays the most powerful potential. In particular, we have proposed an inhibition/antiglobulin ELISA[2,7,10,11] (Table 1, mode 4). The individual steps of the protocol are illustrated in Fig. 2. The procedure normally consists of multiple pipetting, incubating and washing operations, followed by

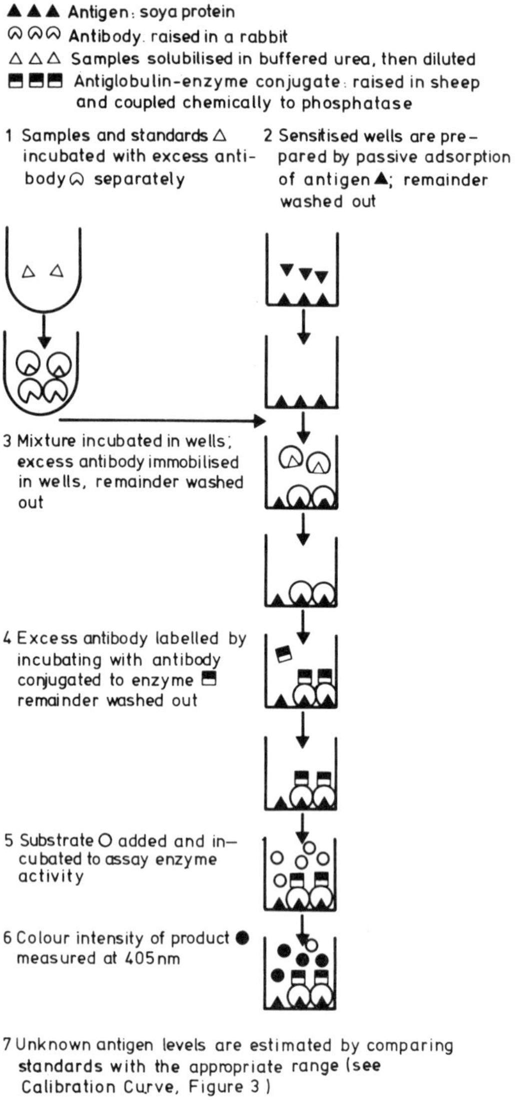

FIG. 2. The determination of soya protein by ELISA: scheme illustrating the simplicity of the individual steps in the procedure. Stages 1 and 5 require adding solutions by pipette and incubating the mixture; stages 2, 3 and 4 involve in addition subjecting the wells to a standardised emptying/washing procedure which can be done in a special semi-automatic washer. The quantitative interactions on which the assay is based occur in a monomolecular layer on the inner surface of the well; normally 96 wells are used simultaneously for blanks, standards and samples at different dilutions. The optical density of the final solution (about 300 μl) is finally measured at stage 6; this can be done *in situ* using a special reader.

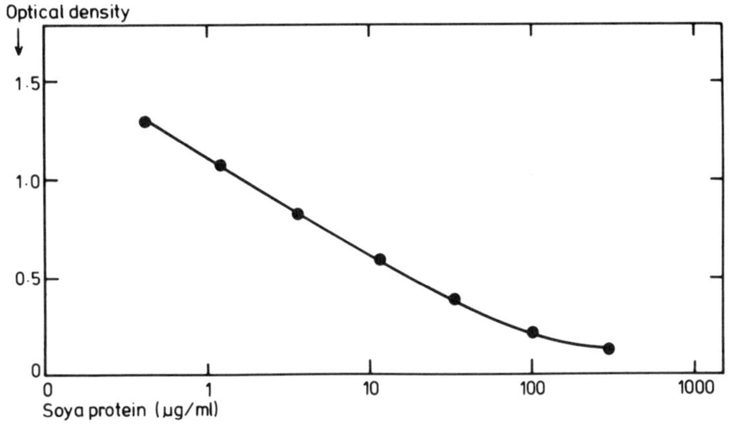

FIG. 3. The determination of soya proteins by ELISA: calibration curve showing the relationship between concentration and observed optical density.

reading the absorbance of the final coloured solution; many samples at several dilutions with their standards and blanks can be simultaneously analysed, particularly with the aid of the semi-automatic equipment now available. The observations lead to standard data illustrated by a calibration curve (Fig. 3), from which final results are calculated. The assay was developed using antibodies to renatured soya protein isolate, but is also successful with commercial antisera to mixed denatured/native protein.[7] It therefore requires only readily available reagents: standard soya protein, the corresponding antibodies and commercial phosphatase-labelled antiglobulin. It is specific for all soya protein ingredients (flour, concentrate, isolate and texturate) in products that are raw, heat-set, canned or dried. It is insensitive to meat, milk, eggs and field bean. It gives useful quantitative data that is being subjected to national and international ring-tests. Other proteinaceous food ingredients can be similarly examined; for instance, ELISA for milk protein in meat products has already been described.[12,13]

Immunoassays for Non-Proteinaceous Components of Foods

The successful development of RIA, EIA and FIA procedures for drugs, antibiotics, hormones, toxins and other clinical analytes invites exploitation by the food analyst whenever such assays are required. The difficulty in their development lies in obtaining suitable antibody preparations: antibodies must be raised, usually to haptens (rather than immunogens), they must display specificity to a particular analyte or group of related analytes (without unwanted cross-reactions), and their titre and avidity must allow a sufficiently sensitive test so that they can be applied to minor and trace food components. However, reports of appropriate immunological reagents for food analysts are now beginning to appear.

Immunoassays can be used to test quantitatively for toxins in foods: for instance, procedures have been reported for aflatoxin M_1 in milk[14] (RIA and ELISA), aflatoxin B_1 in corn, wheat and peanut[15] (RIA and ELISA), trichothecene T-2 toxin in corn and wheat[16] (RIA), staphylococcal enterotoxins[17] (RIA and ELISA) and salmonellae microorganisms[18] (ELISA). Immunoassays have also been recommended for monitoring residual anabolic agents (e.g. diethylstilboestrol) in farm animals.[19,20] Traces of synthetic hexoestrol can be detected by RIA in the urine of cattle at levels less than 10 pg/ml.[21,22] Such assays provide a quick and simple screening procedure when compared to traditional TLC, HPLC, GLC or GLC–MS techniques.

CONCLUSION

While the principles of immunological methods of analysis and their various procedures can only be outlined here, it is evident that they hold great promise in terms of breadth of future application and cost-effectiveness, as well as speed, reliability, specificity and sensitivity. The food analyst came to benefit from exploitation of the technique of GLC in the 1960s, of HPLC in the 1970s and will come to rely equally on the complementary technique of ELISA in the 1980s.

REFERENCES

1. Hitchcock, C. H. S. and Crimes, A. A. (1983). *Analyt. Proc.* (in press).
2. Koh, T. Y. (1978). *J. Inst. Can. Sci. Technol. Aliment.*, **11**, 124–8.
3. Hitchcock, C. H. S., Bailey, F. J., Crimes, A. A., Dean, D. A. G. and Davis, P. J. (1981). *J. Sci. Food. Agric.*, **32**, 157–65.
4. Hayden, A. R. (1978). *J. Food Sci.*, **43**, 476–8.
5. Kang'ethe, E. K., Jones, S. J. and Patterson, R. L. S. (1982). *Meat Sci.*, **7**, 229–40.

6. NEAVES, P., PATEL, P. D. and WOODS, L. F. J. (1982). *Food Res. Assoc. Tech. Circ. No. 777*, BFMIRA, Leatherhead.
7. GRIFFITHS, N. M., BILLINGTON, M. J., CRIMES, A. A. and HITCHCOCK, C. H. S. Data presented to meetings of the Association of Public Analysts at County Hall, Birmingham, September, 1981 and at Leeds 23 April, 1982.
8. OLSMAN, W. J. and HITCHCOCK, C. H. S. (1980). In: *Developments in Food Analysis Techniques—2*, Ed. King, R. D., Applied Science Publishers, London, 225–60.
9. LLEWELLYN, J. W. (1981). In: *Developments in Food Protein—1*, Ed. Hudson, B. J. F., Applied Science Publishers, London, 171–216.
10. CRIMES, A. ., BAILEY, F. J. and HITCHCOCK, C. H. S. (1981). *Analyt. Proc.*, **18**, 164–6.
11. GRIFFITHS, N. M., BILLINGTON, M. J. and GRIFFITHS, W. (1981). *J. Assoc. Publ. Analysts*, **19**, 113–19.
12. TEUFEL, P. and SACHER, V. (1982). *Fleischw.*, **62**, 1474–6.
13. STAAK, C. and KAMPE, U. (1982). *Fleischw.*, **62**, 1477–8.
14. PETSKA, J. J., LI, Y., HARDER, W. and CHU, F. S. (1981). *J. Assoc. Off. Analyt. Chem.*, **64**, 294–301.
15. EL-NAKIB, O., PETSKA, J. J. and CHU, F. S. (1981). *J. Assoc. Off. Analyt. Chem.*, **64**, 1077–82.
16. LEE, S. S. and CHU, F. S. (1981). *J. Assoc. Off. Analyt. Chem.*, **64**, 156–61.
17. FREED, R. C., EVENSON, M. L., REISER, R. F. and BERGDOLL, M. S. (1982). *Appl. Envir.*, **44**, 1349–55.
18. MINNICH, S. A., HARTMAN, P. A. and HEIMSCH, R. C. (1982). *Appl. Envir.*, **43**, 877–83.
19. HEITZMAN, R. J., JOUQUEY, A. and HOFFMANN, B. (1981). *E.E.C. Draft Document VI/6003/81.*
20. HOFFMANN, B. (1978). *J. Assoc. Off. Anal. Chem.*, **61**, 1263–73.
21. HEITZMAN, R. J. and HARWOOD, D. J. (1983). *Vet. Record*, **112**, 120–3.
22. HARWOOD, D. J., HEITZMANN, R. J. and JOUQUEY, A. (1980). *J. Vet. Pharmacol. Therapy*, **3**, 245–54.

9

Microbiological Quality Control

R. SPENCER

J. Sainsbury Ltd, London, UK

ABSTRACT

Microbiological quality control tends to be confused with microbiologists working in microbiology laboratories, busying themselves with a plethora of samples and concerned primarily with details of techniques for counting or detecting microorganisms, together with standards, specifications, etc. Such microbiologists, if sufficiently numerate, might also have regard to the statistical aspects of counting or detecting microorganisms, including sampling tables and control charts. In other words, microbiological quality control tends to be confused with finished product inspection, an essentially wasteful activity, and tends not to be seen as synonymous with the control of the microbiological quality of foods.

The two prime requirements in controlling effectively and efficiently the microbiological quality of foods are a knowledge of the microbiological ecology of the food and a knowledge of the raw materials and of the processes, which together result in the production of the food and its associated microflora. The next requirement is to identify those aspects of the raw materials, the processes, or the finished product, which can affect fundamentally the microbiological quality of that product—and then to introduce stringent controls over these critical aspects. Finished product inspection then becomes of minor importance.

The need to understand the microbiological ecology of the food, and the use of such techniques as recipe hazard analysis and critical control point hazard analysis are discussed with examples.

INTRODUCTION

The first words of the title of this symposium are 'Control of Food Quality' and it would be semantically consistent for this particular contribution to be titled 'Control of the Microbiological Quality of Foods' rather than 'Microbiological Quality Control'. It might be considered that there is no real distinction between 'Microbiological Quality Control' and 'Control of Microbiological Quality'. It is one of the objectives of this contribution to demonstrate that there is a real distinction between these two terms, a distinction that is important, if not indeed fundamental, both in principle and in practice.

'Microbiological Quality Control' is taken to refer to those elements of the system used to ensure that a product attains the desired quality, that are *microbiological* in nature rather than chemical, instrumental, organoleptic, organisational, documentary, etc. By 'Control of Microbiological Quality', is meant *all* elements of the system which are used to ensure that a product attains the desired *microbiological* quality. The use of the term 'Microbiological Quality Control' inevitably focuses attention on microbiological means of achieving the desirable end. Such microbiological means may not always be, and indeed frequently are not, the most effective and efficient means. The use of the term 'Control of Microbiological Quality' focuses attention on the ends to be achieved and allows the most effective and efficient means to be used (be they microbiological or not) for achieving these ends.

Like so much of microbiology, the concepts of the control of the microbiological quality of foods go back to Louis Pasteur and his work in the 1860s. In addition to establishing the concept of infection and destroying the concept of spontaneous generation, he showed that without infection a product such as blood would not undergo putrefaction. Pasteur also demonstrated that the microbiological status of a fluid product could be profoundly influenced by heating the product to a temperature of up to 100 °C, that heating a fluid product under pressure to temperatures of 120 °C could eliminate microorganisms from the product, i.e. sterilise it, and that dry products required temperatures much in excess of 120 °C to sterilise them. He also showed that fluids with an acid reaction when heated to 100 °C remained apparently sterile, whereas in fluids with an alkaline reaction which had similarly been heated to 100 °C, microorganisms would survive and grow. In addition to his work on anthrax and on rabies, Pasteur was concerned with establishing, and indeed succeeded in establishing, procedures for preparing good wine, beer and vinegar.

In the early decades of this century, much microbiological effort was devoted to milk, on the grounds both of the safety of milk and its more general bacterial quality. Milk was a major source of infectious diseases, including enteric diseases (typhoid, paratyphoid and dysentery), septic sore throat and diphtheria, scarlet fever and, of course, tuberculosis, and it became apparent that the most practicable way of preventing milk-borne infectious diseases was by some form of heat-treatment of the milk, usually at temperatures below 100 °C, i.e. pasteurisation. Wilson commented in 1942[1] that if pasteurisation was rendered compulsory and universal, milk-borne diseases would practically cease to exist; the relative absence of milk-borne infectious disease in England and Wales and the not infrequent occurrence of salmonellosis from unpasteurised milk in Scotland is perhaps confirmation of this view.

The quality of milk over a considerable period of time was defined in terms of bacterial counts. It took a microbiologist of Wilson's calibre to correct this situation. In 1935 he wrote:[2] 'The plate count is severely criticised. Ostensibly it measures the number of bacteria in milk but in fact it does not', and later,[3] '(the plate count) is one of the most widely used methods for the bacteriological grading of milk according to cleanliness. It is, however, exposed to criticism on so many grounds that it is doubtful whether its continued use is justifiable.... As scientific bacteriologists we can hardly condone a practice which is little short of bacteriological prostitution'.

Wilson was almost as scathing about the value of the coliform test with milk, commenting[3] that it had been extensively used in the past for the grading of milk without any real appreciation of the fundamental assumptions on which it rests, and concluding: 'It will thus be seen that none of the three premises on which the scientific application of the coliform test to water in this country is based holds true for milk'. Wilson did suggest that the coliform test may be of some empirical value in the control of pasteurisation since the practical absence of coliforms immediately after the process afforded a 'fairly good indication that pasteurisation had been carried out efficiently'. This application of the coliform test was, however, superseded by the phosphatase test. The coliform test continued to be advocated as an index of post-pasteurisation contamination.

Perhaps one of Wilson's major achievements in relation to food microbiology was, however, his advocacy of the methylene blue reduction test as a replacement for bacterial counts in the determination of the bacterial cleanliness of the milk and of its keeping quality. In 1946, the legal plate standard of 100 000/ml for pasteurised milk was replaced in England and Wales by the methylene blue test.

Ice-cream followed a similar route to milk in relation to the control of its microbiological quality. Initially there was emphasis on control by bacterial counts which was superseded by control on the basis of a combination of heating the mix (pasteurisation or sterilisation) and subsequent refrigeration of the final product.

More recently, when it was realised that liquid egg could be an important vehicle of salmonella food poisoning, pasteurisation, together with the use of the alpha-amylase test to ensure that pasteurisation had been carried out, was rapidly introduced as a means of controlling microbiological quality effectively and efficiently.

Hobbs[4] observed in 1967: 'Ice-cream has been a safe commodity in the UK since the institution of the "Heat Treatment" regulations in 1947', and the same could be said of liquid egg following the introduction of similar regulations in 1963.

Whilst, no doubt, there is still much conventional routine microbiology associated with the control of the microbiological quality of milk, cream, ice-cream and liquid egg, the prime means of this control is now not microbiological in nature. It might well be argued that much of the residual conventional routine microbiology results from failure to apply non-microbiological controls effectively, coupled with the innate conservatism of microbiologists. However, with most foods there is even less reliance on non-microbiological controls and even more use of conventional routine microbiology. This attitude is exemplified by Hobbs,[4] who in order to increase the safety of foods recommended 'the provision of unlimited numbers of free samples for examination by public health authorities and, regardless of cost, by the manufacturer'.

CONTROL OF MICROBIOLOGICAL QUALITY

Microbiological Quality

Of all the hazards to health that result from the consumption of food, those that result from the presence in the food of microorganisms or their products must far exceed in terms of human illness those that result from the presence of other toxic substances, such as those natural to the food, those deliberately added as food additives, or those which might contaminate the food adventitiously, such as pesticide or herbicide residues or heavy metals. In England and Wales in recent years there have been more than 10 000 recorded cases per annum of microbial food poisoning or food-borne infections.[5] There are similar figures (adjusted for population size) available for Canada and the USA, and even higher figures for Japan.[6] How many unrecorded cases there are each year in these countries must remain conjecture.

The causative agents of microbiological food poisoning and food-borne infections are many (Table 1). More extensive lists would also include: classic bacterial infections such as anthrax and tuberculosis, *Campylobacter* and *Yersinia* infections; gastro-enteritis caused by enterococci, various enterobacteria including *Proteus* and pseudomonads; parasitic protozoa, such as *Entamoeba histolytica* and *Toxoplasma gondii*, and parasitic worms such as *Taenia* and *Trichinella*: and microbiological toxins, such as that from the dinoflagellate *Gonyaulax* which is responsible for paralytic shellfish poisoning, as well as mycotoxins and scombrotoxin.[7,8,9] Whilst

TABLE 1
REPRESENTATIVE FOOD-BORNE PATHOGENS OR TOXINS
(ADAPTED FROM REFERENCE 7)

Severe hazards
Clostridium botulinum
Salmonella typhi, *S. paratyphi*
Shigella dysenteriae
Vibrio cholerae
Infectious hepatitis virus
Moderate hazards: potentially extensive spread
Salmonella typhimurium and other *Salmonella* species
Vibrio parahaemolyticus
Escherichia coli (enteropathogenic)
Beta-haemolytic streptococcus
Moderate hazards: limited spread
Bacillus cereus
Brucella abortus
Clostridium perfringens
Staphylococcus

many of these latter causative agents are currently rare or even absent in relation to food-borne illness in the Western World, the continuously increasing international trade in processed foods means that they cannot be totally ignored by health authorities nor by commercial organisations engaged in this international trade.

The other dimension of microbiological quality relates to food spoilage, either to the level of consumer unacceptability, with substantial direct economic losses, or to the level of reduced consumer acceptability, with loss of competitive position on the part of the commercial organisation concerned. Whilst there are few data available, it is considered highly probable that such economic damage from microbiological spoilage is, so far as processed foods are concerned, much more substantial than from other forms of spoilage.

Thus, in any general consideration of the control of food quality, priority must be given to the control of microbiological quality: that is to eliminating, so far as is possible, hazards to health and to minimising spoilage. The means which are to be used in this control must be effective, reliable, and cost-efficient. Thus, for any particular food they must be based on a knowledge of the hazards to health likely to be presented by that food and of its potential for spoilage, i.e. on a knowledge of the microbial ecology of foods and of the epidemiology of food-borne disease.

Microbial Ecology of Foods

The range of different types of food available to the consumer continues to grow. A large supermarket might stock over 10 000 different food products and whilst the differences between some products will be minor and of little microbiological consequence, the differences between many of these 10 000 products will have substantial significance to the microbiological quality of the products. These differences will fall into the following five categories:

Infection

This term applies to the number of types of microorganisms in the food at the time of its manufacture (or harvesting, processing, packaging, etc.). These microorganisms might be intrinsic to the food itself, or they might gain access to the food with minor ingredients or from contaminated surfaces, water, air, dust, or from human or animal carriers.

Processing

The infection of the food might be modified in number and/or type by any processes which the food undergoes during manufacture or preparation. The application of heat to the food is particularly likely to modify the microflora, their numbers tending to increase at temperatures below 40–50 °C and to diminish at higher temperatures, with concomitant changes in the relative abundance of different groups of microorganisms. Other processes such as the removal of heat (i.e. cooling and freezing), or removal of water (i.e. concentration or dehydration) may have similar effects. Such processes might also affect the nature of the food.

Intrinsic factors

This term relates to the nature of the food itself. Some factors are chemical or physical, for example, the availability of microbial nutrients, the presence of antimicrobial substances, the pH and buffering capacity, the redox potential, the water activity, the emulsion nature of the food; others are biological, for example, the nature of the food, including both structure and physiology.

Extrinsic factors

This term relates to the conditions in which the food is held during storage. Temperature is clearly a most important factor, not only in its direct effect on microbial growth and thus on the absolute and relative abundance of different groups of microorganisms, but also in the ability of fluctuating temperatures to bring about water migration and hence changes in water activity. Other important factors are the partial pressure of water vapour, with a tendency to dry or moisten the food and thus change the water activity, and the partial pressure of oxygen with its effect on the balance of aerobic, microaerophilic and anaerobic bacteria. The way in which the food is packaged clearly relates to the possible influence of oxygen or water vapour.

Implicit factors

This term relates to the changes which the microorganisms in the food themselves bring about by antagonistic or synergistic effects upon one another, for example, by lowering the pH or redox potential.

The above concepts were first formalised by Mossel and Ingram in 1955 in relation to the spoilage of foods.[10] They are, however, equally applicable to the microbiological safety of foods and continue to provide a very valuable framework within which the microbial ecology of foods and, hence, the control of the microbiological quality of foods can be considered. More recent publications have extensively amplified these concepts in relation both to the general principles involved and also their application to particular foods.[11,12]

Many of the factors which influence the microbiological quality of foods have been known and made use of on an empirical basis for thousands of years. The trends in the food industry now are first, to make use of these factors on a rational basis, particularly by seeking to determine 'safety' quantitatively; secondly, to push the factors to the limits of their effectiveness often in the interests of greater consumer acceptability by, for example, reductions in the concentrations of sodium chloride or acetic acid, or a lower heat process; and, thirdly, to make use of combinations of factors, any one of which at the level used is unlikely to have significant effect, for example, combining low pH, low water activity and the use of preservatives. These trends make it even more important that the microbiologist concerned with controlling the microbiological quality of foods relies less on microbiological inspection of the product and more on controlling those factors outlined above which profoundly affect microbiological quality, and, furthermore, controlling them in the most efficient and effective manner.

Epidemiology of Food-borne Disease

Although many different types of microorganisms have been and continue to be incriminated in food poisoning and food-borne infections, and it would be rash to suggest that any particular food is totally safe, most incidents of food-borne disease are caused by one of only a few types of microorganisms, with only a few types of foods serving as the carrier.

In a survey of food-borne disease in 6 countries (Australia, Japan, Canada, USA, England and Wales), Todd[6] reported that in each country salmonellae, *Staphylococcus aureus* and *Clostridium perfringens* were by far the most common causative organisms, with the exception of Japan where *Vibrio parahaemolyticus* was the most common causative organism and *Cl. perfringens* food poisoning was rare. In all countries except Japan, meat and poultry were the most common carrier foods. Fish and shellfish were by far the most common carrier foods in Japan and the second most common in the USA.

Todd's study, in addition to presenting a broad picture of food-borne disease in the 6 countries, highlighted a number of significant details, for example, the relatively high incidence of food-borne hepatitis A in the USA, together with the importance in that country of salads as a carrier. Further information on the relationship between different microorganisms and different foods in food-borne disease is available.[7,8,9]

In addition to the common relationships between particular food-borne diseases and particular foods, it is important to be aware of the less common relationships. Botulism has been associated with various forms of processed fish in addition to canned vegetables; salmonellosis has been associated with dried milk, food colours, vegetable protein food supplements and chocolate candy in addition to meat, poultry, cream and egg products; staphylococcal intoxication has been associated with bacon and salami in addition to cooked meats and cream products; food-borne hepatitis A is not only associated with sewage polluted shellfish;[13] and there are many other examples.

Another aspect of epidemiology is a consideration of the factors in food processing which contribute to outbreaks of food-borne disease as, for example, for outbreaks of food-borne disease in the USA.[13] Table 2 shows the factors in the manufacturing process which contributed to the outbreak associated with manufactured foods, raw material contamination and a failure of a heat process being the major factors. Table 3 shows that for outbreaks associated with foods prepared in the home or in food service establishments, inadequate refrigeration was a major factor. A further breakdown of the factors responsible for the failure of the heat process for canned foods[14] is shown in Table 4.

Microbiological Examination of Foods

Whatever the means used for the control of the microbiological quality of foods, some reliance must inevitably be put on conventional microbiological examinations of raw materials and ingredients, plant samples, and finished product.

Microbiological procedures

Much has been written pertaining to the microbiological examination of foods and it is not the intention of this contribution to

TABLE 2

FACTORS IN FOOD PROCESSING PLANTS CONTRIBUTING TO OUTBREAKS OF FOOD-BORNE DISEASE

Factor		*No. of outbreaks*
Contamination (if no terminal heat process)	Raw product	35
	Additive	3
	During process	4
Heat process failure		31
Post-process contamination	Raw product	1
	Equipment	5
	Cross-contamination	8
	Workers	8
Factors permitting growth in plant	Inadequate refrigeration	14
	Fermentations	4
	Anaerobic packaging	10
Evidence of growth after product left plant		10

seek to review the many publications available. Areas extensively covered include: the treatment of the food, including its homogenisation and dilution and the use of automated devices; various techniques for determining colony or viable counts such as pour plates, surface spread plates, drop plates (the Miles and Misra diluent drop technique), agar droplets (the technique of Sharpe and Kilsby[15]), and spiral plating; procedures for determining viable counts indirectly by measurement of, e.g. changes in impedance or of ATP concentrations; a plethora of selective and/or diagnostic media for bacteria, yeast and moulds, biochemical and serological tests for the identification of isolated microorganisms including rapid biochemical computer-based identification procedures and highly sophisticated techniques such as pyrolysis–gas–liquid chromatography and enzyme-linked immunosorbent assays; the isolation and identification of viruses from foods, and, the detection and quantification of microbial toxins, e.g. staphylococcal enterotoxins, mycotoxins, histamines. Details of methods are given in several publications,[8,16] some being concerned with particular areas, such as dairy products,[17] canned foods,[18] and frozen foods,[19] and rapid and

TABLE 3

CONDITIONS CONTRIBUTING TO OUTBREAKS OF FOOD-BORNE DISEASE BY FOODS PROCESSED IN THE HOME OR IN FOOD SERVICE ESTABLISHMENTS

Factor	*No. of outbreaks*
Inadequate refrigeration	336
Preparing food far in advance of service	156
Infected persons and poor personal hygiene	151
Inadequate cooking or heating	140
Holding food in warming device at too low a temperature	114
Contaminated raw materials in uncooked foods	84
Inadequate reheating	66
Cross-contamination	58
Inadequate cleaning of equipment	52
Other conditions	160

automated methods in food microbiology have been the subject of several recent reviews.[20-23]

It will be appreciated that the microbiologist concerned with the microbiological quality control of foods has at his disposal a wide range of procedures for detecting or counting microorganisms in food samples or for quantifying their toxins (although not all are suitable for routine use, particularly those for toxins, viruses and parasites). However, such procedures, whatever their range and accuracy, must be *applied* and the results *interpreted* satisfactorily before the procedures themselves are of any real value in determining the microbiological quality of the foods.

TABLE 4

THE 10 MOST FREQUENTLY REPORTED DEVIATIONS FROM THE LOW-ACID CANNED FOODS GOOD MANUFACTURING PRACTICE REGULATIONS

1. Records inadequate
2. Registration and process filing forms incomplete
3. Process deviations not handled properly
4. Faulty temperature-recording devices
5. Scheduled process adequacy not verified
6. Improper venting
7. Initial temperature not controlled
8. Retorts inadequate
9. Reference thermometers not in compliance
10. Critical factors not controlled

Sampling. The first area of concern is that the microbiological procedures used can only be applied to *samples* of food and hence the results obtained on such samples have statistical uncertainties associated with them as a consequence of their having been taken from a mass of food. The principles of statistical quality control are well established and are widely used in industry generally. Regrettably, microbiologists concerned with microbiological quality control tend to be much less familiar with these principles and their applications than they are with strictly microbiological procedures. This is, perhaps, because there is no comprehensive publication concerned with microbiological statistical quality control (although there are many publications which are easily applicable to food microbiology). This defect is partially remedied by the ICMSF publication on sampling for microbiological analysis,[24] although it must be borne in mind that this publication is concerned primarily with finished product inspection in relation to international and national trade. It has limitations, which its contributors fully recognise and indeed draw attention to in relation to the wider aspects of the control of microbiological quality.

Interpretation. The second area of concern relates to the interpretation of the results of the microbiological examinations. There are problems associated with the technical limitations of the microbiological procedures used; there are problems of statistical significance associated with sampling plans; and there are also problems of the relevance of the microbiological results to the chemical and physical nature of the food, its previous history, how it is packaged, how it is to be distributed, and in which form it is to be consumed.

It is usual for foods to be examined microbiologically against some recommended limits, specifications or standards. Such recommendations ought to prescribe the methodology and the sampling plan to be used and have regard to the statistical uncertainties associated with the results obtained; they ought, most importantly, to be related to the nature of the food, its previous history and what is to happen to the food subsequently.

Many microbiological specifications for foods relate to pathogens or their toxins, for example, salmonellae, and it is not unusual for such specifications to state that all pathogens and their toxins shall be absent from the food, possibly prescribing microbial methods and sampling plans for ensuring this. It may fail to be recognised, first, that the microbial method is likely to be less than 100% certain of detecting the pathogen if it is present in the sample examined and that there will be lower limits to the detection of any toxin; secondly, that no sampling plan can guarantee complete absence of the pathogen; thirdly, that previous history of the food might be such that the likelihood of the pathogen or toxin being present is remote; fourthly, that the nature of the food or of its subsequent treatment is such that the pathogen or toxin, if present, is highly unlikely to cause harm; and finally, that the pathogen is so common in the food that it is very likely to be found and for economic or political reasons it is not practicable to ban the food. The concept of a 'Zero Tolerance' for pathogens might be excellent in principle but it is meaningless in practice.

A further consideration is that the expression 'all pathogens' is so general as in practice to be meaningless. It would include viruses, protozoa and exotic pathogens for which isolation procedures are highly technical, or which require special facilities, or which are extremely unlikely to be found in the food.

Many microbiological specifications for foods refer to groups of bacteria which are themselves harmless but which 'indicate' the likely presence of pathogens. The commonest examples of such indicator microorganisms are, of course, coliforms, 'faecal coli' and *Escherichia coli* (excluding of course, enteropathogenic varieties). Much has been published on the appropriateness of examining foods for indicator organisms and on the relative merits of coliforms, *E. coli* or indeed of the Enterobacteriaceae family as indicators of faecal pollution and hence of the presence of, for example, salmonellae. Suffice it to say here that while there might be some value in the use of indicator organisms in particular circumstances, the rationale of such use needs to be very carefully determined, otherwise, at best, the effort expended will be wasted or, at worst, the results obtained will be positively misleading.

By far the most common parameter in a microbiological specification is some measure of the total number of microorganisms, usually bacteria. The usual procedure is to undertake a colony count on a non-selective medium at some prescribed temperature, the parameter being referred to as a 'total plate count', 'total colony count', or 'total viable count'. It will, of course be obvious that such a procedure will not determine all living bacteria but only those capable of growing under the particular cultural conditions chosen. The use of different media, different times or temperatures of incubation, and incubation in different gaseous environments, will give not only results which are quantitatively different but results which differ in their meaning.

Notwithstanding the above, however, a measure of the level of viable microorganisms in a food that has not been produced by fermentation, can be useful on three counts. First, it can provide information about the level of contamination of raw materials or processing equipment, about the efficacy of heat processing, or about the time/temperature conditions under which the food has been held. Secondly, for perishable foods, it can provide information about the likely storage life of the food. Thirdly, foods containing large numbers of microorganisms are more likely than are foods containing low numbers of microorganisms to cause illness, either from specific pathogens, e.g. salmonellae or *Staphylococcus aureus*, or less specifically, for example, because of large numbers of *Proteus* sp. or enterococci.

HAZARD ANALYSIS

Many food companies have quality control programmes for ensuring the microbiological quality of their products. Such programmes, which generally include a substantial amount of microbiological testing of product, have usually evolved on an *ad hoc*, trial-and-error basis, and may contain major deficiencies (see Table 4). Such deficiencies often come to light only *after* a major problem has occurred, for example, an outbreak of botulism from canned foods.[25] These programmes can often be substantially improved in terms of both effectiveness and cost, by the adoption of a logical and systematic approach to the identification and quantification of the risks associated with a particular product and its process, and the subsequent identification of particular points in the process which can critically affect quality and where control action should be concentrated. This is the rationale behind the Hazard Analysis Critical Control Points (HACCP) concept.

The application of hazard analysis to the control of food microbiological quality originated in the USA in 1969 in relation to the control of salmonellae in foods,[26] and was subsequently developed by the US Food and Drug Administration,[25,27,28] by the

National Aeronautics and Space Administration for foods to be used in the Skylab project,[29,30] by the US Natick Research and Development Command[31] and by the Pillsbury Company in the USA[32] for wider applications. Interest has also been expressed by WHO[7] in this approach as a possibly cost-effective means of improving the safety of foods. Its uses in relation to the microbiological quality of frozen foods[33] and canned foods,[34] and in food service establishments[35-38] have been outlined. An application in relation to determining and controlling hazards in domestic recipes—Recipe Hazard Analysis—has been recently suggested.[39]

In relation to the control of salmonellae in foods, an attempt was made to categorise foods on the basis of three product hazard characteristics.[26]

A. The product contains an ingredient that has been identified as a significant potential factor in salmonellosis.

B. The manufacturing process does not include a controlled step that would destroy salmonellae. The processing step could be heat, concentration, pH change or any other change in physical or chemical characteristics which will destroy salmonellae.

C. There is a substantial likelihood of microbiological growth if mishandled or 'abused' in distribution or consumer usage. The intention here was to identify products which are a good medium for growth of salmonellae, either in distribution or as normally prepared for consumer use.

Foods themselves could then be ranked according to the hazard characteristics present. For example, the most hazardous food would be indicated by ABC, meaning that it contains a sensitive ingredient, it has no 'controlling process' and there is potential for abuse. A food of lesser hazard might be one indicated by A00, i.e. it contains a sensitive ingredient but has a controlling process and has no abuse potential.

Ingredients could be further categorised depending upon the likelihood of their being contaminated with salmonellae: the least likely ingredients include sugar, salt, citric acid, and other essentially pure organic and inorganic chemicals, whereas the most likely ones are raw natural materials subjected to no processing, for example, meat or eggs.

This categorisation was in relation to the control of salmonellae, but it is suggested to have greater applicability in relation to hazard analysis. Peterson and Gunnerson have proposed a redefinition of the three product hazard characteristics, as follows:[33]

A. The product contains a ‘sensitive’ ingredient or ingredients which can be assumed to be potential sources of contamination under normal circumstances.
B. The manufacturing process does not contain a controlled processing step that effectively destroys harmful bacteria.
C. There is substantial potential for microbiological abuse in distribution or in consumer handling that could render the product harmful when consumed, as the result of microbial growth.

It is believed that Peterson and Gunnerson do not go far enough in defining general microbial product hazard characteristics, in that:

1. Contamination must refer not only to all microbial pathogens (including viruses) capable of causing disease by the oral route, but also microbial toxins such as staphylococcal enterotoxins and mycotoxins.
2. The controlling manufacturing process must destroy all those microorganisms and their toxins which are considered as important in relation to ingredient contamination.
3. Most importantly, consideration must be specifically given to the possibility of contamination by harmful organisms after any controlling process, together with the opportunity for such contaminating organisms to grow in the product.

It must be reiterated that this form of hazard characterisation can be useful if it emerges as part of a detailed hazard analysis. It could lead to dangerous complacency if it is based on a superficial survey and is then used to preempt a detailed hazard analysis. For example, the likelihood of an ingredient being contaminated might be seriously underestimated; the effect of the process might be overestimated, particularly in relation to toxins or large numbers of contaminating microorganisms, or indeed the process itself might not be under sufficient control; the possibility of post-processing contamination might be overlooked or the ability of any contaminating microorganisms to grow might be underestimated. Equally so, it could lead to unnecessary concern and wasteful activity if the likelihood of growth in the final product is overestimated.

Critical Control Points

In the development of the concept of Critical Control Points, they were first viewed[27] as 'the location(s) or point(s) in a food processing operation at which failure to prevent contamination can be detected by laboratory tests with maximum assurance and efficiency'. Once again the initial emphasis was on microbiological laboratory tests. This view was, however, soon overtaken by regarding Critical Control Points less as points where contamination was likely to occur and could be detected by laboratory tests, but as points where control could effectively be applied to prevent not only contamination but also growth or even survival. For example, Bauman[32] defined them as 'those processing determiners whose loss of control would result in an unacceptable food safety risk'. It might be added 'or an unacceptable risk of spoilage'.

Critical Control Points can take a variety of forms. Raw materials may constitute Critical Control Points depending upon their nature, origin and use. If, however, a raw material is subject to a process step which will reliably eliminate any hazard associated with that raw material, then the raw material ceases to be a Critical Control Point, but the process step might then become one. The possibility of subsequent contamination might establish yet another Critical Control Point, which it might take a further process step to replace.

Heat processes are the most common Critical Control Points, followed by refrigeration. Chemical or physical changes to the food, such as acidification, the incorporation of preservatives, or a reduction of water activity, may also constitute Critical Control Points, particularly in relation to spoilage. The human factor should not, however, be neglected, not only in relation to personal hygiene but also in relation to control procedures and their monitoring. Adequate training, written procedures and effective supervision are important elements in HACCP.

When Critical Control Points have been identified, control needs to be exercised and monitoring of this control to be carried out. Raw materials might require microbiological tests against specifications; process Critical Control Points are usually best controlled and monitored by physical means, for example, by time and temperature and the use of recorders. Where finished product monitoring is necessary, microbiological tests against specifications might be appropriate but again physical or chemical tests for, for example, acidity, water activity, or concentration of preservative, might be more informative as well as more cost-effective. Curtis and Huskey[40] comment that since HACCP techniques emphasise hazard elimination through in-line controls, quality control of finished product is required only to determine if the product has characteristics (e.g. sterility, pH) which preclude development of a hazard.

It will be apparent from the above that for hazard analysis to be an effective approach to controlling the microbiological quality of a food, including spoilage potential as well as risk to health, there is need not only for a detailed knowledge of all the procedures concerned with the production of the food and its subsequent distribution and use, but also for an assessment of the microbiological hazards associated with the production of the food, its distribution and use, an identification of Critical Control Points, and the establishment of monitoring procedures. These latter requirements necessitate an extensive knowledge of the microbial ecology of the food and, associated with this, a knowledge of the epidemiology of microbial food poisoning and food-borne infections. Lastly, where microbiological testing is unavoidable, there is a need not only for appropriate methodology but also to maximise the benefits of the results obtained and ensure that there is an appropriate 'feedback' into the HACCP system, as emphasised by Peterson and Gunnerson.[33]

STATISTICAL CONTROL CHART TECHNIQUES

Reference has already been made to the relative lack of familiarity of food microbiologists in general with statistical techniques. In particular, whereas the use of statistical control chart techniques is standard in many industries, their use by food microbiologists would seem to be uncommon, with the consequence that the results of microbiological examinations of raw materials or of finished products do not yield their full benefits and hence that there are both diseconomies in control and production costs and greater risks of unsatisfactory product being allowed to pass into distribution. Such techniques can be used for both product attributes, i.e. presence or absence of some specific defect, and product variables, i.e. the magnitude of some parameter such as a plate count, and are described in detail in, for example, British Standard 2564.[41]

CONCLUSIONS

This contribution to the Symposium has sought to direct attention to the need for a change in emphasis in the role of the commercial food microbiologist. Traditionally the emphasis has been on microbiological testing of ingredients, plant samples and finished product. This is undoubtedly an important aspect of the commercial food microbiologist's role, particularly when a knowledge of statistics is coupled with a knowledge of microbiological counting, isolation and identification procedures. Important as it is, however, this aspect makes only limited use of what is in principle a most important member of the technical team. From a knowledge of the microbial ecology of foods, of the epidemiology of food-borne disease, and of the physics, chemistry and engineering of food processing operations, the food microbiologist is in a key position to make a major contribution to an effective and efficient system for controlling the microbiological quality of the foods with which he or she is concerned. One system for controlling the microbiological quality of foods is HACCP. It is not the only one and it is not new. It is believed that it has much to offer and that it deserves wider consideration than it is currently receiving. The role of the food microbiologist in the application of HACCP is crucial. The final words will be with Howard Bauman,[42] one of the originators of the HACCP approach, 'microbiologists are critical to the successful development, processing and distribution of a safe food product. Microbiologists are involved—or should be—in the decision making process from conception of idea to final use of the product by the consumer. The corporate microbiologist, of necessity, must have a broad knowledge base far beyond the field of microbiology'.

REFERENCES

1. WILSON, G. S. (1942). *The Pasteurization of Milk*, Edwin Arnold & Co., London.
2. WILSON, G. S., TWIGG, R. S., WRIGHT, R. C., HENDRY, C. B., COWELL, M. P. and MAIER, I. (1935). *Spec. Rep. Ser. med. Res. Coun. Lond. No. 206*.
3. WILSON, G. S. and MILES, A. A. (1942). *Topley and Wilson's Principles of Bacteriology and Immunity*, 3rd edition, Edward Arnold & Co., London.

4. Hobbs, B. C. (1967). In: *Quality Control in the Food Industry*, Vol. 1, Ed. Herschdoerfer, S. M., Academic Press, London.
5. Hepner, E. (1980). *Publ. Hlth Lond.*, **94**, 337.
6. Todd, E. C. D. (1978). *J. Food Prot.*, **41**, 559.
7. World Health Organisation (1976). *Microbiological Aspects of Food Hygiene*, Technical Report Series No. 598, WHO, Geneva.
8. International Commission on Microbiological Specifications for Foods (1978). *Microorganisms in Foods 1. Their significance and methods of enumeration*, 2nd edition, University of Toronto Press, Toronto.
9. Riemann, H. and Bryan, F. L. (1979). *Food Borne Infections and Intoxications*, 2nd edition, Academic Press, New York.
10. Mossel, D. A. A. and Ingram, M. (1955). *J. appl. Bact.*, **18**, 232.
11. International Commission on Microbiological Specifications for Foods (1980). *Microbial Ecology of Foods. Vol. 1. Factors Affecting Life and Death of Microorganisms*, Academic Press, London.
12. International Commission on Microbiological Specifications for Foods (1980). *Microbial Ecology of Foods. Vol. 2. Food Commodities*, Academic Press, London.
13. Bryan, F. L. (1974). *Food Technol.*, **28**(9), 52.
14. Schaffner, R. M. (1982). *Food Technol.*, **36**(12), 87.
15. Sharpe, A. M. and Kilsby, D. C. (1971). *J. appl. Bact.*, **34**, 435.
16. Speck, M. L. (1976). *Compendium of Methods for the Microbiological Examination of Foods*, American Public Health Association, Washington, DC.
17. Marth, E. H. (1978). *Standard Methods for the Examination of Dairy Products*, 14th edition, American Public Health Association, Washington, DC.
18. National Canners Association (1978). *Laboratory Manual for Food Canners and Processors Vol. 1. Microbiology and Processing*, Avi Publishing Company Inc, Westport, Connecticut.
19. Hall, L. P. (1975). *A Manual of Methods for the Bacteriological Examination of Frozen Foods*, Oxford University Press, Oxford.
20. Southern, P. M. (1979). *Food Technol.*, **33**(3), 54.
21. Cox, N. A. and Mercuri, A. J. (1979). *Food Technol.*, **33**(3), 57.
22. Goldschmidt, M. C. and Fang, D. Y. C. (1979). *Food Technol.*, **33**(3), 63.
23. Hood, J. M. and Gibbs, P. A. (1982). In: *Developments in Food Microbiology—1*, Ed. Davies, R., Applied Science Publishers, London.
24. International Commission on Microbiological Specifications for Foods (1974). *Microorganisms in Foods 2. Sampling for microbiological analysis: Principles and specific applications*, University of Toronto Press, Toronto.
25. Kauffman, F. L. and Schaffner, R. M. (1974). *Proc. IVth Int. Congress Food Sci. and Technol.*, **3**, 402.
26. National Academy of Sciences (1969). *An Evaluation of the Salmonella Problem*, National Academy of Sciences, Washington, DC.

27. Food and Drug Administration (1972). *Proceedings of the 1971 National Conference on Food Protection*, US Department of Health, Education and Welfare, Washington, DC.
28. Kauffman, F. L. (1974). *Food Technol.*, **28**(9), 51.
29. Heidelbaugh, N. D., Smith, M. C., Jr. and Rambout, P. C. (1973). *Am. Vet. Med. Assoc., J.*, **163**, 1065.
30. Bourland, C. T., Heidelbaugh, N. D., Huber, C. S., Kiser, P. R. and Rowley, D. B. (1974). *J. Milk Food Technol.*, **37**, 624.
31. Longree, K. (1980). *Quantity Food Sanitation*, 3rd edition, Wiley Interscience, New York.
32. Bauman, H. E. (1974). *Food Technol.*, **28**(9), 30.
33. Peterson, A. C. and Gunnerson, R. E. (1974). *Food Technol.*, **28**(9), 37.
34. Ito, K. (1974). *Food Technol.*, **28**(9), 46.
35. Bobeng, B. J. and David, B. D. (1977). *J. Food Prot.*, **40**, 632.
36. Bryan, F. L. (1979). *J. Environ. Hlth.*, **41**, 198.
37. Bryan, F. L. and McKinley, T. W. (1979). *J. Food Prot.*, **42**, 4.
38. Bryan, F. L., Bartleson, C. A. and Christopherson, N. (1981). *J. Food Prot.*, **44**, 500.
39. Zottola, E. A. and Wolf, I. D. (1981). *J. Food Prot.*, **44**, 560.
40. Curtis, J. E. and Huskey, G. E. (1974). *Food Product Devel.*, **8**(3), 19.
41. British Standards Institution (1955). BS 2564: Control Chart Technique when Manufacturing to a Specification, BSI, London.
42. Bauman, H. E. (1982). *Food Technol.*, **36**(12), 58.

10

Rapid Methods for Microbiological Quality Control of Foods

C. S. GUTTERIDGE

Cadbury Schweppes PLC,
Lord Zuckerman Research Centre, University of Reading, UK

ABSTRACT

Microbiological quality control is required to ensure that food does not contain pathogenic microorganisms or toxins and will not spoil in any discernible way during the shelf-life of the product. The control of microbiological quality during manufacture is a vital procedure but one that takes a great deal of time and resources. For example, some of the methods used to test for the presence of pathogenic microorganisms can take between 3 and 5 days to produce a confirmed negative or positive result. Given that the trend in the food processing industry is towards continuous processes, if a microbiological quality problem becomes apparent the delay in obtaining meaningful results will mean that large quantities of stock will have to be traced, quarantined, tested and, perhaps, destroyed with obvious cost penalties.

Conventional methods for estimating microbial quality require the population of microorganisms present to be cultured on selective or non-selective media then counted and compared with a standard figure. For pathogenic organisms or toxins, specialist identification or confirmation techniques may be required. In recent years several methods have been proposed to accelerate testing for microbial quality. Some detection methods, e.g. direct epifluorescent filtration (DEFT), represent an attempt to speed up a counting procedure—in this case a direct microscopic count. Other methods, e.g. impedance, are not based on counting but utilise some aspect of microbial metabolism.

In this paper the need for rapid methods will be examined and the variety of novel methods proposed for detection and identification of microorganisms will be reviewed. This review will consider in some detail those methods likely to have an impact on the food manufacturing industry in the next five years and will also speculate about techniques likely to make a major impact over a more protracted timescale.

INTRODUCTION

The role of microbiological quality control in food manufacturing is to ensure that food does not contain pathogenic microorganisms or toxins and will not spoil in any discernible way during a period which is the accepted shelf-life of that product. Microbiological tests are conducted to assess the acceptability of the food, a food ingredient or a process and the results of each test are measured against a microbiological criterion each of which is composed of four components:[1]

1. A statement of the contaminant of concern (species or group of microorganisms or their toxins).
2. The analytical method(s) to be used for their detection and/or enumeration.
3. The sampling plan—the number of samples to be taken, for example, of a finished product or an ingredient.
4. The decision criteria, i.e. the microbiological limits appropriate to the sample being tested.

The primary aim of this paper is to examine novel rapid methodology that will have an impact on the second component of this criterion. However, it is important to appreciate that the analytical method used for microbiological testing should not be considered in isolation and for novel methodology to be effective due regard has to be taken of the nature of the problem, the sampling plan and the decision criteria. With this proviso this paper will not explore in much depth the philosophy of microbiological testing but will examine the need for more rapid methods, review those methods likely to find useful application during the next five years and suggest developments which may grow in importance over a more protracted timescale. The current high level of activity in rapid microbiological methods research means inevitably that some selectivity has been applied to choose those methods discussed. The methods selected are those that, in the author's opinion, will feature predominantly in the control of microbiological quality as practised by the food manufacturing industry.

Why Rapid Methods?

The time required to achieve microbiological results using conventional methods can be a serious constraint to testing as a means of control. For example, *Salmonella* testing requires a minimum of 4 days[2] with an additional day needed for investigating and confirming the identity of suspect colonies. A Most Probable Number determination for *Escherichia coli* may require as long as 8 days.[2] Many other important tests take a few days to yield results. Consequently the use of microbiological testing to monitor critical control points usually produces results that are only of retrospective value.

In the case of finished product testing food may have to be warehoused for several days until test results are available. Given the trend in the food manufacturing industry towards continuous processes large quantities of stock may be involved and the costs of stock control and warehousing will escalate. Furthermore, although microbiological incidents are few and far between, if a microbiological quality problem does become apparent, the delay in obtaining results will mean that large quantities of stock will have to be traced, quarantined, tested and perhaps destroyed with obvious cost penalties. Thus, from the food manufacturer's view point the simple answer to the question 'Why do we need rapid methods?' is that it can save significant sums of money. Of course it is vital to establish the reliability of any proposed new method because no responsible manufacturer will wish to prejudice the effectiveness of an extensive programme of microbiological testing and the safety of his products by introducing methods that have not been evaluated properly or even approved officially.

Another area where rapid microbiological methods can produce benefits, although they are less easy to prove, is within a product development function. Responsible manufacturers will assess the stability and microbiological condition of new products, formulations or ingredients. Often these operations are carried out to tight timescales or cost constraints imposed by marketing considerations. The introduction of rapid methods can allow a more thorough evaluation within the same timescales and can circumvent future microbiological incidents.

Finally, the role of rapid methods in a research function can be of significance particularly when applied to screening operations, e.g. for more robust formulations or for novel preservative systems.

REVIEW OF NEW METHODS AND THEIR APPLICATIONS

At the research level three symposia[3–5] demonstrate the wealth of interest in rapid methods within microbiology. Much of this interest is directed at medical microbiology but food microbiologists are becoming more aware of the need and prospects for rapid methodology and this field has recently been the subject of an excellent review.[6] The 'classification' of techniques used by Wood and Gibbs[6] is adopted here.

Cell and Colony Counting Methods

The conventional microbiological quality control approach is to count organisms and compare the results with a standard. Colony counting methods, i.e. plate counts, are by definition not rapid because of the incubation periods necessary for the growth of colony forming units to form colonies. In the last decade there have been many developments in the mechanisation and miniaturisation of colony counting techniques. Methods such as the agar droplet technique,[7] loop dilutions[8] and the spiral plate maker[9] are now established in some food microbiology laboratories.[6] The spiral plate technique is probably the most developed. The apparatus, which was developed in the Food and Drug Administration Laboratories in the USA, dilutes and plates out the sample in a way that allows a wide range of colony counts to be determined on a single plate. Various comparisons of data obtained by the standard plate count and the spiral plate methods have shown a high degree of correlation between the two methodologies[10,11] and in 1981 it became an accepted method of the Association of Official Analytical Chemists.[12] Colony counts can be carried out by a laser counter designed specifically to go with the spiral plater. Overall the method requires less materials than traditional techniques and there is a considerable labour saving in terms of preparation time and time at the laboratory bench. However, because the colonies have to be grown prior to counting it cannot be described as a rapid method *per se*.

Direct observation of microorganisms using a microscope is regarded as the original rapid microbiological method.[6] The use of direct counts in food microbiology is limited by several factors notably the low sensitivity, interference by food particles and the fatigue associated with the examination of the large numbers of samples down a microscope. To overcome some of these problems the direct epifluorescent filter technique (DEFT) has been developed for the estimation of microorganisms in milk and some dairy products.[13,14] The method involves the recovery of organisms from the sample by filtration, staining *in situ* with a fluorescent dye and counting using epifluorescent microscopy. The essential element of DEFT is the filtration step and methodology has to be developed that permits the filtration of a significant quantity of sample. The method devised for raw milk involves pretreatment with trypsin and Triton X-100 at 50 °C for 10 min to lyse somatic cells and disperse fat globules sufficiently to permit membrane filtration through a 0·6 μm polycarbonate filter. The bacteria retained on the membrane are stained with acridine orange and counted. Modifications of this procedure, e.g. by varying the detergent concentration or incubation period, permitted the filtration of a range of dairy products. Figure 1 shows the close agreement between DEFT results and conventional colony counts for three different sources of milk.[13]

As first reported DEFT still had the potential disadvantage of operator fatigue caused by long periods at the microscope. Recently the technique has been semi-automated[15] by using an image analysis system to undertake the counting, and full automation including the sample preparation seems achievable. There is no doubt that DEFT has an important role to fulfil in dairy microbiology and a recent collaborative trial involving 6 laboratories[16] showed that each laboratory obtained a highly significant relationship between DEFT counts and plate counts. Reproducibility between laboratories was more of a problem but the authors believe that this could be improved by rigid standardisation of equipment such as filter towers and batches of stain. The extension of DEFT to the enumeration of microorganisms in other foods has been attempted[17] successfully for fresh meat and fish and some frozen and prepared foods. There is no reason why DEFT could not be more widely used but the filtration methodology will have to be established for each food material to be tested, and in a laboratory handling a wide range of samples the variety of pretreatments required may prove to be impractical.

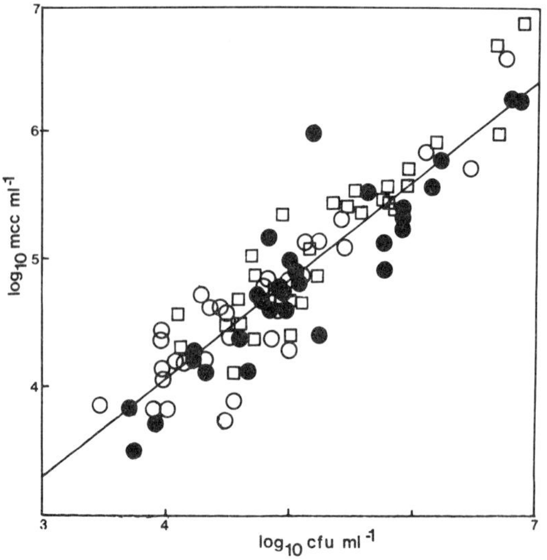

FIG. 1. Correlation between membrane (DEFT) and plate counts for samples of exfarm (○), bulked tanker (●) and silo milks (□). Line represents fitted regression line ($y = 0{\cdot}89 + 0{\cdot}8x$). (Redrawn from reference 14).

Non-counting Methods

The growth of microorganisms to produce colonies on solidified growth media is a powerful amplification procedure which allows the enumeration of microorganisms by eye. The plate count has been described, provocatively,[18] as a 'totally unique datum—nothing in the physical, chemical, biochemical or immunological world corresponds to it'. It is certainly convenient but is inevitably slow and the desire to obtain rapid results has led to interest in a variety of non-counting techniques.

The dairy industry has for a long time used dye reduction tests to assess the bacteriological quality of milk. These tests provide an estimate of the total metabolic activity of the viable microorganisms in a sample. The idea of measuring metabolic activity has spawned some interesting instrumental developments in rapid methods, monitoring direct changes in, for example, the electrical characteristics of a medium (impedance or conductance detection), evolution of gas (radiometry) or evolution of heat (microcalorimetry). Monitoring of electrical changes using impedance or conductance detection is, in the author's opinion, the fastest developing new methodology in food microbiology and will make a considerable impact during the next few years.

Impedimetric detection

Electrical impedance is a measure of the resistance to the flow of alternating electrical current through a conducting material. All microbiological media have an initial impedance and as micro-organisms grow their metabolic activities or products change this impedance. These changes can be monitored continuously by passing a small current through the medium via electrodes and comparing it with either an uninoculated control or an electronic reference. The electrodes are usually stainless steel but must be of a metal that does not produce erratic electrical signals when exposed to culture media but is sensitive to changes in the medium.

The electrical circuit formed by the electrodes in a medium can be represented by the model of a resistor and a capacitor in series. In this model the resistor represents the medium and the capacitor represents the electrode/medium interface. The following relationship is observed:

$$Z^2 = R^2 + \frac{1}{(2fc)^2}$$

where Z = impedance, R = resistance, c = capacitance and f = alternating current frequency.

In practice the actual impedance of the sample is not recorded but rather the ratio of the sample to the reference. This helps to eliminate changes occurring due to physical and chemical effects rather than microbial growth. The detailed physics of impedimetric detection has been described elsewhere[19] but impedance can be considered to consist of a conductance factor (related to resistance) and a capacitance factor. At the present time there are two major manufacturers of impedance monitoring instrumentation—Bactomatic Inc. of Princeton, New Jersey, USA, and Malthus Instruments of Stoke-on-Trent, UK. Both manufacturers produce a range of machines from a relatively unsophisticated 32 (or less) channel instrument that will record continuously the response on a chart recorder, to a 120 plus channel instrument that is fully computer-controlled. Samples are usually incubated in purpose-designed modules but some of this instrumentation allows connections to be made to remote electrode systems. The major

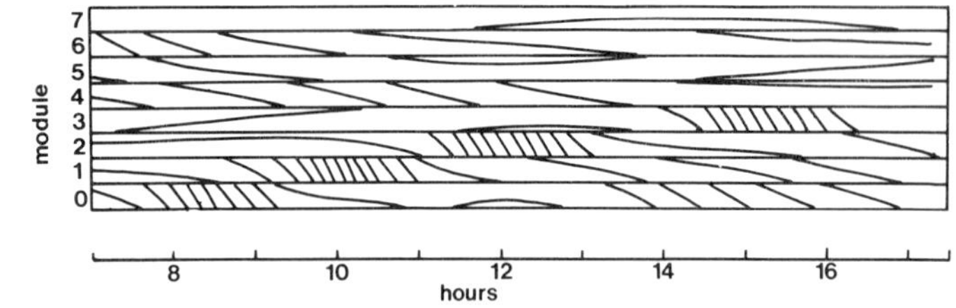

FIG. 2. Typical strip chart output from a Bactometer 32. Modules 0–3 show the growth response of *Salmonella typhimurium* to various levels of disinfectant. Modules 4–7 are controls.

difference between the two manufacturers' products relates to the measurements made. In Bactomatic equipment both the capacitance and conductance factors are measured, but Malthus instruments only measure conductance. The relative merits of these different approaches have yet to be determined fully.

Typical output from a Bactometer 32 and a computerised Bactometer 120 are shown in Figs 2 and 3, respectively.

The technique of impedimetric detection is not new. Some claim it was first reported in 1899,[20] but the subject began to develop when commercial instrumentation appeared during the 1970s. Although it

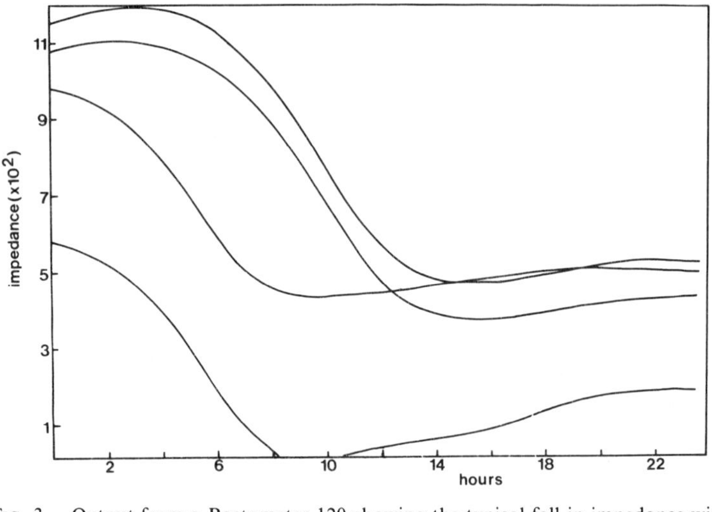

FIG. 3. Output from a Bactometer 120 showing the typical fall in impedance with time associated with the growth of yeasts—in this case four dilutions of *Saccharomyces cerevisiae*.

was first tried in clinical laboratories, it was not long before reports were appearing on the estimation of microorganisms in foods. A typical application was described by Hardy *et al.*[21] who investigated the use of impedance for the detection of excessive microbial contamination of frozen vegetables, i.e. $>10^5$ organisms/g. Fifty-gram samples of the vegetables were puréed with a growth medium, with sterile medium used as a reference. When impedance results were compared with traditional pour plate results for 257 samples of various vegetables, a 92% agreement was obtained. Crucially, the pour plates results were available in 72 h but the impedance results were complete in 6 h.

Impedance has been applied to the assessment of the microbiological quality of milk[22,23] meat,[24–27] and to beer and brewing ingredients.[28,29] In addition it has been used within dairy science to follow acid production in yoghurt cultures and to monitor the activity of starter cultures or detect the effect of bacteriophage. It has also been shown to be capable of estimating mould levels in foods and assaying vitamins.[6] However, the published applications of impedance do not yet reflect the level of activity within food microbiology and the next few years will see an explosion of applications for impedance both for estimating total populations and for enumerating specific groups of organisms.

The overriding advantage of impedance that has attracted the interest of food microbiologists is the speed of analysis. A standard plate count technique can be converted directly to an impedance method with, typically, a 75% reduction in time. Of course if impedance results are to be used as decision criteria then a considerable amount of work will need to be undertaken to produce a standard response curve for each sample type for various levels of inocula. Once this has been accomplished, detection times, i.e. the time taken to observe an accelerating impedance change, can be related directly to the metabolic activity of the microbial population in the sample and usually to the number of organisms present. The sensitivity of current instrumentation is such that an accelerating impedance change can only be detected when the population of growing organisms exceeds 10^5/ml (although this depends on the type of organism and the composition of the medium). Prospects for a second generation of more sensitive instrumentation must be good.

Once impedance-based decision criteria have been established, the computerised instruments can be programmed in a manner suitable for operation within a factory laboratory, so that only those tests where the microbiological limits are exceeded are brought to the attention of the operator. Thus, a non-microbiologist can, with minimal training, interpret the results of microbiological examinations, which may be important for shift working or in small food manufacturing operations where personnel perform a multiple function. One final advantage is that because impedance systems monitor continuously, tests with a specified incubation period can be left to run unattended, e.g. over a weekend.

One area of concern with respect to impedance techniques is our current lack of fundamental understanding about what happens at the electrode/medium interface and which aspects of microbial metabolism produce impedance responses. At the moment microbiologists developing impedance methods are doing so empirically, largely through the direct conversion of conventional methods. It seems obvious that an understanding of the origins of impedance changes at a biochemical level would allow media which will enhance and accelerate impedance changes to be 'engineered' rather than discovered by chance.

Radiometric detection

Radiometric detection is based upon the measurement of $^{14}CO_2$ produced by the microbial metabolism of ^{14}C substrates incorporated into a test medium. The time taken to detection is inversely related to the initial number of organisms in the sample. The method is available commercially as the 'Bactec' (Johnson Laboratories, Maryland, USA) in which headspace gases above the inoculated medium are tested at intervals. The 'Bactec' does not monitor $^{14}CO_2$ evolution continuously, the culture bottles have to be placed in the instrument, but sample handling speeds of 60/h are possible.

The technique has been applied to the estimation of pathogenic organisms[30] and to the enumeration of organisms in foods.[31,32] The detection of excessive levels of yeasts, *Leuconostoc* and *Lactobacillus* in frozen orange juice[32] showed that of 600 samples studied, 44 positives ($>10^4$ organisms/ml) were detected in 12 h and 41 were positive in 8 h. Radiometry has been applied to the problem of detection of *Salmonella* in a novel way[33] using the production of $^{14}CO_2$ from radioactive dulcitol. It was observed that gas production was suppressed by *Salmonella* polyvalent 'H' antiserum and the ratio of gas produced in the absence of antiserum to that produced in its presence was used as the decision criterion.

Radiometric techniques are used widely in clinical microbiology but have not become accepted in the food field. The reasons for this are not clear although there seems to be a general reluctance to use radioactive materials in food quality control laboratories.

Microcalorimetry

The principle of microcalorimetry is to record the heat production as a function of time during microbial growth and metabolism. The power–time curve produced can be characteristic of organisms provided the curves are recorded under strictly controlled conditions.[34] The technique has not been applied extensively but a recent report on the characterisation of commercial yeast strains[35] suggests it may have a wider usage in the food industry, e.g. for the examination of starter cultures.

Very Rapid Methods

Very rapid methods is the term used by Wood and Gibbs[6] to describe methods which measure a structural or metabolic component of the microbial cell. An example is the 'Limulus' assay based upon the observation that minute amounts of endotoxin from the outer membrane of Gram-negative bacteria will coagulate a lysate of amoebocytes from the horseshoe crab (*Limulus polyphemus*). This principle has been used to assay microbial populations.[36,37] For example, Jay[38] used the test for the examination of the microbiological quality of refrigerated ground beef. Endotoxins were extracted by shaking with water and the extracts were assayed by adding an aliquot of Limulus reagent, incubating at 37 °C for 1 h and observing for gelation. Jay suggested that a 0·1 ml inoculum from a 10^3 dilution of good quality ground beef should produce a negative lysate test.

Other methods to estimate rapidly microbial populations are based on the detection of light emitted during the reaction of microbial cell materials with added reagents. Chemiluminescence uses the catalytic effect of porphyrins (haematin) on the chemiluminescent reaction of luminol (5-amino-2,3-dihydro-1,4-aminophthalate) in the presence of hydrogen peroxide. This technique has not, so far, found any great use in food microbiology and its reproducibility has been questioned.[39]

Bioluminescence is based upon the reaction of adenosine

triphosphate (ATP) from microbial cells with the luciferin–luciferase enzyme system from firefly tails. The overall reaction can be summarised as:[40]

$$E + LH_2 + Mg.ATP \longrightarrow E.LH_2 - AMP + pp \qquad (1)$$

$$E.LH_2 - AMP + O_2 \longrightarrow \text{oxyluciferin} + CO_2 + AMP + \text{LIGHT} \qquad (2)$$

where E is luciferase, LH_2 is luciferin, pp is pyrophosphate and AMP is adenosine monophosphate.

Technical aspects of this assay have been reviewed by Thore.[41] The use of the reaction for the rapid estimation of microbial populations was first reported in 1967[42] and its use for foods was suggested in 1970.[43] Sharpe *et al.*[43] reported good results for pure cultures with a value for ATP detected of 10^{-15} g/organism for vegetative cells. Attempts to estimate microbial populations in a range of foods were unsuccessful due to high levels of non-microbial ATP. In order to apply bioluminescence to food microbiology, methods have to be devised to eliminate the interference caused by non-microbial ATP. This can be achieved in two ways:

1. By selective destruction of the non-microbial ATP, or
2. By separation of the microorganisms from the food matrix.

The first approach has been applied to the estimation of yeasts in orange juice[44] by the use of a nucleotide releasing agent, which attacks only the plant cells, followed by an ATPase to destroy the non-microbial ATP that is released. The microbial ATP is then released using a stronger nucleotide releasing agent, and can be assayed.

The second approach has been used successfully for the estimation of microorganisms in raw meats.[6] The procedure developed consists of five stages:

1. Homogenisation (10 g meat in 90 ml buffer).
2. Centrifugation (2000 *g*, 10 s)—removes coarse food particles.
3. Extraction (10 ml of supernatant from 2 is mixed with a buffered cation exchange resin to remove protein).
4. Filtration (5 ml of supernatant from 3 is filtered through a 0·22 μm filter).
5. Assay of microbial ATP on the filter.

Using this procedure the authors were able to show a linear relationship between $\log_{10}$ATP and $\log_{10}$ colony counts with a correlation coefficient of 0·93.

The sensitivity of the ATP method is governed by the detection limit of the photometer used—and there are several commercially available systems. It has been suggested that as few as 200 cells may be detectable but this depends on a variety of factors including the removal of non-microbial ATP, the concentration of microbial cells and the delivery of all of the extracted ATP into the assay vial. Adenosine triphosphate bioluminescence methods have not yet found widespread usage in the food industry but the method is attractive because it has the potential to give instantaneous results and is likely to grow in importance as novel extraction and separation methods become available for different foods.

Extraction Techniques

It can be seen from the description of ATP bioluminescence that techniques to separate microorganisms from foods can form a crucial part of a novel methodology. In general food microbiology lacks novel rapid methods to effect the separation and collection of microorganisms from solid materials. Since the presence of food particles does not interfere with traditional plate count techniques there has been little motivation to develop new approaches. However, novel detection methods may require 'cleaner' samples and the available obvious techniques are not directly applicable to food homogenates. With filtration, however, there is scope for innovation as has already been described for DEFT.

Membrane filtration has been used in food microbiology for a long time but has only been effective for relatively clean suspensions. Also a membrane filter has a limited counting range compared to a pour plate. In 1974 Sharpe and Michaud[45] introduced the concept of the hydrophobic grid membrane filter (HGMF). The HGMF is a membrane base upon which a hydrophobic grid is applied to divide the membrane into individual growth compartments. The net effect is to increase significantly the reliable counting range of a membrane filter and the HGMF count can be determined by an MPN calculation.[46] The concept has now been commercialised in the Iso-Grid HGMF system (QA Laboratories, Toronto, Canada) which uses a 0·45 μm membrane with 1600 growth compartments contained within a filter housing. Above the membrane, in the same housing, is a prefilter—usually a 5 μm or 10 μm stainless steel mesh. Prefiltration using this stainless steel grid was shown to have no effect on the recovery of microorganisms from 87 food samples.[47] One hundred and nine foods were tested through the complete system and 68 could be filtered without additional treatment. Of the remaining 41, 39 were rendered filterable with an appropriate enzyme or surfactant treatment.

Iso-Grid based methods have now been developed for indicator organisms,[48] *Salmonella*,[49] aerobic plate counts and yeasts and moulds.[50]

Although the use of HGMF does not produce a rapid method *per se*, it does offer advantages in terms of reductions in material costs and savings in labour. It should also be viewed as a positive step towards the development of an improved separation methodology. Currently the HGMF system is used in conjunction with conventional cultural methods although counting and subsequent subculturing has been automated. It would seem, however, a logical step to attempt to combine the Iso-Grid approach with rapid methods such as ATP bioluminescence.

The use of ion-exchange chromatography for the separation of microorganisms from foods has already been demonstrated as part of the ATP bioluminescence estimation of the microbial population of raw meats. It has been suggested that ion-exchange chromatography or even hydrophobic interaction chromatography could have a wide usage for the separation of microorganisms from food systems[6] but the difficulties must not be underestimated. A population of 10^6 organisms/g represents only 1 ppm of the total mass of a food sample and to expect to find unique conditions for the extraction of microorganisms by ion-exchange is a tall order.

Identification

The novel methods described so far, are all directed at detection or enumeration of microorganisms in foods. A certain amount of identification is undertaken in food laboratories, usually to confirm the isolation of pathogenic microorganisms. In recent years several different commercial systems have been introduced for rapid identification, principally of Gram-negative fermentative organisms but also for some other groups. Kits such as the API 20E (API Laboratory Products Ltd, Basingstoke, UK), Enterotube (Roche Diagnostics Ltd, Nutley, New Jersey, USA) and Micro-ID (General

Diagnostics Ltd, Morris Plains, New Jersey, USA) are basically miniaturised collections of standard laboratory tests usually backed by a substantial computerised data base. In these kits the concentration of the inoculum and the test reagent(s) produces a real reduction in test time, usually to <24 h and in some cases to as little as 4 h. Although these kits were developed for identification in clinical laboratories they have found wide application in food laboratories, although isolates from foods can have different characteristics from those from clinical sources and mis-identifications can occur.[51]

Identification in a food laboratory is, rightly or wrongly, a lesser activity compared to the enumeration of microorganisms, although it can be a critical step in the confirmation of pathogens, as illustrated by its role in the detection of Salmonellae.

THE *SALMONELLA* PROBLEM

The detection of *Salmonella* organisms in foods is a lengthy but vital procedure carried out in many quality control laboratories. The development of an accepted reliable rapid test, completed in hours rather than days, remains one of the most intractable problems in food microbiology and serves to illustrate some of the areas in which new thinking in methodology may be required and applied.

A conventional scheme for the confirmation of *Salmonella* is shown in Table 1. Because the test has to be sufficiently sensitive to detect a single viable *Salmonella* cell it contains lengthy periods of pre-enrichment (to allow the recovery of sublethally stressed cells) and selective enrichment to increase the number of *Salmonella* cells present. The scale of the detection problem has been brought into focus by Sharpe[18] who calculated that the mass of a single *Salmonella* cell was 2×10^{-14} g and this had to be detected in 25 g or 250 g of material—a signal to noise ratio way beyond the capabilities of even the most sensitive analytical instrumentation! The latter part of the procedure is conventional microbiology using culturing techniques to achieve an isolation and subsequent identification. Final confirmation is usually carried out by serology.

The complete procedure takes 5 days although presumptive data can be available in 3 days. Many workers have tinkered with the methodology in this scheme trying, for example, different enrichment media, etc. At best this type of development will only shorten the test

TABLE 1
METHOD FOR THE CONFIRMATION OF THE PRESENCE OF *Salmonella* ORGANISMS IN FOOD

1. *Pre-enrichment*
   25 g sample added to 250 ml of brilliant green milk broth or lactose broth or buffered peptone water incubated at 37 °C, 6–18 h.
2. *Selective enrichment*
   10 cm^3 pre-enrichment broth diluted in 90 ml mannitol selenite and/or tetrathionate broth incubated at 37 °C, 18–24 h.
3. *Selection and presumptive identification*
   Enrichment broth streaked out on to two selective agars, e.g. XLD agar, bismuth sulphite agar. Incubated at 37 °C, 24 h; colony appearance observed.
4. *Confirmation*
   Microscopy.
   Typical colonies inoculated into confirmatory media or rapid identification mini-kit. Incubated at 37 °C, 4–24 h.
   Serology.

by a few hours. If a dramatic reduction in *Salmonella* testing time is to be achieved it seems that it will result from the application of serology during or after the enrichment phases. Three approaches are worthy of consideration at the present time:

1. Fluorescent antibody.
2. Enrichment serology.
3. Enzyme immunoassay.

With each of these procedures samples are pre-enriched and selectively enriched and are then subcultured in a non-selective medium (elective culturing).

The fluorescent antibody method for *Salmonella* was first reported in 1957.[52] Subsequent improvements to the method enabled a collaborative trial to be conducted in 1975[53] with official recognition coming in 1976. The procedure requires 24 h pre-enrichment, 24 h selective enrichment and 4 h post-enrichment. Smears are made from the post-enrichment broth and are tested, results being available on the afternoon of day 3. The major drawbacks of the fluorescent antibody test are the occurrence of false-positive reactions (at an overall rate of 1–9 %) and the operator fatigue inherent in the screening of large numbers of samples by microscopy. At the present time the value of the procedure is as a presumptive screening test and all positive results need to be confirmed by conventional procedures.[54]

Enrichment serology was first described by Sperber and Deibel.[55] The method involves pre-enrichment (18 h), selective enrichment (24 h), elective enrichment (6–8 h) followed by serological testing (2 h). Salmonellae are detected in the elective broth culture by a modification of the Spicer–Edwards H agglutination technique. Several publications have reported excellent agreement between the enrichment serology procedure and traditional methods for the analysis of a variety of food products,[56–58] although the period of elective enrichment seems critical.[59] Despite favourable published reports on the sensitivity of the technique it has not received universal acceptance and its sensitivity has not been confirmed in some laboratories.

An enzyme linked immunosorbent assay (ELISA) for *Salmonella* was first developed by Krysinski and Heimsch[60] and was improved by Minnich.[2] The protocol of ELISA techniques has been described elsewhere.[61] In Minnich's procedure a broth culture is introduced into a cuvette or microtitre well. To this is added an equal volume of diluted Spicer–Edwards purified IgG preparation. After 1 h at room temperature the cells are washed and then reacted with diluted goat antirabbit alkaline phosphatase conjugate. After 1 h the cells are again washed then treated with alkaline phosphatase substrate. The production of a yellow colour indicates a positive result. Minnich applied the method originally to post-enrichment cultures (i.e. after selective enrichment) and his experiments indicated that the assay could detect 10^5–10^6 Salmonellae/ml.

Minnich's comparative analysis of 98 food samples is summarised in Table 2. The ELISA method detected 20 positive samples while only 13 of these were detected by standard methodology. These 13 positives were also detected by applying ELISA and enrichment serology to post-enrichment cultures. The results indicate that Minnich's ELISA test has a rate for false-positives of 7 %, which he attributed to the failure of certain serotypes to replicate during selective enrichment to sufficiently high numbers to be detected. The possibility of applying ELISA to pre-enrichment cultures is extremely attractive because confirmed results could be obtained during the afternoon of day 2. Also the ELISA methodology lends itself readily to automation.

In the future the serological approach to the detection of

TABLE 2

COMPARATIVE ANALYSIS RESULTS OF TESTING 98 FOOD SAMPLES FOR *Salmonellae* BY VARIOUS ANALYTICAL METHODS (ADAPTED FROM REFERENCE 2)

Result	*ELISA*		*Fluorescent antibody*	*Enrichment serology*	*Standard method*
	Pre[a]	*Post*[b]			
Positive	20	13	23	13	13
Negative	78	85	75	85	85
False-positive	7	0	10	0	0
False-negative	0	0	0	0	0

[a] Positive identified from pre-enrichment.
[b] Positive identified from post-enrichment.

Salmonella is certain to become more prevalent. Currently problems do exist with cross-reactions with other Gram-negative bacteria but current research into monoclonal antibodies[62] will yield antisera with low cross-reactivity. The extraction of low numbers of *Salmonella* from a complex food matrix remains a considerable obstacle to the development of a test that will be complete in a working day. One solution would be to use the specificity of serology in the extraction process but how this can be achieved in practice remains to be determined.

DISCUSSION

The Need for Good Microbiology

The review of methods and the discussion of the *Salmonella* problem illustrate the breadth of activity in the field of rapid microbial methods at the present time. Nevertheless it is important to remember that no test, however rapid, is of value if its microbiological aims are suspect. As an example consider the fermentation test which is used by the beverage industry to assess the microbiological quality of preserved fruit materials (bases and concentrates). An outline of this test is given in Table 3. At first sight it appears slow (14 days) and is interpreted rather subjectively. Since it consists simply of a dilution with sucrose it would appear to be an ideal candidate for acceleration by the use of impedance or even ATP bioluminescence. However, the whole basis of the test is suspect

TABLE 3

OUTLINE OF THE FERMENTATION TEST FOR BENZOATE AND SULPHUR DIOXIDE PRESERVED FRUIT MATERIALS

1. Dilute 10 cm^3 sample with 94 ml 9·6% w/v sucrose.
2. Incubate at 25 °C for up to 14 days.
3. Observe for fermentation, e.g. by:

   a. A yeast smell.
   b. Bubbles of gas.
   c. Clearing.
   d. Deposit of yeast cells.
   e. A yeast taste.
   f. Presence of yeast cells (microscopy).
   g. Reduction of specific gravity.

because the addition of extra sucrose is likely to encourage the growth of preservative resistant yeast which would normally have been inhibited. Consequently accelerating this test as it stands would not improve the quality control of fruit materials and what is needed is a more detailed understanding of the microbiology of preservative resistance, leading to a new test with better defined and obtainable objectives. Making a poor test work faster is no help to the efficiency of food microbiology.

Future Prospects

In the next five years there is no doubt that faster microbiological methods will be available for adoption by the food industry. It seems likely that the techniques of impedance, DEFT and ATP bioluminescence will lead this revolution and, depending on the nature of the work, should replace most plate count procedures. It is unlikely that these techniques have a role to play in the confirmation of pathogens or the detection of toxins, but new specific serological procedures will become available as a direct result of the interest in and development of monoclonal antibodies. There is currently no universal panacea on the horizon to revolutionise the extraction of microorganisms from foods. This subject needs desperately some innovation and there is a danger that the momentum gained on novel detection and enumeration methods will be lost because extraction methodology fails to keep apace.

On a longer timescale it can be envisaged that more sensitive instrumentation, tuned in to markers of metabolic activity, will become available. This could take the form of, for example, improved impedance equipment or novel biosensors based on enzymes.[63] However, it would be surprising if food microbiologists did not adopt some of the techniques of the analytical chemistry laboratory—notably gas chromatography, mass spectrometry and high pressure liquid chromatography. Gas chromatography has already been used to a small extent in food microbiology, e.g. for the detection of *Clostridium botulinum* in canned mushrooms by analysis of short-chain fatty acids[64] and for the identification of sporeformers and non-sporeformers as the probable cause of swollen cans of low-acid foods.[65]

The use of analytical instrumentation is not common practice in food microbiology laboratories which is hard to understand considering the dependence of food chemistry quality control on these techniques. In the future some cross-fertilisation is bound to occur, stimulated by a fall in the capital cost of gas chromatography–mass spectrometry systems in particular. Obviously a great deal of work has to be done to identify chemically those substances which are removed or produced by growing microorganisms or relate directly to the number of viable microorganisms present. It is clearly not going to be easy but at this stage it has not even been attempted. Perhaps the time has come to recognise the inadequacies of the 'unique datum of the plate count'[18] and to replace current methods in food microbiology by a more chemical approach in which microorganisms are treated as packets of organic polymers amenable to analysis, rather than mysterious agents of spoilage and disease.

REFERENCES

1. Codex Alimentarius Commission (1980). *General Principles for the Establishment and Application of Microbiological Criteria for Foods*, Report of 17th Session of Committee on Food Hygiene, FOA, Rome.
2. Silliker, J. H. (1982). *Food Technol.*, **36**, 65–70.
3. Heden, C. G. and Illeni, W. J. (1975). *New Approaches to the Identification of Micro-organisms*, John Wiley & Sons, New York.
4. Johnston, H. H. and Newsom, S. W. B. (1976). *Second International Symposium on Rapid Methods and Automation in Microbiology*, Learned Information (Europe Ltd), Oxford.
5. Tilton, R. C. (1982). *Rapid Methods and Automation in Microbiology*, American Society for Microbiology, Washington, DC.

6. Wood, J. M. and Gibbs, P. A. (1982). In: *Developments in Food Microbiology—1*, Ed. Davies, R., Applied Science Publishers, London, 183–214.
7. Sharpe, A. N. and Kilsby, D. C. (1971). *J. Appl. Bact.*, **34**, 435–40.
8. Kitchell, A. G., Ingram, G. C. and Hudson, W. R. (1973). In: *Sampling—Microbial Monitoring of Environments*, SAB Tech., Series 7, 43–61.
9. Gilchrist, J. E., Campbell, J. E., Donelly, C. B., Peeler, J. T. and Delaney, J. N. (1973). *Appl. Microbiol.*, **25**, 244–52.
10. Donelly, C. B., Gilchrist, J. E., Peeler, J. T. and Campbell, J. E. (1976). *Appl. Environ. Microbiol.*, **32**, 21–7.
11. Jarvis, B., Lach, V. H. and Wood, J. M. (1977). *J. Appl. Bact.*, **43**, 149–58.
12. AOAC Method 56 1981 (1981). *Spiral Plate Method for Bacterial Count of Foods or Cosmetics, 46. 110-46. 116*, *J. Assoc. Off. Anal. Chem.*, **64**, 528.
13. Pettipher, G. L., Mansell, R., McKinnon, C. H. and Cousins, C. M. (1980). *Appl. Environ. Microbiol.*, **39**, 423–9.
14. Pettipher, G. L. and Rodrigues, U. M. (1981). *J. Appl. Bact.*, **50**, 157–66.
15. Pettipher, G. L. and Rodrigues, U. M. (1982). *J. Appl. Bact.*, **53**, 323–9.
16. Pettipher, G. L., Fulford, R. J. and Mabbitt, L. A. (1983). *J. Appl. Bact.*, **54**, 177–82.
17. Pettipher, G. L. and Rodrigues, U. M. (1982). *Appl. Environ. Microbiol.*, **44**, 809–13.
18. Sharpe, A. N. (1980). *Food Microbiology. A Framework for the Future*, Charles C. Thomas, Springfield.
19. Richards, J. C. S., Jason, A. C., Hobbs, G., Gibson, D. M. and Christie, R. H. (1978). *J. Phys. E: Sci. Instrum.*, **11**, 560–8.
20. Stewart, G. N. (1899). *J. Exp. Med.*, **4**, 235.
21. Hardy, D., Kraeger, S., Dufour, S. W. and Cady, P. (1977). *Appl. Environ. Microbiol.*, **34**, 14–17.
22. Cady, P., Hardy, D., Martins, S. B. and Selby, M. J. (1978). *J. Food Prot.*, **41**, 277–93.
23. O'Connor, F. (1979). *J. Food Sci. Technol.*, **3**, 93–100.
24. Martins, S. B. and Selby, M. J. (1980). *Appl. Environ. Microbiol.*, **39**, 518–24.
25. Wood, J. M., Lach, V. H. and Jarvis, B. (1977). *J. Appl. Bact.*, **43**, xiv.
26. Bell, C. (1980). *Food Flavourings, Ingredients, Packaging and Processing*, **2**, 32.
27. Firstenberg-Eden, R. (1983). *Food Technol.*, **37**, 64–70.
28. Lawless, P., Shaw, J. and Kraeger, S. J. (1974). *Proc. Am. Soc. Microbiol. Ann. Mtg*, **74**, 8.
29. Evans, H. A. V. (1982). *J. Appl. Bact.*, **53**, 423–6.
30. Previte, J. J. (1972). *Appl. Microbiol.*, **24**, 535–9.
31. Rowley, R. B., Previte, J. J. and Srinivasa, H. P. (1978). *J. Food Sci.*, **43**, 1720–2.

32. Hatcher, W. S., Di Bennedetto, S., Taylor, L. E. and Murdock, D. J. (1977). *J. Food Sci.*, **42**, 636–9.
33. Stewart, B. J., Eyles, M. J. and Murrell, W. G. (1980). *Appl. Environ. Microbiol.*, **40**, 223–30.
34. Perry, B. F., Beezer, A. E. and Miles, R. J. (1979). *J. Appl. Bact.*, **47**, 527–37.
35. Perry, B. F., Beezer, A. E. and Miles, R. J. (1983). *J. Appl. Bact.*, **54**, 183–9.
36. Jorgensen, J. H., Carvajal, H. F., Chips, B. E. and Smith, R. F. (1973). *Appl. Microbiol.*, **26**, 38–42.
37. Coates, D. A. (1977). *J. Appl. Bact.*, **42**, 445–9.
38. Jay, J. M. (1977). *J. Appl. Bact.*, **43**, 99–109.
39. Strange, R. E. (1972). *Adv. Microbiol. Physiol.*, **8**, 105–41.
40. McElroy, W. D. and DeLuca, M. (1978). In: *Bioluminescence in Action*, Ed. Herring, P. J., Academic Press, London.
41. Thore, A. (1979). *Sci. Tools*, **26**, 30–4.
42. Levin, G. V., Chen, C. S. and Davis, E. (1967). *Aerospace Med. Res. Lab.*, **TR**, 67–71.
43. Sharpe, A. N., Woodrow, M. N. and Jackson, A. K. (1970). *J. Appl. Bact.*, **33**, 758–67.
44. Vanstaen, H. (1980). *Lab. Practice* (December), 1281–3.
45. Sharpe, A. N. and Michaud, G. L. (1974). *Appl. Microbiol.*, **30**, 519–24.
46. Sharpe, A. N. (1982). In: *Rapid Methods and Automation in Microbiology*, Ed. Tilton, R. C., American Society for Microbiology, Washington, DC, 53–7.
47. Entis, P., Brodsky, M. H. and Sharpe, A. N. (1982). *J. Food Prot.*, **45**, 8–11.
48. Brodsky, M. H., Entis, P., Sharpe, A. N. and Jarvis, G. A. (1982). *J. Food Prot.*, **45**, 292–6.
49. Entis, P., Brodsky, M. H., Sharpe, A. N. and Jarvis, G. A. (1982). *Appl. Environ. Microbiol.*, **43**, 261–8.
50. Brodsky, M. H., Entis, P., Entis, M. P., Sharpe, A. N. and Jarvis, G. A. (1982). *J. Food Prot.*, **45**, 301–4.
51. Griffiths, M. W. and Phillips, J. D. (1982). *J. Appl. Bact.*, **53**, 343–50.
52. Thomason, B. N., Cherry, W. B. and Moody, M. D. (1957). *J. Bacteriol.*, **74**, 525–32.
53. Anon. (1975). *J. Assoc. Off. Anal. Chem.*, **58**, 417–19.
54. Thomason, B. N. (1981). *J. Food Prot.*, **44**, 381–4.
55. Sperber, W. H. and Diebel, R. H. (1969). *Appl. Microbiol.*, **17**, 533–9.
56. Fantasia, L. D., Sperber, W. H. and Deibel, R. H. (1969). *Appl. Microbiol.*, **17**, 540–1.
57. Mohr, H. R., Trenk, H. L. and Yeterian, M. (1974). *Appl. Microbiol.*, **27**, 324–8.
58. Surdy, T. E. and Haas, S. O. (1981). *Appl. Environ. Microbiol.*, **42**, 704–7.
59. Boothroyd, M. and Baird-Parker, A. C. (1973). *J. Appl. Bact.*, **36**, 165–72.

60. Krysinski, E. B. and Heimsch, R. C. (1977). *Appl. Environ. Microbiol.*, **33**, 947–54.
61. Voller, A., Bidwell, D. E. and Bartlett, A. (1980). In: *Manual of Clinical Immunology*, 2nd edition, Ed. Rose, N. R. and Friedman, H., American Society for Microbiology, Washington, DC, 359–71.
62. Anon. (1983). *Biotechnol. News*, **3**, 5–6.
63. Mosback, K., Mandenius, C. F. and Danielsson, B. (1983). In: *Biotech '83*, Online Publications, Northwood, 665–78.
64. Mayhew, J. W. and Gorbach, S. L. (1975). *Appl. Microbiol.*, **29**, 297–99.
65. Schafer, M. L., Peeler, J. T., Bradshaw, J. G., Hamilton, C. H. and Carver, R. B. (1982). *J. Food Sci.*, **47**, 2033–7.

11

Sensory Quality Control

R. HARPER*

Formerly Department of Food Science,
University of Reading, UK

ABSTRACT

Sensory quality control may be discussed from many different points of view. Quality control has itself undergone a number of changes during the last 20 years, with greater emphasis now on quality information and quality assurance. This includes a proper specification of what is required in a particular product. There is much scope for increasing use of the specification of quality in sensory terms. Special attention is given to general principles, with occasional examples. Other contributors will no doubt include reference to sensory quality in dealing with particular foods.

The relevant sensory method(s) depends upon many factors, including whether raw materials, natural (unprocessed) foods, materials in processing, or finished products are concerned. The term 'Quality' itself has a number of different meanings. Attention is concentrated on sensory quality and its importance. However, it is important to separate the sensory-descriptive aspects—including those implicit in establishing differences or uniformity—from likes or dislikes and preferences.

A selection from the literature on sensory quality and its specification and control is reviewed, including nearly 70 references. The selection, which still omits many which are both relevant and important, takes some account of international contributions. The need for special techniques did not exist before the rise of modern transport systems and a food industry, which has become more and more science based. However, with a few conspicuous exceptions, the

* Present address: 29 Harrow Court, Bath Road, Reading RG1 6JF, UK.

procedures used and the problems involved as a routine in the food industry are not well documented in open publications. A few of the exceptions are noted, but the bulk of the literature concentrates on research, much of it carried out in external institutions, rather than within the food industry itself. Contemporary developments include progressive standardisation of both terminology and methods, and a marked increase in the use of sensory profiles in the product specification. The link with the consumer is also becoming important. The number of symposia, short courses and workshops is increasing. However, steps must be taken to ensure that high professional standards are maintained in the complex tasks involved in sensory quality control.

ASPECTS OF QUALITY

Some Definitions

The word 'Quality' and other terms associated with it mean different things to different people. Dictionary definitions are too numerous to be helpful and include too many alternatives. Among these are (i) degree of excellence, and (ii) the opposite of quantity. Personally, I prefer (iii) fitness for intended purpose, which depends upon the context, including the particular food, or point in the manufacturing or distribution chain, of immediate interest. To these three possibilities, which might be elaborated further, the word 'Qualities' in the plural very conveniently introduces the idea of 'Sensory Qualities'. It is with these and their particular functions that the present analysis is concerned.

Quality control is closely associated with inspection techniques and with sequential statistical procedures, particularly associated with physical or chemical measurements, but also including attributes (e.g. specific defects, which are present or absent). The use of quality control charts dates back to the middle 1930s,[1] but the earliest example incorporating sensory data in my own collection of reprints deals with selecting the most consistent members of a taste panel scoring dried egg, subject to different treatments.[2] Gradually, the idea of quality control, with its implication of the wasteful rejection of what does not come within the specified tolerance limits, has given place to that of quality assurance, which implies a tighter control of the processes of production, distribution and storage.

Perhaps the distinction is more one of degree rather than kind, with current emphasis more on quality specification and quality information.

Sensory Quality

The specification of quality, at any point in the food chain, involves many different topics or subjects not really effectively represented by a simple list, since that might imply that one set of considerations is more important than another. Other contributors may deal with the physical, chemical, microbiological, public health and legal aspects of quality in food. Here, attention is concentrated on the sensory aspects.

Any one, or any combination, of the senses may be involved and it is convenient to separate these into the order in which they are normally affected. Without taking account of the influence of one of the senses on what is perceived by another, the order is, roughly:

Sight (Colour and Appearance)
Smell (Aroma)
Taste (Taste + Smell = Flavour)
Touch (Mouthfeel) and Muscle Sensitivity (Texture)
Hearing (Sounds)

Each of the senses involves its own group of sensory qualities. Just a few terms will cover the range of taste sensations. In contrast, hundreds of terms may be relevant to describe odours or flavours. Each food will involve its own selection of terms, many specific to that food. The total number required to describe efficiently a particular food or drink will also vary widely, in some instances between 40 and 50 terms (now often referred to as 'descriptors') may be necessary, particularly in research investigations.

SENSORY METHODS

The term 'Sensory Methods' is reserved here for a number of specialised techniques for dealing with different aspects of what we perceive, including its expression in numerical form, where relevant. The current state of development of these methods has been outlined elsewhere.[3] For the sake of brevity only two aspects of these methods are considered here, namely: (i) Difference tests, and (ii) Descriptive profiles. They are taken in this order since this corresponds with the order in which these two methods have been developed, systematically.

Difference tests are concerned with the evaluation or detection of small differences in terms of probabilities. The detection or recognition of very weak stimuli, the measurement of which constitutes the conventional thresholds and their determination will not be considered here, although such measures are of critical importance in relation to taints and off-flavours. However, these measures are also essentially probabilistic and could be fitted into the framework of the difference tests assuming a particular stimulus-concentration is being evaluated against a neutral background.

In contrast, descriptive profiles usually involve assigning numerical values to a range of sensory qualities, relevant to the particular sample of food concerned, at substantial levels of perception. These two groups of methods are now considered in further detail.

Difference Tests

Three examples of the difference tests are considered, namely: the Triangular test, the Duo-trio test and the Paired Comparisons test. Each of these tests requires a particular set of conditions, and the choice depends upon these conditions, including the question asked.

The Triangular Test deals with the situation of an unknown type of difference. It involves the presentation of three samples in a specified order, two of which are the same, (e.g. XXY and the other 5 arrangements). The task is to pick out the odd sample and the existence of a difference is evaluated in terms of a significantly greater number of 'correct' judgements than would be expected by chance (0·33). The method is particularly appropriate as one means of investigating various drinks, since the two identical samples XX can be taken from the same bulk. The method was popularised in the late 1940s when its use at the Carlsberg Breweries was reported,[4,5] although its use in Sweden as early as 1923 has been noted.[6]

The Duo-trio test is also particularly relevant for drinks. In this case, the 'duo' consists of two identical samples of an accepted standard (S), the third sample (X) now being evaluated in relation to (S). Orders of presentation (S)SX and (S)XS are balanced and the task of the assessor is to indicate which of the second two (SX or XS) is the same as the standard (S). In this case, the chance of making a correct judgement by guessing is 0·5, and the results obtained are evaluated by referring to published tables of significance. This test was the first to be standardised by Committee E-18 (sensory evaluation) of the American Society for Testing and Materials[7] following its extensive use in maintaining product uniformity at Schenley's Distilleries.[8] More recently the use of two initial presentations of the standard in the arrangements (SS)SX or (SS)XS has been recommended.[9]

Finally, a brief reference is made to the Paired Comparisons test. This has a very long history, going back to the pioneers of psychophysical investigations in the second half of the 19th century. In this method, the basis of judgement between the two samples (AB or BA) has to be made explicit in advance. This could be either in terms of some specific sensory quality (e.g. sweetness) or in terms of preference. As in the previous tests, the results are evaluated statistically using prepared tables. Following modifications in the experimental design the use of the method can be extended to include the intercomparison of a number of samples, and the type of judgement might consist of the evaluation and the degree of similarity or difference between the members of each pair. In this instance more sophisticated methods of analysis are appropriate including the use of multidimensional scaling for which computer programs are available. Simple paired comparisons could be used in many situations, including market research—in which case interest centres primarily on preferences. The more complex system involving many pairs is most likely to find use in research projects.

Descriptive Profiles

Descriptive profiles represent a standardised development of the ordinary processes of spontaneous description. Two different aspects are involved, the development of a vocabulary covering the relevant sensory qualities and the choice of a method of indicating the degree or extent to which any particular food or drink has these sensory qualities. Strictly speaking, this represents a form of biological measurement, using man as an instrument. It is the end-product of the interaction between a physical or a chemical stimulus and the human sense organs, as expressed in terms of a mark on a scale or the equivalent statement by the assessors. The relevant list of terms will be product-specific.

In principle this approach could be used in connection with any one of the senses, but the discussion will be confined to odour and taste (=flavour) and after-taste, and to mouthfeel and texture. The reason for this is that similar formal developments have not taken place to the same extent with sight and hearing, although the importance of these two senses in sensory quality is fully appreciated. In any case, sight and hearing are very much more cultivated in education and experience than taste, smell and touch and it could be argued that normal, everyday language is likely to be adequate to describe colour and appearance, and probably the sounds made by foods when they are eaten. In contrast, untrained people have very limited skill when it comes to describing tastes, smells and tactile or muscle sensations. (Muscle sensations have their own technical term, which dates back to the last century, *kinaesthesis*.) Without training, most people will find it difficult to bring to mind more than a few descriptive terms and are most likely to fall back on terms like 'delicious', 'nice' or 'nasty'. These are expressions of likes and dislikes, or preferences and contribute very little to any form of description or specification in standardised terms. It is for this reason that the practice has arisen of preparing check-lists for different foods, each term being associated with a simple scale to indicate how strong each of the listed characteristics is found to be. Different experts may use slightly different scales, such as 0–5 or 0–10, with corresponding verbal equivalents for the points on the scales, while others use a line upon which the appropriate position of each sample can be marked. Each quality or 'descriptor' is evaluated separately. The total number of terms used depends upon the particular food being evaluated, the list having been built up carefully both from the literature and from preliminary discussions, often of the 'round table' form.

Some products may be covered adequately by a small number of terms, others may require between 40 and 50 terms. Once the list has been established in principle, meaning and understanding can be helped by the development of reference standards, made up to represent as far as possible some of the terms. This is a matter for experimental demonstration. Many chemical substances, for example, require a number of 'descriptors' to characterise them. In addition, qualitative and quantitative differences between individuals in their sensitivities to a substantial number of such stimuli means that perfect agreement between the individual members of the panel is unlikely. This is one of the criticisms made against the pioneer version of the Flavour Profile[10] of the 1950s, in which each of the agreed characteristics is assigned a single number to indicate its intensity, on a consensus basis. Of course, it could be argued that agreement in meaning has been achieved by previous training, but alternatively any deviant individuals would gradually be excluded from the panel.

Other developments should be noted. These include the extension of the method to cover texture, in the early 1960s.[11,12] The systematic development of comprehensive lists of terms, coupled with the independent evaluation of the product by each assessor, dates back to the investigation of odour characterisation and odour classification (1964–1967) which eventually yielded a list of some 44 terms capable of covering in a representative manner the complete range of odour qualities.[13] An increasing number of practical applications followed, with minor modifications, including the development of specific vocabularies for particular foods or drinks. In rough sequence, examples include: the characterisation of bilberry juice,[14] canned meat products,[15] beers,[16,17] soft drinks,[18] wines[19] and watercress.[20]

ON CURRENT PRACTICES

This section is concerned mostly with current practices in the UK. It is based upon a survey reported in 1977 by Muller[21] at a symposium on 'Sensory Quality Control: Practical Approaches in Food and Drink Production', jointly organised by the Sensory Panel of the Food Group of the Society of Chemical Industry (SCI) and the Institute of Food Science and Technology (IFST). The survey was conducted mainly among the members of the Sensory Panel (a special interest group within the Food Group of the SCI). To that extent the sample was inevitably biased and included practically all individuals or representatives committed to the importance of systematic methods of sensory analysis. Other aspects of this symposium are discussed in the next section. In the survey 218 questionnaires were sent out, including 10 to directors of the main research institutes. The response rate was 25% in the case of the members of the Sensory Panel of the Food Group and 70% for the individual directors of the research institutes. The results for industry and the research institutes were separated, and no special category was assigned to teaching institutions, from which a few of the replies must have come. Among the more striking conclusions at this time were the following:

1. Most of the sensory testing in industry dealt with finished products (72%), raw materials coming a long way second

(23%) and materials in processing, only 6%. The figures for the research institutes were in the same order.

2. With only minor differences, the emphasis in testing was placed on flavour in the mouth (100%), aroma, using the nose only (90%), and colour (including appearance) (90%). Texture was considered to be less important and was separated under three headings: in the mouth (75%), by appearance (60%) and by hand (28%). Separate analyses in terms of products would alter these average figures (See original for details).
3. Scoring or rating for overall quality was used by 58% and for separate qualities or attributes by 51%. Flavour profiles were prepared by only just over 6%.
4. Of the difference tests, the most frequently used was the Triangular test (28%), with the Paired Comparison test close behind (21%). Only one respondent referred to the use of the Duo-trio test.

It is now almost seven years since this survey was carried out and the time is ripe for the preparation of an up-to-date picture of current practices. Until this is done, Muller's findings represent the best information available about practices in the UK.

HISTORICAL BACKGROUND

At this point, thoughts on the subject of sensory quality control go back to the late 1940s. The date is convenient, but arbitrary. A more detailed account of developments in the UK was presented at an earlier symposium in this series.[22] Here, the net is cast wider and includes some of the principal developments in the USA as well as the UK and a few from other countries. For convenience a list of some of the main developments is given in Table 1.

Limitations of space allow only a selection of the events included to be discussed in further detail, the choice being greatly influenced by personal experience. This began with a series of studies of the skills of cheesemakers and cheesegraders during the immediate post-war years.[23] Although these studies were primarily concerned with manipulative skills (e.g. the role of the hand and the pressure of the thumb in traditional methods of making and grading cheese), several reviews on food grading and related topics were made.[24,25] About this time, a symposium on 'Organoleptic Tests in the Food Industry' provided an opportunity for some of the war-time innovations to be discussed critically from the sensory point of view. The products discussed included dried egg[26] and dried vegetables.[27] Of the latter, Tomkins wrote 'Had tasting tests been allowed to determine the issue, much inedible dried vegetable would never have been produced'.

Some Developments in the USA

Turning for a while to developments in the USA, reference must be made to the establishment of the Food Acceptance Branch of the Quartermaster Food and Container Institute (QMF and CI) for the Armed Forces, in Chicago in 1943. For 20 years this was one of the major organisations concerned with development and use of sensory methods. Numerous reports and publications could be listed from this source. Reference has already been made to the development and promotion of Flavour Profiles by Arthur D. Little, Inc. of Cambridge, Massachusetts. One of the first publications on this subject appeared in 1949 and many others have followed. As early as 1951 a comprehensive review on sensory methods for measuring differences in foods was prepared within the United States Department of Agriculture (USDA).[28] This publication contained over 300 references. About the same time a programme for the analysis of the sensory properties of foods was initiated with the transfer of the Department of Food Technology from the Berkeley Campus to the Davis Campus of the University of California. Within a few years this became internationally well known. In 1959, the Department of Dairying was combined with Food Technology to become the Department of Food Science and Technology. By 1964 nearly 100 papers from this group were noted,[29] and a year later the first textbook on the sensory evaluation of food to appear in the English language was produced by Amerine, Pangborn and Roessler.[30] In the middle 1970s the Sensory Evaluation Division of the Institute of Food Technologists was formed to coordinate the growing interest and activities. At the time of the first news letter, there were over 350 members and by 1982 the number exceeded 1000. A convenient point to end is to note the continuing growth in the literature. On the American scene the last complete volume of the *Journal of Food Science* contained over 60 papers on different aspects of sensory analysis and its applications.

TABLE 1
SELECTED DEVELOPMENTS IN SENSORY ANALYSIS 1940–1983

UK	*Elsewhere (mostly the USA)*
	1943–63. QMF and CI Food Acceptance Branch, Chicago. Numerous studies and reports.
1946–50. Personal studies of skills of cheesemakers and cheesegraders. NIRD.	1945. Earliest paper using control chart with sensory data.
1947. Symposium: Organoleptic Tests in the Food Industry. SCI.	
	1949. First identified report on Flavour Profiles. Author D. Little Inc.
	1951. USDA Review: Sensory Methods for Measuring Differences in Foods.
1953. Symposium: Flavour assessment. SCI and others.	
1955. Final end of food rationing in the UK.	
1957. Symposium: The Quality Control of Food. SCI (Food Group)/Assoc. Pub. Analysts.	1957. First textbook on sensory evaluation (in Polish).
	1958. QMF and CI Manual: Sensory Testing Methods.
	1958. ASTM Committee E-18 (Sensory Evaluation of Materials and Products) formed. Many subsequent publications.
1960. Symposium: Food Assessment and Food Acceptance. British Psychiatric Society.	1962. Le Magnen's *Technical Vocabulary* (in French).
	1963. First reports on texture profiles. General Foods, New York.
1964. International review on sensory evaluation.	
1964–67. Project: Odour Characterisation and Odour Classification. FRI, Norwich.	1965. Publication of *Principles of Sensory Evaluation of Food*, Amerine, Pangborn and Roessler.
1967–72. Publication of *Quality Control in the Food Industry* (3 volumes) edited by Herschdoerfer.	1968. First international symposium: Sensory Evaluation of Food: Principles and Methods. Gothenburg.

TABLE 1—*contd.*

UK	*Elsewhere (mostly the USA)*
1968. Formation of BSI Committee on sensory analysis.	
1974. Formation of Sensory Panel of SCI Food Group.	
1975. BS 5098 on terminology published.	1975. First news letter, Sensory Evaluation Division, IFT (370 members—increased to over 1 000 by 1982).
1977. Symposium: Sensory Quality Control: Practical Approaches in Food and Drink.	
1980: BS 5929 Part 1 on sensory methods published.	
1982. Symposium: Sensory Quality in Foods and Beverages: Its Definition, Measurement and Control. SCI. Jubilee.	1981. This volume of the *Journal of Food Science* contains over 60 papers on different aspects of sensory analysis.
1983. The present symposium.	

An Early Symposium

Reverting back to developments in other countries, particularly in the UK it is important to note that here (in the UK) food rationing did not end completely until 1955 by which time 'quality consciousness' and discrimination was beginning to return. This is well illustrated by the fact that the first symposium expressly on the subject of 'Quality Control of Food' took place in 1957 and was published in 1960.[31] This included 15 papers on different aspects of food quality, several contributions involving a substantial sensory component. At this stage terms like 'subjective assessment' or 'organoleptic tests' were often used; the present day equivalents 'sensory evaluation' or 'sensory analysis' were yet to emerge. Picking out a few details, the paper on chocolate and confectionery referred to 25 years' accumulated experience with sensory tests used in process modifications and in routine quality control. The importance of using trained assessors was stressed.[32] However, a few contributors were somewhat ambivalent about sensory tests, especially the question of how such information can be expressed in numbers, at the same time recognising that for many purposes, sensory data are indispensable. Several recurrent themes were discussed by others and the contributors and the topics have continued to appear in recent presentations (that is until now). Thus, Harries discussed the quality control of food by sensory assessment, in the light of his knowledge and experience with the Ministry of Agriculture, Fisheries and Food. Many of the theoretical considerations which would be examined today are covered in outline. Score sheets, setting out the key features of several products are listed.[33] About one-third of Adam's contribution on standards of quality in canned fruit and vegetables dealt with sensory quality.[34] Particular emphasis was placed upon a scoring system based on the separate contributions for colour, texture, absence of defects, size, grade and flavour of canned products. An overall score out of 100 provided the basis of commercial grades. This system became the substance of an internal document known as QC6, available to the industry as members of what is now referred to as the Campden Food Preservation Research Association. Even at this point the development of taints had been investigated for some five years, chiefly using the Triangular test. The results were made available to the industry, such tests being rare in the research or quality control departments of the canneries.

Another recurrent topic, with a long history, was that of quality control in the fish industry. In the treatment of this subject a substantial part was devoted to the score sheet developed for evaluating the characteristics of white fish from pristine freshness to the stages of decomposition. Separate score sheets were available for raw and for cooked fish. That for raw fish was divided into four groups, each with its own range of scores, as follows: General appearance (5–0), Flesh, including belly flaps (5–0), Odours (10–0), and texture (5–1). The corresponding groups for the cooked fish were: Odour (10–0), Texture (5–1) and Flavour (10–0). In each instance, a comprehensive description was provided for every numerical category, the high score corresponding to the perfectly fresh condition, the lower values to increasing loss of freshness.[35] This method was first formalised in 1953,[36] building upon earlier knowledge and information. This is a particularly good example of a complex system of scoring in so far as the description of sensory quality changes as the scores decrease. This contrasts with the profile approach, discussed earlier, in which scores (0–5 or 0–10, for example) refer to the changes in intensity of each individual quality or 'descriptor'—to use the present day terminology.

The last paper in this symposium dealt with the basic statistics, mostly confined to physical or chemical measurements.[37]

An International View

Brief reference should be made at this point to a series of 17 papers arranged and edited for *Laboratory Practice* on the current state of sensory evaluation in several different countries. This included 9 contributions from the UK, 5 from the USA and one each from Australia, Denmark and Poland. This collection represented the range of personal contacts at that time and in retrospect a number of other countries might well have been included. However, it is doubtful whether more space could have been found for a more extended treatment of the subject. Publication in book form of what was a highly original collection was considered, but the estimated demand failed to justify this action. A careful comparison of current problems and practices with those of the 1960s would be instructive. In addition to my personal overview,[38] Peryam[39] outlined the sensory testing carried out at the Quartermaster Food and Container Institute in Chicago until its closure in 1963. Pangborn[40] traced the developments which took place in the Department of Food Science and Technology at Davis in California. Tilgner[41] provided a similar outline of developments at the Polytechnic in Gdansk, Poland, which go back to the 1950s and include the first text book *Qualitative and Quantitative Sensory Analysis* published (in Polish) in 1957. Sullivan and Caul[42] of Arthur D. Little, Inc. reviewed the application of their Flavour Profile to packaging problems. Taste testing in the Commonwealth Scientific and Industrial Research Organisation (CSIRO) in Australia was surveyed by Christie,[43] and Harries[44] brought the survey of the work of the Ministry of Agriculture, Fisheries and Food in London up to date. The second special number of *Laboratory Practice* began with an introductory review of the sensory evaluation of animal foods by Hammond.[45] Baker[46] then dealt with the special problems of taste and odour in water. The next three papers dealt with wines, spirits and beers, with contributions by Amerine and Ough[47] on Californian wines, Brandt[48] on quality control in the distilled spirits industry and Trolle[49] dealt with judgement of quality in beer with regard to taste and smell. Lea[50] surveyed the sensory evaluation of dried milk and dried egg, summarising the effective use of scoring systems and tracing significant work on both subjects back to the early 1940s. Next, Spencer[51] extended the reports of work on the freshness of fish to sensory assessment under commercial conditions in the docks, as compared with the earlier laboratory studies. Another interesting innovation was a survey of sensory testing at J. Lyons and Company Ltd by McCowen.[52] This included an experimental study of the effects of changes in the sugar and fruit purée content of water ices on preferences (likes or dislikes, in this instance) and an application of multidimensional scaling of the sensory qualities of teas. The last contribution in this series consisted of a review by Baines and Shewan[53] of the pioneer studies involved in the development of sensory methods for evaluating the quality of white fish.

Textbooks on Quality Control

Another significant development relating to quality control in the food industry was the appearance of the three-volume series, edited by Herschdoerfer,[54] between 1967 and 1972. However, with a few exceptions, which will be noted, the 23 separate and often extensive contributions concentrated mostly on the non-sensory aspects of food quality. The exceptions include the chapter by Gridgeman, dealing explicitly with sensory assessment in quality control. This 48 page review covers most aspects of the subject, including a number of the examples which have already been discussed in the present survey. Indeed, it is gratifying to find that in discussing the aims of sensory analysis Gridgeman[55] chooses to paraphrase a review of my own published in 1955.[25] It is also of interest to note that a number of Gridgeman's references go back to the 1930s, again confirming the long established roots of sensory analysis. The first volume also includes a chapter by Steiner,[56] 111 pages in length. Although this contains a section on quality control charts, most of the applications throughout the chapter deal with physical or chemical rather than sensory variables. One exception concerns the application of sequential methods to the analysis of defectives, which could include those identified by sensory methods. The same procedure has often been used in combination with the Triangular test to select discriminating panel members.

The remaining two volumes have been scrutinised less intensely.

They are mainly concerned with particular products, details of some of which have already been touched upon. Otherwise, most of the detailed information concerns the non-sensory aspects of quality specification and quality control. However, selected paragraphs and pages are informative about these aspects and Volumes 2 and 3 still merit further scrutiny. The same is true of the two volumes by Kramer and Twigg,[57] summarising American experience in the broader aspects of quality control in the food industry.

The First International Symposium

Attention should be drawn to many other events and publications before the present time is reached. Sensory evaluation is said to have come of age with the first fully international symposium organised by the Swedish Food Research Institute (SIK) in 1968. Regrettably, no formal proceedings were published, although some individual contributions were published separately. These included a general impression of the symposium by Pangborn[58] and a composite review by Tilgner[59] of the past, present and future developments in sensory analysis which included his opening address at the international symposium. His treatment of the subject covered 62 pages and included 280 references, without being comprehensive. Indeed, the most comprehensive bibliography available on the sensory evaluation of food is prepared by Drake and Johannson[60] for the international symposium and published in 1969. This two-volume document was divided into four parts: (1) Physiology, (2) Psychology, (3) Methods, and (4) Applications. Most of the entries include a brief summary by the authors. A supplement covering the period 1968–1973 was prepared later.

Reverting to Tilgner's review,[59] this included reference to a number of European and other contributions to the subject, which might easily be overlooked since they naturally appeared in their own languages. For example, one of the most comprehensive vocabularies was edited by Le Magnen[61] in 1962. He was also the prime mover in a French symposium on different aspects of sensory analysis, as early as 1964. This involved some 38 contributions, the publication of which ran to 606 pages. Reference was also made to the *Handbook for Sensory Testing in Industry* prepared by the Japanese Union of Scientists and Engineers in 1962.

Other Organisations

Special reference should be made to the activities of various standards organisations. Priority in time again goes to the USA with the establishment of Committee E-18 (Sensory Evaluation of Materials and Products) of the American Society for Testing and Materials (ASTM). This committee became active in the early 1960s after having been in existence since 1958. A whole range of relevant publications have already been published, including a recent review of the Committee's current activities.

Since 1968, international activities have been focused by Working Group 2 (Sensory Analysis of Agricultural Food Products) of Committee TC34 of the International Standards Organisation (ISO). Different national standards organisations have worked on different topics assigned to them. Naturally, international deliberations take much longer than the national ones to reach the stage of formal and approved publication. So far, two such publications from the British Standards Institution (BSI) (Committee FAC/20—Sensory Analysis) have appeared. The first, BS 5098: 1975, deals with terminology,[62] the second, BS 5929: 1980, deals with sensory methods.[63] Both these publications are strongly recommended so as to promote standard practices and to make use of the wide experience of the many contributors. Further information about the ISO's activities and those of the contributing national organisations such as AFNOR, BSI, DIN and others should be examined to provide an up-to-date picture. It should be remembered, however, that most of the committees in mind have been concerned with general principles and methods, rather than with particular commodities. Most standards organisations also have their commodity committees and the primary internal function of the sensory committees has been to provide the commodity committees with expert knowledge about the sensory methods and their use. In most instances, certainly in the case of the BSI committee, the question of consumer preferences has been excluded from the terms of reference. The main topics considered in the whole programme have been terminology, the use of the difference tests, the measurement of thresholds, different types of scales capable of quantifying well-spaced levels of sensation, and the various profiling systems. These are recurrent themes in the specification and control of quality in food.

Recent Symposia

One of the most useful symposia specifically concerned with sensory quality control has already been referred to in outlining

Muller's survey of practising in the food industry in the UK. Further comments are necessary on some of the other contributions. My own introductory paper on our senses and how we use them has been superseded and amplified in a later publication.[64] The remaining papers deal with industrial applications, beginning with Pridmore's analysis of statistical concepts underlying sensory quality control.[65] He emphasises proper specification including the relevance of Flavour Profiles to provide important details. As with many other industrial or commercial applications, comparative judgements are considered to be very important, with some form of control product as a point of reference. However, with natural or manufactured products and their associated sensory qualities, special steps have to be taken to minimise systematic changes in 'the control'. In addition, the question of the consumer's response, including the comparison between the company's and the competitor's product(s), is always of central interest. Other important topics discussed include an up-to-date review by Howgate on the measurement of fish freshness by sensory methods, referred to here deliberately as 'objective sensory methods'.[66]

Presswood outlined what is involved in butter and cheese grading. A system, re-introduced after the end of food rationing (1955) continued to be used until 1975 when in England (but not in Scotland) independent grading for commercial purposes was set aside and taken over by 'the trade' itself*. Personally, this change is viewed with regret and it is not unusual to find ordinary cheese on the market which does not come up to the standards of the previous system. However, if this meets the requirements of the consumer, would it be reasonable to protest? Although not a part of this contribution, note should be taken of the recommendations of the International Dairy Federation (IDF)[67] in 1981. This consisted of a scoring system for butter and dried milk, the document for cheese not yet having been finalised at that time. The terminology used is derived largely from the ISO. The system is an interesting development. Scores within the range 5–1 are given under selected major headings—Appearance, Consistency and Flavour–in the case of butter and deductions are made from a score of 5 for departures from the ideal, highest quality

* Since preparing this survey the English Country Cheese Council have just announced (July 1983) the introduction of the Cheese Mark applicable to the products of prescribed quality from all creameries in England and Wales.

under each of the separate headings. In this instance an international vocabulary is provided, consisting of 36 terms: Appearance (12), Consistency (5) and Flavour (19). The scores also represent quality classes, thus: 5 = (I); 4 = (I −); 3 = (II); 2 = (II −) and 1 = (III). The five quality classes are designated as Very Good, Good (defects under this heading can only be very small deviations from the ideal type), Fair (slight defects), Poor (evident defects) and Very Poor (strong defects). A score of zero is not listed in the table setting out these details, but is interpreted as 'unfit for human consumption in its present condition'. No formal instructions are given about combining the separate scores. It would appear that they are looked at separately and an overall judgement made with the proviso that the lowest score given to any one of the three categories (Appearance, Consistency and Flavour) 'should in international trade, be decisive for the final classification'. The relative importance of each group of attributes is not discussed. This contrasts markedly with most traditional grading schemes, which usually assign a number of points to the several categories, depending upon how important these are considered to be, and deductions are made for departures from what is considered to be ideal. The separate scores would be totalled and the boundaries between the various quality grades would determine the final category.

Reverting to the 1977 symposium, other contributions merit equal attention from this comprehensive outline of commercial and industrial practices, to which the reader should refer. Topics covered include milling and baking, meat products, tea buying and blending, soups, confectionery, fruit juices and soft drinks, oils and fats, and ice-cream. The last two papers deal with sensory testing more as a management tool, Hicks concentrating on consumer product specification,[68] and Wren dealing with the sensory quality of beers.[69] Hicks refers especially to individual and group differences in preferences, giving several different examples. He also stresses how a product with a number of different attributes may be valued by some for one attribute and by others for a different attribute. This would fit in well with the earlier definition of quality—or at least an important aspect of it—as fitness for intended purpose. Wren's paper includes details of a Flavour Profile Specification of a draught bitter beer with numerical values for Aroma, Palate and After-palate in respect of 20 specified sensory qualities. In respect of each of these, where relevant, target values and upper and lower limits are provided.

CONCLUDING REMARKS

The nature of sensory quality and the special methods necessary for its control and specification have been examined. This has involved tracing some of the developments over the last 40 years. A selection of the available literature has been detailed and a few examples examined in further detail. With a few conspicuous exceptions, ignoring examples consisting of vague generalities, most of the published literature deals with research investigations, rather than with industrial or commercial practices. Attitudes may be changing, as illustrated in some of the more recent symposia.

Among the striking conclusions is the fact that many of the basic questions and some of the methods were formulated many years ago. What is new is the expanding interest and application of sensory methods, including progressive movements towards their standardisation. A particular growth area during the last 15 years has been in the development of profiling methods and their successful application to product specification. Much of the relevant information has, in the past, been obtained from trained assessors, sometimes highly trained. Currently, the interest extends to further consideration of the responses of the consumer. This, and the increasing number of short courses which are becoming available, make it necessary to sound a note of caution to ensure that high professional standards are maintained. Perhaps this analysis and reference to some of the starred items in the list of references which follows will help to achieve this end.

REFERENCES

Items have been starred in the following list simply so that the reader who wishes to have a fuller appreciation of sensory analysis and its applications, may do so quickly. The 1977 Symposium, first referred to in reference 9, should be read in full.

1. Dudding, B. P. and Jennett, W. J. (1942). *Quality Control Charts*, British Standards Institution, London (BS 600R: 1942, being a revision of BS 600: 1935).
2. Marcuse, S. (1947). *Food Ind.*, **19**, 316–18.
*3. Harper, R. (1982). In: *Food Flavours. Part A. Introduction*, Eds. Morton, I. D. and MacLeod, A. J., Elsevier, Amsterdam, 79–120.
4. Bengtssen, K. and Helm, E. (1946). *Wallerstein Lab. Comm.*, **9**(28), 171–80.

5. HELM, E. and TROLLE, B. (1946). *Wallerstein Lab. Comm.*, **9**(28), 181–94.
6. MELDAHL, H. F. (1964). Personal communication.
7. AMERICAN SOCIETY FOR TESTING AND MATERIALS (1967). *Document No. E-339-67*. ASTM, Philadelphia, PA.
8. BRANDT, D. A. (1964). *Lab. Pract.*, **13**(8), 717–19, 733.
*9. HICKS, D. (1977). In: *Sensory Quality Control: Practical Approaches in Food and Drink Production*, Eds. Symons, H. G. and Wren, J. J., SCI (Food Group, Sensory Panel) IFST (UK), London, 119–26.
10. CAUL, J. F. (1957). *Adv. Food Res.*, **7**, 1–40.
11. SZCZESNIAK, A. S. (1963). *J. Food Sci.*, **28**(4), 385–9.
12. BRANDT, M. A., SKINNER, E. Z. and COLEMAN, J. A. (1963). *J. Food Sci.*, **28**(4), 404–9.
13. HARPER, R., BATE-SMITH, E. C., LAND, D. G. and GRIFFITHS, N. M. (1968). *Perfum. and Essent. Oil Rec.*, **59**, 22–37.
14. VON SYDOW, E., ANDERSON, J., ANJOU, K., KARLSSON, G., LAND, D. G. and GRIFFITHS, N. M. (1970). *Lebensm.-Wiss u. Technol.*, **3**, 11–17.
*15. PERSSON, T., VON SYDOW, E. and AKESSON, C. (1973). *J. Food Sci.*, **38**, 386–92.
16. WREN, J. J. (1972). *J. Inst. Brewing*, **78**, 69–75.
*17. CLAPPERTON, J. F. (1973). *J. Inst. Brewing*, **79**, 495–508.
18. CHAUHAN, J. (1982). *Characterisation and Discrimination of Soft Drinks by Sensory Methods*, Ph.D. Thesis, University of Reading.
19. NOBLE, A. C., WILLIAMS, A. A. and LANGRON, S. P. (1983). In: *Sensory Quality in Foods and Beverages. Definition, Measurement and Control*, Eds. Williams, A. A. and Atkin, R. K., Ellis Horwood Ltd, Chichester (for the Society of Chemical Industry, London), 324–34.
20. SPENCE, R. M. (1982). *J. Food Technol.*, **17**(5), 633–48.
*21. MULLER, J. G. (1977). In: *Sensory Quality Control, Practical Approaches in Food and Drink Production*, Eds. Symons, H. G. and Wren, J. J., SCI (Food Group, Sensory Panel) and IFST (UK), London, 28–36.
*22. HARPER, R. (1977). In: *Sensory Properties of Foods*, Eds. Birch, G. G., Brennan, J. G. and Parker, K. J., Applied Science Publishers, London, 167–87.
23. HARPER, R. (1952). *Brit. J. Psychol., Monog. Supp. No. 28*, Cambridge University Press, Cambridge, 1–64.
24. HARPER, R. (1949). *Food*, **18**, 207–10.
25. HARPER, R. (1955). *Applied Statistics*, **4**(3), 145–61.
26. BATE-SMITH, E. C. (1948). *Chem. and Ind.*, **67**(7) 107.
27. TOMKINS, R. G. (1949). *Chem. and Ind.*, **68**(11), 167–8.
28. DAWSON, E. H. and HARRIES, B. L. (1951). *Agric. Inform. Bull. No. 34*, US Department of Agriculture, Washington, DC, 1–134.
*29. PANGBORN, R. M. (1964). *Lab. Practice*, **13**(7), 610–16.
30. AMERINE, M. A., PANGBORN, R. M. and ROESSLER, E. B. (1965). *Principles of Sensory Evaluation of Food*, Academic Press, New York and London, 1–602.
31. ANON. (1960). In: *Quality Control of Food*, SCI Monograph No. 8, Society of Chemical Industry, London, 1–176.

32. LIPSCOMB, A. G. (1960). *ibid.*, 22–40.
33. HARRIES, J. M. (1960). *ibid.*, 128–37.
34. ADAM, W. B. (1960). *ibid.*, 45–59.
35. CUTTING, C. L. and BURGESS, G. H. O. (1960). *ibid.*, 59–77.
36. SHEWAN, J. M., MACKINTOSH, R. G., TUCKER, C. G. and EHRENBERG, A. S. C. (1953). *J. Sci. Food Agric.*, **4**, 283.
37. STEINER, E. H. (1960). In: *Quality Control of Food*, SCI Monograph No. 8, Society of Chemical Industry, London, 145–62.
38. HARPER, R. (1964). *Lab. Practice*, **13**(7), 599–604.
39. PERYAM, D. R. (1964). *ibid.*, 605–9.
40. PANGBORN, R. M. (1964). *ibid.*, 610–16.
41. TILGNER, D. J. (1964). *ibid.*, 617–24.
42. SULLIVAN, F. and CAUL, J. (1964). *ibid.*, 625–41.
43. CHRISTIE, E. M. (1964). 630–7.
44. HARRIES, J. M. (1964). 638–41.
45. HAMMOND, J. (1964). *Lab. Practice*, **13**(8), 700–4.
46. BAKER, R. A. (1964). *ibid.*, 705–11.
47. AMERINE, M. A. and OUGH, C. S. (1964). *ibid.*, 712–16, 738.
48. BRANDT, D. A. (1964). *ibid.*, 717–19, 738.
49. TROLLE, B. (1964). *ibid.*, 720–2.
50. LEA, C. H. (1964). *ibid.*, 723–8.
51. SPENCER, R. (1964). *ibid.*, 729–33.
52. MCCOWEN, P. (1964). 734–8.
53. BAINES, C. R. and SHEWAN, J. M. (1965). *Lab. Practice*, **14**(2), 160–3.
54. HERSCHDOERFER, S. M. (Ed.) (1967–1972). *Quality Control in the Food Industry*, Vols 1–3 Academic Press, London and New York.
55. GRIDGEMAN, N. T. (1967). In: *Quality Control in the Food Industry*, Vol. 1, Ed. Herschdoerfer, S. M., Academic Press, London and New York, 235–83.
56. STEINER, E. (1967). In: *Quality Control in the Food Industry*, Vol. 1, Ed. Herschdoerfer, S. M., Academic Press, London and New York, 121–234.
57. KRAMER, A. and TWIGG, B. A. (1970). *Fundamentals of Quality Control for the Food Industry*, AVI Pub. Co. Inc., Westport, Conn., 1–556.
58. PANGBORN, R. M. (1969). *Food Technol.*, **23**(5), 108–10.
*59. TILGNER, D. J. (1971). *Adv. Food Res.*, **19**, 215–77.
60. DRAKE, B. and JOHANSSON, B. (1969). *Sensory Evaluation of Food. Annotated Bibliography*, Vols 1 and 2, SIK Report No. 255 (see also Supplement 1968–1973, SIK Report No. 350), Swedish Institute for Food Preservation Research, Gothenburg, Sweden.
61. LE MAGNEN, J. (Ed.) (1962). *Vocabulaire Technique des Charactères Organoleptiques et de la Dégustation des Produits Alimentaires*, Centre Nationale de la Recherche Scientifique, Paris, 1–86.
*62. BS 5098: 1975. Glossary of Terms Relating to Sensory Analysis of Foods, British Standards Institution, London, 1–13.
*63. BS 5929:1980. Methods for the Sensory Analysis of Foods: Part 1. Introduction and General Guide to Methodology, British Standards Institution, London, 1–13.

64. HARPER, R. (1982). In: *Food Flavours: Part A*. Introduction, Eds. Morton, I. D. and MacLeod, A. J., Elsevier, Amsterdam and London, 79–120.
65. PRIDMORE, W. A. (1977). In: *Sensory Quality Control: Practical Approaches in Food and Drink Production*, Eds. Symons, H. W. and WREN, J. J., SCI (Food Group, Sensory Panel) and IFST (UK), London, 19–27.
66. HOWGATE, P. (1977). In: *Sensory Quality Control: Practical Approaches in Food and Drink Production*, Eds. Symons, H. W. and WREN, J. J., SCI (Food Group, Sensory Panel) and IFST (UK), London, 41–8.
67. INTERNATIONAL DAIRY FEDERATION (1981). *International IDF Standard 99:1981. Sensory Evaluation of Dairy Products*, IDF, Brussels, 1–7.
68. HICKS, D. (1977). In: *Sensory Quality Control: Practical Approaches in Food and Drink Production*, Eds. Symons, H. W. and Wren, J. J., SCI (Food Group, Sensory Panel) and IFST (UK), London, 119–26.
*69. WREN, J. J. (1977). In: *Sensory Quality Control: Practical Approaches in Food and Drink Production*, Eds. Symons, H. W. and Wren, J. J., SCI (Food Group, Sensory Panel) and IFST (UK), London, 127–33.

12

Potato Storage and Quality

G. LISIŃSKA and G. SOBKOWICZ

Agricultural Academy, Institute of Storage & Food Technology, Wrocław, Poland

ABSTRACT

The changes in contents of dry matter, starch, reducing sugars, vitamin C and the darkening of raw tuber flesh of several potato varieties stored for a long time under different conditions were studied. The quality of chips made from stored potatoes was also studied.

It is concluded that an 8-month period of potato storage at temperatures of 7°C and 13°C and at 85–95% relative humidity causes total weight losses of tubers, changes in dry matter and starch contents and a decrease in vitamin C content.

Chips from stored potatoes absorbed lower amounts of oil than chips from fresh potatoes; their texture was inferior and their colour was generally darker than that of chips from fresh tubers. The changes of chemical composition of tubers and the quality of chips made from them were highly dependent on potato variety, temperature and storage time.

INTRODUCTION

Potato tubers are perishable materials and difficult to store, because they contain about 75% water. However, most uses of potatoes involve both short- and long-term storage. The purpose of potato storage is not only to minimise losses but also to allow treatment which retains and develops desired qualitative features of the potatoes according to their destination. Potato industries, such as starch factories, alcohol distilleries and dehydrated potato-fodder industries, operating seasonally, reduce the storage time to minimum by eliminating the spring campaign and processing early, in September. Potatoes for food purposes are processed in most industries for 8 to 10-month periods. A problem of adequate potato storage therefore arises.

Potato tubers immediately after harvesting and conditioning periods are usually of high quality. This quality decreases when the storage time is extended. Potato storage, even under the best conditions, affects the chemical composition of the tubers, which consequently results in deterioration in the colour and other sensory properties of the finished products.

CHEMICAL COMPOSITION OF THE STORED TUBERS AND QUALITY OF CHIPS

Changes in the specific gravity of the stored tubers depend on temperature, relative humidity and storage time.[1-4] The increase in specific gravity during long-term storage results from greater water loss in the evaporation process than losses of dry matter content during respiration. The main factors increasing dry matter losses are mechanical damage to the tubers, sprouting, high storage temperature and low humidity. Tubers with damaged skin and flesh, or sprouting tubers, respire more intensely, thus increasing the use of carbohydrates in the oxidation process.

Figure 1 shows the dry matter and starch contents in the tubers of 4 varieties and total weight losses of the tubers under various conditions of storage during an 8-month period. No additional treatments, such as sprout inhibitors or irradiation, were used. Total losses of tuber weight were high even during the first months of storage, particularly in the tubers stored under the conditions of low humidity. By the end of 8 months of storage the losses amounted to 20% of the initial tuber weight. Changes in the dry matter and starch contents depended on potato variety, e.g. Aba and Leda varieties during 6 months of storage were more stable and changes were greater only in the later storage months, while Certa and Kora varieties increased their dry matter and starch contents throughout the whole storage period. Changes in the ratio of dry matter to water after long-term storage in rooms of comparatively high temperature (7 °C and 13 °C) unfavourably affected the consistency of chips made

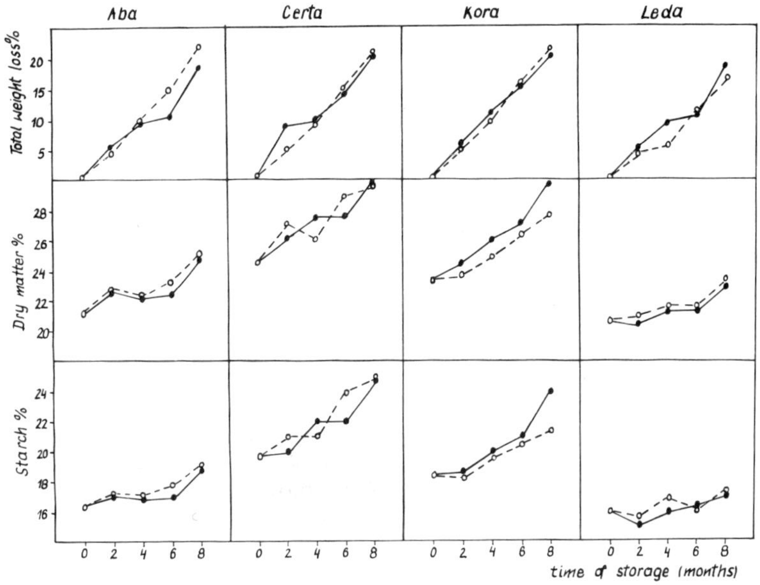

FIG. 1. Effects of storage conditions and time on total weight loss, dry matter and starch contents of 4 potato varieties (means of 3 yr). ●, 7 °C, RH 85–90 %; ○, 13 °C, RH 90–95 %.

from these tubers (Fig. 2). Higher dry matter content in the tubers stored for longer periods resulted in decreased oil absorption of the chips (Fig. 3).

Total carbohydrate content in potato dry matter undergoes a slight change during potato storage. The transformation of starch to sugars in the tubers stored under various conditions has been studied and reported by many authors. The decrease in starch content of tubers

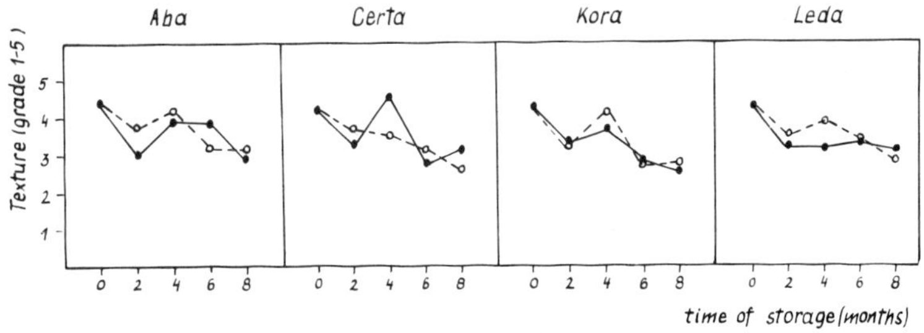

FIG. 2. Effects of storage temperatures and time upon chip texture of 4 potato varieties (means of 3 yr). ●, 7 °C; ○, 13 °C.

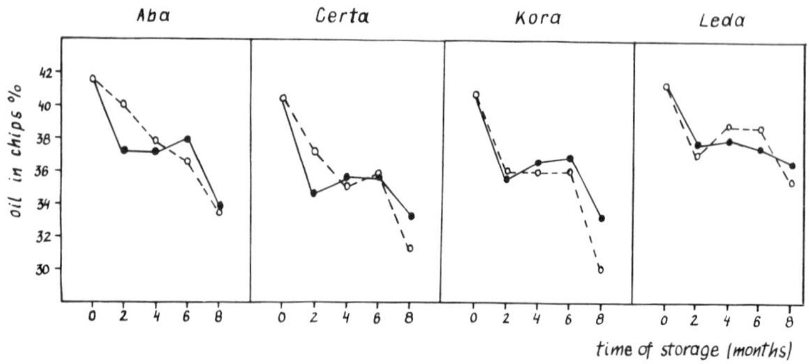

FIG. 3. Effects of storage temperatures and time upon oil content of chips from 4 potato varieties (means of 3 yr). ●, 7°C; ○, 13°C.

stored at low temperatures is accompanied by an increase in sugar content.[5–13] Moreover, in the tubers moved to rooms of higher temperatures, the starch content increases, together with a decrease in the sugar content.[5,6,14,15] Sugar content and composition do not only depend on temperature but also on potato variety,[10,15] maturity,[10,16,17] storage time,[12,18] irradiation,[19] use of sprout inhibitors[20] and types and concentration of gases in the surrounding atmosphere.[8,9,21]

Variability of the reported factors affecting changes in chemical composition of tubers, especially sugar content, is accounted for by the fact that authors have suggested optimal temperature ranges for storage of potatoes used both as fresh food material and for processing purposes.[22–36] Our studies (Fig. 4) proved that chips made from the tubers stored for 2 months at 13 °C were lighter in colour than from tubers stored at 3 °C and then reconditioned at 18 °C or 15 °C. The results encouraged us to carry out further investigations on the long-term storage of the potatoes for chip production purposes, at the high temperatures of 13 °C and 7 °C. The results of the chip colour determinations (made from tubers stored for 8 months) are shown in Fig. 5. Reactions of several potato varieties to the conditions and the storage time were different. Storage of Certa and Kora varieties at 13 °C did not affect the chip colour significantly as their colour was similar to that of the product obtained from fresh raw material. Chips made from the tubers of these varieties stored at 7 °C, but for a period longer than 2 months, also developed the right colour. Chips made from the tubers of Aba

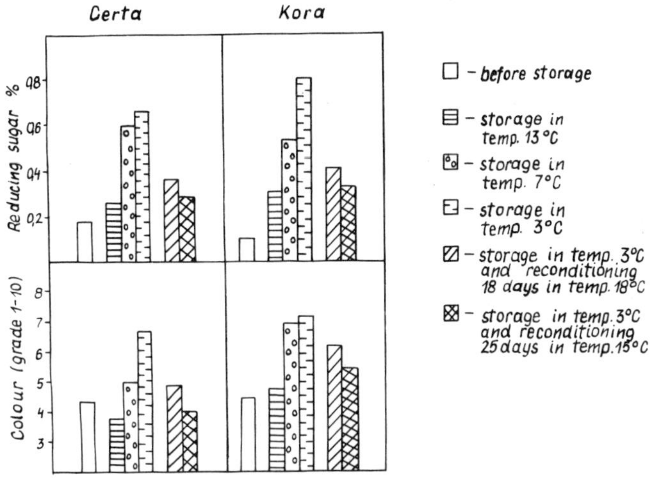

FIG. 4. Effects of storage temperatures upon reducing sugar content and chip colour of 2 potato varieties.

and Leda varieties, stored at 7 °C, were too dark, while tubers of the same varieties stored at 13 °C could be used directly in chip production; the Aba variety could be used during the first 6 months of storage, the Leda variety after 4 months of storage.

Storage conditions (especially temperature) influence the content and composition of nitrogen compounds in the tubers.[37] Habib and Brown's investigations[38,39] proved that in the tubers stored at high temperatures, the content of amino acids increased, whereas in the tubers reconditioned at 21 °C, the quantities of these compounds

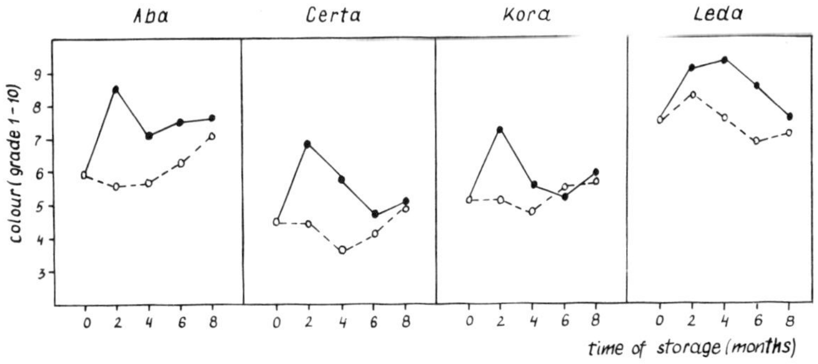

FIG. 5. Effects of storage temperatures and time upon chip colour of 4 potato varieties (means of 3 yr). ●, 7 °C; ○, 13 °C.

rapidly decreased. Lisińska[40] found that the metabolism of nitrogen compounds in the stored tubers depends on the same factors as the metabolism of carbohydrate compounds.

Potatoes are the cheapest and most common source of vitamin C. A problem exists in finding adequate storage conditions under which vitamin C content would remain the same as at the initial stage of storage.

Many data on the changes of ascorbic acid content in tubers can be found in the literature,[41–44] some authors[45] reporting that vitamin C losses are reduced in the tubers stored at lower temperatures. Great effects on vitamin C content of stored tubers are caused by the following: potato maturity during harvesting, potato variety and storage time.[46,47] The results of study (Fig. 6) prove that vitamin C content in tubers is reduced when storage time is long, and the greatest changes occur after the first 2 months, to reoccur between the sixth and eighth months. No influence of temperature on vitamin C content has been found.

During storage, potatoes may undergo some changes in the contents of organic acids.[48] Sweeney *et al.*[49] found that the content of citric acid decreases in stored tubers, while the quantity of malic acid increases. Gould and Deppen[50] maintain that the sum of organic acids in the stored tubers is three or four times as great when the temperature falls from 10 °C to 0 °C. Concentration of organic acids in the tubers should be considered when potato quality is to be determined. A catalytic role is attributed to these compounds in

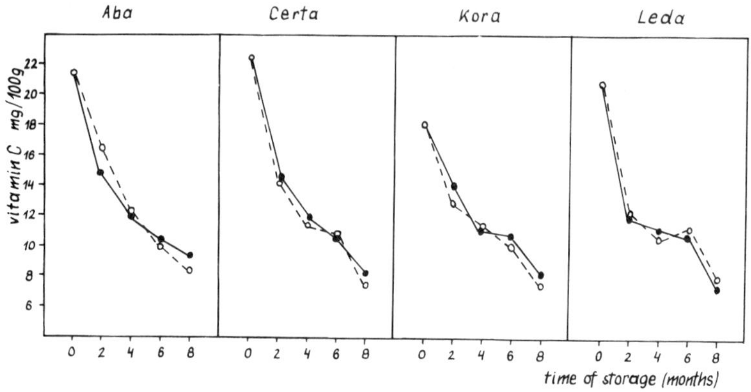

FIG. 6. Effects of storage temperatures and time upon vitamin C content of 4 potato varieties (means of 3 yr). ●, 7 °C; ○, 13 °C.

TABLE 1

DARKENING OF RAW TUBER FLESH BEFORE AND AFTER 5 MONTHS OF STORAGE OF POTATOES IN LOW PILES AND HIGH PILES WITH FORCED VENTILATION AND 10 DAYS RECONDITIONING (GRADE 1–10)

Variety	*Before storage*	*After storage*		*After reconditioning at 22°C*	
		Low piles Minimum temperature 3°C; maximum temperature 8°C	*High piles Minimum temperature 4°C; maximum temperature 9°C*	*From low piles*	*From high piles*
Noteć	3·1	2·2	3·6	3·5	4·1
Lenino	2·8	2·2	3·4	3·2	4·0

browning reactions, and even direct participation in the Maillard browning reaction with sugars.

Flesh darkening of raw and cooked tubers is an unfavourable phenomenon in the raw material destined for direct consumption and for processing purposes. Potato susceptibility to flesh darkening may increase during storage, with rapid environmental changes, such as temperature, relative humidity, carbon dioxide content, etc.[51] Studies of tubers stored under industrial conditions in low piles and high piles with forced ventilation (Table 1) proved that 5 months of storage did not affect potato susceptibility to darkening of the raw tuber flesh, whilst rapid temperature changes during reconditioning did.

The results presented above, concerning chemical composition of the stored tubers and quality of the finished products, prove that storage is one of the most important stages in food production. Only proper storage of the raw material with regard to its destination can yield high quality tubers and food products.

REFERENCES

1. Samotus, B., Kołodziej, Z., Niedźwiedź, M., Leja, M. and Czajkowska, B. (1973). *Potato Res.*, **16**, 61–8.
2. Schippers, P. A. (1971). *Am. Potato J.*, **48**, 313–20.
3. Talley, E. A. and Porter, W. L. (1970). *Am. Potato J.*, **47**, 214–24.
4. Fitzpatrick, T. J., Talley, E. A., Porter, W. L. and Murphy, H. J. (1964). *Am. Potato J.*, **41**, 75–81.
5. Burton, W. C. and Wilson, A. R. (1978). *Potato Res.*, **21**, 145–63.

6. Hyde, R. B. and Morrison, J. W. (1964). *Am. Potato J.*, **41**, 163–9.
7. Iritani, W. M. and Weller, L. D. (1976). *Am. Potato J.*, **53**, 57–65.
8. Lisińska, G. (1973). *Zesz. Nauk. WSR—Wroc. Rol. XXX*, **103**, 61–70.
9. Lisińska, G. (1973). In: *Molecular Structure and Function of Food Carbohydrate*, Eds. Birch, G. G. and Green, L. F., Applied Science Publishers, London, 208–15.
10. Mića, B. (1977). *Stärke*, **29**, 368–72.
11. Zeehringer, M. V., Cunningham, H. H. and Sparks, W. C. (1966). *Am. Potato J.*, **43**, 305–14.
12. Zgórska, K. (1979). *Ziemniak*, 183–206.
13. Zgórska, K. and Frydecka-Mazurczyk, A. (1976). *Biul. Inst. Ziemniaka*, **18**, 163–87.
14. Iritani, W. M. and Weller, L. D. (1978). *Am. Potato J.*, **55**, 425–30.
15. Samotus, B., Niedźwiedź, M., Kołodziej, Z., Leja, M. and Czajkowska, B. (1974). *Potato Res.*, **17**, 64–96.
16. Samotus, B. and Dzierżak, D. (1968). *Hod. Rośl. Aklim.*, **12**, 673–86.
17. Samotus, B. and Schwimmer, S. (1962). *J. Food Sci.*, **27**, 1–4.
18. Kubicki, K. (1974). *Nowe Rol.*, **21**, 21–3.
19. Burton, W. G. (1975). *Potato Res.*, **18**, 109–15.
20. Kamienobrodzki, W. and Lisińska, G. (1968). *Zesz. Nauk. WSR-Wroc. Rol. XXV*, **77**, 45–51.
21. Harkett, P. J. (1971). *Potato Res.*, **14**, 305–11.
22. Shallenberger, R. S., Smith, O. and Treadway, A. H. (1959). *J. Agric. Food Chem.*, **7**, 274–7.
23. Smith, O. (1961). *Eur. Potato J.*, **40**, 174–81.
24. Lyman, S. and Mackrey, A. (1961). *Am. Potato J.*, **38**, 51–7.
25. Stevenson, F. J. and Cunningham, C. E. (1961). *Am. Potato J.*, **38**, 105–13.
26. Clegg, M. D. and Champan, H. W. (1962). *Am. Potato J.*, **39**, 176–84.
27. Clegg, M. D. and Champan, H. W. (1962). *Am. Potato J.*, **39**, 212–16.
28. Hyde, R. H. and Walkof, C. (1962). *Am. Potato J.*, **39**, 266–70.
29. Lauer, F. and Shaw, R. (1970). *Am. Potato J.*, **47**, 275–8.
30. Schippers, P. A. (1975). *Potato Res.*, **18**, 479–94.
31. Sobkowicz, G. and Lisińska, G. (1979). In: *Sugar, Science and Technology*, Eds. Birch, G. G and Parker, K. J., Applied Science Publishers, London, 241–57.
32. Gould, W. A., Baroudi, A. and Hair, B. L. (1978). *Am. Potato J.*, **55**, 375–6.
33. Gould, W. A., Confar, N. S., Stone, W. E., Fenercioglu, H., Hair, B. L., Huber, F. V., Stover, J. G. and Pisarczyk, J. M. (1979). *OARDC Res. Circ.*, **250**, 28–32.
34. Hair, B. L. and Gould, W. A. (1979). *OARDC Res. Circ.*, **250**, 35–8.
35. Hill, M. K. and Gould, W. A. (1977). *J. Food Sci.*, **42**, 927–30.
36. Huber, F. V. and Gould, W. A. (1979). *OARDC Res. Circ.*, **250**, 43–5.
37. Fitzpatrick, T. J. and Porter, W. L. (1966). *Am. Potato J.*, **43**, 238–48.
38. Habib, A. T. and Brown, H. D. (1956). *Food Technol.*, **10**, 332–6.
39. Habib, A. T. and Brown, H. D. (1957). *Food Technol.*, **11**, 85–9.
40. Lisińska, G. (1975). *Zesz. Nauk. AR-Wroc. Rol. XXXI*, **109**, 165–73.

41. AUGUSTIN, J., JOHNSON, S. R., TEITZEL, C., TOMA, R. B., SHAW, R. L., TRUE, R. H., HOGAN, J. M. and DEUTSCH, R. M. (1978). *J. Food Sci.*, **43**, 1566–70 and 1574.
42. BOLILYI, P. P., KOROBIEWSKAJA, A. P. and MICZKO, W. N. (1977). *Kartofiel Owoszczi*, **23**, 9–10.
43. KNÖTZ, P. (1979). *Lebensm.-Ind.*, **26**, 63–5.
44. SHAKHAR, V. C., IRITANI, W. M. and ARTECA, R. (1978). *Am. Potato J.*, **55**, 663–70.
45. HEILINGER, F. and VAN VLIET, W. F. (1960). *Eur. Potato J.*, **39**, 182–7.
46. KUBICKI, K. (1974). *Nowe Rol.*, **21**, 21–3.
47. SIMEK, J. (1978). *Ved. Pr. Vyzk. Ustavu Bramb. CSAZV v Havlićkove Brode*, **7**, 113–19.
48. SHERMAN, M. and EWING, E. E. (1982). *Am. Potato J.*, **59**, 165–79.
49. SWEENEY, J. P., HEPNER, P. A. and LIBECK, S. V. (1969). *Am. Potato J.*, **46**, 463–9.
50. GOULD, W. A. and DEPPEN, J. (1969). *Ohio Report, OARDS*, **54**, 54–5.
51. KUBICKI, K. (1973). *Zasady przechowywania ziemniaków*. Państwowe Wydawnictwo Rolnicze i Leśne, Warszawa.

13

Factors Affecting the Quality of Dairy Products

P. A. MORRISSEY, P. F. FOX and D. M. MULVIHILL
Department of Dairy and Food Chemistry,
University College, Cork, Republic of Ireland

ABSTRACT

Milk, an important component of Western diets, shows considerable compositional variation which has an important bearing on consistency and functional properties such as heat stability, rennet clotting times, foamability, etc. The quality of milk must also be considered from the point of view of public health, since it may act as a vector for chemical and biological toxins, e.g. pesticides, antibiotics, mycotoxins and heavy metals. From the processing viewpoint, the main microbiological problems with milk produced under modern conditions are associated with psychrotrophic Pseudomonads, *which produce heat-stable proteinases and lipases and may cause problems in high heat products and butter, respectively.*

The quantitative and qualitative variations in the protein constituents can affect the manufacturing properties of milk. However, in the case of heat stability, some of the problems can be counteracted by controlling preheat treatment and the use of conventional and non-conventional additives. Cheese quality is best controlled by careful attention to milk quality, choice of milk clotting enzyme and type of starter organisms used. Sodium chloride concentration is critical for the development of proper flavour, texture and quality of all cheese varieties. The quality of butter is affected by the fatty acid composition of milk fat, level of salt and pro-oxidants.

Heat treatment of protein systems, particularly in the presence of reducing sugars, induces some loss of lysine with the formation of Maillard compounds. In some cases lysinoalanine, which has been found to cause kidney damage when fed to rats, may also be formed.

The influence of moisture content or water activity on the Maillard reaction, lipid oxidation and microbial growth is very significant.

High protein dairy products, e.g. caseins, caseinates, whey protein concentrates and isolates, and lactalbumin are used in the food industry for the functional characteristics they bestow on the end-product. It is therefore essential to establish their functional properties in a quality control programme. However, many difficulties are experienced in choosing methods for assessing functional properties which are affected by several processing factors.

INTRODUCTION

Milk is a rich source of the principal nutrients and has been used as a major dietary component by Man since prehistoric times. In Western European and North American diets, milk and dairy products supply a considerable portion of dietary protein, lipids, vitamins and minerals.[1] Milk is widely used internationally as a dietary supplement, mainly as a source of high quality protein. However, milk and its products are probably more frequently used for their highly desirable organoleptic attributes.

Because milk is an animal product, it may unfortunately act as a vector for the transmission of diseases from animal to Man unless due precautions are taken. Milk is also a good source of nutrients for microorganisms and, because of its physical nature, it is highly susceptible to bacterial spoilage. Further, the composition of milk is highly variable[2] and partly because of its physical state, is very amenable to adulteration and to physical and chemical deterioration.

The average composition of cows' milk is usually reported as water 87 %, fat 3·6 %, lactose 4·9 %, protein 3·5 % and ash 0·7 %.[2] Most of the constituents of milk, e.g. 100 % of the fatty acids C_4 to C_{14} and 50 % of C_{16}, lactose, the principal proteins and numerous minor components, including a variety of enzymes and sugar derivatives are synthesised by the cells of the alveolar epithelium, while other components—minerals, vitamins, some proteins and water—are transferred directly from the blood stream into the alveolar lumen.[3] The composition of milk is influenced by a number of factors including breed, individuality, stage of lactation, udder infection, plane of nutrition, season of the year and environmental factors.[2,4] Milk production in New Zealand, Australia and Ireland is very seasonal; the ratio of peak to trough production in Ireland is ~16:1 compared with ~2:1 in most European countries. This seasonality of milk production causes major technological problems which arise from variations in the concentration and/or physico-chemical characteristics of all the principal milk constituents for lactational (physiological) and/or nutritional reasons, and/or production practices (e.g. alternate or every-third-day collection of milk). Seasonal variations in the concentration of the principal constituents in Irish milk include: fat 3·2–5·0%, total protein 2·6–4·5%, and casein 2·0–3·0%.[5] In addition to these, changes in the fatty acid and milk protein profiles and in the properties of casein micelles also occur. The technologist is frequently able to minimise gross compositional variations by standardising milk or by modifying the manufacturing process. However, the heat stability, rennet clotting time, alcohol stability, cheese and casein yields and butter hardness are influenced by the more subtle compositional variations which, in general, cannot be controlled at the processing stage.

The quality controller must choose the correct analytical procedures in order to monitor compositional changes and must recognise limitations in the chosen analytical methods. For example, the infrared method for fat determination, compared with the Gerber method, significantly underestimates total milk fat produced by cows fed protected tallow, owing to an increase in the average molecular weight of milk fatty acids.[6] The presence of free fat may cause problems in the determination of fat by the Milko–Tester method.[7] The prescribed standard Gerber method for the determination of fat in skim milk underestimates the fat content by 0·03% when compared with the reference Rose–Gottlieb method.[8] Variations in the content of different protein fractions influence the dye binding capacity[9] and may result in some error. Recent work in our laboratory suggests that the International Dairy Federation (IDF) acetic acid/acetate method[10] may significantly overestimate non-casein nitrogen in late-lactation milk. The problems encountered in determining the moisture content of milk products will be reviewed later.

The quality of milk and dairy products must be considered from the point of view of (a) hygiene and public health, (b) chemical, physical and organoleptic deterioration by chemical, physical and biological agents, (c) consistency of functional properties and (d) nutritional quality. In a brief article like this it is not possible to review such a broad area in any depth, rather, we have chosen to review some selected topics in some depth and the review will be confined to quality problems encountered in countries with an advanced dairy industry.

HYGIENE AND PUBLIC HEALTH

Where milk is pasteurised and when precautions are taken to avoid post-pasteurisation contamination, it is unlikely that milk will be a significant vector for the transmission of pathogens. Further, the principal products are quite unsuitable for the growth of pathogens due either to low pH or low water activity. However, milk and dairy products may be vectors for chemical and biological toxins unless due precautions are taken. Among the more important of these substances are: (i) residues of herbicides, pesticides and antibiotics; (ii) mycotoxins; (iii) heavy metals; (iv) nitrosamines.

There is considerable interest in the potential contamination of milk and milk products by the growing use of a wide range of pesticides, herbicides, polychlorinated biphenyls, polychlorinated dibenzodioxins and polycyclic aromatic hydrocarbons.[11] According to an IDF report,[12] the maximum levels of chlorinated insecticides reported from many countries do not pose a health hazard when measured against the maximum limits recommended by WHO/FAO. Much concern has, however, been aroused by the detection of polychlorinated biphenyls in milk and milk products.[12] Although the levels found in milk are low[12] and have been traced to accidental contamination of cattle feeds, their unique stabilities make them very important in the food chain.

Increasing attention is also focused on the problem of heavy metals in our food and environment. The concentrations of these metals in milk and milk products generally range from less than 1 μg/kg to a few mg/kg.[13] It is generally accepted that concentrations of the highly toxic metals mercury, cadmium and arsenic in milk are well below the maximum established limits,[13,14] while copper may be present at levels likely to catalyse lipid oxidation in butter and other dairy products.[15] The relationship between sodium intake and hypertension has been a major source of concern.[16] Since cows' milk contains about 3 times the sodium content of human milk, the dietary sodium chloride levels in infant and toddler formulations need to be assessed carefully and probably replaced by potassium chloride which is known to have an ameliorating effect on hypertension.[17] When preparing food formulations there is always the great danger that sodium chloride may be used accidentally in place of sugar and fatalities have occurred in several hospital nurseries.[18]

The iodine levels in some milk and milk products have increased substantially in recent years with the widespread use of iodophors.[19] According to a recent review,[20] dairy products contribute 38–50% and 56–85% of dietary iodine for adults and children, respectively. Sources of iodine include animal feedstuffs, test dips and cleaning solutions and the additive effect of iodine from these sources, as well as intentional direct addition, could increase the iodine content of milk to $>500\,\mu g$/litre which could lead to an increase of thyroid disorder. It has been shown that the levels of iodine could be reduced considerably by a good extension service and public relations rather than by the imposition of penalties.[21]

The discovery of aflatoxin M_1 (AFM_1) in milk and its source have been reviewed.[22,23] When aflatoxin B_1 (AFB_1) is ingested by dairy cows, a portion of it is metabolised to AFM_1 which carries over into milk. Experimental 'carry-over' studies[22] indicate that the ratio of the concentration of AFB_1 in the feed to that of AFM_1 in milk is approximately 300:1. Thus, the maximum prescribed limits (EEC regulations) of $20\,\mu g$/kg and $10\,\mu g$/kg of AFB_1 in concentrate feeds and dairy rations should preclude detectable AFM_1 levels in milk. Unfortunately, AFM_1 is stable in raw milk and processed milk products and is unaffected by pasteurisation or processing of milk into cheese, yoghurt or evaporated milk.[24] A five- to eight-fold enrichment of AFM_1 in cheese over that in the milk from which it was made has been reported.[25]

Penicillium roqueforti, which is used in the production of roquefort and similar types of cheese, has been shown to produce a number of trace metabolites including festuclavine,[26] roquefortine, isofumigaclavines A and B[27] and roqueforti toxin.[28] Roquefortine is reported to be a neurotoxin when administered intraperitoneally to mice[27] and there is evidence that some of these toxins may present a hazard to Man. Roquefortine at levels of 162–651 ng/g was found in all of 12 samples of cheese and at 18 and 72 ng/g in two samples of Blue cheese dressing.[29]

The use of nitrate and nitrite as food additives has become a cause of serious concern, (a) as potential precursors of carcinogenic nitrosamines[30,31] and (b) as possible carcinogens *per se*.[32] The practice of adding nitrate to cheese milk in the manufacture of Gouda- and Edam-type cheeses to inhibit the development of clostridia and thus prevent late-blowing of cheese must be questioned. Most of the data to date indicate that the levels of nitrosamines in cheese are below 10 μg/kg and are probably more generally in the range of 1–5 μg/kg.[33] One group of workers[34] concluded that there is no relationship between the occurrence of nitrosamines and addition of nitrate. Spray-drying of cheese whey to which nitrates has been added may lead to nitrosamine formation.

DETERIORATION OF MILK AND MILK PRODUCTS

The constituents of liquid milk products exist either in true solution or in the colloidal state. The colloidal constituents, i.e. the lipids and proteins, are intrinsically unstable, chemically and physically, and undergo deterioration induced by microbial, enzymic, chemical or physical agents.

Microbiological

Until relatively recently, mesophilic lactic acid bacteria and coliforms were the principal spoilage microorganisms in raw milk. However, with the widespread use of prolonged refrigerated storage of milk on farms and at dairy factories, psychotrophic pseudomonads, which secrete extracellular heat-stable proteinases and lipases, now cause serious problems.[35–40] The heat-stable proteinases may cause bitterness in pasteurised and UHT-sterilised products as well as reduced yield of Cottage cheese. However, these proteolytic psychrotrophs do not affect Cheddar cheese quality and have effectively been ruled out as causative agents of age-gelation in UHT products. Psychrotrophic contamination may be prevented by proper hygiene and their growth markedly reduced by using low storage temperatures, thermisation[41] or activation of the lacto-peroxide/thiocyanide system.[42]

Enzymatic

Milk, as secreted, contains about 30 indigenous enzymes.[43] These enzymes are fortuitous in milk, and gain access to milk either as a result of breakdown of the secretory cells or due to the method of 'export' of milk constituents from the secretory cells through the apical cell membrane into the alveolar lumen during which the membrane is gradually removed to form the fat globule membrane and is replenished by intracellular membranes brought to the apex on protein export. Only a few indigenous enzymes are active in milk, and possibly dairy products, under certain conditions.

Lipolysis

Technologically, the most important enzyme in milk is lipoprotein lipase, which will be referred to as lipase. Lipase was first isolated from milk by Fox and Tarassuk.[44] A lipoprotein lipase was identified in bovine milk[45] and isolated by Egelrud and Olivecrona;[46] it appears that the lipase previously isolated[44] is in fact a lipoprotein lipase,[47] which appears to be the only significant indigenous lipolytic enzyme in milk.

The triglycerides in milk occur predominantly in globules and are protected from lipase, which is distributed mainly in the fat-free phase, by the fat globule membrane (FGM). The FGM is a relatively delicate structure and if it is damaged by homogenisation, agitation, freezing or temperature fluctuations, the lipase gains access to its substrate and hydrolysis of the triglycerides ensues. Short chain fatty acids ($<C_{10}$) have a strong peppery, bitter, goaty or unclean flavour while the longer chain acids have a soapy flavour. The relationship between the flavour of milk and its free fatty acid (FFA) content has been examined and reviewed by many workers.[48–50] For milk and cream, the generally acceptable threshold values are 1·2–1·5 meq/100 g fat for trained experts and 2·0–2·2 meq/100 g fat for the average consumer.[48] Fatty acids of chain length C_4 to C_{12} appear to be mainly responsible for lipolysed flavour, with each contributing fairly equally to the development of the defect.[51]

Free fatty acids are also important contributors to the flavour of some dairy foods, e.g. Blue and hard Italian cheeses;[52] lipolysis in these cheeses may be caused by indigenous milk lipase but more frequently by added exogenous lipase, usually pregastric esterase.

The FGM may be damaged by any of several processing operations to which milk is subjected. Among the treatments which induce lipolysis are: aeration, especially due to the suction of air at milking machine teat-cups;[53] pumping, particularly with aeration and type of pump;[54,55] pipeline milkers, particularly where features such as elbows, joints, in-line fittings and vertical risers are incorporated;[54,56,57] homogenisation, freezing and thawing. The contributions of the major factors during milking, transportation and storage in promoting lipolysis have been calculated and discussed.[58,59] The milks of a minority of individual cows undergo lipolysis without any specific activation treatment; lipolysis is induced simply by cooling. This phenomenon, referred to as spontaneous rancidity, was previously considered[60] to be due to a second lipase, termed membrane lipase, but it now appears that such milks contain a higher than normal level of blood serum[61] which activates the lipoprotein lipase and it is suggested that spontaneous lipolysis could be caused by leakage of blood components into the milk. Hydrolytic rancidity in milk is very significant commercially and has been the subject of considerable research and review.[48,62,63]

Indigenous milk lipase is completely inactivated by HTST pasteurisation, although somewhat higher temperatures are required for complete inactivation in cream. Since milk is now normally pasteurised during the manufacture of most dairy products, indigenous milk lipase is of significance only in raw milk. However, post-pasteurisation contamination is a common cause of microbial lipolysis in milk products.[37] If lipolysis occurs post-manufacture, due to enzymes elaborated by psychrotrophic bacteria and which have a high specificity for short chain acids,[49] rancid flavour can be detected at quite low acid degree values.[64,65] For this reason, measurement of C_4 and C_6 may give the best indication of hydrolytic rancidity in butter.[49]

Proteolysis

It is now fully accepted that milk contains an indigenous alkaline proteinase and probably an acid proteinase and peptidases also. Work on the isolation, characterisation and significance of these enzymes has been reviewed recently.[38,39,66,67] The present evidence indicates that the alkaline milk proteinase is plasmin (fibrinolysin) which is probably transferred from blood to milk via leaky junctions; thus, the level of proteinase in milk is particularly high during mastitic infection and in late lactation. The proteinase is predominantly attached to the casein micelles and is thus concentrated in cheese and casein. The proteinase is a serine proteinase with a pH optimum at ~pH 7·5 and hence its activity in acid dairy products is quite low. The enzyme is quite heat-stable and is completely inactivated only by heating at 130 °C for ~40 s; it is in fact activated by heating at 73 °C for 15 s, probably due to the thermal inactivation of an indigenous trypsin inhibitor.

The industrial significance of alkaline milk proteinase is still uncertain. In milk, plasmin acts preferentially on β-casein which is hydrolysed at 3 sites adjacent to lysine residues 24, 105 and 107 giving rise to 6 peptides: γ^1, γ^2 and γ^3-caseins and the proteose peptones 5, 8-fast and 8-slow. β-Casein is the most hydrophobic of the caseins and dissociates from the casein micelles on cooling; plasmin also dissociates on cooling and hence cold storage of milk results in more extensive hydrolysis of β-casein. Plasmin hydrolyses α_{s1}-casein and especially α_{s2}-casein but κ-casein is very resistant, which is fortuitous in view of the key micelle-stabilising role played by κ-casein. The principal whey proteins, in the native state, are also resistant to plasmin; in fact β-lactoglobulin is a competitive inhibitor. In addition, milk proteinase may be the probable cause of proteolysis in UHT-sterilised milks but apparently is not responsible, at least directly, for age-gelation of UHT milks.[68] Considerable levels of γ-caseins are formed in cheese, almost certainly due to the action of milk proteinase;[69] however, the significance of this proteolysis to the flavour and texture of cheese is unknown. The action of plasmin alters the gel-forming properties of casein micelles and hence the quality of cheese gels is adversely affected.

The acid proteinase, with a pH optimum of 4·0, is less well characterised but it may be a significant contributor to proteolysis in cheese.

Other enzymes

Xanthine oxidase, particularly in the denatured state, may be involved in lipid oxidation.[70] The possibility of using superoxide dismutase, indigenous or added, to inhibit lipid oxidation in dairy products has been mooted,[52] and sulphydryl oxidase plays a role in the amelioration of cooked flavour arising from sulphydryl groups exposed on protein denaturation.[52] It is unlikely that any of these enzymes is significant in milk or milk products.

Lipid Oxidation

Lipid oxidation and resultant flavour impairment seriously limits the storage potential of most fat-containing foods, including dairy products.[71] It is a critical factor in limiting the shelf-life of UHT-cream[72] and is a problem in the manufacture of whole milk powder.[73] Flavour defects also arise in butter, but are generally confined to salted, ripened cream butter.

Lipid oxidation in milk and milk products is caused by autoxidation of unsaturated fatty acids and its mechanisms have been reviewed extensively.[74–78] The resultant off-flavours have been variously described by consumers as metallic, oily, tallowy, cardboardy, mushroomy, fruity, etc., and are due to the production of a range of volatile compounds including alkanals, alk-2-enals, alk-2,4-dienals, alk-1-en-3-ones, dicarbonyls, β-dicarbonyls and alkan-2-ones.[79]

Lipid oxidation in milk and milk products is accelerated by many factors including light, air or oxygen, ascorbic acid, temperature, copper, iron and halides. Modern methods of displaying butter at retail outlets in illuminated cabinets tend to promote lipid oxidation.[80] Levels of copper, which play a dominant role among the pro-oxidants in milk,[71] show seasonal variations and have a considerable influence on the keeping quality of Irish ripened cream butter as evidenced by the limited storage stability of butter produced between October and February.[81] Copper contamination of butter and other dairy products can arise due to the presence of metals in the packaging materials.[82] Sodium chloride acts as a pro-oxidant especially in ripened cream butter[83,84] but its pro-oxidant properties cannot be explained on the basis of high levels of trace metals known to catalyse lipid oxidation.[80]

Bovine milks vary considerably in susceptibility to oxidation[71] and some may in fact develop spontaneous oxidised flavour. This phenomenon has been extensively studied in the USA and is considered to be an enzymatic reaction involving xanthine oxidase;[85] variation in the levels of indigenous superoxide dismutase may have a minor effect on oxidative stability.[86] Methods for measurement of lipid oxidation have been reviewed;[87,88] the principal methods used for dairy products are the thiobarbituric acid (TBA) test[89] and the peroxide value.[90,91] The TBA method is not considered to be reliable due to interaction of malonaldehyde (the main compound responsible for colour formation in the test) and closely related compounds with amino acids, proteins, etc.[92] The peroxide value is limited to the initial stage of oxidation since the hydroperoxides decompose readily. Good correlations, however, have been reported between peroxide values and the organoleptic flavour score for butter[80] and cream.[72] In recent years, considerable effort has been expended on examination of volatiles and trace components that characterise and contribute to food flavour and off-flavours.[93–95] A direct gas chromatographic method for determining volatiles, without prior enrichment,[95] has been used to separate and identify volatiles from salad oils and shortenings,[96] and vegetable oils.[96] In several of these investigations, the data correlated well with flavour-scored samples.[88,96,97] Certain flavour-related 'markers' such as pentane, pentanal, octane, hexanal, *trans*-2-heptenal, 2,4-heptadienal and 2,4-decadienal were identified.[88,94] We feel that this direct gas chromatographic technique may offer a novel approach to quality control in the butter and milk powder industries. The separation and measurement of individual volatile carbonyl-dinitrophenylhydrazones, isolated from whole milk powder, has recently been achieved by HPLC, using a reverse phase C_{18} column and isocratic elution with methanol:water (80:20).[98] This method also shows considerable promise.

Maillard Browning

Mild heat treatment of foods rich in reducing sugars, such as milk and milk products, may lead to Maillard browning, with change in product colour and loss of lysine.[99] A comprehensive review on browning in milk and its products was written in 1955,[100] and Maillard browning has been treated in a comprehensive manner at a recent conference.[101] Classically the Maillard reaction occurs between an aldo- or a keto-sugar and the amino group of an amino acid. The overall reaction has been divided into three stages. The early reaction involves the formation of the Amadori compound, 1-amino-1-deoxy-2-ketose, which is biologically unavailable[102] and loss of nutritive value occurs without any observable colour or flavour changes.[103] In some food systems, such as milk, the Maillard reaction stops practically at this stage as long as heating conditions are not too drastic or the reaction time too prolonged. The second stage involves: dehydration by loss of 3 molecules of water to form furfurals or by loss of 2 to reductones; fission, mainly by dealdosilation; and Strecker degradation, the interaction of amino acids and dicarbonyls. The final stage consists of the conversion of furfurals, fission products, reductones and Strecker aldehydes into melanoidin pigments, with further involvement of amines. The dehydration occurring in the second stage could account for the observed increase in moisture content of milk powder which occurs even in totally impermeable containers.

The Maillard reaction increases with temperature and time. Water content has a pronounced effect on the reaction, while acid pH values inhibit and alkaline values accelerate the reaction.[99] The loss of lysine in milk products depends on the type of heat treatment and also on the composition of the product, and varies in the range: spray-drying, 0 %; UHT process, 0 %; in-can sterilisation, 10–15 %; roller-drying, 45–75 %. Lactase-treated milks and milks in which lactose has been replaced by glucose are much more sensitive to heat: lysine losses increase from 0–2 % to 55 % on spray-drying.[102] The importance of composition and drying conditions is also highlighted in a recent report from Sweden which examined the effect of replacing sucrose by glucose or fructose in milk and cereal-based infant foods.[104] The presence of glucose or fructose at the drying stage invariably resulted in protein damage, and the loss was increased when the drying time was extended.

Maillard reactions also occur during storage. A 10 % loss of available lysine was observed in a sample of dried milk stored at 10 °C for 12 months,[105] while 13 % blockage of lysine was observed after 1 week and 36 % after 8 weeks when spray-dried milk was stored at 60 °C.[102] The increased moisture content observed when browning occurs can adversely affect the solubility of the powder, increase the α/β-lactose ratio and probably induce emulsion destabilisation.

Racemisation of L- to D-amino acids and concurrent formation of lysinoalanine (LAL) in foods treated with heat and/or alkali can also impair the nutritional quality and safety of foods by: (a) decreasing the amount of essential L-amino acids; (b) decreasing digestibility and bioavailability of proteins; and (c) forming toxic products.[106,107] Lysinoalanine produces lesions in the renal tubular cells of rats. Perhaps the most serious significance of LAL in the diet is the recent observation[108,109] that it is generated in a variety of home-cooked foods and commercial preparations when heated under non-alkaline conditions. High values of LAL were reported in milk-based infant formulae which may be significant because these products may be the sole nutrients for infants. In general, LAL causes only a slight reduction in nutritive value and products which are rich in LAL are generally used more as ingredients than as protein source.[110] Thus, the Maillard reaction may be more important in terms of loss of available lysine,[111] particularly in infant foods, while the possible harmfulness of LAL on humans is an open question.[109]

Heat Stability

The milk protein system is remarkably heat stable at pH values $>$ $\sim$6·4: milk of standard concentration can withstand heating at 140 °C for $\sim$20 min at pH 6·7–6·8 before coagulation occurs. Such stability is much more than is required to survive the thermal processing to which unconcentrated milk is normally subjected. The heat stability of milk, which is one of the few classical problems in dairy chemistry awaiting a satisfactory explanation, is influenced by a wide range of compositional and processing factors which have been extensively reviewed.[112,113] These are of little practical significance for unconcentrated milk.

However, the heat stability of milk decreases markedly on concentration and the stability of milk concentrated 2·5-fold is marginally adequate to withstand the time–temperature conditions used in commercial sterilisation, even when optimum processing conditions are used. With a few exceptions, notably preheating, the factors that influence the heat stability of unconcentrated milk also influence the stability of concentrates. The two factors most widely used to increase heat stability, viz. preheating and stabilising salts (usually orthophosphates and, less frequently, citrates and carbonates), have been used commercially for $\sim$80 yr. These methods are used in the manufacture of heat-stable milk powders suitable for recombination into UHT-milks, evaporated milk, coffee whiteners, etc. The precise mechanism of the stabilising action of preheating is unknown but it almost certainly involves denaturation of whey proteins and possibly some precipitation of tri-calcium phosphate.[112] Heating at 90 °C for 10 min prior to concentration has been the conventional preheating practice, but heating at 120–130 °C for 2 min gives improved stability,[114] while UHT-preheating (150 °C for 3 s) gives best results, although special plant is required. Reduction of pH by 0·06–0·12 pH units prior to preheating accentuates the efficacy of the process.[115]

The action of stabilising salts appears to be via the sequestration of Ca^{2+} and pH adjustment.[116] Variations in the content of indigenous urea in milk account for 70–90 % of the variability in the heat stability of unconcentrated milk[117] and addition of exogenous urea markedly increases stability.[118] However, urea is reported to be ineffective on concentrates, but it appears that the preheat treatment applied to milk greatly affects the response to added urea[119] and the heat stability of milk reconstituted from milk powder is related to its urea content.[119,120] Urea appears to be an effective stabiliser only in the presence of a carbonyl compound, including lactose,[121,122] but the mechanism of this synergistic action is unknown.

The heat stability of unconcentrated and concentrated milks are markedly improved by various small aldehydes and sugars[121–123] and their efficacy is further improved by addition of urea.[122] Diacetyl, which is a natural constituent in fermented dairy products and a permitted additive for margarine, is also a very potent stabiliser whose efficacy is increased by urea. The use of these additives in heated milk and milk products, while technologically feasible, may be totally undesirable nutritionally and toxicologically, since carbonyls react with ε-NH_2 groups and dicarbonyls react with arginine; it is postulated that urea converts lysine to homocitrulline which may then react with carbonyls. The technological, nutritional and toxicological aspects of the use of some of these stabilisers are currently being investigated in our laboratory.

The manufacture of milk powders suitable for use in recombined evaporated milk and similar products is now receiving considerable attention.[124] The powders used must generally be 'heat-stable' but there is no satisfactory method of predicting the stability of the reconstituted products and, in practice, heat-stable powders are selected on the basis of pilot batches of reconstituted products. It is still not possible to set out to manufacture a powder with predetermined heat stability characteristics, although the odds can be improved by adopting certain manufacturing procedures.

MOISTURE IN MILK PRODUCTS

It is now generally recognised that the manner in which water interacts with other food constituents affects the readiness with which it may be removed during dehydration, influences the reconstitution of dehydrated foods and affects product stability and keeping quality. The association of water with food systems is best described by the term water activity (a_w) which is defined[125] as the ratio of the partial vapour pressure of water in air (P) to the vapour pressure of water vapour in saturated air (P_s) at the same temperature:

$$a_w = P/P_s = \frac{\%RH}{100}$$

and may also be defined as the relative humidity (RH) at equilibrium divided by 100.

The relationship between water activity or relative humidity and moisture content is best described by a sorption isotherm.[126] Dehydrated foods fall within the region of low water activity ($a_w = 0$–$0{\cdot}5$) while semi-moist food products have $a_w = 0{\cdot}6$–$0{\cdot}9$.

Water sorption phenomena in foods have been extensively reviewed.[126–130] The control of water activity is a basic food processing technique and the moisture content can be used to predict the storage stability of a food.[127,131] An excellent 'food stability map as a function of a_w' which summarises many of the reactions responsible for deterioration of dehydrated foods has been described.[127] The optimal a_w for stability of dehydrated foods occurs in the range 0·2–0·3[132,133] where water is strongly absorbed in a monomolecular layer which is usually referred to as the BET monolayer.[134]

Microbial activity can generally be neglected if a_w is less than 0·7.[125] Most bacteria do not grow below $a_w = 0{\cdot}91$, most moulds and yeasts are inhibited between 0·88 and 0·8, although some xerophilic organisms can grow down to 0·6.[135] The minimum a_w for production of mycotoxins has been reported as 0·81, while toxin formation by *Clostridium botulinum* does not occur below 0·94. Environmental factors affect the water activity required for microbial growth; in general, pH, nutritional adequacy, oxygen pressure and temperature influence the tolerance for a_w.[135]

Butter and cheese are the principal dairy products with high water activities and are thus likely to undergo microbial spoilage. Addition of sodium chloride (~2%) to butter lowers the a_w sufficiently to prevent growth of both desirable and undesirable bacteria. The a_w of cheese is ~0·99 during the early stages of manufacture and does not interfere with the growth and activity of starter microorganisms. However, growth of starters, which have a minimum a_w for growth in the 0·93–0·94 range, is halted by the addition of sodium chloride.[136] The optimum level of sodium chloride for Cheddar cheese, best expressed on a salt-in-moisture basis, is ~4·9%. Propionibacteria, which are responsible for eye formation in Emmentaler cheese and probably for the development of the so-called late fermentation defect, are very sensitive to a_w changes in the range 0·99–0·95.[137] The influence of a_w on the metabolic activity of starter bacteria has not been studied thoroughly. The potential for 'osmotic manipulation' from the standpoint of both suppressing bitter flavours and enhancement of proper flavour in cheese deserves further consideration.

Enzymic activity is also influenced by a_w.[138] In general, most enzymes are inactivated when a_w is reduced to 0·85. However, lipases remain active at a_w values below 0·3, even as low as 0·1,[139,140] which may be important in certain dairy products. Available information concerning the influence of a_w on proteolysis in cheese indicates that the hydrolysis of β-casein by chymosin is strongly dependent on sodium chloride concentration;[141,142] at 5% sodium chloride, β-casein hydrolysis is significantly reduced while α_{s1}-casein hydrolysis is maximal in the presence of 5–10% sodium chloride. Similar results have been reported for protein breakdown in soft cheeses.[143] Fox and Walley[142] concluded that changes in substrate rather than enzyme were responsible for the reduced proteolysis of β-casein in the presence of sodium chloride.

Apparently the active sites of enzymes function even at very low a_w, but the size, mobility and physical state of the substrate become increasingly important as water is removed.[140]

The Maillard reaction occurs with maximum velocity at $a_w = 0{\cdot}3$–$0{\cdot}7$[133,139] depending on the kind of food.[144] Water not only accelerates the reaction but also shortens the induction period.[133] Acceleration of the reaction is due to faster diffusion and increased dissolution of reactants.[133] At higher a_w the reaction rate decreases due to dilution of the reactants and probably also due to product inhibition.[144] In milk powder, browning reactions reach a maximum at $a_w = 0{\cdot}6$–$0{\cdot}7$[139] and are generally not important from a practical viewpoint if $a_w < 0{\cdot}2$. At very low a_w ($<0{\cdot}1$), fat oxidation becomes a practical problem[139] but is at a minimum at or near the monolayer moisture level, i.e. $a_w = 0{\cdot}2$–$0{\cdot}3$. Like other reactions, the rate of oxidation also increases as a_w increases above the monolayer value.[133] The effect is attributed to changes in availability, mobility and hydration of metal catalysts and peroxide intermediates.[133]

Activity of water is of special importance in the determination of the moisture content of foods. The problem of accurate moisture determination lies in the difficulty of removing the tightly bound BET monolayer water.[145] The techniques used for measurement of the moisture content of foods have been reviewed.[145] The basic problem in oven-drying methods is that volatilisation of non-aqueous substances occurs and products such as whey powders have been shown to undergo partial hydrolysis.[146–148] On the other hand, the

BET monolayer water may not be removed in oven drying procedures. According to Thomasow *et al.*[147] the water of hydration of α-lactose is only partly removed by the standard oven-drying methods.

The toluene distillation method for moisture determination is widely used in the milk powder industry and the results invariably approach the true moisture content. However, reading accuracy (i.e. the water volume) is limited and solvent material may be trapped within the water layer. The Karl Fischer method determines the total (free and bound) quantity of water in the product and is widely acceptable as the standard for comparative purposes.

For various empirical methods of moisture determination, deviation from the true water content appears to occur at values corresponding to the BET monolayer level and a predetermined factor is frequently added to the value obtained for the oven-dried sample to obtain the true water content. The mean values obtained for dried milk by the Karl Fischer and toluene distillation methods are reported to be almost identical[149] but other workers[150] have found that oven-drying at 102 °C underestimates moisture contents of skim and whole milk powders by, on average, 0·33 % and 0·49 % compared with either the Karl Fischer or toluene distillation methods. Walley *et al.*[151] reported a somewhat wider range (0·3–1·1 % moisture) of differences between toluene and oven methods on 334 samples; the authors suggest, in agreement with previous findings,[152] that the difference between the toluene and oven methods is due to the variable amount of crystalline lactose in the powder. It is often suggested for process control and routine testing that the oven method could be made comparable with the toluene method by heating for a longer period. This idea is incorrect in principle since one method measures total moisture, while the other measures free moisture, and secondly, longer heating times lead to errors from decomposition and volatilisation.

QUALITY OF VARIOUS PRODUCTS

Butter

Butter is one of our staple foods and consequently comes under close scrutiny by the consumer. The main attributes which influence quality are flavour, colour and spreadability. Flavour deterioration is generally due either to lipolysis or lipid oxidation. Sodium chloride content and pH are the two critical factors which distinguish between the susceptibility of salted and unsalted sweet and ripened cream butters to post-manufacture lipid autoxidation, microbial growth and associated lipolysis.[63] In general, low pH and high sodium chloride content are inhibitory to post-manufacture microbial growth and associated lipolysis but are conducive to lipid autoxidation.[63] Lipolytic defects are the primary cause of deterioration in unsalted sweet cream butter, unsalted ripened cream butter and salted sweet cream butter in order of decreasing risk. On the other hand, copper-induced lipid autoxidation is the primary cause of flavour deterioration in salted, ripened cream butter.[63]

The spreadability of butter is one of its most important physical properties, particularly with the advent of soft margarines.[153] The factors affecting hardness and methods of improving spreadability have been widely investigated.[154–158] Butter manufactured under constant processing conditions shows marked variation in consistency, being hard in winter and soft in summer.[154,157–163] The proportion of palmitic acid is higher in winter than in summer, while the proportion of oleic acid or oleic plus stearic is lower;[158,161] variations in the ratio of unsaturated to palmitic acids appear to be the major factor that influences fluctuations in butter hardness.[154,158,159,163] Changes in the fatty acid profile have been related to seasonal fluctuation in the liquid fat content of milk[156] and to butter hardness.[159] The proportion of liquid fat in butter may be increased by: (a) addition of a low melting point fraction of fractionated butter fat,[157] (b) blending low and high melting point butter fat fractions, (c) production of a milk fat high in polyunsaturated fats through feeding protected polyunsaturated lipids,[164–166] and (d) special temperature treatment of cream before manufacture. The possibility of modifying the rheological properties of butter by means of processing technology, fractionation of milk fat and blending with other fats has been reviewed.[167] The 'Alnarp' method of temperature treatment, which involves cooling cream to 8 °C, warming to 19 °C and then slowly cooling to 16 °C ('8-19-16'), or modifications thereof, has been applied successfully to improve butter spreadability[158] and appears to be the most attractive method in process control; it may be the only economic way. Fracturing and lack of cohesion of butter layers which produces undesirable butter texture and causes such products to be downgraded,[168] is a further rheological problem encountered in butter related to the proportion of liquid fat in butter fat.

The problem of butter consistency, which to the consumer is synonymous with spreadability, has been a major cause for concern over the years. Numerous objective methods have been developed to evaluate consistency.[167,169–172] The most frequently applied methods are based on sectility, extrusion or penetration. None of these methods really reproduces the effect of spreading butter on bread and the state of the art may best be summed up by a recent IDF report[172] which states that 'evaluating the consistency of butter is a rather unruly subject, and many aspects of it are a matter of opinion rather than of fact'. However, some of the methods, e.g. sectility methods, are used on a routine basis for assessing product hardness.[173] This area should receive further attention.

Cheese

The IDF lists 510 varieties of cheese that can be classified into approximately 20 families;[174] undoubtedly there are many varieties absent from this list, especially in those countries that are not members of the IDF. In many respects, cheese is at the same time the most interesting and most difficult group of dairy products to manufacture: the wide range of varieties makes a comprehensive knowledge of cheese difficult to acquire. An entire presentation could be devoted to the problem of cheese manufacture and consequently only a few of what we consider to be the most significant aspects, particularly of Cheddar cheese, will be considered here.

Milk must be of high bacteriological quality, with a psychrotrophic count $< 10^7$, and contamination of milk for Swiss and Dutch cheese with *Clostridium tyrobutyricum*, which causes late gas blowing, must be avoided. The first step in manufacture of the vast majority of cheese varieties involves coagulation of milk with a proteolytic enzyme preparation, rennet, which hydrolyses the casein micelle-stabilising component, κ-casein. Because of the shortage of the traditional source of rennet, i.e. calf vells, a number of rennet substitutes have found more or less general acceptance, viz. bovine and porcine pepsins and the acid proteinases from *Mucor meihei* and *M. pusillus*. Chicken pepsin and proteinase from *Endothia parasitica* have to date had limited acceptability. Acceptable rennet substitutes must possess low general proteolytic activity in order to avoid excessive proteolysis during gelling and ripening which leads to poor cheese yields and bitterness. The main focus of attention of research on rennets at present appears to be on the use of genetic engineering to genetically modify microbial species to secrete 'chymosin', or more likely, prochymosin, and some success in this regard has been reported.[175] Coagulation of milk by immobilised rennets has been reported; however, immobilised rennets have short lives and other technological problems are also likely to arise.[52] Rennet and rennet substitutes have been reviewed extensively elsewhere.[176–178]

With the exception of the enzymatically induced coagulation of the caseinate system, which is a *sine qua non* for cheese manufacture, the attainment of the proper rate of acidification and the proper final pH is probably the most critical operation in cheese manufacture; it controls, in particular, the rate of syneresis of the curd and hence the moisture content of the cheese, which, together with the direct effect of pH and sodium chloride, regulates the activity of bacteria and enzymes in cheese.

The international cheese industry still generally uses mixed-strain starters which consist of unknown mixtures of strains of *Streptococcus lactis*, *S. cremoris*, probably *S. diacetyllactis* and possibly *Leuconostoc* spp. and for some varieties, *S. thermophilus* and *Lactobacilli* spp. Bacteriophage infection is the cheese manufacturer's principal concern, and in an effort to reduce such infections and thus obtain more predictable starter performance, single-strain starters were introduced in New Zealand in the 1930s. The majority of early single-strain starters were chosen for their fast acid-producing properties in the interest of reducing cheese manufacture time, but these tended to produce bitter cheese. Bitterness is avoided by using a blend of fast (*S. lactis*) and slow (*S. cremoris*) acid producing strains.

Paired single-strain starters were replaced in New Zealand by single-strain cocktails containing 6 carefully selected, matched, phage-unrelated single-strain cultures in the interest of producing better flavoured cheese. The principal advantages of defined starters (singles, pairs, cocktails) are a reproducible rate of acid production and phage resistance. However, these defined strain starters have not been generally accepted internationally, although single-strain systems are being investigated and used on a trial basis in a number of countries at present.

The third important factor in cheese manufacture is the control of composition, i.e. control of moisture content and especially the level and distribution of sodium chloride.[179] In Cheddar cheese, a moisture content of ~37% is probably optimal but this may be increased or decreased by ~1% to accelerate or retard the rate of ripening. Sodium chloride plays a key role in cheese ripening[180] and in the development of proper flavour and texture: (i) it has a direct influence on flavour, (ii) it modifies osmotic pressure and water activity (already discussed), (iii) it promotes curd syneresis. Unfortunately, sodium chloride distribution in cheese appears to be poor.[181] Depending on variety, cheeses are salted by mixing dry sodium chloride with milled curd, e.g. Cheddar-type cheese; by surface application of dry sodium chloride, e.g. Blue and hard Italian varieties; or by submersion in brine, e.g. Dutch and Swiss varieties. Considerable interblock and intrablock variation in sodium chloride content occurs with direct salting unless adequate mixing is practised.[181] In surface-salted cheese varieties a sodium chloride gradient exists from the surface to the centre for a considerable time which has an important bearing on the ripening of Blue[182,183] and Romano-type (Guinee, T. P. and Fox, P. F., unpublished work) cheese varieties. The influence of sodium chloride concentration and gradient on the biochemistry of Swiss cheese has been reviewed.[184]

The quality (flavour and texture) of cheese is still assessed subjectively by trained graders who presumably reflect consumer preferences with respect to quality; personal preferences represent a major problem here. In spite of very extensive research on cheese flavour and aroma and a lesser amount on cheese texture, it is still not possible to employ objective, instrumental methods to assess cheese quality. Undoubtably, research in these areas will continue and would appear to be a commercially valuable, although frustrating, area.

Cheese ripening is a slow, unpredictable and expensive operation ranging from periods of approximately 4 weeks up to 2 or more years. Maturation involves proteolysis, lipolysis, glycolysis, as well as secondary changes, by rennet, starter and non-starter micro-organisms. There is increasing interest in accelerating and regulating cheese ripening. The various possible approaches have been reviewed[185,186] and the most promising techniques in the short–medium term appear to be temperature profiling and the use of exogenous enzymes. Starters especially designed by genetic engineering hold long-term prospects. If these techniques prove to be commercially successful, it should be possible to exercise much better quality control programmes in the cheese industry.

Milk Powder

During the last two decades the manufacture of milk powders suitable for a wide range of uses has received considerable attention.[124,187,188] Such powders require defined physical and chemical properties and strict adherence to purchase specifications, which are becoming increasingly stringent,[188,189] makes severe demands on quality control systems. However, it is accepted that modern technology makes it possible to meet these requirements.[188] The properties of spray-dried milk powders and how they relate to processing conditions have been reviewed,[190] while a series of experiments was conducted recently[189] to determine the effects on powder quality of processing variables and regression equations relating various quality parameters to drier operating variables established. The particle size, bulk density, moisture content, solubility index, free fat, scorched particles, reconstitution properties, flow properties, whey protein index and heat stability are among the major parameters of importance in quality control. However, available lysine, hydroxymethylfurfural, protein efficiency ratio and taste panel assessment should also be considered in the quality profile. Seasonality of milk production in Ireland[191] and elsewhere has a major influence on the protein content of milk powder (range 32·4–41·93 %) and this may cause considerable problems if a protein standard is incorporated in specifications for skim milk powders for EEC intervention.

Based on the American Dry Milk Institute (ADMI) Specifications,[192] skim milk powders are classified as low, medium or high heat powders on the basis of undenatured whey protein nitrogen (UWPN). The accuracy and reliability of the ADMI turbidity method have been criticised[193,194] and several workers[191,195,196] have shown that seasonal variations in the amount of total and individual whey proteins in raw milk make it impossible to satisfy ADMI standards at certain times of the year. It is suggested[188,197] that powders should be classified on the basis of the proportion of undenatured whey protein to total protein in the reconstituted milk. It is recommended that a wider range of analyses be performed to ensure that powders possess the properties required, e.g. viscosity, rennetability and heat stability.[188]

FUNCTIONAL DAIRY PROTEINS

An important consideration in a quality control programme for many dairy companies is the determination and control of the functional properties of protein-rich milk products intended for use as functional proteins in a wide range of foods. The functional properties of high-protein milk products and their use as food ingredients have been reviewed.[198–207] General functional properties of proteins important in food process applications are outlined in Table 1. From the quality control viewpoint, the principal problems encountered are how these functional attributes should be assessed and how the results of laboratory assessments relate to the performance of the protein in actual food process applications.

It is evident from the literature[208,209] that the methods used to determine basic functional properties, even in model systems, are not standardised. In extrapolating from a model to a food system, some researchers have used a utility or food test, i.e. an evaluation of a functional property under test conditions that mimics a food preparation in all particulars.[209] The usefulness of this approach may be limited unless the test procedure is closely designed to meet the particular end application; also, the cost of utility tests may be prohibitive. The primary producers of functional milk proteins may not be in a position to evaluate their functionality in other than model systems but the question arises as to the best model system to use. It appears that researchers in the area of functional evaluation have made little or no attempt to follow standard procedures but have employed model systems that suit their particular needs, or more often, to suit the equipment available. Perusal of the range of

TABLE 1
FUNCTIONAL PROPERTIES OF PROTEINS IMPORTANT IN FOOD PROCESS APPLICATION

Colour, flavour, odour, texture, turbidity.
Solubility, dispersibility, water absorption/retention, viscosity, swelling, gelation, syneresis.
Emulsification, fat adsorption, foaming, whipping, stabilisation.
Aggregation, elasticity, cohesion, adhesion, chewiness, texturisability, dough formation, extractability
Compatibility with other food components.

methods used to evaluate the principal functional properties of high-protein milk products will clearly demonstrate the difficulties involved in the evaluation and control of protein functionality.

Solubility

Solubility is a very important functional property of proteins and its determination under a variety of environmental conditions (pH and ionic strength) can give valuable information on the processing history of the product and on its potential value in applications involving foam or emulsion formation, where solubility is a prerequisite.

Several methods used to evaluate the solubility of functional milk proteins are summarised in Table 2. Product concentration used has varied from 0·5 to 5%; solutions have been prepared in water or in buffers, sometimes of unstated concentration or ionic strength, and the methods of dispersion are seldom reported. Some researchers determine solubility at one pH only, while others use a range of pH values; temperatures and holding times are rarely reported and the methods of separation of insoluble protein vary from filtration to centrifugation at forces ranging from 1000 to 65 000 *g* for 5–40 min. Solubility is usually reported as the protein remaining in the filtrate or supernatant, although other methods, e.g. volume of sediment[210] have been used.

Viscosity

The viscosity of a protein solution is highly sensitive to the history of the protein and to the techniques used in its measurement.[220] The rheological characteristics of concentrated skim milk, caseins and caseinates, whey protein concentrates and isolates, and co-precipitates are dependent on concentration, dispersion conditions, including solvent and equilibration time, pH, ionic strength, temperature and shear rate used in the measurement.[211,212,217,221–230] The relationships between these factors and viscosity are complex because of the non-ideal behaviour of the solutions. Processing and compositional factors, e.g. temperature and pH of precipitation, temperature of drying, calcium content and the extent of its replacement by sodium or its sequestration by chelating agents and the presence of reducing agents, also affect viscosity. All these factors should be considered when determining viscosity as a functional property.

Water Absorption

Proteins are capable of binding large amounts of water via hydrogen bonding to polar groups, and this interaction is important to other functional properties such as swelling, hydration, gelation, viscosity and solubility. As water binding varies with the number and type of polar groups and since conformational factors influence the nature and availability of these hydration sites, any environmental factor that affects either polarity or conformation may affect water absorption or hydration.

Many terms are used to describe the uptake of water by functional proteins, the terminology in any particular instance being related to the method of determination. Four principles are usually used to evaluate the uptake of water by proteins:[231] (i) sorption isotherms; (ii) swelling; (iii) water uptake measured as water content of protein precipitate obtained by filtration or centrifugation, under conditions of excess water; and (iv) water saturation of the protein under conditions of limited solvent. These, as well as other methods, have been applied to high-protein milk products.

On equilibration at 84% relative humidity, casein binds ~21·6 g water/16 g nitrogen.[232] In milk powders, water is bound primarily by the casein fraction at low a_w but is also bound to lactose at higher values of a_w.[233] Bound water, measured as that which remains unfrozen at −40 °C, when assayed by differential scanning calorimetry of concentrated aqueous dispersions of whey protein concentrates, containing 65–75% water, varied between 0·5 and 1·2 g water/g solid. Products containing high lactose and salts, e.g. whey powder, have high water binding capacities at high a_w but below $a_w \sim 0{\cdot}7$ water sorption by these products is due primarily to the macromolecular components in the whey and consequently water binding capacity decreases markedly.[234]

Thermal denaturation has little, if any, effect on sorbed water.[234] The 'water absorptive capacity' of dried milk products, measured using a Brabender farinograph, varied from 96 to 128 g water/100 g protein; preheat treatment had no noticeable effect on water absorption.[235] Values for lactic casein varied from 97 to 115, increasing as particle size decreased; sodium caseinate had a very high value of 215, while calcium caseinate and lactalbumin had values of 159 and 96, respectively. Water absorption values for co-precipitates ranged from 111 for insoluble preparations to 345 for soluble samples. Short,[236] also using a Brabender farinograph, found that the water

TABLE 2

METHODS USED TO DETERMINE THE SOLUBILITY OF FUNCTIONAL DAIRY PRODUCTS

Product	*Solution preparation*	*pH and holding time prior to separation*	*Method of separating insoluble material*	*Method of determining and expressing results*	*Reference*
Co-precipitate	8·0 g dispersed in 200 ml H_2O using an Ultra-Turrax mixer for 5 min at 30 °C	Adjusted to pH 7·0 with NaOH. Heated to 80 °C by mixing with Ultra-Turrax (15 min). Cooled to 30 °C.	Centrifugation: 14 000 *g* × 5 min; sediment resuspended in H_2O and re-centrifuged.	Millilitres of sediment (0–14)	210
Casein, ammonium caseinate	5 g/95 g H_2O	—	Centrifugation: 4 500 *g* × 10 min.	Nitrogen (N) in supernatant determined by micro-Kjeldahl (MK). Total solids in supernatant determined by Majonier.	211
Whey protein concentrate (WPC)	0·5–1 % in H_2O	3·2–8·3 × 30 min	Filtration	N in filtrate by MK, also pH 4·6 soluble N.	202
	1 % in buffer (unstated)	2·0, 4·0, 6·0, 8·0	Filtration	N in filtrate by MK.	202
	1 % in phosphate buffer	2·0–9·0	Centrifugation: 1 000 *g* × 10 min.	N in supernatant by MK.	202

WPC	5·0% in H_2O	4·6 with $NaCH_3COO/CH_3COOH$; 40°C × 10 min.	Centrifugation: 15 000 *g* × 40 min.	N in supernatant by MK.	212
WPC	1·0% in H_2O	4·6	Centrifugation: 1 000 *g* × 10 min.	N in supernatant by MK.	213
WPC	50 g/kg H_2O	Neutral	Centrifugation: 2 500–3 000 *g* × 15 min.	N in supernatant as % of total N.	214
WPC	2·0% in H_2O	2·0–12·0 with HCl/NaOH	Centrifugation: 3 150 *g* × 30 min.	N in supernatant by MK.	215
WPC	2·0% dispersed in H_2O using a Virtis 45 mixer for 2 min at 8 500 rpm	2·0–8·0 with HCl/NaOH	Centrifuged in a 50 ml graduated solubility Index tube at 1 200 *g* × 20 min.	N in top 10 ml of supernatant termed N solubility index.	216
Whey protein (WP) isolate or WP hydrolysate	2·0% in H_2O	7·0 × 1 h	Centrifugation: 3 000 rpm × 10 min (centrifuge unspecified).	N in supernatant by MK.	217
WP or WP hydrolysate	2·0% in H_2O	3·0–7·0 with 1 N HCl/NaOH × 1 h	Centrifugation: 3 000 rpm × 15 min (*g* unknown).	N in supernatant by MK.	218
WP isolate	1·0% in H_2O	3·0, 4·5, 8·0 with 1 N HCl/NaOH × 30 min	Centrifugation: 3 000 *g* × 10 min.	N in supernatant by MK.	219

absorption capacity of lactalbumin varied from 88 to 180 g water/100 g protein depending on the surface characteristics of the particles, particularly roughness or porosity. The term 'water affinity' has been used to describe the ability of whey proteins to hold water after being heat-denatured at 85 °C for 5 min;[212] the viscosity of the resulting gel is correlated with 'water affinity'. Swelling characteristics of proteins, as an estimate of water absorption, are strongly dependent on pH and ionic strength.[237] Caseinate, whey protein concentrate and soy protein isolate show different swelling characteristics which may be related to functionality. The water binding properties of milk proteins in model meat systems, i.e. in a utility test, have been found to correlate with the solubility, viscosity and swelling characteristics of the proteins.[238] Replacing some meat protein by either caseinate or whey protein concentrate (WPC) caused a pronounced increase in moisture loss as measured by centrifugation at 40 000 *g* for 30 min. When the meat system was heated to 80 °C, the caseinate showed a higher moisture loss than the WPC due to gelation of the latter.[238] Addition of sodium chloride influences the functional properties and performance of proteins in model systems.[239] The excess (i.e. unabsorbed) water method is not applicable to soluble proteins, since they go into solution, but the water saturation method is reported to be satisfactory and values for the water hydration capacity of 2·33 and 0·97 ml/g of caseinate and whey protein concentrate, respectively, have been obtained with this method.[240]

Gelation

Interaction of proteins to form a matrix or gel capable of immobilising large amounts of water is a very important functionality of proteins in food processing. Gelation is induced either by the action of heat or divalent cations or both and is a physical manifestation of protein denaturation processes which depend on the type and concentration of protein, processing conditions used to induce gelation, pH and ionic environment.[241,242] From the quality control viewpoint, the aspects of interest in regard to functional milk proteins are the conditions of temperature, time, pH and ionic environment required for gel formation and the physical characteristics of the matrix once a gel has formed.

The heat-induced gelation of WPC has been investigated in a

number of model systems. Among the criteria used to describe the gelling capacity of whey protein preparations are: gelation time, as observed visually;[243] the gelation temperature, measured as the temperature at which it is possible to invert a tube containing the protein solution without movement of contents;[214,244] and least coagulable protein concentration, determined by heating the sample in a boiling water bath for 30 min, cooling for 5 min and judging coagulation to be complete if the coagulum is not fluid.[244] Viscosity measurements have also been used to study gelation.[21]

Gelling ability of WPC improves with increasing protein concentration and temperature; however, if heated above a critical temperature, solutions do not gel until cooled.[243,244] Both gelling time and least coagulable protein concentration are influenced by pH; around pH 5, a precipitate rather than a gel is formed and increasing pH increases both gelling time and least coagulable protein concentration[243,244] with a concomitant decrease in gel strength.[245] Methods used to determine the rigidity of heat-induced whey protein and other milk protein gels include visual comparison of gel strength with standard gels,[245] several rheological techniques using penetrometers of unspecified dimensions and shape,[214,246] a curd firmness meter[217] or the Instron Universal testing machine[227,244,245,247] and the scanning electron microscope.[248] The rigidity of gels is influenced by protein concentration, temperature and pH; addition of sodium chloride up to 0·5 M, or calcium chloride up to 30 mM, increases gel strength considerably. Addition of cysteine up to 25 mM increases gel strength by 200 %, but higher levels of cysteine (75 or 100 mM) cause a reduction in strength with virtual destruction of gelation in the presence of 100 mM cysteine.[244]

Emulsification

Functional dairy proteins are widely used as emulsifiers in the food industry.[199–202,249] Two main approaches have been adopted in determining the emulsifying properties of proteins in model systems: (i) measurement of the emulsifying capacity, i.e. the maximum amount of oil emulsified by a protein dispersion before emulsion inversion occurs, i.e. when the emulsion changes from an oil-in-water to a water-in-oil emulsion; and (ii) measurement of the emulsion stability, i.e. the ability of the formed emulsion to remain unchanged over a period.[250] With the former approach, a variety of methods

TABLE 3

METHODS USED TO ASSESS THE EMULSIFYING PROPERTIES OF FUNCTIONAL DAIRY PROTEINS

Protein dispersion	*Oil*	*Emulsion preparation*	*Emulsifying properties reported*	*Reference*
Whey protein concentrate (WPC) in 1·0 M NaCl	Corn oil	Oil added at 0·8 ml s^{-1} to protein dispersion in an Osterizer at 'blend' speed.	Emulsifying capacity (EC): g oil required to produce infinite electrical resistance.	202
Non fat dry-milk (NFDM), 0·2–1·7 g protein/100 ml distilled H_2O; adjusted to pH 3·0–10·0.	Corn oil	Oil added at 0·40–2·0 ml s^{-1} to protein dispersion in a variable speed Waring blender.	EC: ml oil required to reach phase inversion measured by noting the drop in amperage requirements of the blender motor due to the drop in viscosity.	252
Potassium caseinate or NFDM; 4·25 mg protein per 25 ml buffer; pH 5·5–10·4; μ (ionic strength) = 0·55 and 0·3	Soybean oil	Oil added at 0·9 ml s^{-1} while mixing with a 'Lightening' stirrer at 1 750 rpm.	EC: g oil/mg protein at phase inversion as determined by a drop in viscosity. Emulsion stability (ES): time elapsed between formation and breakdown of emulsion.	253
NFDM, 6·7 g in 100 ml 3·5% NaCl	Corn oil	Oil added at 1·0 ml s^{-1} to protein dispersion in a Waring blender at maximum speed. 54 g oil/100 ml dispersion mixed at maximum speed × 3 min.	EC: ml oil/g protein at phase inversion determined by change in amperage to blender motor. ES: emulsion heated at 77 °C × 40 min, centrifuged at 4 300 rpm × 15 min, scored subjectively.	254
Sodium caseinate, 5 g/90 ml 3·3% NaCl	Soybean oil	50 g oil added to protein dispersion, stirred at 1 000 rpm.	ES: emulsion heated to 85 °C × 15 min, cooled and centrifuged in graduated tube at 3 000 rpm × 15 min; determine % oil separated (free fat).	255
Sodium caseinate, 0·1–2·0% in H_2O	Coconut oil	Molten oil (to 4%) added to protein dispersion with agitation in a Waring blender. Mixture homogenised (single state) at 140 kg/cm^2.	ES: % fat in aqueous, lower phase determined by the Gerber method following quiescent storage for 24 h or centrifugation at 2 000 rpm × 15 min.	256

Sodium caseinate, 0–1·0%; NFDM, 0–15% in H_2O	Milk fat	50 g emulsion blend containing 25% fat heated at 62 °C × 15 min; emulsified with an ultrasonic instrument.	ES: emulsion poured into tube of Atlab Emulsion Test Viewer to '100' mark. Creaming read directly at % upper phase separated. $\text{Stability index} = \frac{\text{total solids in bottom half}}{\text{total solids of original sample}} \times 100$	257, 258
Sodium caseinate, WPC; 2·5% protein in H_2O or 0·2 M NaCl, pH 7·0	Soybean oil	Emulsions containing 40% oil prepared using: (a) Sorvall omni-mixer, speeds up to 15 000 rpm; (b) Ultra-Turrax, speeds up to 20 000 rpm; (c) Ultrasonic Sonifer cell disruptor horn operating at 20 kHz; (d) Single Piston Valve Homogeniser.	$\text{Stability rating} = \frac{\text{\% fat in test solution}}{\text{\% fat in original emulsion}} \times 100(\%)$ Bottom 5 ml of aqueous phase on storage of emulsion for 24 h at 20 °C or centrifugation at 180 g × 15 min.	251, 259, 260
WPC, 1·5% protein in H_2O	Vegetable oil	Oil (to 40%) added to stirred protein solution; mixture homogenised 4 times using a single piston homogeniser at a pressure of 6·9 MPa and at a rate of 9 litre/h.	$\text{Stability index (SI)} = \frac{\text{\% fat in top 2 ml of emulsion}}{\text{\% fat in bottom 2 ml of emulsion}}$ After overnight storage at 4 °C or centrifugation at 180 g × 15 min.	261
Whey protein, 1·0–8·0% (W/w) in H_2O, pH 3·0–9·0 containing 0–600 mM NaCl	Coconut oil	Emulsions containing 10, 20 and 40% oil prepared with a Polytron PT20 at 19 500 rpm for 8 min.	$\text{Stability rating } (SR_1) = \frac{F_1}{F_0 \times 100}$ $(SR_2) = \frac{F_2}{F_0 \times 100}$ F_0 = % total fat in emulsion, F_1 = % fat in bottom 3 ml of emulsion after storage for 1 day at 20 °C F_2 = % fat in bottom 3 ml of emulsion after centrifugation at 180 g × 10 min.	262

TABLE 4

METHODS USED TO ASSESS THE FOAMING PROPERTIES OF FUNCTIONAL DAIRY PROTEINS

Protein dispersion	*Preparation of foam*	*Foam capacity*	*Foam stability*	*Reference*
10·0 g WPC + 5 g egg white solids in 100 ml H_2O.	Whip at high speed in a Hamilton Beach Mixer.	% overrun (O/R) $= \frac{\text{wt of certain volume mix} - \text{wt same volume whipped mix}}{\text{wt same volume whipped mix}} \times 100$	Drip volume after 1 h from foam placed in Buchner funnel.	202
WPC, 5·0–35·0%, total solids (TS) pH: 5·0–8·0; fat: 1·0–3·0%.	Whip for 10 min at top speed in a Hamilton Beach Mixer.	% O/R $= \frac{\text{wt of a volume of liquid}}{\text{wt same volume of foam}}$	Time for first drop of fluid to drip from foam placed in a Buchner funnel.	212
WPC, 4% w/w protein in H_2O	Whip for 90 s at speed 2 in a Habort Mixer and at speed 3 until end-point.	% O/R $= \frac{\text{wt of certain volume of liquid} - \text{wt same volume of foam}}{\text{wt same volume of foam}} \times 100$	Time for leakage of first drop of liquid from foam in a glass funnel.	213
WPC, 100 g protein/kg solution in H_2O; pH: 6·0, 8·5	Whip for 6 min at full speed in a Kenwood Chef Mixer.	% O/R $= \frac{\text{whip volume} - \text{initial volume}}{\text{initial volume}} \times 100$	Time required for first drop to fall from whip in a 1 mm mesh funnel.	214
WPC, 100 g protein/kg solution in H_2O; pH: 6·0, 8·5	200 ml air injected through a sintered glass disc into 100 ml solution in 2 min.	Foaming power $= \frac{\text{volume retained air}}{\text{volume injected air}}$		214
Whey protein isolate (WPI), 11% protein in H_2O.	Whip for 5 min at full speed in a Kenwood Chef Mixer.	Specific foam volume, ml/g $= \frac{\text{volume of foam}}{\text{wt foam}}$	Volume drained from foam in 30 min through a 1 mm nylon mesh.	219
WPC, 10% (w/v) in H_2O; natural pH.	Whip for 15 min at full speed in a Kenwood Chef Mixer.	% O/R $= \frac{\text{volume whip} - \text{volume liquid mix}}{\text{volume liquid mix}} \times 100$	Stability at time $x = \frac{V_F - V_X}{V_F} \times 100$ V_F = liquid volume following whip collapse and V_X = liquid volume drained from whip in a standard Imhoff cone at time X.	227

WPI, 5% in H_2O; pH: 9·0	Whip for 20 min at full speed in a Hamilton Beach Mixer.	Foam volume/foam wt, ml/g	Drainage volume through a wire screen at time intervals.	244
WP or WP hydrolysate, casein; 4% protein in H_2O; pH: 6·5, 8·5.	Whip in a Kitchen Aid Mixer.	Specific volume, ml/g	Time to collect liquid = half wt of foam following inversion of foam on 12·5 mm mesh screen.	265
WPC, 30% total solids in H_2O; pH: 3·5–7·3	Whip for 10 min at top speed in a Hamilton Beach Mixer.	$\% \text{ O/R} = \frac{\text{wt volume of liquid}}{\text{wt equal volume of foam}}$	Leakage time, taken as the time for appearance of one drop of liquid drainage from a standard wt of foam.	266
Sodium caseinate, WP, 1% (w/w) protein in H_2O; pH: 7·0	(1) Stirring method: solution stirred for 1 min with a rotating blade homogeniser at 10 000 rpm. (2) Bubbling method: nitrogen gas bubbled through solution at 15 ml/min for 3 min. (3) Shaking method: 25 ml solution stirred for 1 min in a 50 ml graduated cylinder using a 'swing arm agitator'.	1 and 2: foaming power = $100(L+G/L-1)$ where $L+G$ = foam volume, L = volume of liquid phase of foam. 3: foam volume.		267

have been used to determine the inversion point and with the latter, oil separation and creaming are among the indices of stability applied.[251] One of the major problems encountered in studies on emulsifying properties is the effect of the method of emulsion preparation on its properties; such factors as protein concentration, pH, ionic strength and equipment used in emulsion preparation all have a major influence on the properties of emulsions.[251] Despite the influence of these factors it can be seen from Table 3 that in studies on the emulsifying properties of dairy proteins, conditions for protein dispersion preparation, oil used and method for emulsion formation have varied widely as have the methods of determining inversion point in studies of emulsifying capacity and the methods for determining and reporting emulsion stability.

Whippability/Foamability

Foams are formed by the dispersion of a gas in a liquid and the envelopment of the gas cells by surface-active agents which cause entrapment of the gas in the liquid phase. Foams are important in many foods, e.g. whipped toppings and creams, meringues, souffles, mousses, ice-cream, etc. Proteins are the most useful surface-active agents for use in foods where stable foams are required. Two approaches have been used in studies on the foaming characteristics of proteins in model systems: (i) bubbling air through the protein solution, and (ii) incorporating air into the protein solution by mechanical agitation. With both techniques the object is to measure (i) the ability of the protein solution to form a foam, usually termed 'Foaming Capacity' and (ii) once the foam has been formed, to determine its stability over time, termed 'Foam Stability'.

The assay conditions used are critical, as are factors such as protein concentration, pH, temperature, ionic strength and presence of sugars and lipids, known to influence foaming properties.[198,200,214,263,264] Any processing conditions that cause protein denaturation and/or leave residual (milk) lipid in the protein preparation may also influence foaming. Different equipment has been used to prepare foams and in many cases little attention has been paid to factors known to influence foaming (Table 4). Various 'units' have been used to describe both 'Foaming Capacity' and 'Foam Stability'.

REFERENCES

1. Porter, J. W. G. (1980). Doc. 125, IDF, Brussels, 14–21.
2. Johnson, A. H. (1974). In: *Fundamentals of Dairy Chemistry*. 2nd edition, Eds. Webb, B. H., Johnson, A. H. and Alford, J. A., AVI Publishing Co. Inc., Westport, Conn., 1–57.
3. Larson, B. L. and Smith, V. R. (1974). *Lactation. A comprehensive Treatise*, Vol. 1, Academic Press, New York.
4. International Dairy Federation (1980). Doc. 125, IDF, Brussels.
5. McGann, T. C. A. and O'Connell, J. A. (1971). *Dairy Research Series* (3), An Foras Taluntais, Dublin, Republic of Ireland.
6. Franke, A. A., Dunkley, W. L. and Smith, N. E. (1977). *J. Dairy Sci.*, **60**, 1870–4.
7. Harding, F. and Morris, J. L. (1973). *J. Soc. Dairy Technol.*, **26**, 91–3.
8. Chambers, B. G. and Foley, J. (1968). *Ir. J. Agric. Res.*, **7**, 209–15.
9. Tarassuk, N. P., Abe, N. and Moats, W. A. (1967). *The Dye Binding of Milk Proteins*, Technical Bulletin No. 1369, United States Department of Agriculture, Washington, DC.
10. International Dairy Federation (1964). International Standard IDF 29, Brussels.
11. Self, R. (1979). *Biomed. Mass Spect.*, **6**, 261–373.
12. International Dairy Federation (1979). Doc. 113, IDF, Brussels.
13. International Dairy Federation (1978). Doc. 105, IDF, Brussels.
14. Hubbard, A. W. (1978). *Nutr. Rev.*, **36**, 224–30.
15. Smith, G. J. and Dunkley, W. J. (1960). *J. Dairy Sci.*, **43**, 278–80.
16. Select Committee on Nutrition and Human Needs (1977). *Dietary Goals for the United States*, United States Government Printing Office, Washington, DC.
17. Meneely, G. R. and Battarbee, H. D. (1976). *Am. J. Cardiol.*, **38**, 768–85.
18. Gauthier, B., Freeman, R. and Beveridge, J. (1969). *Aust. Paediatr. J.*, **5**, 101–5.
19. Dunsmore, D. G. (1976). *Aust. J. Dairy Technol.*, **31**, 125–8.
20. Hemken, R. W. (1980). *J. Am. Vet. Med. Assoc.*, **176**, 1119–21.
21. Bruns, R. J. and Tullock, D. N. (1982). *Aust. J. Dairy Technol.*, **37**, 115–17.
22. Stoloff, L. (1980). *J. Food Prot.*, **43**, 226–30.
23. Applebaum, R. S., Brackett, R. E., Wiseman, D. W. and Marth, E. H. (1982). *J. Food Prot.*, **45**, 752–77.
24. Stoloff, L., Trucksess, M., Harelin, N., Francis, O. J., Hayes, J. R., Polan, C. E. and Campbell, T. C. (1975). *J. Dairy Sci.*, **58**, 1789–93.
25. Brackett, R. E. and Marth, E. H. (1982). *J. Food Prot.*, **45**, 597–600.
26. Ohmono, S., Sato, T., Utagawa, T. and Abe, M. (1975). *Agric. Biol. Chem.*, **39**, 1133–4.
27. Scott, P. M., Merrien, M. A. and Polonsky, J. (1976). *Experimentia*, **32**, 140–2.

28. WEI, R. D., SCHNOES, H. K., HART, P. A. and STRONG, F. M. (1975). *Tetrahedron*, **31**, 109–14.
29. WARE, G. M., THORPE, C. W. and POHLAND, A. E. (1980). *J.A.O.A.C.*, **63**, 637–41.
30. SCANLAN, R. A. (1975). *CRC Crit. Revs. Food Technol.*, **5**, 357–402.
31. CROSBY, N. T. and SAWYER, R. (1976). *Adv. Food Res.*, **22**, 1–71.
32. NEWBERNE, P. M. (1979). *Science*, **204**, 1079–81.
33. GRAY, J. I., IRVINE, D. M. and KAKUDA, Y. (1979). *J. Food Prot.*, **42**, 263–72.
34. SEN, N. P., DONALDSON, B. A., SEAMAN, S., IYENGAN, J. R. and MILES, W. F. (1977). Paper presented at the Symposium on Nitrosamines in Cheese, Ottawa, Canada.
35. COGAN, T. M. (1977). *Ir. J. Food Sci. & Technol.*, **1**, 95–105.
36. LAW, B. A. (1979). *J. Dairy Res.*, **46**, 573–88.
37. COUSINS, M. A. (1982). *J. Food Prot.*, **45**, 172–207.
38. VISSER, S. (1981). *Neth. Milk & Dairy J.*, **35**, 65–88.
39. FOX, P. F. (1981). *Neth. Milk & Dairy J.*, **35**, 233–53.
40. SUHREN, G. (1981). F-Doc. 85, IDF, Brussels, 1–8.
41. SCHIPPER, C. J. (1975). Doc. 86, IDF, Brussels, 113–15.
42. BJÖRCK, L. (1978). *J. Dairy Res.*, **45**, 109–18.
43. FOX, P. F. and MORRISSEY, P. A. (1981). In: *Enzymes and Food Processing*, Eds. Birch, G. G., Blakeborough, N. and Parker, K. J., Applied Science Publishers Ltd, London, 213–32.
44. FOX, P. F. and TARASSUK, N. P. (1968). *J. Dairy Sci.*, **51**, 826–33.
45. KORN, E. D. (1962). *J. Lipid Res.*, **3**, 246–50.
46. EGELRUD, T. and OLIVECRONA, T. (1972). *J. Biol. Chem.*, **247**, 6212–17.
47. FLYNN, A. and FOX, P. F. (1980). *Ir. J. Food Sci. & Technol.*, **4**, 173–6.
48. DEETH, H. C. and FITZ-GERALD, C. H. (1983). In: *Developments in Dairy Chemistry—2: Lipids*, Ed. Fox, P. F., Applied Science Publishers Ltd, London (in press).
49. CONNOLLY, J. F., MURPHY, J. J., O'CONNOR, C. B. and HEADON, D. R. (1979). *Ir. J. Food Sci. & Technol.*, **3**, 79–92.
50. KUZDZAL-SAVOIR, S. (1980). Doc. 118, IDF, Brussels, 53–66.
51. SCANLAN, R. A., SATHER, L. A. and DAY, E. A. (1965). *J. Dairy Sci.*, **48**, 1582–4.
52. FOX, P. F. (1982). In: *Use of Enzymes in Food Technology*, Ed. Dupuy, P., Lavoisur Publishers, Paris, 135–57.
53. JUDGE, F. J., FLEMING, M. G., O'SHEA, J. and RAFTERY, T. F. (1977). *Ir. J. Agric. Res.*, **16**, 115–22.
54. KELLEY, L. A. and DUNKLEY, W. L. (1954). *J. Milk Food Technol.*, **17**, 306–12, 319.
55. MEIN, G. A., HICKEY, M. W. and BROWN, M. R. (1974). *19th Int. Dairy Congr.*, **1E**, 18–19.
56. JELLEMA, A. and SCHIPPER, C. J. (1975). Doc. 86, IDF, Brussels, 138–40.
57. WORSTORFF, H. (1975). Doc. 86, IDF, Brussels, 156–61.
58. FLEMING, M. G. (1979). *Ir. J. Food Sci. & Technol.*, **3**, 111–29.
59. ANDERSON, M. (1983). *J. Soc. Dairy Technol.*, **36**, 3–7.
60. TARASSUK, N. P. and FRANKEL, F. N. (1957). *J. Dairy Sci.*, **40**, 418–30.

61. Olivecrona, T. (1980). Doc. 118, IDF, Brussels, 19–25.
62. Downey, W. K. and Cogan, T. M. (1975). Doc. 86, IDF, Brussels.
63. Downey, W. K. (1980). Doc. 118, IDF, Brussels, 4–18.
64. Deeth, H. G., Fitz-Gerald, C. H. and Wood, A. F. (1979). *Aust. J. Dairy Technol.*, **34**, 146–9.
65. Woo, A. H. and Lindsay, R. C. (1980). *J. Dairy Sci.*, **63**, 1058–64.
66. Humbert, G. and Alais, C. (1979). *J. Dairy Res.*, **46**, 559–611.
67. Reimerdes, E. H. (1982). In: *Developments in Dairy Chemistry—1: Proteins*, Ed. Fox, P. F., Applied Science Publishers Ltd, London, 271–88.
68. De Koning, P. J. and Kaper, J. (1981). *Neth. Milk & Dairy J.*, **35**, 323–7.
69. Richardson, B. C. and Pearce, K. N. (1981). *N.Z.J. Dairy Sci. & Technol.*, **16**, 209–20.
70. Allen, J. C. and Humphries, C. (1977). *J. Dairy Res.*, **44**, 495–507.
71. Wilkinson, R. A. (1964). *Theories of the Mechanisms of Oxidized Flavour in Dairy Products*, Internal Report No. 4, Division of Dairy Research, CSIRO, Melbourne, Australia.
72. Downey, W. K. (1968). *J. Dairy Res.*, **35**, 429–38.
73. Pyle, J. R. (1975). In: *Winter School of Dairying*, Eds. Baker, B. C., Muller, L. L. and Griffin, A. T., Australian Society of Dairy Technology, Melbourne, 59–65.
74. Schultz, H. W., Day, E. A. and Sinnhuber, R. O. (1962). *Symposium on Foods: Lipids and their Oxidation*, AVI Publishing Co. Inc., Westport, Conn.
75. Lundberg, W. O. (1961). *Autoxidation and Antioxidants*, Interscience, New York.
76. Simic, M. G. and Karel, M. (1980). *Autoxidation in Food and Biological Systems*, Plenum Press, London.
77. Downey, W. K. (1969). *J. Soc. Dairy Technol.*, **22**, 154–62.
78. Richardson, T. and Korycka-Dahl, M. (1983). In: *Developments in Dairy Chemistry—2: Lipids*, Ed. Fox, P. F., Applied Science Publishers Ltd, London (in press).
79. Day, E. A. (1965). *Food Technol.*, **19**, 1585–90.
80. Foley, J., O'Donovan, D. and Cooney, C. M. (1971). *J. Soc. Dairy Technol.*, **24**, 38–45.
81. Downey, W. K. (1975). *Dairy Research and Review Series*, No. 7, An Foras Taluntais, Dublin, Republic of Ireland.
82. Parodi, P. W. (1963). *Aust. J. Dairy Technol.*, **18**, 25–8.
83. Wiley, W. J. (1939). *J. Dairy Res.*, **10**, 300–9.
84. McDowell, A. K. R. (1955). *J. Dairy Res.*, **22**, 349–64.
85. Aurand, L. W., Chu, T. M., Singleton, T. A. and Shen, R. (1967). *J. Dairy Sci.*, **50**, 465–71.
86. Hicks, C. L. (1980). *J. Dairy Sci.*, **63**, 1199–210.
87. Gray, J. I. (1978). *J. Amer. Oil. Chem. Soc.*, **55**, 539–46.
88. Angelo, J. A. St., Legendre, M. G. and Dupuy, H. P. (1980). In: *Autoxidation in Food and Biological Systems*, Eds. Simic, M. G. and Karel, M., Plenum Press, London, 171–83.

89. King, R. L. (1962). *J. Dairy Sci.*, **45**, 1165–71.
90. Hill, G. L. and Thiel, C. C. (1946). *J. Dairy Res.*, **14**, 340–53.
91. Holloway, G. L. (1966). *Aust. J. Dairy Technol.*, **21**, 74–6.
92. Kwon, T. W. and Menzel, D. B. (1965). *J. Food Sci.*, **30**, 808–13.
93. Buttery, R. G. and Teranishi, R. (1961). *Anal. Chem.*, **33**, 1439–41.
94. Dupuy, H. P., Brown, M. L., Legendre, M. G., Wadsworth, J. I. and Rayner, E. T. (1978). In: *Lipids as a Source of Flavour*, Ed. Supran, M. K., American Chemical Society Symposium Series, American Chemical Society, Washington, DC, **75**, 60–7.
95. Dupuy, H. P., Fore, S. P. and Goldblatt, L. A. (1971). *J. Amer. Oil Chem. Soc.*, **48**, 876.
96. Dupuy, H. P., Rayner, E. T. and Wadsworth, J. I. (1976). *J. Amer. Oil Chem. Soc.*, **53**, 628–31.
97. Dupuy, H. P., Rayner, E. T., Wadsworth, J. I. and Legendre, M. G. (1977). *J. Amer. Oil Chem. Soc.*, **54**, 445–9.
98. Touhy, J. J. and Barrett, L. (1982). *Ir. J. Food Sci. & Technol.* (Abstract), **6**, 191.
99. Mauron, J. (1981). In: *Progress in Food and Nutrition Science. Maillard Reactions in Food*, Vol. 5, Ed. Eriksson, C., Pergamon Press, Oxford, 5–35.
100. Patton, S. (1955). *J. Dairy Sci.*, **38**, 457–78.
101. Eriksson, C. (Ed.) (1981). *Progress in Food and Nutrition Science. Maillard Reactions in Food*, Pergamon Press, Oxford.
102. Finot, P. A., Deutsch, R. and Bujard, E. (1981). In: *Progress in Food and Nutrition Science. Maillard Reactions in Food.* 5, Ed. Eriksson, C., Pergamon Press, Oxford, 345–55.
103. Hurrell, R. F. and Carpenter, K. J. (1974). *Br. J. Nutr.*, **32**, 589–604.
104. Abrahamsson, L., Bengtsson, O., Hambraeus, L. and Holm, H. (1979). *J. Food Technol.*, **14**, 429–40.
105. Luquet, F. M., Mouillet, L., Boudier, J. F. and Vincent, J. P. (1982). Doc. 142, IDF, Brussels, 154–5.
106. Masters, P. M. and Friedman, M. (1979). *J. Agric. Food Chem.*, **27**, 507–11.
107. Friedman, M., Zahnley, J. C. and Masters, P. M. (1981). *J. Food Sci.*, **46**, 127–31, 134.
108. Sternberg, M., Kim, C. Y. and Schwendi, F. J. (1975). *Science*, **190**, 992–4.
109. Dworschak, E. (1980). *CRC Crit. Rev. Food Sci. Nutr.*, **13**, 1–40.
110. Finot, P. A. (1983). *Nutr. Abstr. and Rev.*, **53**, 67–80.
111. De Koning, P. J. and van Rooijen, P. J. (1982). *J. Dairy Res.*, **49**, 725–36.
112. Fox, P. F. and Morrissey, P. A. (1977). *J. Dairy Res.*, **44**, 627–46.
113. Fox, P. F. (1982). In: *Developments in Dairy Chemistry—1: Proteins*, Ed. Fox, P. F., Applied Science Publishers Ltd, London, 189–228.
114. Kelly, P. M. (1982). *J. Dairy Res.*, **49**, 187–96.
115. Newstead, D. F. (1977). *N.Z.J. Dairy Sci. & Tech. 50th Jubilee Conference*, Special Issue, 89–93.

116. SWEETSUR, A. W. M. and MUIR, D. D. (1980). *J. Soc. Dairy Technol.*, **33**, 101–5.
117. HOLT, C., MUIR, D. D. and SWEETSUR, A. W. M. (1978). *J. Dairy Res.*, **45**, 183–90.
118. MUIR, D. D. and SWEETSUR, A. W. M. (1977). *J. Dairy Res.*, **44**, 249–57.
119. MUIR, D. D. and SWEETSUR, A. W. M. (1978). *J. Dairy Res.*, **45**, 37–45.
120. KELLY, P. M. (1982). *Effect of Seasonal and Process Changes on the Heat Stability of Skim Milk Powders*, National University of Ireland, Dublin.
121. MUIR, D. D., SWEETSUR, A. W. M. and HOLT, C. (1979). *J. Dairy Res.*, **46**, 381–4.
122. SHALABI, S. I. and FOX, P. F. (1982). *J. Dairy Res.*, **49**, 197–207.
123. KUDO, S. (1980). *N.Z.J. Dairy Sci. & Technol.*, **15**, 197–200.
124. INTERNATIONAL DAIRY FEDERATION (1982). Doc. 142, IDF, Brussels.
125. SCOTT, W. J. (1957). *Adv. Food Sci.*, **7**, 83–127.
126. LABUZA, T. P. (1968). *Food Technol.*, **22**, 263–72.
127. LABUZA, T. P. (1971). In: *Proc. 3rd Int. Congr. Food Sci. and Technol.*, Institute of Food Technologists, Chicago, 618–35.
128. LABUZA, T. P. (1975). In: *Water Relations of Foods*, Ed. Duckworth, R. B., Academic Press, London, 22–38.
129. ROCKLAND, L. B. and STEWART, G. F. (1981). *Water activity: Influences on Food Quality*, Academic Press, London.
130. FENNEMA, O. R. In: *Principles of Food Science. Part 1. Food Chemistry*, Ed. Fennema, O.R., Marcel Dekker Inc., New York, 13–39.
131. LABUZA, T. P., MCNALLY, L., GALLAGHER, D., HAWKES, J. and HURTADO, F. (1972). *J. Food Sci.*, **37**, 154–9.
132. SALWIN, H. (1959). *Food Technol.*, **13**, 594–5.
133. LABUZA, T. P., TANNENBAUM, S. R. and KAREL, M. (1970). *Food Technol.*, **24**, 543–50.
134. BRUNNANER, S., EMMET, P. H. and TELLER, E. (1938). *J. Amer. Chem. Soc.*, **60**, 309–19.
135. TROLLER, J. A. (1979). *Food Technol.*, **33**, 72–5.
136. BROWN, A. D. (1976). *Bact. Rev.*, **40**, 803–46.
137. RÜEGG, M., GLÄTTLI, H. and BLANC, B. (1978). *20th Int. Dairy Congr.*, **E**, 593–4.
138. ACKER, L. W. (1969). *Food Technol.*, **23**, 1257–70.
139. LONCIN, M., BIMBENET, J. J. and LENGES, J. (1968). *J. Food Technol.*, **3**, 131–42.
140. SCHWIMMER, S. (1980). *Food Technol.*, **34** , 64–74, 82.
141. RÜEGG, M. and BLANC, B. (1981). In: *Water Activity: Influence on Food Quality*, Eds. Rockland, L. B. and Stewart, G. F., Academic Press, London, 791–811.
142. FOX, P. F. and WALLEY, B. F. (1971). *J. Dairy Res.*, **38**, 165–70.
143. NOOMEN, A. (1978). *Neth. Milk & Dairy J.*, **32**, 26–48.
144. EICHNER, K. and KAREL, M. (1972). *J. Agric. Food Chem.*, **20**, 218–23.
145. KARMAS, E. (1980). *Food Technol.*, **34**, 52–9.

146. DE MOOR, H. and HENDRICKX, H. (1970). *18th Int. Dairy Congr.*, **1E**, 436.
147. THOMASOW, V. J., MROWETZ, G. and DELFS, E. M. (1972). *Milchwissenschaft*, **27**, 76–81.
148. AAS, G. (1966). Doc. 73, IDF, Brussels.
149. DELLA-MONICA, E. S. and HOLDEN, T. E. (1968). *J. Dairy Sci.*, **51**, 40–3.
150. HENDRICKX, H., DE MOOR, H. and DE CORDIER, J. (1969). Cited in *Dairy Sci. Abstracts*, **31**, 462.
151. WALLEY, B., O'CONNOR, C. B. and NAGLE, M. (1977). *Irish Agric. & Creamery Rev.*, **30**, 11–12.
152. BOON, P. M. and WOODHAMS, D. J. (1974). *N.Z.J. Dairy Sci. & Technol.*, **9**, 151–5.
153. RICHARDS, E. (1982). *J. Soc. Dairy Technol.*, **35**, 149–53.
154. DEMAN, J. M. and POULSEN, N. (1968). *Milchwissenschaft*, **23**, 463–7.
155. MCDOWELL, A. K. R. and CREAMER, L. K. (1970). *N.Z.J. Dairy Sci. & Technol.*, **5**, 14–20.
156. NORRIS, G. E., GRAY, I. K. and DOLBY, R. M. (1973). *J. Dairy Res.*, **40**, 311–21.
157. FOLEY, J. (1978). *J. Soc. Dairy Technol.*, **31**, 21–7.
158. CULLINANE, N. and EASON, D. (1981). *Farm and Food Res.*, **12**, 7–9.
159. RUSSEL, R. W. (1970). *18th Int. Dairy Congr.*, **1E**, 204.
160. GRAY, I. K. (1973). *J. Dairy Res.*, **40**, 207–14.
161. HALL, A. J. (1970). *Dairy Ind.*, **35**, 20–3, 24.
162. RICHARDSON, T. and MCGANN, T. C. A. (1964). *Ir. J. Agric. Res.*, **3**, 151–7.
163. DEMAN, J. M. and WOOD, F. W. (1959). *J. Dairy Res.*, **26**, 17–23.
164. SCOTT, T. W., COOK, J. L., FERGUSON, K. A., MCDONALD, I. W., BUCHANAN, R. A. and HILLS, G. L. (1970). *Aust. J. Sci.*, **32**, 291–3.
165. TAYLOR, M. W. and NORRIS, R. (1975). *N.Z.J. Dairy Sci. & Technol.*, **12**, 166–70.
166. WOOD, F. W., MURPHY, M. F. and DUNKLEY, W. L. (1975). *J. Dairy Sci.*, **58**, 839–45.
167. MORTENSEN, B. K. (1983). In: *Developments in Dairy Chemistry—2: Lipids*, Ed. Fox, P. F., Applied Science Publishers Ltd, London (in press).
168. BRADY, J. P., BUCKLEY, J. and FOLEY, J. (1978). *J. Food Technol.*, **13**, 469–75.
169. KLEPACKI, J. (1978). *20th International Dairy Congress*, **E**, 407–8.
170. DIXON, B. D. and PARELCH, J. V. (1979). *J. Text Studies*, **10**, 421–34.
171. BOARD, P. W., AICKEN, K. and KUSKIS, A. (1980). *J. Food Technol.*, **14**, 277–83.
172. INTERNATIONAL DAIRY FEDERATION (1981). Doc. 135, IDF, Brussels, 1–11.
173. DEUTSCHE INDUSTRIENORM, 10331, 1977.
174. INTERNATIONAL DAIRY FEDERATION (1981). Doc. 141, Brussels.
175. NISHIMORI, K., KAWAGUCHI, Y., HIDAKA, M., UOCUMI, T. and BEPPU, T. (1981). *J. Biochem.*, **90**, 901–4.
176. NELSON, J. H. (1975). *J. Dairy Sci.*, **58**, 1739–50.

177. STERNBERG, M. (1976). *Adv. Appl. Microbiol.*, **20**, 135–57.
178. GREEN, M. L. (1977). *J. Dairy Res.*, **44**, 159–88.
179. LELIEVRE, J. and GILLES, J. (1982). *N.Z.J. Dairy Sci. & Technol.*, **17**, 69–75.
180. THOMAS, T. D. and PEARCE, K. N. (1981). *N.Z.J. Dairy Sci. & Technol.*, **16**, 253–9.
181. FOX, P. F. (1974). *Ir. J. Agric. Res.*, **13**, 129–35.
182. GODINHO, M. and FOX, P. F. (1981). *Milchwissenschaft*, **36**, 476–8.
183. GODINHO, M. and FOX, P. F. (1982). *Milchwissenschaft*, **37**, 72–5.
184. MOCQUOT, G. (1979). *J. Dairy Res.*, **46**, 133–60.
185. LAW, B. A. (1978). Doc. 108, IDF, Brussels, 40–5.
186. INTERNATIONAL DAIRY FEDERATION (1982). F-Doc. 86, IDF, Brussels.
187. INTERNATIONAL DAIRY FEDERATION (1979). Doc. 116, IDF, Brussels.
188. JENSEN, G. K. and NIELSEN, P. (1982). *J. Dairy Res.*, **49**, 515–44.
189. BLOORE, C. G. and BOAG, I. F. (1982). *N.Z.J. Dairy Sci. & Technol.*, **17**, 103–20.
190. WOODHAMS, D. J. and MURRAY, M. J. (1974). *N.Z.J. Dairy Sci. & Technol.*, **9**, 172–8.
191. WALLEY, B. and O'CONNOR, C. B. (1980). *Farm and Food Res.*, **11**, 82–3.
192. AMERICAN DRY MILK INSTITUTE INC. (1971). *Standards for the Dry Milk Industry including Methods of Analysis*, Bulletin No. 916, ADMI, Chicago.
193. SANDERSON, W. B. (1970). *N.Z.J. Dairy Sci. & Technol.*, **5**, 46–8.
194. O'SULLIVAN, A. C. and O'CONNOR, F. (1971). *Dairy Ind.*, **36**, 340–4.
195. DELLA-MONICA, E. S., HOLDEN, T. F., CALHOUN, M. J. and ACETO, N. C. (1965). *J. Dairy Sci.*, **48**, 1585–90.
196. SANDERSON, W. B. (1970). *N.J.Z. Dairy Sci. & Technol.*, **5**, 48–52.
197. MCGANN, T. C. A., O'CONNELL, J. A. and MCFELLY, R. (1975). *J. Soc. Dairy Technol.*, **28**, 23–7.
198. MORR, C. V. (1976). *Food Technol.*, **30**, 18–22, 42.
199. MORR, C. V. (1979). *N.Z.J. Dairy Sci. & Technol.*, **14**, 185–94.
200. MORR, C. V. (1979). *J. Dairy Res.*, **46**, 369–76.
201. MORR, C. V. (1982). In: *Developments in Dairy Chemistry—1: Proteins*, Ed. Fox, P. F., Applied Science Publishers Ltd, London, 375—99.
202. MORR, C. V., SWANSON, P. E. and RICHERT, R. L. (1973). *Science*, **38**, 324–30.
203. MULLER, L. L. (1982). In: *Developments in Dairy Chemistry—1: Proteins*, Ed. Fox, P. F., Applied Science Publishers Ltd, London, 315–37.
204. BURGESS, K. J. and COTON, G. (1982). In: *Food Proteins*, Eds. Fox, P. F. and Condon, J. J., Applied Science Publishers Ltd, London, 211–24.
205. EVANS, E. W. (1982). In: *Developments in Food Proteins—1*, Ed. Hudson, B. J. F., Applied Science Publishers Ltd, London, 131–69.
206. FOX, P. F. and MULVIHILL, D. M. (1982). *J. Dairy Res.*, **49**, 679–93.

207. Fox, P. F., Morrissey, P. A. and Mulvihill, D. M. (1982). In: *Developments in Food Proteins—1*, Ed. Hudson, B. J. F., Applied Science Publishers Ltd, London, 1–60.
208. Kinsella, J. E. (1982). In: *Food Proteins*, Eds Fox, P. F. and Condon, J. J., Applied Science Publishers Ltd, London, 51–103.
209. Pour-El, A. (1981). In: *Protein Functionality in Foods*, Ed. Cherry, J. P., American Chemical Society Symposium Series, No. 147, American Chemical Society, Washington, DC, 1–19.
210. Hayes, J. F., Dunkerley, J. and Muller, L. L. (1969). *Aust. J. Dairy Technol.*, **24**, 69–74.
211. Girdhar, B. K. and Hansen, P. M. T. (1974). *J. Food Sci.*, **39**, 1237–43.
212. McDonough, F. E., Hargrove, R. E., Mattingly, W. A., Posati, L. P. and Alford, J. A. (1974). *J. Dairy Sci.*, **57**, 1438–43.
213. Richert, S. H., Morr, C. V. and Cooney, C. M. (1974). *J. Food Sci.*, **39**, 42–8.
214. Haggett, T. O. R. (1976). *N.Z.J. Dairy Sci. & Technol.*, **11**, 244–50.
215. Hidalgo, J. and Gamper, E. (1977). *J. Dairy Sci.*, **60**, 1515–18.
216. Jost, R. and Monti, J. C. (1977). *J. Dairy Sci.*, **60**, 1387–93.
217. Molder, H. W. and Emmons, D. B. (1977). *J. Dairy Sci.*, **60**, 177–84.
218. Monti, J. C. and Jost, R. (1978). *J. Dairy Sci.*, **61**, 1233–7.
219. Burgess, K. J. and Kelly, J. (1979). *J. Food Technol.*, **14**, 325–9.
220. Shen, J. L. (1981). In: *Protein Functionality in Foods*, Ed. Cherry, J. P., American Chemical Society Symposium Series, No. 147, American Chemical Society, Washington, DC, 89–109.
221. Towler, C. (1974). *N.Z.J. Dairy Sci. & Technol.*, **9**, 155–60.
222. Hayes, J. F. and Muller, L. L. (1961). *Aust. J. Dairy Technol.*, **16**, 265–9.
223. Hayes, J. F., Southby, P. M. and Muller, L. L. (1968). *J. Dairy Res.*, **35**, 31–47.
224. Roeper, J. (1977). *N.Z.J. Dairy Dairy Sci. & Technol.*, **12**, 182–9.
225. Towler, C. (1976). *N.Z.J. Dairy Sci. & Technol.*, **11**, 140–1.
226. Towler, C., Creamer, L. K. and Southward, C. R. (1981).*N.Z.J. Dairy Sci. & Technol.*, **16**, 155–165.
227. Johns, J. E. M. and Ennis, B. M. (1981). *N.Z.J. Dairy Sci. & Technol.*, **15**, 79–86.
228. Hayes, J. F., Muller, L. L. and Frazer, P. (1969). *Aust. J. Dairy Technol.*, **24**, 75–8.
229. Southward, C. R. and Goldman, A. (1975). *N.Z.J. Dairy Sci. & Technol.*, **10**, 101–12.
230. Southward, C. R. and Goldman, A. (1978). *N.Z.J. Dairy Sci. & Technol.*, **13**, 97–105.
231. Hutton, C. W. and Campbell, A. M. (1981). In: *Protein Functionality in Foods*, Ed. Cherry, J. P., American Chemical Society Symposium Series, No. 147, American Chemical Society, Washington, DC, 177–200.
232. Hagenmaier, R. (1972). *J. Food Sci.*, **37**, 965–6.
233. Berlin, E., Anderson, B. A. and Pallansch, M. J. (1968). *J. Dairy Sci.*, **51**, 1912–15.

234. Berlin, E., Kliman, P. G., Anderson, B. A. and Pallansch, M. J. (1973). *J. Dairy Sci.*, **56**, 984–7.
235. Knightbridge, J. P. and Goldman, A. (1975). *N.Z.J. Dairy Sci. & Technol.*, **10**, 152–7.
236. Short, J. L. (1980). *N.Z.J. Dairy Sci. & Technol.*, **15**, 167–76.
237. Hermannson, A.-M. (1972). *Lebensm. Wiss. u. Technol.*, **5**, 24–9.
238. Hermannson, A.-M. and Aoøkesson, C. (1975). *J. Food Sci.*, **40**, 595–602.
239. Hermannson, A.-M. and Aoøkesson, C. (1975). *J. Food Sci.*, **40**, 603–10.
240. Quinn, J. R. and Paton, D. (1979). *Cereal Chem.*, **56**, 38–40.
241. Schmidt, R. H. (1981). In: *Protein Functionality in Foods*, Ed. Cherry, J. P., American Chemical Society Symposium Series, No. 147, American Chemical Society, Washington, DC, 131–47.
242. Hermannson, A.-M. (1979). In: *Functionality and Protein Structure*, Ed. Pour-El, A., American Chemical Society Symposium Series, No. 92, American Chemical Society, Washington, DC, 81–103.
243. Hillier, R. M. and Cheeseman, G. C. (1979). *J. Dairy Res.*, **46**, 113–20.
244. Sternberg, M., Chiang, P. J. and Eberts, N. J. (1976). *J. Dairy Sci.*, **59**, 1042–50.
245. Schmidt, R. H., Illingworth, B. L. and Ahmed, E. M. (1978). *J. Food Sci.*, **43**, 613–15, 621.
246. Kalab, M., Voisey, P. W. and Emmons, D. B. (1971). *J. Dairy Sci.*, **54**, 178–81.
247. Dunkerley, J. A. and Hayes, J. F. (1980). *N.Z.J. Dairy Sci. & Technol.*, **15**, 191–6.
248. Kalab, M. and Harwalkar, V. R. (1973). *J. Dairy Sci.*, **56**, 835–42.
249. Morr, C. V. (1981). In: *Protein Functionality in Foods*, Ed. Cherry, J. P., American Chemical Society Symposium Series, No. 147, American Chemical Society, Washington, DC, 201–15.
250. Tornberg, E. (1979). In: *Functionality and Protein Structure*, Ed. Pour-El, A., American Chemical Society Symposium Series, No. 92, American Chemical Society, Washington, DC, 105–23.
251. Tornberg, E. and Hermannson, A.-M. (1973). *J. Food Sci.*, **42**, 468–72.
252. Crenwelge, D. D., Dill, C. W., Tyber, P. T. and Landmann, W. A. (1974). *J. Food Sci.*, **39**, 175–7.
253. Pearson, A. M., Spooner, M. E., Hegarty, G. R. and Bratzler, L. J. (1965). *Food Technol.*, **19**, 1841–5.
254. Smith, G. C., Juhn, H., Carpenter, Z. L., Mattil, K. F. and Cater, C. M. (1973). *J. Food Sci.*, **38**, 849–55.
255. Inklaar, P. A. and Fortuin, J. (1969). *Food Technol.*, **23**, 103–7.
256. Sabharwal, K. and Vakaleris, D. G. (1972). *J. Dairy Sci.*, **55**, 277–82.
257. Smith, L. M. and Dairiki, T. (1975). *J. Dairy Sci.*, **58**, 1249–53.
258. Smith, L. M. and Dairiki, T. (1975). *J. Dairy Sci.*, **58**, 1254–62.
259. Tornberg, E. (1978). *J. Food Sci.*, **43**, 1159–62, 1565.
260. Tornberg, E. and Lundh, G. (1978). *J. Food Sci.*, **43**, 1553–8.
261. Hayes, J. F., Stranagham, B. and Dunkerley, J. A. (1979). *N.Z.J. Dairy Sci. & Technol.*, **14**, 259–64.

262. Yamauchi, K., Shimitzu, M. and Kamuya, T. (1980). *J. Food. Sci.*, **45**, 1237–42.
263. Kinsella, J. E. (1981). *Food Chem.*, **7**, 273–88.
264. Cherry, J. P. and McWatters, K. H. (1982). In: *Protein Functionality in Foods*, Ed. Cherry, J. P., American Chemical Society Symposium Series, No. 147, American Chemical Society, Washington, DC, 149–76.
265. Kuehler, C. A. and Stine, C. M. (1974). *J. Food Sci.*, **39**, 279–382.
266. De Vilbiss, E. D., Holsinger, V. H., Posati, L. P. and Pallansch, M. J. (1974). *Food Technol.*, **28**, 40–8.
267. Kitabatake, N. and Doi, E. (1982). *J. Food Sci.*, **47**, 1218–21, 1225.

14

Meat Quality and its Control

MOGENS JUL

Danish Meat Products Laboratory,
Ministry of Agriculture, Copenhagen, Denmark

ABSTRACT

The quality of meat is perceived differently by meat processors, the distributing trade, consumers and scientists. Thus, for meat processors, abnormal quality of pork, i.e. PSE (pale-soft-exudative) and DFD (dark-firm-dry), are important because the former gives lower cooking or curing yield, while the latter may affect keeping time adversely. Consumers are less aware of these defects. The meat trade in the USA insists on marbled beef, although the advantage is not noticeable tastewise. Consumers buy it simply because it is marked 'choice' and they assume that this conformation grade is equivalent to a superior taste. The trade in the UK requires very well trimmed lean pig carcasses, although more of the pork is sold cut up so that this is of little or no relevance for the consumer.

Scientists for years have had a somewhat unrealistic desire to measure quality objectively, mainly by chemical or physical tests although these have little or only moderate correlation to consumer perception of quality. Partly as a consequence of this, scientists have turned to sensoric tests, which have been carried to a degree of sophistication where they also bear little relationship to consumer perception except in cases of off-taste.

Meat quality needs to be controlled first at the producing level. Much can be achieved by selecting an appropriate breed. Age is also important for taste and texture but also often conflicts with the trade's demand for a certain animal size and the producers' need for rapid growth. The meat processor often compensates for defects in meat quality by sophisticated curing techniques, i.e. use of phosphate, massaging equipment, etc. The fresh meat distributor may greatly influence quality by appropriate ageing, a factor often neglected for pigs and poultry. Consumers might control quality by discriminating selection but are so price conscious that largely only such improvements are possible which do not lead to increased costs. Also, it must be realised that consumer selection is more dictated by appearance and convenience than by taste and texture at time of eating. Consumers may control quality considerably by selecting home preparation methods; much improvement in, say, pork quality is possible by appropriate selection of cooking methods. Consumers may at times be highly quality conscious and willing to pay high prices for quality, viz. in cases where a superior product is clearly identified in the trade, appropriately promoted and marketed under circumstances which stress its superior quality, e.g. the Danish 'Antonius' pork.

INTRODUCTION

In this paper it is intended to review the various means whereby man can control—in the sense of influencing—the quality of meat from domesticated animals and products thereof, as quality is experienced by the trade, and by the consumer. The strategies and methods for quality control of these products are discussed elsewhere.[1] The quality concept is here limited to organoleptic quality and yield. Other aspects of meat quality such as nutritional value (retention of protein quality and of vitamins, minerals, etc.) are also not included since they are not included in the traditional concept of quality. These aspects are discussed by the author in reference 2. Also, the safety of meat products, i.e. the presence or absence of contaminants such as herbicides, pesticides and pharmaceuticals, toxic material such as mycotoxins, and naturally present, possibly harmful components, etc., are not included. This subject was reviewed by Hamm.[3] Finally, the contribution of veterinary meat control and hygiene safety of meat and meat products to quality are not considered under the quality concept as here discussed. To some extent, these aspects also are discussed elsewhere by the author.[1]

MEAT QUALITY

Considerable uncertainty exists about what is meant by meat quality, even if the above mentioned limitations are accepted.[4] The author suggests that the term must refer to the satisfaction which the production of meat gives to (i) the producer, (ii) the processor, (iii) the trade, and (iv) the ultimate consumer. It is not always accepted that meat quality must include the former three. However, it seems clear, for instance, that the existence of a meat industry and a meat trade in Denmark has given very valuable contributions to the standard of living and the gross domestic product in Denmark and thus has given considerable satisfaction in Denmark over and above the satisfaction which Danish meat or meat products may have given the ultimate consumers. These parts of meat quality are probably mostly—but not exclusively—measurable in economic terms. Conversely, the consumer's satisfaction is measurable only in subjective terms; it is often considered as limited to appearance, taste and texture. It is, however, clear that other factors, e.g. packaging, convenience and certainly price, will also affect consumer satisfaction. Since many sectors of society, primarily animal producers, processors, trade and consumers, are interested in meat quality, many attempts to measure it have been made. The use of some, especially economic parameters, has been fairly successful while attempts to measure objectively the subjective value of meat have at times failed to such a degree that producers, processors and the trade have been misled.

OBJECTIVE MEASUREMENT

It seems to be almost in the nature of science that one strives to find objective measurements for anything with which one has to work. Since animal husbandry research and meat producers needed guidance in breeding and feeding work, attempts to measure growth, feed conversion rates, etc., in animal husbandry were introduced quite early. Obviously, such factors as meat production per kilogram of feed, ratio of high-priced to low-priced cuts, days from birth to slaughter weight, were easy to measure in objective terms and were in the early days the main guidance for animal producers. Other factors, of course, also forced themselves upon research, e.g. resistance to disease, inter-calving time, litter size, etc.; these were of economic importance for the producer, and they were therefore also considered quite early.

Since some meats and some cuts of meat are sold at higher prices than others, and therefore presumably are more appreciated by the consumer, it was obvious that other factors also were of importance for the meat producer. It seemed that mainly taste and texture were involved. Therefore, enormous efforts were made to measure these. Many attempts have been and are being made to identify the preferred—and the undesired—flavour components in meats with an aim to measuring meat quality through chemical analyses. So far these attempts have been unsuccessful.

Very characteristic for meat preference also is meat texture. This seemed to be a factor which might easily be measured by physical methods. Numerous methods exist for the measurement of water binding and shear strength, etc., for meat. Some of these measurements have shown a moderate degree of correlation with quality as it is perceived by the processors, the trade and the consumer.

Another factor was, for instance, fatness. In earlier days of food scarcity, even in the industrialised countries, fat was actually a desired part of the meat animal. Today, this is rarely the case. Thus, in the pig industry, fat deposits, which seemed easily determined by measuring back fat thickness, became important measurements. They correlated fairly well with the wishes of the trade because they reflected with acceptable accuracy the ratio between expensive and less expensive cuts. From the 1950s to today, the average back fat thickness in Danish pigs was reduced from 32 mm to about 21 mm. However, eventually, this resulted in some confusion because pig breeding and pig feeding techniques developed animals with low back fat measurements but large amounts of belly fat. Thus, an extra measurement was introduced, and soon belly fat was also on the decline. Then, suddenly, complaints regarding so-called slight-of-lean (sol), absence of meat in the loin muscle, were received from the UK in spite of the low back fat measurements made on the sides in Denmark. This led to an additional measurement in the grading system, the side fat measurement. Almost instantaneously, the farming system responded and the frequency of sol declined, from an average of about 28 mm in the 1950s to about 15 mm today.[5]

Today, Danish pigs are not graded directly according to fat measurement, but according to per cent of meat in the side, an index compounded on the basis of several meat and fat layer measurements.

Even less sophisticated grading systems, for example that adopted in the EEC, correlate well with fat content. In the EEC system, the highest grade has 58 % meat in the carcass while the lowest grade has only about 41 %.

On the other hand, fat not easily measured is often overlooked. Thus, in the poultry industry, feeds containing relatively large amounts of fat were preferred by animal producers for a considerable period without it being realised that their use may lead to additional fat deposits which are often lost or discarded in the evisceration of the poultry; at any rate, they are not desired by the consumer. Thus, what is a gain for the producer may be a loss to the processor or the consumer. Similarly, the reduction of visible fats in pig carcasses through selective breeding using fatty tissue measurements as a guidance was accompanied by a lowering of the fat content in the lean parts of the carcass, seemingly correlated with a lower taste value of the meat. Thus, a chemical determination of fat in the lean tissue might also correlate somewhat with quality.

Colour seemed to be another important factor, especially in consumer choice at the point of purchasing. Many attempts have been made to measure colour objectively, i.e. by spectrometers and various other colour measuring instruments, and a fair degree of correlation with subjective evaluations has been obtained. Today, several countries are experimenting with combining the electrical probes, used for fat and lean measurements, with optical probes. Such measurements may correlate quite well with the other meat quality criteria.

SUBJECTIVE MEASUREMENT

While economic measurements are generally, but not always exclusively, accepted as final, it is obvious that other objective measurements are relevant only to the degree to which they correspond to the often mainly or purely subjective satisfaction which the processor, the trade and the ultimate consumer receives. Already in the early days of animal husbandry and meat research, it was customary to evaluate the animal and the meat not only by weight, etc., but by looking at it and tasting it. This was normally done by experienced people, animal judges and meat specialists. In so far as the meat trade is concerned, this led to carefully organised visual judging of the quality of carcasses, i.e. by meat judging teams, trained carcass graders, etc. When the performance of these groups is considered closely, it will be seen that their performance is of value mainly for the meat trade. Thus, the visual classification of a beef carcass is very valuable for the beef trade, and the best classified carcasses obtain the higher prices. This is mainly because better carcass conformation correlates fairly well with the ratio of valuable to less valuable cuts, i.e. is a measure of carcass value for the meat trade. However, once a carcass is cut up into steaks, etc., a high carcass grade may have little or no correlation with the eating quality of the meat itself, i.e. one may get a tough or tasteless cut from an animal of the highest grade. Therefore, a second grading system may be introduced. In the USA, two grades exist for the grading of beef cattle. One is the yield grade, whereby the carcass as a whole, e.g. conformation, etc., is estimated. In addition, a quality grade exists, whereby marbling, etc., is evaluated to determine the value of the meat for the consumer. The yield grade for beef considers such factors as the colour and the marbling of the cut surfaces and the meat is graded quality according to these. Both the trade and the consumer were prepared to pay more for those cuts which received a better quality grade in this regard. Actually, the correlation between quality grade and eating quality has proved not to be very good.

The satisfaction which the ultimate consumer obtains is obviously to a considerable degree related to the texture and taste. Since the judgement by individuals is, or at least may appear to be, quite erratic, many attempts were made to rationalise subjective measurement of these factors. As a result, quite detailed techniques for sensoric taste tests were developed. In these, one generally uses taste panels, often 6 to 12 people, with considerable experience in the evaluation of taste, colour and tenderness. They are given various well-defined scales, or are asked to use ranking or comparison methods whereby even very small differences in colour, taste or texture may be detected. The results are calculated statistically. Today, the technique is developed to a very high degree of sophistication. In the process, however, it often appears as if its purpose is no longer clear. Most sensoric panels are well-equipped to determine whether small differences exist between samples or if an off-taste is present, but they are generally not very useful for, and sometimes not even intended for, the measurement of quality as perceived by the consumer. Thus, a sensoric panel may say that one sample has a gamier taste than another but be unable to say which may be preferred. Often, of course, even different groups of consumers would have different preferences. Thus, the sensoric technique is often of only limited use as a guidance in efforts to measure or improve meat quality.

Other factors which make the interpretation of the findings of sensoric panels even more complicated lie in the fact that consumer satisfaction is a very ill-defined combination of various impressions; even the visual impression of the package at the time of purchasing or advertising may be extremely important. For such reasons also, it is very difficult or near impossible for any sensoric panel to give an overall evaluation of quality as actually perceived by the user.

GUIDANCE AS REGARDS MEAT QUALITY

It is thus obvious that the situation as the author sees it is complex. Nevertheless, meat producers, meat processors and the meat trade must have guidance. It is often overlooked that the main guidance is actually received through economic indicators as mentioned above, reactions in the trade and from the consumer's actual selection. Thus, since quite yellowish chickens are preferred in France, the poultry supply system has moved towards the production of such birds, while the reverse is the case in Denmark, where a very whitish appearance is preferred.

Therefore, in any attempts to advise on meat quality, one has to make use of the above mentioned techniques as well as of any signals which may be obtained from the trade or from observing consumer habits in attempts to guide animal producers and meat processors in their efforts to produce meat of a better quality or at a lower price. Because of the complexities, one may end up with the very simple and also simplistic definition of meat quality which was paraphrased by the British animal husbandry research worker, John Hammond, who said that quality is 'that for which the producer is prepared to pay the most'. In a somewhat pragmatic fashion, the author considers it his duty to help improve meat quality without necessarily defining or measuring it.

INFLUENCE OF BREED

The farmer's choice of animal breed has, as might be expected, considerable influence on the quality of the meat. Some breeds simply give a better proportion of expensive to inexpensive cuts. This is one of the advantages of the Danish Landrace pig. The taste of its meat is no better than that from other breeds, but when, for instance, a British grocer cut up half a Wiltshire bacon side from Denmark, he had more gammon and more loin, less forend and less fat than from bacon from other breeds. For this reason, he was willing to pay more for that type of pig meat. The Belgian Pietrain breed gives an even more favourable ratio in this regard, but has a high frequency of carcasses with very light, watery meat, so-called PSE (pale-soft-exudative) meat, and is therefore not often selected in pig production.

SELECTION

As already mentioned, purely economic factors have had a very powerful influence on meat quality. Once a breed was chosen, animal husbandry science and producers have strived by careful selection and progeny testing, performance evaluation, etc., to produce meat as cheaply as possible. Enormous gains were obtained; thus, the Danish Landrace pig in 1930 could produce 1 kg of live weight on 3·4 feed units where the requirement in 1980 was 2·7 feed units, obviously a considerable gain for the agricultural community, but actually an advancement, the benefit of which—as practically all benefits from higher productivity in farming—was passed on to the consumer completely. The latter is illustrated by the fact that farm income today is relatively much lower than income in other trades. Also, in 1960, an average hourly wage in Denmark would buy 1 kg of pig meat, while today it will buy 2 kg in spite of the artificially high feed prices which the Danish farming community has to pay since Denmark's entry into the Common Market in 1973.

Progress, mainly through selective breeding, has been equally impressive in poultry production. Thus, in 1958, 11 weeks and 3·1 feed units were required to produce 1 kg of chicken broiler while, today, it requires 6 weeks and less than 1·8 feed units. The advantage of this productivity increase was also passed on to the consumer, who today pays 50% more for chicken than 35 yr ago, while the rate of inflation over the same period probably has been close to 800%.[5]

CROSSBREEDING

Selection by a few economic indicators proved not to be the ultimate solution in animal production; thus, it turned out that the impressive results which were obtained by selective breeding with the Landrace Danish pig had adverse consequences on meat quality. While the Landrace pig had the above mentioned great advantages as regards carcass conformation, it showed a tendency to a high frequency of PSE and so-called DFD (dark-firm-dry) meat. These were factors which to a certain extent affected consumers, and even more the meat industry, in that PSE meat gives a lower curing yield and DFD meat may show lower keeping quality, especially where cuts of meat are vacuum packed for refrigerated storage. Other economic factors were more decisive for the animal producers themselves. It turned out that litter size could be improved and the strength of the animal, e.g. resistance to some disease, increased by crossbreeding. The result was that crossbreeding of first Landrace with Yorkshire and lately three-crossbreeding with Landacre–Yorkshire and Hampshire or Duroc, respectively are preferred. It seems that meat quality as measured by frequency of PSE and DFD has also been improved, but more important for pig producers is the improvement in litter size, health and general strength of the animals.

MANAGEMENT IN ANIMAL HUSBANDRY

The production of meat animals, especially calves, pigs, and poultry, has been subject to a very high degree of rationalisation. In most industrialised countries, this has resulted in what is often referred to as intensive production. Thus, especially sows but also pigs and at times calves may be kept in very close indoor confinement, often without straw or other bedding, at times without daylight. Similarly, laying hens are kept in cages, quite limited in size and with a wire net floor. Many attempts have been made to ascertain whether such methods of production have adverse effects on meat quality but no evidence has so far become available. Thus, the effect on quality must, at the most, be very small.

The farming community generally argues that as long as the animals grow well, are not more affected by disease than normally, show no visual signs of animal discomfort, growth rates are high, etc., the conditions can be expected to be humane. Further, animal producers generally like their animals, like to work with them, show concern for their well-being, etc. Therefore, they feel that accusations of inhumane treatment are unjustified.

On the other hand, urban—often very volatile—groups especially tend to feel differently. Among them there is today a considerable reaction against the use of such methods. Since consumer satisfaction, in any regard in the view of the author, is an important component of meat quality, such reactions, even if purely emotional, need to be given consideration. The author feels that consumers are entitled to access to meat and meat products produced under conditions of which these consumers approve. In so far as management methods are concerned, this has in some instances been implemented. Thus, in France, the Government has issued rules for the production of so-called 'Label' products. For chicken, these stipulate that chicken must be reared in flocks not exceeding 3000 and not more than 12 000 birds may be maintained per production unit. Each chicken must have $0{\cdot}1\ m^2$ of space. Further, after 6 weeks, the chicken must have a specified amount of free range area, $2\ m^2$ per animal. Also, and this is more connected with taste concepts, the chicken must not be less than 12 weeks old at the time of slaughter, where the ordinary bird from modern producers is 6–7 weeks old. This results in a slightly tastier, but also tougher bird. On a blind test, as many prefer the regular chicken as the 'Label' bird. However, some consider the assurance of getting a mature bird worth the higher price, about 50% above that of chicken from the intensive production. Similarly, rules for 'Label' calves require that they must not be kept in close confinement, must have free range grazing opportunity and access to suckling from their mother or another female.

In poultry raising, one important factor, which affects meat quality, was discovered in management. Often, broiler chickens were raised on wood shavings from timber which had been preserved with tetrachlorophenols. This resulted in a microbial formation of tetrachloroanisoles in the bedding, which was transmitted to and gave a very objectionable, musty, off-taste, to the meat.

FEED

In the above, reference was made to the improved feed utilisation by animals developed by selection and crossbreeding. Obviously, feed may also influence meat quality. Thus, it is widely known that the use of non-defatted fish meals may result in a slightly rancid ('metallic' or 'fishy') off-taste of pig meat, veal, and poultry. Similarly, using a high percentage of maize instead of, for instance, barley in pig feed may result in a taste of the pig meat preferred by many fresh pig meat consumers. However, it also results in rather soft fatty tissue, to which at least the Danish and British trades object. Feed has other characteristics; unsaturated fatty acids—even in such small concentration that they do not affect the eating quality of the fresh meat adversely—may result in a greatly reduced keeping quality of the pig meat if frozen.

Fully developed ruminants are less affected by the composition of fats because deposit fats are mainly synthesised in their digestive system. Other factors in feed may, however, affect meat quality. Thus, some kinds of wild plants sometimes eaten by free range cattle may result in an objectionable taste of beef.

TRANSPORT TO SLAUGHTER

In the early 1930s, the British meat research worker, Dr E. H. Callow, published his findings that pigs slaughtered on the farms gave hams of better keeping quality than pigs slaughtered in a central slaughtering plant. He demonstrated that the cause was exhaustion during transport, which caused the glycogen reserves in the blood to be broken down into pH-reducing lactates which were then lost with the blood during exsanguination. Therefore, the meat had a higher pH than normally, and, as a result thereof, a lower keeping quality. He also demonstrated that feeding the animals sugar immediately prior to their transport could eliminate this disadvantage simply because sufficient carbohydrate would then be present in the blood to allow for normal formation of lactates and the corresponding desired pH fall.

Meat research has to a considerable extent concentrated on factors surrounding these phenomena and has disclosed rather more intricate interactions. Exhaustion of an animal in the last hours before slaughter may result in DFD (dark-firm-dry) meat. This has been clearly demonstrated for pigs, cattle, calves and turkeys. On the other hand, excitement immediately prior to slaughter may result in a very rapid lactate formation immediately after slaughter and a very rapid pH fall, resulting in PSE meat. Much research has gone into determining the consequences of and methods for the prevention of these abnormal meat qualities which obviously are closely related to each other. It seems sometimes overlooked that both are of limited importance for consumers. Thus, there are occasional consumer complaints about toughness, which is often due to the PSE, in pig meat, but hardly any reaction to DFD pig meat. On the other hand, as mentioned above, these abnormal qualities may be very unsatisfactory for the industry, since PSE may result in increased weight loss during chilling and excessive weepage in prepackaged retail cuts as well as decreased yield in curing and cooking industrially; DFD results in unsatisfactory keeping quality of vacuum packed meat. The latter is really not acceptable in the beef trade where vacuum packaging of prime cuts for refrigerated storage and shipment is widely used. On the other hand, DFD meat, which has a high pH and high water binding capacity, is often considered very desirable in the meat curing industry, and is even preferred in sausage making. This means that the factor is of little relevance where low quality beef is concerned, e.g. cull cows. On the other hand, regular beef cattle carcasses are generally used primarily for fresh meat cuts; only the less desirable parts are used for sausage making and meat curing. Since obviously the whole animal has to be treated in the same way, most trade objects to meat animals showing signs of DFD and often even refuses to accept such meat.

Sugar feeding may be used to prevent the DFD occurrence in pigs, but will result in a corresponding increase in PSE which is equally objectionable. Because of the special characteristics of the ruminant's digestive system, this technique has had no effect.

One obvious method of trying to eliminate the adverse effect of transport is to lair the animals at the slaughtering plant prior to slaughter. Some countries even require by law that beef animals be rested 24 h or more at the slaughtering facility prior to slaughter. However, in this it was overlooked that lairing of animals rarely has the desired effect. Thus, when pigs are kept overnight in slaughter house pens, they find themselves under unfamiliar conditions and among animals to which they are not accustomed. Stress and fighting will be the result, and the frequency of DFD meat will increase. Much the same is found for cattle. Since some resting may reduce the frequency of PSE meat, it has been determined that a rest of from 2 to 4 h is the optimum for pigs under Danish conditions. However, other considerations enter into the picture. Lairage space is expensive. Very early morning transport is not always possible; operating a plant after a certain hour of the day is expensive because of overtime regulations, etc. Therefore, economic factors may often prevent the plants from giving the animals optimum treatment.

In New Zealand and Australia, it is considered that the best beef quality is obtained by so-called 'tail-board' slaughtering, i.e. slaughtering as quickly as possible after the animal is received at the slaughtering facility.

Another approach is to eliminate excessive transport. Thus, the trend is definitely away from live markets to direct delivery from producer to slaughtering facility. Also the handling and transport of the animals themselves have considerable influence. Many efforts have been made to improve trucks and at times rail road cars for animal transport. Especially for pigs, well-ventilated vans are recommended with coarse floor covering to prevent the animals from slipping during transport, covered for protection against sun and very cold weather, etc.

In the slaughtering plants, much effort has been made to arrange for gentle handling of the animals, well-designed pens and raceways and even toys like old rubber tyres for diversification, etc.

ENZYME INJECTION

In the USA, use is sometimes made of injecting an enzyme preparation into beef animals about 30 min prior to slaughter. This ensures that the enzyme, which is a papain derivative, is distributed fairly evenly in the carcass. The injection has no apparent effect on the animal; the enzyme itself is only active at temperatures above about 50 °C. The enzyme has no effect as long as the meat is cold-stored, but once heating (in cooking) takes place, tenderisation is rather quick. This treatment results in a definite improvement in tenderness, especially of otherwise less tender cuts such as shank, thigh meat, etc. Under the trade name of 'Proten', the method is in use by some companies in the USA and a few other countries. Most countries prohibit it because they consider it undesirable and humanely questionable to inject such an active substance into a live animal.

STUNNING

In most industrialised countries, stunning the animals prior to slaughter is obligatory, except for certain ritual slaughter. This may be considered as an improvement in meat quality in so far as it complies with a very generally held public opinion. Nevertheless, it is somewhat questionable whether many stunning methods are, in fact, more gentle to the animal than a careful slaughter by sticking could be. However, such details could not be explained to the general public, and stunning is required by law. Stunning may result in a decreased meat quality, especially because it often causes internal haemorrhages and bleedings. Also, high voltage stunning of pigs, now the method generally preferred by authorities, may result in a four-fold increase in the number of PSE carcasses.[6] Meat research is at present studying details of these phenomena as related to the various permissible stunning methods. It is likely that more attention should be given to methods developed in Australia and New Zealand, i.e. 'head to feet' and 'head to back' electrical stunning and non-penetrative percussion stunning.

SLAUGHTER

The sticking and slaughtering of the animals may have an influence on meat quality. Thus, for chicken it has been demonstrated that the scald, which is carried out prior to plucking, can have a very considerable effect on tenderness. Thus, scalding broilers for 180 s at 60 °C resulted in meat which was characterised as objectionably tough by taste testers, while controls scalded at the same temperature for 60 s were characterised as pleasantly tender. Quite similarly, splitting calves immediately after slaughter resulted in meat which was characterised by taste tasters as very tough, while splitting the carcasses two days after slaughter had no adverse affect on tenderness. Even splitting after 1 day's chilling at 8 °C resulted in the majority of the animals being characterised as tough or very tough while splitting after 2 days at 8 °C did not result in any carcass designated as tough. Conceivably, other factors in the slaughtering process might also have an influence on meat quality. Therefore, several experiments have been carried out comparing farm-slaughtered animals to those slaughtered at a modern slaughtering facility. When precautions such as those mentioned above are taken, no differences have been found in meat quality. On the other hand, modified slaughtering methods might yet improve meat quality over that obtained by farm slaughtering. No such factors have yet been demonstrated, except where the absence of adequate chilling in home slaughtering can result in hot-shortening and, as a consequence, tough meat.

The choice of slaughtering methods, however, is not without problems. Thus, especially in the UK, there is a considerable trade in non-eviscerated, so-called 'New York dressed' poultry. Similarly, in France only partly eviscerated, so-called 'defilé' poultry is in considerable demand by the consumer. These products have a taste somewhat different from fully eviscerated birds but a completely acceptable shelf life. The remaining question is whether the need for a complete *post mortem* veterinary inspection, which includes the entrails and the body cavity, is considered necessary, in which case complete evisceration would be required. It does appear as if no health consideration is involved. Therefore, this becomes a matter of public preference, i.e. whether the public feels that the entrails and body cavity of poultry should be inspected as an extra, although seemingly unnecessary, precaution.

BLEEDING

In slaughtering, much effort is made to bleed the animal as quickly and completely as possible. It seems that the public feels this proper and desires it. A less intensive bleeding of the animal will result in a slightly darker meat but the difference would not be noticeable by the public. Sometimes hygienic requirements state that blood should be removed as completely as possible. This is assumed to result in an improved keeping quality of the meat, but such an effect has not been demonstrated. It would be somewhat surprising if there were any improvement since remaining blood as well as the other meat juices left in the carcass have much the same composition as the blood. Another reason for complete bleeding is that the blood may contain bacteria. This is the case only for animals suffering acute infectious diseases, which will result in the animal being condemned at the veterinary meat inspection. Further, it may be kept in mind that about 50 % of the blood is left in the carcass. This question is further complicated by the fact that nowadays much effort is made to utilise blood in meat products or in other ways for human consumption and there is no reaction to that. Animals could very well be slaughtered in such a way that less blood were eliminated during bleeding. This could result in a slaughter yield improved by about 1 % and thus in 1 % lower meat prices, since the price paid for the blood is very low. However, public resistance has prevented any efforts in this direction.

CHILLING

Meat hygiene specialists generally desire that the slaughtered animal be chilled as quickly and completely as possible in order that bacterial growth may be retarded as much as is practical. Very rapid chilling of at least large animals has also been seen as in the interest of the slaughtering plant because chilling is normally performed in air. Then, very low air temperatures, i.e. for pigs down to −30 °C, result in very low weight losses during chilling, e.g. 0·6 % for pigs instead of possibly 2·2 % for slow, air blast chilling.

However, after the rather widespread acceptance of this technique, it became clear that very rapid chilling could result in tough or even very tough and unacceptable meat. Workers in New Zealand explored this phenomenon and determined that optimum tenderness of meat was obtained by chilling at air temperatures around 8–12 °C, i.e. a very slow chill. The tenderness of the meat was additionally improved by conditioning the carcass at relatively high temperatures, i.e. 15–18 °C for some 48–72 h. With reasonable precautions as regards microbial activity, such chilling and conditioning could be used without keeping quality problems and resulted in very tender and desirable meat. However, implementing these methods was expensive because it required very large cooler space and held the animals up for several days prior to their further use, in New Zealand normally freezing.

New Zealand workers then demonstrated that the use of so-called electrical stimulation (ES), i.e. exposure of the animals to an electric current very soon after slaughter would result in quite tender meat even if chilling was commenced very rapidly after slaughter. Electrical stimulation is now in very widespread use, especially in cattle and sheep slaughtering facilities. It probably has not resulted in better meat than traditional slaughter and chilling, but it has permitted a very rapid transfer of the animals either to fast chillers or to freezers and thus resulted in a considerable economic advantage.

TENDERISATION

It is well known that especially beef should be aged for a considerable period, e.g. 2 weeks at 2 °C or another appropriate time–temperature combination which may even be 20 °C for 2 days, if adequate precautions are taken. This will result in much more tender and better tasting beef. A similar factor applies to pig meat where optimum meat quality may be obtained after about 4 days of ageing the carcasses at 4 °C. However, this quality improvement has not been sufficient to be perceived by the general public. Therefore, ageing of pig meat prior to its sale is not generally used. A similar effect is found for poultry. Again, it is not normally perceived directly by the consumer, and no preference is given to ageing *per se* among poultry processors. However, the public has shown a considerable preference for fresh poultry over frozen poultry, even if it is generally more expensive in Europe. It is of general assumption that the freezing process has an adverse effect on meat quality, but carefully conducted sensoric tests have demonstrated no such difference, i.e. not even the best trained taste panel can pick out the frozen birds among otherwise similarly treated fresh birds. However, a superior taste and texture of the non-frozen birds can be explained by the fact that when poultry is distributed in the fresh form this offers an obvious explanation for a superior taste, but the quality superiority is actually a result not of the elimination of the freezing process but of the time lag between slaughter and consumption, which obviously must occur in distribution in the fresh state and which actually results in an ageing process.

DISTRIBUTION METHOD

The methods used for fresh meat distribution also have an influence on meat quality. Fresh meat keeps much longer when vacuum packed, provided, of course, that its shape is such that practically all air can be eliminated. The remaining oxygen will then very quickly be used up by the continued metabolism of the meat. Thus, no aerobic microbial growth will take place. When anaerobic or facultative aerobic flora develop, this will mainly result in a slow lactate formation but no putrefactive odours develop even after quite long storage.

However, vacuum packing results in a meat colour to which the public is not accustomed, i.e. the very dark red colour of myoglobin instead of the pinkish colour of oxymyoglobin. The normal colour is restored when the meat is exposed to air for about half an hour. After that there is no difference in appearance between vacuum packed and non-vacuum packed meat. In either case, no taste or texture difference can be determined. Nevertheless, the consumer reaction, which is purely a reaction to the appearance of the meat at the point of purchase, has so far prevented meat from being sold in this form. Experiments are presently going on in several countries to see if the public can become accustomed to meat of this appearance since very considerable savings could be achieved in meat distribution in vacuumised form without any adverse effects on its eating quality.

HOME COOKING

It is worth keeping in mind that the ultimate satisfaction that the consumer receives, for obvious reasons, is also very dependent on the methods employed in cooking. Everyone is aware of the choices: 'rare, medium or well-done'. Less known, however, are the various other methods whereby cooking can very considerably improve upon or adversely affect the final result. One method used for tenderisation is use of meat tenderisers, i.e. enzyme preparations which are spread on the meat shortly before cooking. Also mechanical treatment, i.e. heavy pounding of the cut up meat, may improve its tenderness. Further, tough meat is, of course, often simply used for ground meat, in which case toughness is made much less noticeable.

More indirect methods may also be used. Thus, marinating meats will often result in a certain tenderisation of the meat and is therefore mainly applied to less tender pieces. Finally, the choice of cooking method itself is decisive; thus, a slow cooking to the lowest acceptable end temperature in the centre of the meat will often result in a more tasty and tender product than quick cooking. On the other hand, extended broiling may adversely affect the meat by excessive drying of the surface. It is not without justification that the meat industry in its promotional programmes puts a great deal of effort into advocating optimal home cooking methods. Ultimate consumer satisfaction will depend very much on the latter.

FEEDBACK

The most important means of improving meat quality is probably the provision for a proper feedback of information all the way back, through the meat supply route, a subject dealt with in some detail by the author.[1] Thus, it was the reaction in the British bacon trade which called the attention of the Danish pig industry to the slight-of-lean problem. This again led to the development at the Danish Meat Research Institute of the optical probe which at an early period permitted the on-line grading for side back measurement. The subsequent deduction in price to the pig producer quickly led to a response and the problem was eliminated. Quite similarly, it was complaints in the US market over tough lamb that led to the investigations at the Meat Industry Research Institute, New Zealand, of cold-shortening, conditioning, and, eventually, electrical stimulation.

Three problems exist in this regard. The animal marketing system should preferably be such that the producer of an animal can be identified by eartags, tattooing, etc., at the time at which the animal's quality is first evaluated, i.e. normally at the time of grading. Preferably, the producer should not only be informed as regards to grade, he should also be paid accordingly. As a further sophistication, each animal should be identifiable individually in order that the producer, from his records of the prior history of an animal, may determine possible reasons for high or low grading and take corrective steps. However, many animal marketing systems do not lend themselves easily to such measures.

An example is seen in the Danish pig industry where each pig producer gets a notification of any sign of disease noted by the veterinary meat control. Yet to come is an identification of each animal so conclusions from the animal's history can be drawn. The same applies to the data as regards slaughter weight and meat percentage.

Quality problems further down the supply route may be more difficult to trace. Thus, when some Danish poultry slaughtering plants increased scalding temperature, this resulted in tough birds, but no consumers in Japan or the Middle East were likely to realise that this was the cause of the toughness they found in some Danish birds. Yet, it was complaints from the market place, not the routine quality control, that discovered the problem which science soon explained and the official poultry plant quality inspection then eliminated.

Another problem is that of determining consumer preference. Many, often quite unrestrained consumers' spokesmen, often articulate very strongly their views as to the preferences they believe the consumers have. These opinions are mostly verbal and often difficult to translate into meat quality terms. More important, however, they bear little relationship to consumer behaviour in the market place. Thus, in Denmark, there has continuously been a cry for improved meat products. Several factories tried to comply, but the product lines, which really were of superior quality, failed in the market place.

Even well-informed consumers often misjudge what they themselves will select in the purchasing situation. This is why most conventional market research is of questionable value. The best, but by no means unfailing guidance is often received from experienced marketeers. The best research tool is probably test marketing, a tool rarely available in most phases of research and development work or in direct steps to improve quality.

Another source of information, of course, lies in consumer complaints. However, this tool must be interpreted with caution. Some consumers complain quite unrestrainedly, others never do. Among the latter are two groups, one somewhat indifferent to quality, and another which simply does not buy the product again.

RESEARCH, ADVICE AND TRAINING

It is generally assumed that quality improvement in an industry will come from research efforts. Traditionally this was referred to the activities of universities. Today, it is clear that the main contributions of these lie in the provision of well-trained academic staff for the industry. Beyond this, some more fundamental studies at universities, especially in the biochemical field, have eventually led to quality improvements. Further, especially North American universities, with their tradition for including extension in university programmes, have done a great deal to solve some of the day to day needs of industry.

In Europe, Australia and New Zealand, large contributions have been made by the various central mission-orientated animal husbandry, veterinary and meat science research institutes, some government financed, some industry financed, and many with a mixed type of funding. Their transdisciplinary and considerable resources have resulted in a very substantial impact.

An important factor may be industry's own research and development departments. However, meat being traditionally an empirical industry, only the largest concerns have been able to make substantial contributions except in the field of product development.

A very important factor is also vocational and middle level training. Much relating to quality hinges on how well the farmer, the superintendent in a plant, and even the distributor, understands the factors which influence quality. In meat processing, this factor is often neglected.

It is often overlooked that information and advice given by suppliers, be it suppliers of feedstuffs, veterinary medicine, machinery, food adjuncts and additives, packaging material, etc., has an enormous influence on quality. The author feels that this source of information may possibly be that which affects quality the most. This factor is, of course, not without its problems because it is a biased source of information.

Conversely, it is surprising how relatively modest efforts are exerted by buyers (i.e. meat packaging plants, food chains, etc.) in giving advice to their suppliers (i.e. farmers, meat processors, etc.) directed towards economic and other quality improvement, e.g. better feed utilisation, higher curing yields, cheaper packaging materials, better appearance, etc. In addition, some such steps are directed towards the elimination of defects, e.g. off-taste, toughness, etc. There is comparatively little inducement towards quality improvement.

QUALITY CONTROL

Both governments and industry maintain quite elaborate controls, most of which are aimed at maintaining hygienic quality and the absence of defects. Because of the elusive nature of quality as experienced by the consumers, the contribution of quality controls towards improving, or even preventing a gradual fall in quality, is modest.

SUPERIOR QUALITY GRADES

In the view of the author, a very important means of serving the consumer better lies in the introduction of superior quality products. These must be marked distinctly and their quality must be rigidly monitored and policed. This gives the consumer a choice. The confidence in the controlled quality of the superior products will appeal to the more critical consumers and create for these products a certain market share. There is then less reason for concern as regards the quality of the regular products, which then may be assumed to be satisfactory at the price for which they are sold. The successes of the 'Label' system in France and the Danish 'Antonius' pig (cf. reference 4) suggest that this may be a useful model to develop.

REFERENCES

1. Jul, M. (1983). *Quality Control in the Meat Industry. Manuscript No. 238*, Danish Meat Products Laboratory, Copenhagen, 24 pp., mimeographed.
2. Jul, M. (1982). *Nutritional Value and Sensory Evaluation of Meat.* Danish Meat Products Laboratory, Copenhagen, 32 pp., mimeographed.
3. Hamm, R. (1983). *Residues of Pollutants and Pharmaceuticals in Meat.* Bundesanstalt für Fleischforschung. Kulmbach, 11 pp., mimeographed.
4. Jul, M. and Zeuthen, P. (1980). *Prog. Fd. Nutr. Sci.*, **4**(6), 1–132.
5. Boegh-Soerensen, L., Jul, M. and Jensen, J. H. (1978–81). *Konserveringsteknik* (*Food preservation technology*), Vols 1 and 2, DSR, Copenhagen.
6. Danish Meat Research Institute (1983). *Annual Report 1982.* Slagteriernes Forskningsinstitut, Roskilde.

15

The Application of Modelling and Control to Food Processing Operations

N. D. P. DANG and R. R. SMITH

Leatherhead Food RA, Leatherhead, Surrey, UK

ABSTRACT

The traditional methods used by engineers for the conception, design, operation and control of food processing equipment have undergone significant changes in the past few years. The advent of both large-scale and microcomputing equipment has permitted vastly more detailed and realistic analyses to be carried out with a reasonable degree of effort and cost. More fundamental physical principles are employed and new techniques become possible. With the better understanding that has accrued food processes are better controlled, resulting in improved efficiency and quality control.

This paper reviews the methods for model building, presents current modelling trends in food systems studies, provides examples of applications of modelling, discusses the advantages and disadvantages of process control in the food industry, and identifies the technology associated with present day control applications.

The paper concludes with a description of present research activities at the Leatherhead Food RA regarding modelling and control activities, together with experiences to date.

INTRODUCTION

Process analysis is the gathering of process information, the analysis of this information by suitable methods, the synthesis and decision making thereafter, all employing a mathematical framework. Mathematics is used to give a concise, quantitative and descriptive relationship of the process under examination.

Process analysis entails the application of scientific methods to the recognition and definition of problems and the development of procedures for their solution. In detail, this involves: (a) a mathematical definition of the problem for the given physical situation; (b) subjective deduction to produce a mathematical model; and (c) synthesis and presentation of results to ensure full comprehension. This kind of conceptual representation of a process cannot completely encompass all the fine details of the process. Only some of the process's attributes and relationships can be set down, hopefully those that are easily measured and are significant from the viewpoint of their effect on the process.

The formation of a mathematical model symbolising a physical system can be a significant step towards understanding the complexities of the system. It is emphatically stressed that modelling should not be regarded as a goal in itself, but rather as a means towards the ultimate objective of understanding and making the process more efficient.

The use of mathematical models to describe a process has been successfully accomplished in many process industries, notable examples being the chemical and petrochemical industries. The application to food processing has been comparatively slow as the processes have tended to be 'traditional' and the nature of the industry 'conservative'. To compound the problem, many product characteristics are not easy to quantify, making it appear unreasonable to approach it mathematically. However, there are many distinguishable features that are common in both chemical and food processing. This enables the food process engineer to borrow the technologies already available. Coupled with his knowledge and appreciation of food composition and properties, he can apply modelling techniques to the unit operations of food manufacture, and thereby can design his process with greater confidence and reliability. This leads to quantitative calculations and deductions, a better design, optimisation of the design, optimal operating conditions, and improved process control.

MODEL BUILDING PROCEDURES

For any given process, a number of models can be developed to suit a range of needs and applications. The models would vary markedly in the order of complexity. The degree of complexity and detail incorporated into the model depends to a great extent on the problem to be solved, on the amount of basic information and data available, as well as on the ultimate uses of the model. The latter is perhaps the most important.

The general steps required for the structuring of a model can be outlined as follows (Fig. 1):

1. The first and most important step is defining the problem. This is invaluable in establishing a definite goal for the ensuing analysis and in outlining a path from the problem to the solution.
2. The second applies to the theory that governs the physical phenomena of the process. Every attempt must be made to thoroughly comprehend the mechanics of the process. Should a theory not be available or established, one should be postulated and its validity tested during the validification stage.

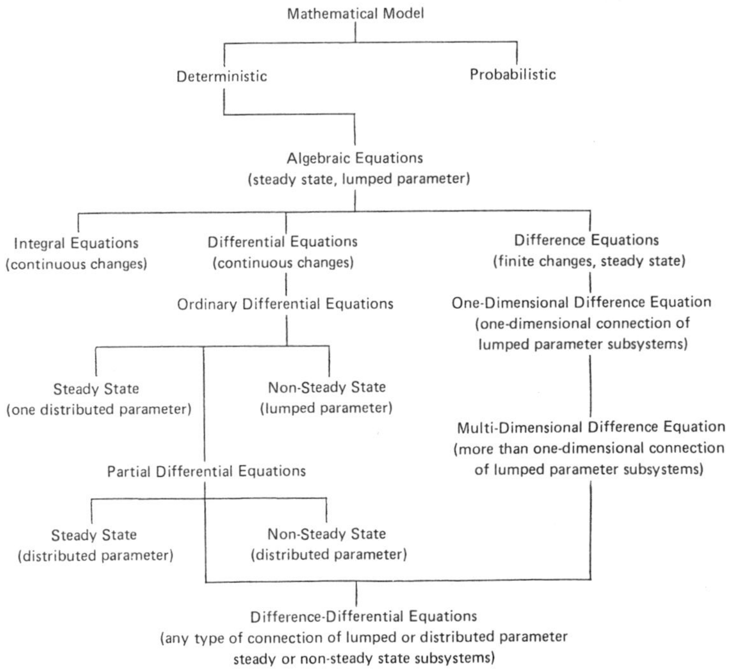

FIG. 1. Classification based on mathematical structure.

3. The exact functional relationships between interacting variables and their dependent parameters must be known. Selection of the correlation is based on theory, experimental results, and/or statistical analysis. This procedure is sometimes necessary as many processes are too complex to be presented satisfactorily by theory-based models. Empirical models are suitable and appropriate substitutes, especially when there is a lack of scientific information about the process.
4. After a process is developed, the mathematical equations must be solved. The algorithm used during this stage will depend entirely on the types of equations present in the model.
5. Verification of the model is undertaken after the computation stage. Experiments are performed to obtain results for comparison. The validity of the theory and/or hypothesised model must always be tested against actual experimental data. This check provides an indication of the true understanding of the process and the justification for the assumptions used during modelling. Any unexpected discrepancies, those not due to experimental errors, must be rationalised to ensure absolute compatibility of both the model and the experimental results. If, however, results agree poorly, the model must be revised, with resultant revision of theory and thoughts, or another approach used. Where no correction of the model is required, the formulated model can be used for analysis, simulation, design, control and optimisation.

The general strategy of analysis of complex processes, given above, follows a fairly well-defined pathway consisting of commonsense steps. These steps are designed to develop an approach of structuring and analysing processes wherever possible through mathematical models. This approach provides for more rigorous analysis and tends to make subjective judgements more formal and thorough.

Real problems are usually ill-defined and do not lend themselves easily to precise specification. One major premise in process analysis is that an entire process can be broken down into distinguishable subsystems and that relationships exist among the subsystems which, when assembled into a whole, can simulate the process. Subsystems do not have to correspond to any basic physical subdivisions of a real process. The only reason for the splitting is that a process can be so complex that it can be neither understood nor described properly as a whole. By proper manipulation and adjustment of the subsystems, an attempt can be made to obtain a reasonable representation of the whole process based on fairly simple, well-known principles for the parts.

Process analysis has some significant limitations which must be recognised. The first is related to the availability of data and the accuracy of the data. That is, the success of modelling depends heavily on the basic information available to the analyst. System studies are only as accurate as the physical and chemical data that go into a model. The second is the type of tools available to solve the mathematical equations that compose the model. In general, these are taken from the field of mathematics. There are structures which present day mathematics cannot solve. Thirdly, if the building blocks for the model are not physically realisable, the danger exists that a concept intended merely as a technique of analysis can become endowed with a physical reality for which no evidence exists. There is an inherent risk of attaching to a model a general aura of validity that it does not merit. Another danger in the use of models is to assume that they represent the real process beyond the range of the variables that the model was originally intended to encompass. Such extrapolation may be a valuable aspect of the model, but the conclusions reached may also be very misleading.

CLASSIFICATION OF MODELS

There is no universal way of presenting or classifying models. In this section a classification method that proves useful to the engineer in visualising and solving problems is given. It is made from the viewpoint of the nature of the equations in the model, and hence oriented toward the solution of models.

Some commonly used groupings are, in opposite pairs:[1]

(i)	analytical	empirical
(ii)	deterministic	probabilistic
(iii)	linear	non-linear
(iv)	steady state	non-steady state
(v)	lumped parameter	distributed parameter
(vi)	continuous	discrete
(vii)	single variable	multi-variable (or state space)

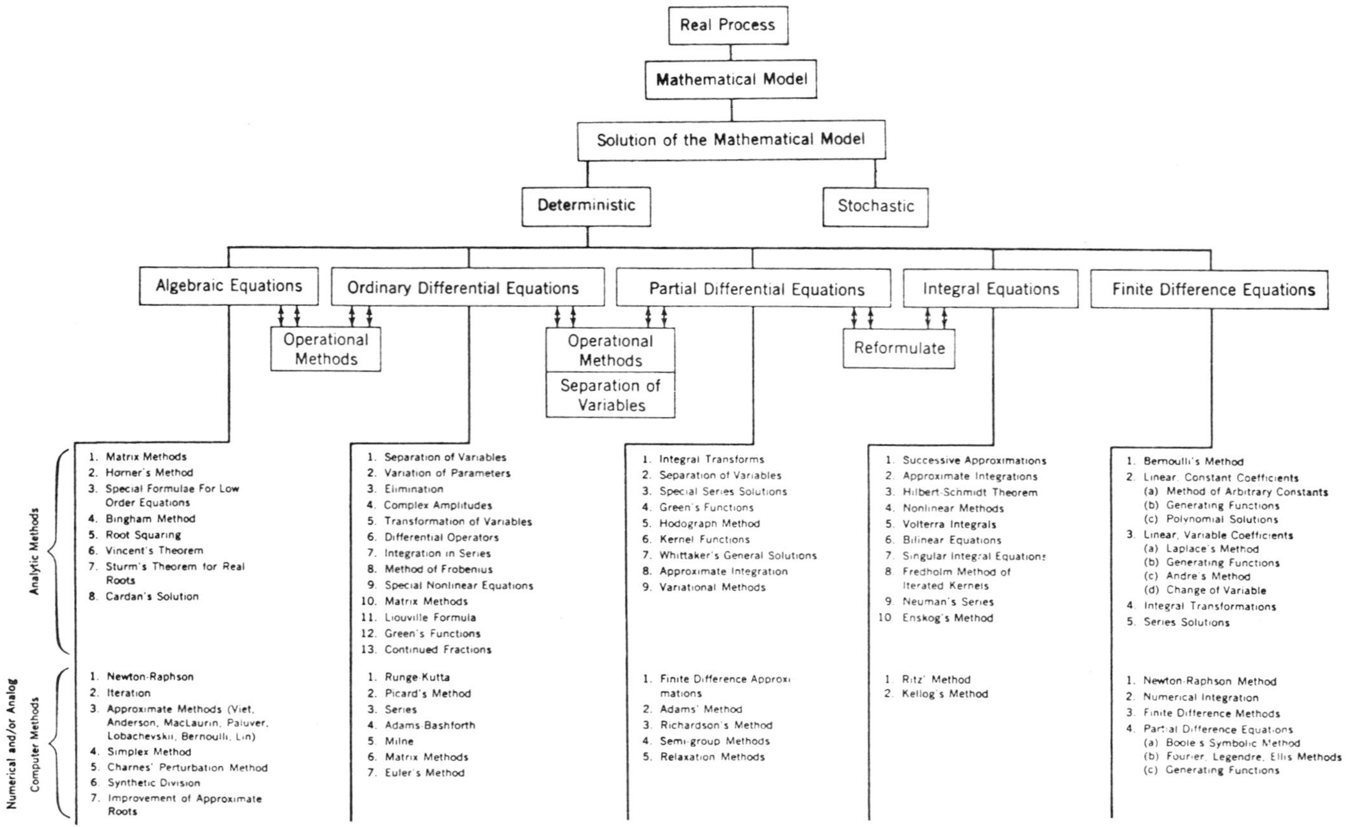

FIG. 2. Mathematical tools.

Another classification scheme is shown in Fig. 2; this acts as a guide to the techniques of solution of model equations. The degree of complexity of solving the equations increases from top to bottom of the figure.

MODELLING OF FOOD ENGINEERING SYSTEMS

In recent years, there has been a proliferation of articles describing the modelling of food processing systems appearing in technical journals and conference proceedings.[2] A global assessment of modelling efforts to date as it relates to food engineering systems draws attention to four particular unit operations: extrusion-cooking, evaporation, drying and freeze-drying.

Extrusion-cooking

Extrusion-cooking is defined as the process by which moistened starchy and/or proteinaceous materials are plasticised and cooked in a tube by a combination of pressure, heat and mechanical shear stress. The high temperature within the extruder promotes gelatinisation of the starchy components, denaturation of proteins, and stretching and restructuring of tractile components. This is followed by exothermic expansion of the extrudate, which is shaped by the opening in the die to form ropes, strips or tubes which are subsequently cut into shaped segments of the desired lengths. Many popular cereal foods consumed daily are now produced in this way. It has been amply demonstrated over the years that extrusion-cooking can minimise nutrient loss, texturise and shape food products under conditions of high production rate and low cost.

The work on modelling which has hitherto been applied to food extruders and food extrusion borrows heavily from the results of scientific and technological progress made in the plastics extrusion industry. There is a common feature between the characteristics of plastics and food materials when being extruded. The modelling of polymer extrusion is very advanced indeed. The objective of food engineers should therefore be to utilise this state of knowledge and apply it to biopolymers. The similarity between plastics and food materials (biopolymers) is obvious when it is observed that during extrusion-cooking the foodstuff changes from particles of various sizes to a plastic mass.

Current and past research efforts are directed at formulating rheological models of a range of food products, collecting operating data (which in itself is not an easy thing to do), and developing models (using both empirical and simplified theoretical approaches) for some types of extruders (particularly the Brabender and capillary extruders).

Evaporation

Many food processes rely heavily on evaporation as the concentration operation to facilitate product storage, preservation or transportation. In food processing, this refers to the removal of water from a food material (in liquid form) by the transfer of heat and the vaporisation of the water which is subsequently removed from the system. Evaporation is a process that involves simultaneous heat and mass transfers, and also includes a substantial number of phenomena of a physical–chemical nature which affects the composition and properties of the food product.

Modelling of evaporators or the evaporation process, as applied to the food industry, has been confined to sugar and tomato juice concentration. Some studies were reported on sugar crystallisation and distribution. Models that were developed tended to be too simplistic, incorporating many assumptions that did not necessarily reflect the physics of the actual process, and had rather limited use.

It is anticipated that an in-depth modelling of an evaporator would provide significant advancement in the mode of operation of these vessels, especially in the confectionery and jam-making industries. At the present time, the vessels are designed more on an historical than on a scientific basis.

Drying

Drying is a process in which water is removed from a food material (usually in solid form) by the application of heat. Heat is transported to the material to be dried (e.g. a slab, a piece of material, a droplet) by radiation, conduction or convection from the external surroundings. Part of the radiation is transmitted directly from the surroundings to the material. The other two forms of heat transfer take place via the medium immediately surrounding the material to be dried to the material itself. Mass transfer from the material occurs by diffusion. The mechanisms of heat and mass transfer between the immediate surroundings and the material take place via convection and dispersive mixing of the drying medium. Inside the material, heat and mass transfer may take place by a multitude of transport mechanisms.

The reasons for drying are as diverse as the materials that are dried, and the theoretical foundations behind the drying process. The diversity also extends to the methods used for drying.

Developments in drying cover the three main areas of:

(a) The description of isotherms.
(b) The transport equations for heat and mass transfer.
(c) The formulation of models for the drying operation.

Progress on the understanding of the fundamental aspects of drying is hampered by the complications arising out of the interaction of heat and mass transport inside the drying material. This needs to be resolved, together with formulating a unified sorption isotherm, transport equations and balance equations. Only then can temperature profiles, moisture content and profiles, and drying times be confidently predicted.

Freeze-drying

Freeze-drying is a process of food dehydration whereby water vapour is removed by sublimation from a frozen solid material, usually under low pressure and the action of radiant heat. Once dried, the hygroscopic food product can be stored in an air-tight container at ambient temperature. The food can be reconstituted easily and rapidly by the addition of water. The principal advantage of freeze-drying lies in the high quality of the product; this is due in part to the minimal amount of thermal degradation induced, the retention of volatile materials responsible for the flavour, and the structural rigidity of the dried product. However, the process suffers from being both slow and expensive. The cost factor is evenly proportioned between the energy for sublimation, energy to support the vacuum atmosphere, and the labour and overhead costs. It is not surprising, therefore, that considerable interest has arisen in investigating the factors that mainly affect the freeze-dryer (which is most amenable to control) and the mechanics of the freeze-drying process.

The heat and mass transfer conditions and equations in the product during freeze-drying have been a dominant subject for study. New formulations of the progress of the sublimation process, taking into account the simultaneous mass and heat flows, have been presented; there are now some very complicated mathematical models available, the theoretical predictions of which are generally supported by experimental evidence. These models now include the variation in transfer properties of the dried layer of product with time.

Much attention is also placed on the question of aroma retention in freeze-dried products.

There has also been a recent upsurge in studies relating to the optimal operation of a freeze-dryer, based on models developed for the drying process.

RESEARCH ACTIVITIES AT THE LEATHERHEAD FOOD RA

Nearly two years ago, the Ministry of Agriculture, Fisheries and Food (MAFF) sponsored a long term research programme at the Leatherhead Food RA on modelling. The primary objective is to demonstrate to the food industry the benefits to be gained from the use of modelling techniques to optimise the control of manufacturing processes. As a result of this effort, the Leatherhead Food RA has established a team with the necessary skills and expertise to offer advice to anyone in the food industry.

Current modelling study is concentrating initially on the vacuum evaporation process using a batch boiling pan, a process that has wide uses in the jam and confectionery industries. In the early stages, sucrose/glucose syrup mixtures were used, with subsequent extensions to fruit, vegetable and meat formulations. A mathematical model of this unit operation is now completed; so too is the design and construction of a pilot vacuum boiling pan plant used for validating the model.[3] Presently, the results obtained indicate that the model does represent the process adequately. Henceforth, work will be aimed at using the model for process control, to investigate design improvements and optimise processing conditions.

ACKNOWLEDGEMENT

The authors would like to thank the Ministry of Agriculture, Fisheries and Food for sponsoring the research work being carried out at the Leatherhead Food RA, and the Director of the Leatherhead Food RA for permission to publish the work presented herein.

REFERENCES

1. HIMMELBLAU, D. M. and BISCHOFF, K. B. (1968). *Process Analysis and Simulation*, Wiley, New York.
2. DANG, N. D. P. (1982). *BFMIRA Scientific and Technical Surveys, No. 132*, Leatherhead Food RA, Leatherhead.
3. DANG, N. D. P. (1982). *BFMIRA Research Report, No. 387*, Leatherhead Food RA, Leatherhead.

16

Control of Quality of Starch and Starch Products

W. Kempf and G. Tegge

Federal Research Centre of Grain and Potato Processing, Detmold, Federal Republic of Germany

ABSTRACT

A review of starch and starch-derived products requiring intensive quality control is given. Quality control includes three main points here considered: quality criteria, quality standards and quality analyses. Their meanings and importance are explained. It is shown that quality control is not an end in itself but an inevitable problem to be solved for each single material. The quality standards for starch products in the Federal Republic of Germany do not have the status of law but more that of an agreement between industry and consumers in the form of 'General Directions'. Some of these standards are explained from the technological point of view.

The superposed role of standardisation of analytical methods is emphasised because it is known that different methods for a single determination can lead to widely differing results. German Industry Standards (DIN) constituting international standards of special importance are mentioned.

With reference to quality control, two methods are described of technological importance. They concern yield determinations of grain maize and wheat flour. Both methods give clear graphic descriptions of recovery rates of the different products by imitating the starch recovery processes. By investigating raw materials in this way it can be shown 'what must be done' instead of 'what should have been done'.

For quality control of starch and starch products, including source, modified, and saccharified materials, respectively, three different terms and fields are to be noted, i.e. *quality criteria*, *quality standards* and *quality analysis*. These terms are sometimes mixed-up, and cause misunderstandings and differences of opinion, so we would like to try to clarify them.

Regarding the quality criteria of starch products there are three aspects, namely:

1. The product itself, depending on the source material.
2. Its properties and those of intermediate and final products.
3. Associated materials of intermediate and final products.

In the quality control of starch and starch products we have to deal with more than 500 final products besides numerous source materials and many intermediate and by-products. A large number of final products is the result of saccharification of starch or starch-containing materials. Each one of them shows particular and specific properties and more or less wanted or unwanted 'contaminations', which require determination. Multiplication of the large number of different materials by the determination methods leads us to a nearly astronomical number of combinations. There is thus a necessity for classification and standardisation of quality control even though the economic field and importance of the starch industry are not as great as those of many others.

The main source material of the starch industry is maize (or corn as maize is called in the USA) with about 70 % of the total, and there are two important quality criteria, i.e.

1. The amount of extractable starch.
2. The processing behaviour and properties.

Similar criteria are of interest for the wheat starch industry with respect to wheat flour or whole wheat grain as source material, and for the potato starch industry.

Properties of unmodified starches are primarily located in their rheological behaviour, i.e. swelling power, gelatinisation, viscosity, gelling, retrogradation, film formation etc., and these properties are far more complicated after different processes of modification. Potato starch is of greatest interest for industrial/technical purposes and the majority of wheat starch is used for foods and baking goods while maize starch can be of interest for both fields of application. The modified properties can be determined in any case by special analytical methods, but give rise to many new problems. All this comes under the term quality standards. Quality analysis has its main importance in the field of starch saccharification. For this purpose a starch of low content of protein and fat or—more precisely—of soluble protein and fatty acids must be preferred. Without regard to the price, potato starch should have preference, as its protein content is very low and it gives rise to no unwanted side reactions or discoloration of saccharification products. For some of these products mineral substances can affect adversely hygroscopicity, clearness and crystal yield of different intermediate products, and especially final products like syrups, candies and beverages. Certain contents of alkali and alkaline earth salts lower quality by causing hygroscopicity or turbidity, and heavy metals, iron and copper cause discoloration.

From all mentioned aspects one may see that quality control is not an end in itself but an inevitable problem to be solved for each material. The quality standards are very difficult to establish because customers' requirements can be very different and sometimes are carried to excess. To quote an example: why do we need a shining white starch without any protein content for making a chocolate pudding cream with the aid of two or three eggs? Quality standards

TABLE 1

'GENERAL DIRECTIONS FOR STARCH AND CERTAIN STARCH PRODUCTS' (ASSOCIATION FOR FOOD LAW AND FOOD SCIENCE, BONN-BAD GODESBERG, FEDERAL REPUBLIC OF GERMANY)

Individual starches	*Starch products*
Maize starch	Edible potato starch
Wheat starch	Sago
First grade	Pregelatinised starches
Second grade	Maltodextrins
Rice starch	Starch sugar
Milo starch	
(Sorghum starch)	*Appendix I*
Potato starch	Gluten
Sweet potato starch	Pregelatinised flours
(Batata starch)	
Tapioca starch	*Appendix II*
(Manioc starch)	Glucose syrup
(Cassava starch)	Dried glucose syrup
	Dextrose monohydrate
	Anhydrous dextrose

TABLE 2

'GENERAL DIRECTIONS FOR STARCH AND CERTAIN STARCH PRODUCTS—PART 1: CEREAL STARCHES' (ASSOCIATION FOR FOOD LAW AND FOOD SCIENCE, BONN-BAD GODESBERG, FEDERAL REPUBLIC OF GERMANY)

	Maize	*Wheat A*	*Wheat B*	*Rice*	*Milo starch*
Colour	White to yellowish	White	White to grey–brown	White to yellowish	White to greyish
Smell	Neutral	Neutral	Neutral	Neutral	Neutral
Taste	Neutral	Neutral	Neutral	Neutral	Neutral
Humidity (%)	14	14	14	14	14
Crude protein (%)	0·5	0·5	5	0·5	0·5
Crude fat (%)	0·1	0·1	0·5	0·1	0·1
Mineral matter (%)	0·3	0·3	1·0	1·0	0·3
Sulphur dioxide (mg/kg)	50	50	50	50	50

All data are presented as maximum limits and refer to starches with maximum moisture content.

TABLE 3

'GENERAL DIRECTIONS FOR STARCH AND CERTAIN STARCH PRODUCTS—PART 2: TUBER AND ROOT STARCHES' (ASSOCIATION FOR FOOD LAW AND FOOD SCIENCE, BONN-BAD GODESBERG, FEDERAL REPUBLIC OF GERMANY)

	Potato	*Sweet potato*	*Tapioca*
Colour	White	White to greyish	White to greyish
Smell	Neutral	Neutral	Neutral
Taste	Neutral	Neutral	Neutral
Humidity (%)	21	18	18
Crude protein (%)	0·1	0·2	0·3
Crude fat (%)	Traces	Traces	Traces
Mineral matter (%)	0·5	0·5	0·5
Sulphur dioxide (mg/kg)	50	50	50

All data are presented as maximum limits and refer to starches with maximum moisture content.

for starches in the Federal Republic of Germany are very broad-minded as they are established with the aid of the starch producing industry. They are known as 'General Directions for Starch and Certain Starch Products' and are given in Table 1. Remarkable is the complete absence of modified starches, except the pregelatinised starches, from these regulations. Furthermore, one may see from Table 2 that permitted levels of 'contaminants of cereal starches' are high enough to cover any reduction in quality by the starch producing industry. Similar 'Directions' are shown in Table 3 for tuber and root starches from potatoes, sweet potatoes and tapioca (or cassava). Accepted humidity is higher, but limits for protein and fat are very much lower compared with cereal starches with regard to the nature of resource plants. Table 4 shows some 'Directions' for starch

TABLE 4

'GENERAL DIRECTIONS FOR STARCH AND CERTAIN STARCH PRODUCTS—PART 3: HYDROLYSIS PRODUCTS' (ASSOCIATION FOR FOOD LAW AND FOOD SCIENCE, BONN-BAD GODESBERG, FEDERAL REPUBLIC OF GERMANY)

	Dry substance (%)	*Dextrose* (*D-glucose*) (%)	*Sulphated ash* (%)	*Sulphur dioxide* (*mg/kg*)
Glucose syrup	Minimum 70	Minimum 20[a]	Maximum 1·0	Maximum 20 (400)
Dried glucose syrup	Minimum 93	Minimum 20[a]	Maximum 1·0	Maximum 20 (150)
Dextrose monohydrate	Minimum 90	Minimum 99·5	Maximum 0·25	Maximum 15
Anhydrous dextrose	Minimum 98	Minimum 99·5	Maximum 0·25	Maximum 15

[a] Dextrose equivalent (DE).

All data refer to hydrolysis product dry-substance.

saccharification products. For glucose syrups two different sulphur dioxide limits are given, depending on the use of the products. For 'normal' glucose syrups the sulphur dioxide content is limited to 20 ppm. Glucose syrups for exceptional use and for the commercial production of sweets are limited to 400 and 150 ppm sulphur dioxide, respectively.

Legislation, of course, plays an important and superimposed role. On the other hand, all criteria are of little relevance, if it is not known by which analytical method the material in question should be determined, as it is known that different methods can lead to widely differing results. As far as feedstuffs are concerned, there are feed laws in the Federal Republic of Germany which comprise all analytical methods to be used. The same is the case with regard to the Feed Law of the EEC.

For foods the Federal Health Office in Berlin is collecting standardised analytical methods and investigation processes. For starch and starch products there are standardised methods as German Industry Standards (DIN) which are partly included in

TABLE 5

ANALYTICAL METHODS FOR STARCH AND STARCH PRODUCTS MAINLY USED IN THE FEDERAL REPUBLIC OF GERMANY: NATIONAL METHODS

Deutsche Industrie-Normen (DIN), Deutsches Institut für Normung e.V. (DIN), Berlin (German Industry Standards (DIN), German Institute for Standardization (DIN), Berlin)
'Standard-Methoden für Stärke und Stärkeerzeugnisse', Arbeitsgemeinschaft für Getreideforschung e.V., Detmold ('Standard Methods for Starch and Starch Products,' Association of Cereal Research, Detmold)
'Standard-Methoden für Getreide, Mehl und Brot,' Arbeitsgemeinschaft für Getreideforschung e.V., Detmold ('Standard Methods for Grain, Flour and Bread,' Association of Cereal Research, Detmold)

'Standard Methods for Starch and Starch Products' and 'Standard Methods for Grain, Flour and Bread', both edited by the Association of Cereal Research, Detmold (Table 5). In the international sphere there are, besides EEC Regulations, the Standard Methods of ISO, CIRF, ICC and ICUMSA, of particular importance. All of them are well distributed and accessible so that they need not be explained extensively (Table 6).

Quality control of starch products and source materials comes into very close association with technology, and can prove its usefulness. Instead of showing what was wrong during manufacture, these methods are able to show what should be done to avoid low qualities and low yields, and could serve as examples for other industrial process planning. The point in question is to determine the processability of source materials into starch and what yields of final and by-products can be predicted. Such methods are developed for source materials such as maize, wheat flour and potatoes and represent nothing more than imitations of industrial/technical recovery processes.

In the yield determination of maize, investigation of general

TABLE 6

ANALYTICAL METHODS FOR STARCH AND STARCH PRODUCTS MAINLY USED IN THE FEDERAL REPUBLIC OF GERMANY: INTERNATIONAL METHODS

EEC Regulations, Commission of the European Community (EC), Brussels, Belgium
ISO International Standards, International Organization for Standardization (ISO), Geneva, Switzerland
Standard Analytical Methods, Corn Industries Research Foundation (CIRF), Washington, DC, USA
Standard Methods, International Association for Cereal Chemistry (ICC), Vienna, Austria
ICUMSA Methods for Sugar Analysis, International Commission for Uniform Methods of Sugar Analysis (ICUMSA), Brunswick, Germany

TABLE 7

QUALITY CONTROL OF MAIZE—GENERAL CONDITIONS AND ANALYTICAL COMPOSITION

General conditions
Foreign matter
Mould
Breakage
Foreign material
Impurities
Test weight (g/1 000 kernels)
Test volume (ml/1 000 g kernels)
Analytical composition
Moisture
Dry-substance
Crude starch
Crude protein
Crude fat
Crude fibre
Mineral matter
Total dry-substance
Acidity
pH-value

quality (Table 7) with respect to foreign matter is the first step, combined with estimation of test weight and test volume. The second step contains a chemical investigation of the composition using more or less modified classical methods.

It might seem to be very important to know all corresponding data, but the practical expert in the factory does not only want to know how much starch is in the maize kernels, but *how much of this starch* can be recovered and sold. The yield estimating method imitates the starch recovery process by using not more than 50 g of source material, follows the technical diagram and splits up the steeped maize kernels into the 5 essential technological fractions instead of their chemical components, i.e.

Steeping water dry matter (soluble-substance)
Germs
Fibre ('fodder')
Gluten (proteineous fraction)
Starch

TABLE 8

QUALITY CONTROL OF MAIZE—YIELD DETERMINATION AND EVALUATION

Starch	*Germs*
Loss	Moisture
Recovery	Crude fat
Appearance	Acid number
Smell	Free fatty acids
Taste	(expressed as oleic acid)
Moisture	
Crude protein	
	Fibre
Gluten	Moisture
Moisture	Crude starch
Crude protein	
Evaluation	*Steep-water dry-substance*
Starch yield	
Starch recovery	*Total yield*

The total yield, of course, must be controlled and should be as close to 100% as possible.

Quality criteria must be determined proving that clean separation of fractions is possible without difficulties (Table 8). Final evaluation of the 'efficiency' quotient (starch recovery/starch content) gives a clear picture of the qualification of a maize charge to be processed. Recovery rates and starch yields are given in Table 9. Many consulting engineering and constructing companies have given their guarantee for yield of starch after technological investigation of maize to be processed with the aid of this method carried out in our institute, and could be protected against subsequent financial claims.

TABLE 9

REVIEW OF MAIZE SAMPLES WITH REGARD TO STARCH YIELD AND RECOVERY RATE AND EXPRESSED IN % DRY-SUBSTANCE

Starch yield[1]	*Recovery rate*[2]
Above 68: superior	Above 96: superior
65–68: good	93–96: good
62–65: sufficient	91–93: sufficient
Below 62: unsuitable	Below 91: unsuitable

Similar tests can be carried out with wheat flour as the mainly used basic material for the wheat starch industry. The yields of first and second grade starch are especially of great importance. Another important question to be answered is that of properties of the gluten fraction recovered from wheat flour. High quality wheat flour is able to form a strong and plastic wet gluten structure which keeps nearly like caoutchouc and makes recovery of nearly gluten-free starch. Other flours give crumbling, greasy structures of the gluten, and their processing in starch factories can only be done after adding sodium chloride or other auxiliary materials, or by decreasing of temperature.

This is only a short glance at the field of quality control of starch and starch products. Determination of degree of substitution of modified starches or sugar composition of starch saccharification products is a further widespread field of very complicated character. In all cases quality control should never be done in absence of ulterior motive, but in close connection with practical uses to make production profitable and to make quality sure in the fullest sense of the word and of benefit to the customer.

REFERENCES

1. PELSHENKE, P. F. and LINDEMANN, E. (1954). *Stärke*, **6**, 177–82.
2. KEMPF, W. (1964). Unpublished work.

17

The Evaluation of Canning Processes from External Temperature History

R. H. SKINNER*

Formerly National College of Food Technology, University of Reading, UK

ABSTRACT

Because of the difficulties associated with measuring temperature at the centre of a can of foodstuff during heat sterilisation, the ability to reliably evaluate the sterilising effect of the process from the measurement of temperature outside the can would be of great potential value. The theoretical model for conductive heat transfer is of only limited applicability because some measure of convection is involved with the majority of products and also because, even by today's standards, the complexity of the associated computation remains less than ideal for routine use.

For this reason the various empirical models for can-centre temperature history which have been proposed over the years are still of potential interest. However, all suffer from a serious limitation in that, irrespective of reliability, they offer solutions only for a hypothetical process in which external temperature remains constant at the processing level throughout the period between two instants when it changes from and to ambient levels.

The paper suggests a model in which the dependence of can-centre temperature upon external temperature history is simulated by the response of a linear dynamic system to an applied input. Such a system is defined by an appropriate differential equation and by using numerical integration a solution can be obtained irrespective of the nature of the applied input.

One criterion for specifying the product-dependent parameters of

* Present address: 49 Farncombe Hill, Godalming, Surrey GU7 2AU, UK.

the model is discussed and representative comparisons between measured and predicted temperature histories presented.

It is suggested that, if these parameters can be reliably established for a given pack, then, in principle, a suitable data logging system should enable a sterilising value, computed either retrospectively or in real time, to be assigned to every such pack leaving a production steriliser.

INTRODUCTION

The evaluation of the sterilising effect of a thermal process applied to a canned foodstuff, from its external temperature history implicitly falls into two stages: first, the determination of internal temperature history from the external, and secondly, the evaluation of sterilising effect from known thermal destruction data for some target microorganism.

Two approaches are possible to this two-stage problem. The first is to calculate thermal destruction by a process of integration throughout the can to obtain a probability for microbial survival from a given initial loading. The second method determines an upper bound for survival probability based on the temperature history at the can-centre, which is assumed to be the slowest heating point.

Since the objective of processing is to reduce the probability of survival below an acceptable limit, the second method, although failing to give a specific probability, does not suffer in comparison with the first and offers two advantages by virtue of requiring only the temperature history at a single point. First, this temperature history may be formulated theoretically or empirically in terms of only a single variable, time, and secondly, it may, alternatively, be directly measured.

A theoretical basis for formulation exists only in the case of foods which heat by pure conduction and in this case solutions are in the form of a complex infinite series.[1] The can-centre is at sterilisation-effective temperatures during the later stages of heating, when the first term of this series is an adequate approximation, and also in the early stages of cooling, when numerous terms must be used.

When any measure of convection is involved there is no longer a practicable theoretical basis for calculating temperature, though normally in the later stages of the heating of such packs, the centre temperature is frequently found to approach the external temperature exponentially, giving a correspondence with the first term of the theoretical solution.

For the heating phase it is thus possible to formulate a simple expression for the temperature–time relationship in either case and this is achieved using two parameters f and j which, in the theoretical case, depend on the thermal properties of the foodstuff and the pack geometry, respectively. A great deal of effort has been expended by many investigators in seeking to establish a comparable relationship for the early stages of the cooling phase and one or two may be used with a measure of confidence.[2] However, they have all been limited to the situation where the external temperature changes to its cooling level very rapidly, which is far from being the case with most continuous processes.

A DYNAMIC SYSTEM MODEL

I have elsewhere described[3] a new approach in which, rather than regarding the process as two unrelated phases, it is treated as a single dynamic system empirically represented by a second-order differential equation in which the constants involved are dependent only on the parameters f and j. Such a system possesses a considerable advantage in the fact that it will offer a solution for processes comprising any sequence of continuous and sudden changes in external temperature.

This model proved generally satisfactory in matching measured data for processes involving appreciable convection, but was less satisfactory when compared with theoretical temperature histories for conduction processes. The limitation arose from the fact that the two exponential terms which constitute the solution of any equation of the type used could not adequately approximate the several terms from the theoretical solution needed in the early part of cooling. Nevertheless, the temperature curve in this region was broadly of the correct nature and it proved possible, without introducing any new parameters, to modify the model specification to correct this discrepancy and obtain agreement in a much wider range of processes. These included processes in which external temperature changed linearly both during come-up and during cooling and for which no other model known to the author offers a solution.

The model temperatures were evaluated using the analytical solution functions of the differential equation. For every change in the external temperature function, a new solution function had to be superimposed upon those already in use, and this effectively limited the complexity of external temperature history which could be employed. The modified model specification was also a contributing factor to this limitation.

USE OF NUMERICAL INTEGRATION

The novel part of this paper consists of reporting the advantages which follow upon employing numerical rather than analytical solutions of the model-defining equation.

First, the number of exponential terms in the solution functions of a linear differential equation is equal to its order, so that it is to be expected that the matching of the early part of the cooling phase could be progressively improved by increasing the order of the system. Such increases of order would make the program for evaluation of the solution functions unrealistically complex but by employing numerical integration each unit increment in order requires only the addition of a single program statement of extreme simplicity.

Secondly, as a consequence of this increase in order of the system, the supplementary factor in the model specification can be dropped so that there is no longer any constraint on the external temperature history. If the behaviour of any pack can be matched by appropriate choice of process-independent model parameters then, in principle, a suitably designed data logging system for temperature at sufficient locations within a steriliser and for conveyor speed, should enable a sterilising value to be computed, either retrospectively or in real time, for every can leaving the steriliser.

MODEL FORMULATION

The parameters involved in the new model are most conveniently selected by making reference to the simple instantaneous jump in external temperature from 1 to 0 on a normalised scale, with the can-centre initially in thermal equilibrium at $\theta = 1$.

We are seeking a differential equation which would yield an analytical solution for θ in terms of time, t, of the form:

$$\theta = a_1 \exp(-p_1 t) + a_2 \exp(-p_2 t) + \cdots + a_n \exp(-p_n t) \quad (1)$$

with $p_1 < p_2 < p_3 \ldots$ This differential equation will be:

$$\theta^{(n)} + b_{n-1}\theta^{(n-1)} + \cdots + b_1\theta^{(1)} + b_0\theta = 0 \quad (2)$$

where $\theta^{(n)}$ is the nth derivative of θ with respect to t and b_{n-r} is the sum of products of all possible combinations of r factors taken from $p_1, p_2, \ldots, p_n$, e.g. $b_{n-1} = p_1 + p_2 + \cdots + p_n$ and $b_0 = p_1 p_2, \ldots, p_n$.

The established approximation for small values of θ is

$$\theta = j10^{-t/f} \quad (3)$$

so that for the new model to be identifiable with this, we must take $a_1 = j$ and $p_1 = 2{\cdot}303/f$.

This fixes only 2 of the $2n$ parameters involved so that additional criteria are required to determine values for those remaining. To simplify this problem the arbitrary but, it is felt, not unrealistic criterion that the exponential factors shall be in increasing geometrical progression has been introduced, reducing the number of undetermined quantities to n. Initial thermal equilibrium suggests making the first $n-1$ time derivatives initially zero and this, taken with the requirement that $\theta = 1$ when $t = 0$, leads to a system of n simultaneous equations which can be solved for the exponent ratio factor p_{r+1}/p_r leading to values for all the equation coefficients. Since the equation, rather than its solution, forms the basis of computation, there is no need to determine the coefficients a_r.

Having chosen the model parameters it becomes necessary, for computational purposes, to express eqn (2) in terms of actual temperature, T, rather than reduced temperature, θ, and we obtain:

$$T^{(n)} + b_{n-1}T^{(n-1)} + \cdots + b_0 T = b_0 T_1 \quad (4)$$

where T_1 is external temperature. An algorithm for solution of the equation with $n = 3$ is given below. h is the time increment between successive evaluations of T and T_0 is the initial centre temperature.

$t = 0 : T = T_0 : T^{(2)} = T^{(1)} = 0$

LOOP $t = t + h$

$T^{(3)} = b_0(T_1 - T) - b_1 T^{(1)} - b_2 T^{(2)}$

$T^{(2)} = T^{(2)} + hT^{(3)}$

$T^{(1)} = T^{(1)} + hT^{(2)}$

$T = T + hT^{(1)}$

GOTO LOOP

MODEL PERFORMANCE

The order of equation was selected by comparing models of increasing order with a variety of theoretical and measured processes. It was evident that, in general, matching improved with increasing order but that beyond 5th order, improvement became marginal and so 5th order was selected as standard. In this case the system of equations for determining the index ratio, k, reduced to:

$$k^{10} - j(k^4 - 1)(k^3 - 1)(k^2 - 1)(k - 1) = 0$$

A short iterative procedure at the start of the model program performs the necessary solution of this equation which has only a single root in the range $0 < k < 100$. k has the values 2·67, 3·76 and 21·2 for $j = 2{\cdot}04$, 1·5 and 1·05, respectively. No root > 1 exists for $j = 1$ which is to be expected since this value of j is only obtainable with a first-order system.

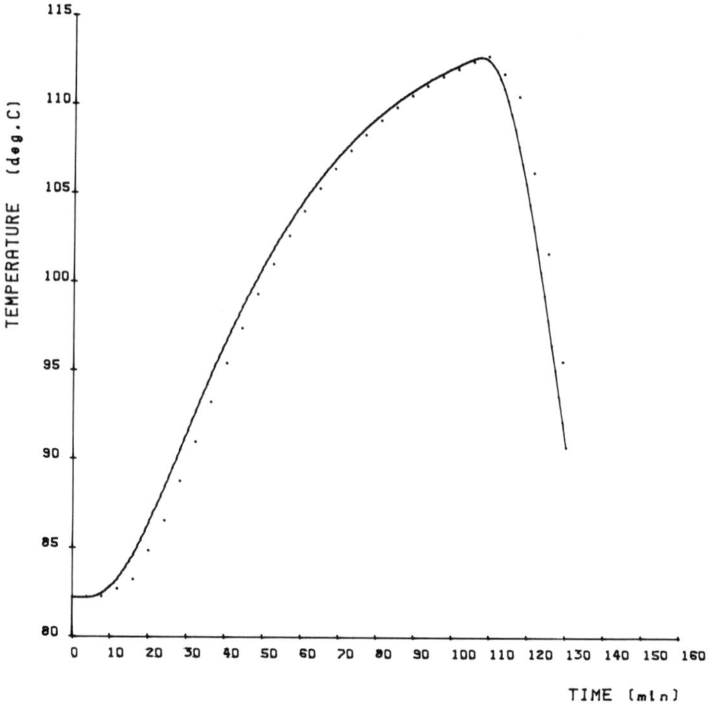

FIG. 1. Performances of the model in two theoretical processes.

Figures 1 and 2 show the performance of the model in two theoretical hot-fill processes using $f = 78{\cdot}3$ min and $j = 2{\cdot}04$. The continuous curves represent the model whilst the individual points are theoretical values. Figures 3 and 4 show typical comparisons between model and measured temperatures for real processes. The values of j and f employed here were obtained in each case by subjecting an identical pack to a rapid come-up process. Temperatures were measured by fine wire thermocouples and for the purpose of model evaluation the three sections of the external temperature history were represented by separate cubic equations fitted by polynomial regression to a selection of measured temperatures. Eighteen such processes have been investigated and no surprise will be occasioned by the fact that agreement between model and measurement is often far less good than in the illustrations, yet these are fully representative of the best 40 % of results.

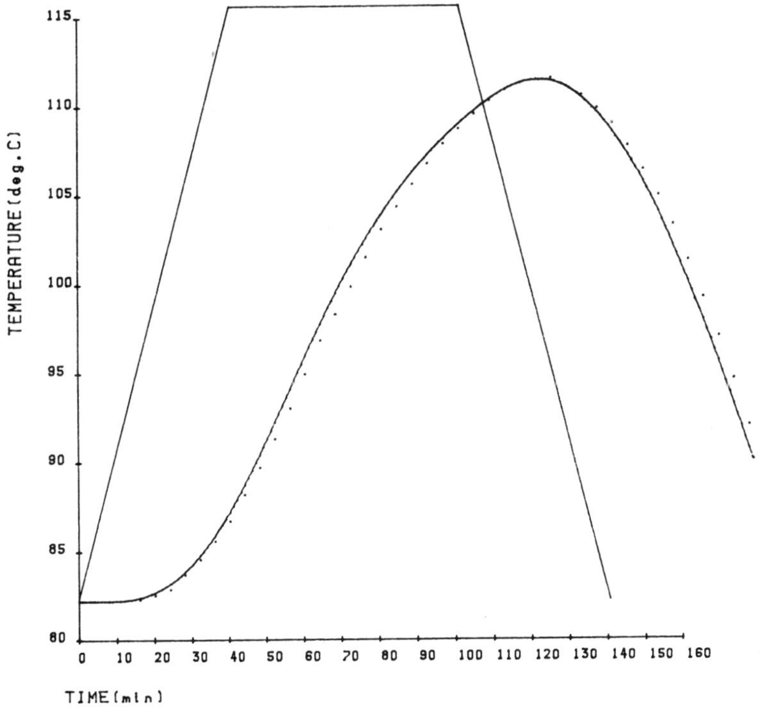

FIG. 2. Performances of the model in two theoretical processes.

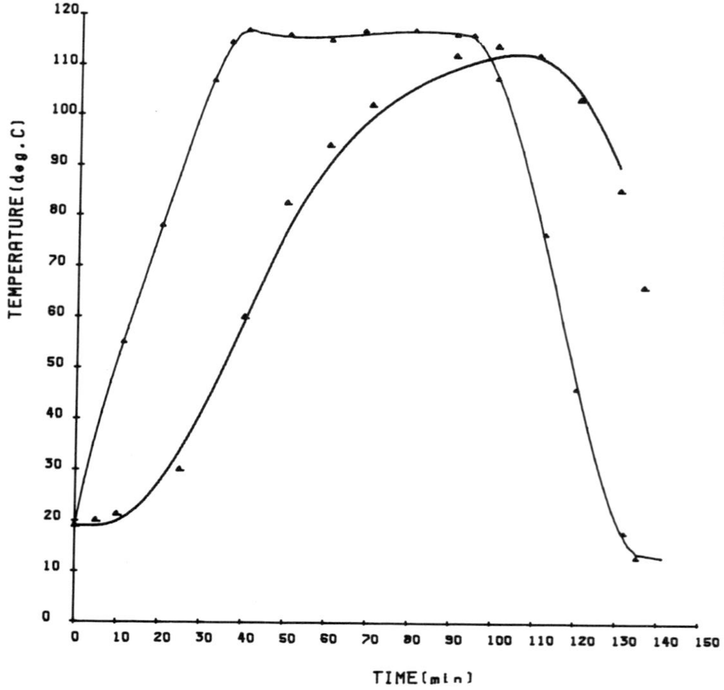

FIG. 3. Performances of the model in simulating two real processes.

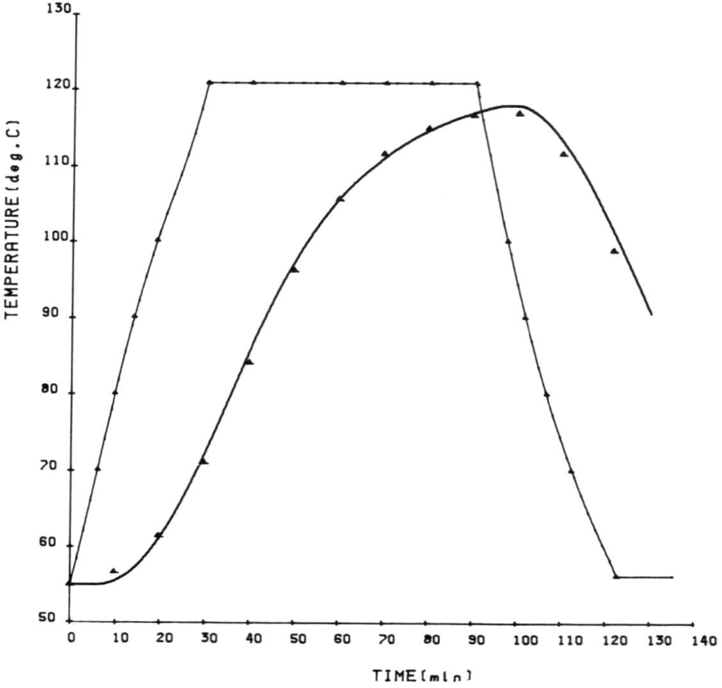

FIG. 4. Performances of the model in simulating two real processes.

CONTINUOUS PROCESS EVALUATION

It has been suggested above that if the adequacy of this model can be established for any pack, then it should be possible to assign a sterilising value to any such pack emerging from a continuous steriliser and this concluding section suggests how this might be achieved.

The computation would be carried out simultaneously for a number of sample cans, say 10, uniformly spaced within the steriliser with values for intermediate cans assigned by interpolation. As one can left the plant its sterilising value would be logged and its place taken by one at the entry point. A number of temperature sensors, 8 would probably suffice, would enable the computer to store a table of temperatures at fixed points from which a value for any desired

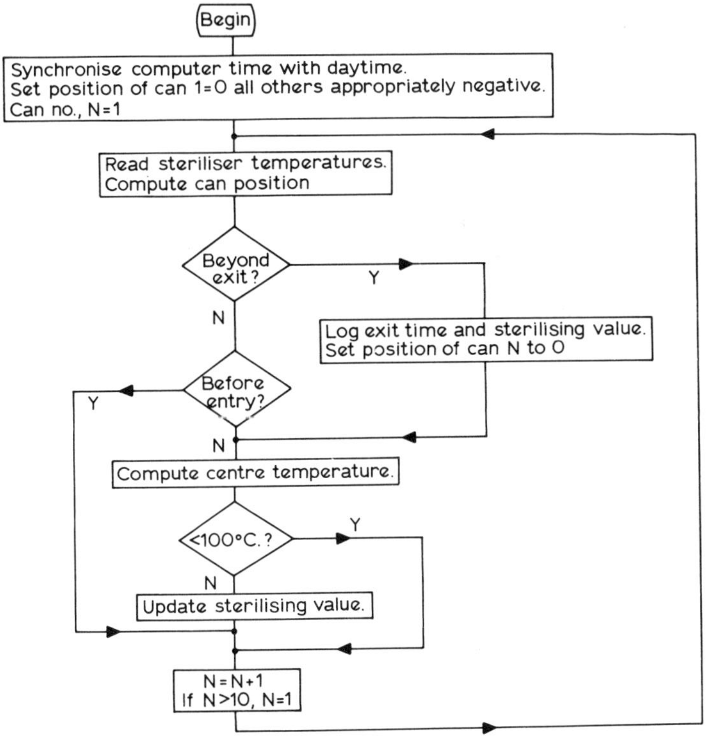

FIG. 5. Flow diagram for on-line computation.

location could be interpolated. A table of conveyor speeds over a period of a few minutes should also be allowed for, although, should the computation speed be sufficiently rapid, a single instantaneous value would be adequate. The computer's internal clock would be related to daytime at start-up and used with conveyor speed data to determine the can positions. It would not be necessary to use a fixed interval between computations for successive cans provided that a table containing the time of the last update for each can was maintained.

Figure 5 shows a suggested flow diagram for this computation.

ACKNOWLEDGEMENT

I am indebted to J. O'Flynn for empirical data employed in the model assessment.

REFERENCES

1. Carslaw, H. S. and Jaeger, J. C. (1959). *The Conduction of Heat in Solids*, Clarendon Press, Oxford.
2. Skinner, R. H. and Jowitt, R. (1977). In: *Mathematical Modelling in Food Processing*, Ed. Anon., Lund Institute of Technology, Sweden, 203–22.
3. Skinner, R. H. (1979). In: *Food Microbiology and Technology*, Ed. Jarvis, B., Christian, J. H. B. and Michener, H. D., Midicina Viva, Parma, Italy, 309–22.

18

Some Aspects of the Chemical Basis of Fruit and Vegetable Quality

R. S. SHALLENBERGER

New York State Agricultural Experiment Station, Cornell University, Geneva, New York, USA

ABSTRACT

To illustrate the chemical basis of processed fruit and vegetable quality, three examples are given. The first is a heat-induced flavour defect in processed table beets, the second a metabolically induced flavour defect in carrots, and the third is inferior colour, flavour and texture in processed apple products. The chemical origin of these problems and their solution has interesting cause–effect relations.

INTRODUCTION

In the sense that foods are an organisation of chemical systems, food quality logically has a chemical basis. It includes food nutritive value, wholesomeness, colour, flavour and texture. The former two attributes are of primary importance, but also of no significance whatsoever if the colour, flavour and textural attributes are not appropriate. If the latter three attributes are not appropriate, the food will not be consumed. This seems to be the principal realm of food chemistry, and the chemical basis of food quality.

The types of chemistry involved in studies to ascertain and establish food quality are of the usual types such as organic and inorganic, enzymic and non-enzymic. In addition there is a type of chemistry probably best described as psychochemical, which involves studies on the sweetness of the sugars, the sourness of the acids, appropriate sugar/acid ratios and so forth. Psychochemistry also involves the study of unusual, off and unbalanced flavours in foods.

The origin of some of these, and the correction of the problem, usually involves intriguing cause and effect relations, several of which will be mentioned subsequently.

There is also a type of chemistry related to food quality that is best described as psychophysical. The colour attributes of the plant pigments (greenness of the chlorophylls, redness of the anthocyanins, etc.) and the textural attributes of the plant polymers are examples. A general principle seems to be that whenever one quality attribute, such as colour, is aberrant, the other two (flavour and texture) will be out of synchronisation also. To elaborate upon this thesis I would like to mention several food quality problems with fruits and vegetables for processing that were essentially food chemistry problems which had rather neat practical solutions. One problem had, in the final analysis, an alteration in the fertiliser programme as the solution, another an alteration in the raw product storage practice, and still another by rescheduling of the harvest programme.

OFF-FLAVOUR IN BEET PURÉE

Table beet processors are occasionally troubled by the sporadic occurrence of an off-flavour in the processed beets variously described as medicinal, astringent and bitter. A salient feature of this defect is that it is not detectable in the raw beet, but forms during processing, suggesting that the defect is heat-induced. To follow up on this idea, beet purée as a baby food was selected for study because the time–temperature programme used to ensure sterilisation is rather drastic and involves holding the purée at around 93·3 °C for some time before filling into jars and then retorting for 45 min at 118·3 °C.[1] When silicic acid chromatography showed that the pyrrolidonecarboxylic acid content of the bitter purées was nearly double that of the acceptable samples, we felt that we were on the right track, and therefore executed a systematic study of the glutamine–pyrrolidonecarboxylic acid system.[2]

In this particular case, prior knowledge more or less directed the course of our studies. We knew, for example, that table beets were capable of accumulating copious amounts of the half-amide of glutamic acid, or glutamine. We also knew that L-glutamine was essentially tasteless, and under relatively mild conditions could be quantitatively converted to pyrrolidonecarboxylic acid (PCA).

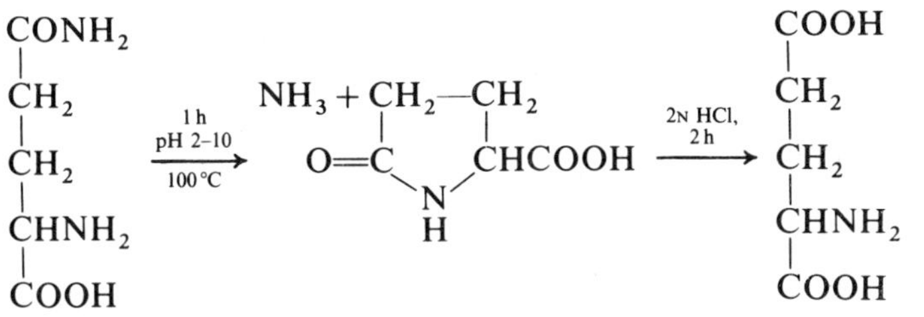

Glutamine PCA Glutamic acid

The fact that PCA can itself be hydrolysed to glutamic acid served as a convenient method for its determination. Then, by assembling purées with a wide range of PCA content, we were able to demonstrate the correlation between off-flavour intensity and PCA content (Fig. 1). Figure 2 shows that the panel could significantly detect ammonium pyrrolidonecarboxylate in purées when 50 mg had been added. Thus, while the glutamine–PCA transformation was characteristic of the type of reactions leading to off-flavour, it was not the sole cause, which was to be expected. Other ammonium salts of organic acids are not particularly pleasing to taste.

With the cause of the off-flavour established, we next turned our attention to minimising the reaction.

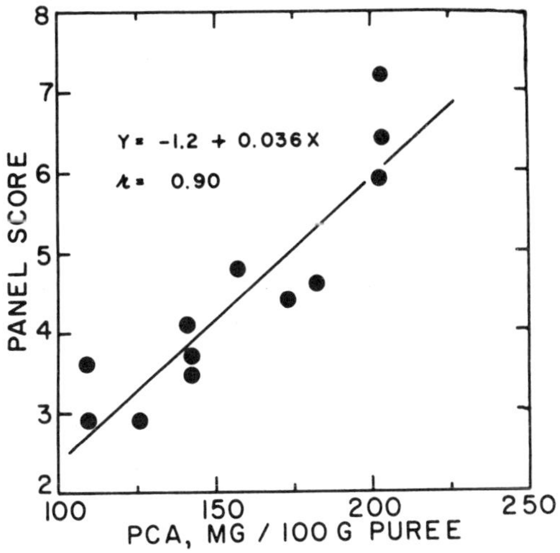

FIG. 1. Relation between off-flavour scores for beet purée and concentration of pyrrolidonecarboxylic acid.

With table beets grown for processing, as well as with other crops, the profit column can only be entered when the yield per hectare is satisfactory. This is ensured, in turn, by the rate of nitrogen fertilisation. For beets, the usual practice is to broadcast at the rate of 68 kg nitrogen per hectare in the spring, followed by a side-dressing in midsummer, and then by a second side-dressing in the autumn to keep the tops up.[3] However, whenever the autumn season is characterised by cool, wet weather, nitrogen uptake continues and is

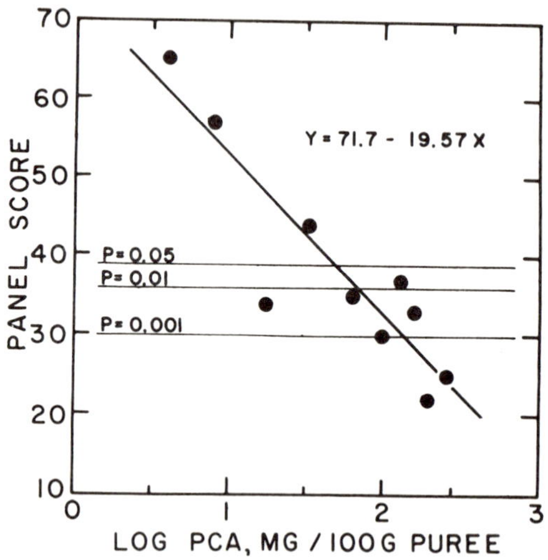

FIG. 2. Effect of ammonium pyrrolidonecarboxylate added to beet purée upon the triangle-intensity score.

held in reserve by the accumulation of glutamine. This is when the problem seems to occur. It also seems to occur when beets held in common storage are frozen, again leading to the accumulation of glutamine, probably for osmotic purposes in this case. In any event, there does not seem to be any solution to the problem. If one could anticipate the weather, perhaps the grower could hold off on his second side-dressing, or the beets could be held in refrigerated storage. A processing solution recommended was to leach the glutamine from the puréed beets in a holding tank prior to sterilisation.

OFF-FLAVOUR IN PROCESSED CARROTS

Along somewhat similar lines, our research unit was approached with a flavour defect in carrots. In this particular case, we did not have prior knowledge to assist us, and the flavour defect was unusual in that it occurred in the raw carrots, and carried over into the processed product. It too was described as bitter, hot, soapy and so forth, and was quite serious as the carrots were inedible. As the defect occurred in the raw material, the first approach taken towards finding a solution to the problem was horticultural. In spite of the fact that field experiments are not the easiest of studies to conduct, it was established that none of the following factors were involved: date of planting, soil type, chemical weed control programme, insecticides applied, soil fumigation practices, drainage, the incidence of plant disease, date of harvest and major and minor element fertilisation.[4]

It was then observed that when carrots harvested from a given field were stored in refrigerated houses they soon turned bitter, whereas those held in common storage (piled on the ground outside the processing plant) would not, indicating a metabolic source of the off-flavour induced by the refrigerated storage. In the refrigerated storage, humidity, temperature and air circulation were eliminated as the cause. However, carrots stored in closed containers and receiving only air from *outside* the storage would not turn bitter, while the others would. The causal and triggering agent therefore moved in the air, i.e. a physiologically active gas was responsible, and the scene was set for solution of the problem.

In the meantime, some progress was being made in the laboratory. Sondheimer[5] had found that hexane extracts of bitter carrots had a strong ultraviolet absorption spectrum associated not only with bitterness, but with the occurrence of 3-methyl-6-methoxy-8-hydroxy-3,4-dihydroisocoumarin which served as a rapid objective test for the bitterness and eliminated the need for our taste panel, which was rapidly losing the faith anyway.

It was also found that the so-called bitter principle was steam-distillable, and distillates of bitter carrots were murky and cloudy due to water insoluble components, whereas those from non-bitter carrots were quite clear. Extraction and purification of the steam-distillable bitter fraction yielded a light-yellow oil.[6] When a few microlitres of this oil were placed upon the tip of the tongue of panellists, the sensation perceived was seemingly analogous to the detonation of a bushel of carrots in the oral cavity within just a few microseconds. The 'bitter carrot' flavour problem was not a 'bitter flavour' problem at all, in the quinine sulphate bitterness sense, but a sensory response to an overabundant concentration of natural carrot root flavour.

To make what is by now a relatively long story somewhat shorter, the use of prior knowledge finally came into play. Obviously, a physiologically active gas in refrigerated storage was initiating the accumulation in excess of natural carrot flavour compounds. The first physiologically active gas to come to mind was ethylene, and as soon as ethylene came to mind, so did apples (it was known, for example, that apples are capable of emitting enough ethylene to defoliate roses). In all cases where carrots were bitter in refrigerated storage, ethylene could be detected and apples were present. In those cases where ethylene could not be detected, and apples were not present, the carrots had been stored when apples were present.[4] Thus, the solution to a very complex practical problem turned out, in the final analysis, to be quite simple. As opposed to the case for the bitter beets, where the ultimate solution was weather control, the solution for bitter carrots was merely to avoid storing them with apples.

UPGRADING COMMERCIAL PACKS OF PROCESSING APPLES

At one time the quality of the apple slices produced for the baking industry from New York's processing varieties was not competitive. The slice colour, flavour and texture were decidedly inferior even though New York produces about one-half of the processed apple products in the USA. Usually, but not always, slices made from the New York processing varieties Rhode Island Greening and Baldwin were flaccid, greenish in hue, and quite tart. As a consequence, they usually received a Standard or 'C' grade for quality by the United States Department of Agriculture (USDA) grading standards which qualified them for a decidedly inferior price.

The usual practice for harvesting processing apples was found to be a matter of convenience and practicality. Apple growers in New York normally start to harvest the variety Rhode Island Greening about the first or second week in September. Picking crews on hand are thus kept busy, and when the dessert varieties, such as McIntosh, begin to show proper colour, the crews concentrate on harvesting these varieties. They then return to complete harvesting the Greening variety. However, during an unusually cold growing season, or an unusually hot growing season, either of which seems to be the usual case, apple maturation rate is significantly retarded, and dessert varieties are slow to develop colour. As a consequence, the processing crop (Rhode Island Greenings are always green) may be harvested in early September even though their maturation rate is significantly retarded also. Therefore, apple maturity studies as related to processing quality were initiated.

It was found, during an initial two year pilot study, that the major processing variety, Rhode Island Greening, reached *minimum* maturity for processing as Fancy or Grade A apple slices on about 1 October or thereabout, or when 3000 heat units had been accumulated. Yet, the entire Greening crop during that two year study had been harvested one month earlier. Of course, apples may be harvested somewhat early, and further ripened in storage, but experience showed that the overall increase in quality was slight. Ripening in storage resulted in textural changes, but the colour and flavour were not improved.

During the course of the maturity and processing studies, various measures of maturity were employed to indicate *processing quality*. It was found, for example, that when the pressure needed to penetrate the apple flesh with a 1·11 cm head (Magness–Taylor instrument) dropped to between 66·7 and 90 N, the apples were at minimum maturity for processing. However, the variability experienced with this instrument was quite large and the rate of change of pressure test prior to and at harvest was too low to provide reliable differences. However, it was also found that when the Brix/acid ratio had increased to between 15 and 20, this too corresponded to minimum maturity for processing. This chemical test, although not as convenient, had narrower variability. This test also correlated well with the accumulation of heat units throughout the growing season.[7]

As these findings were judged to have important applications to the New York apple processing industry the decision was made to apply the maturity estimation procedures on a large scale. The primary object of the large-scale programme was simply to take the usual quality of the processed apple pack from a standard grade to the Fancy grade by carefully selecting the minimum harvest date when the variety Rhode Island Greening would begin to yield the Fancy pack processed products.

To keep variables to a minimum, canned apples slices were selected as the product to be produced commercially since the importance of the quality of a single variety is manifested only in slices. Nine growers having 12 Greening orchards and an estimated crop of 1173 tonne of apples agreed to participate. A leading canned apple slice processor made the necessary arrangements to procure the apples, and altered his processing schedule to permit canning of the slices at minimum maturity (or better) in order to insure a Fancy apple slice pack.

METHOD

Four orchards, designated as North (N), South (S), East (E) and West (W) were selected as pilot orchards. These bracketed the apple growing region along Lake Ontario, as shown in Fig. 3. Weekly samples were taken from these orchards for recording the pressure test, Brix/acid ratio, and also for processing throughout the study as

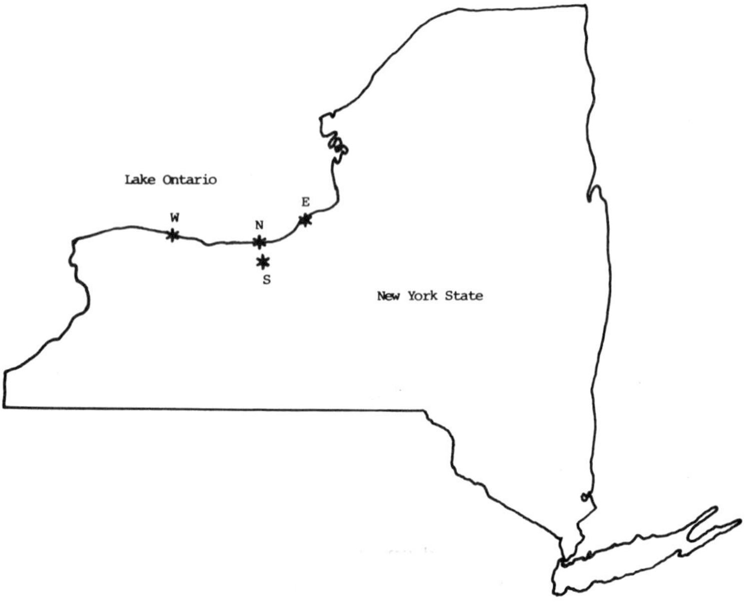

FIG. 3. Location of the 4 pilot apple orchards along the Ontario Lake plateau of New York State. The distance between the eastern and western orchards is about 100 miles.

canned apple slices in the pilot plant at Geneva, New York State. Samples were also taken from the 8 remaining orchards for recording the Brix/acid ratio only. It was felt that the maturity of all orchards could be estimated from the more complete records kept on the 4 pilot orchards.

As indicated by heat unit calculation for a central point, pressure test and Brix/acid ratio determinations, growers were informed that they would be told when their fruit would reach minimum maturity for processing as Fancy pack apple slices with some certainty 2 weeks before harvest should begin. They would be informed with absolute certainty 1 week before harvest should begin. In turn, the processor agreed to keep track of the apples from the pilot orchards when they arrived at the processing plant so further ripening in storage could be followed. The processor also agreed to process the apples when the Geneva studies indicated a Fancy product would be obtained.

RESULTS

Sampling of the 12 orchards for recording objective measures of maturity and for processing as slices began the first week of September. By 15 September, as determined on the basis of heat unit calculations, pressure test and Brix/acid ratios, the growers were informed that their crops would probably process as Fancy pack slices if harvested the first week in October. By 21 September, it was established that the minimum date for obtaining an average pressure test and a Brix/acid ratio of 15–20 would be 5 October, and harvesting should begin on that date. Figure 4 illustrates the manner in which this decision was made for 12 orchards on the basis of the changing Brix/acid ratio. Excluding orchard No. 6, which was the northern pilot orchard, the Brix/acid ratio for 11 remaining orchards ranged from 13 to 17 or averaged 15 on 5 October. The growers commenced harvesting around 5 October which was, for many, 3 weeks later than in previous years.

The behaviour of orchard No. 6 needs further explanation since the slow maturation rate illustrated substantiates previous results. Orchard No. 6 was harvested on 26 September or 9 days before the suggested minimum date. The Brix/acid ratio was raised to about 14 by further ripening in common storage, but when the pressure test fell to 71 N, the processor was informed that he should process the No. 6

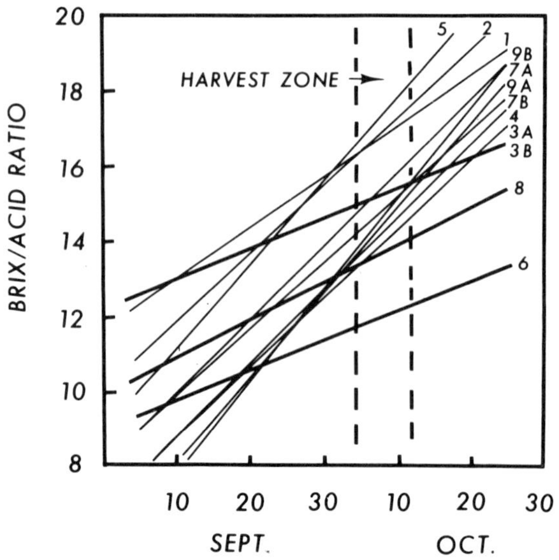

FIG. 4. Rate of maturation of Rhode Island Greening apples as measured by Brix/acid ratio in 12 orchards.

lot. The quality of the processed product resulting was judged lowest in this lot.

During storage of the crops from the 4 pilot orchards at the processing plant, pressure tests, Brix/acid ratio and samples for pilot plant processing continued to be taken. When the objective indices attained a reading of 15–20 Brix and 90 N, the processor was informed that he should process these lots.

Orchard No. 1, the eastern-most pilot orchard, needs special mention, particularly so that it may be contrasted with the results of the one orchard in which the apples were harvested early. At the start of the sampling in September, it was found that orchard No. 1 had apples that were among the most mature of the 12 orchards studied. Moreover, the apples appeared to be maturing fairly rapidly. However, the grower operating orchard No. 1 had an exceptionally heavy crop of McIntosh apples, and was unable to begin harvesting the Greenings until after 15 October. Since this crop had a Brix/acid ratio of 19 on 15 October, the processor was informed that the apples from orchard No. 1 should be processed as soon as they arrived at the plant. Instead of being harvested at minimum maturity to yield a Fancy product, this orchard was harvested at optimum maturity; and

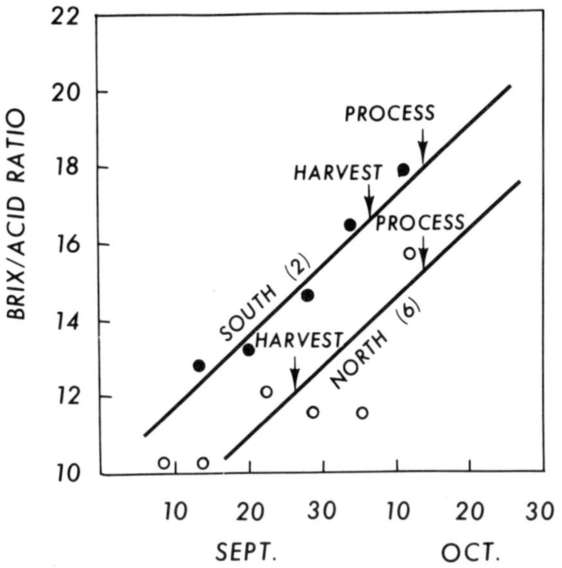

FIG. 5. Detailed information on the rate of maturation of Rhode Island Greening apples as measured by changing Brix/acid ratios for the North and South Pilot orchards.

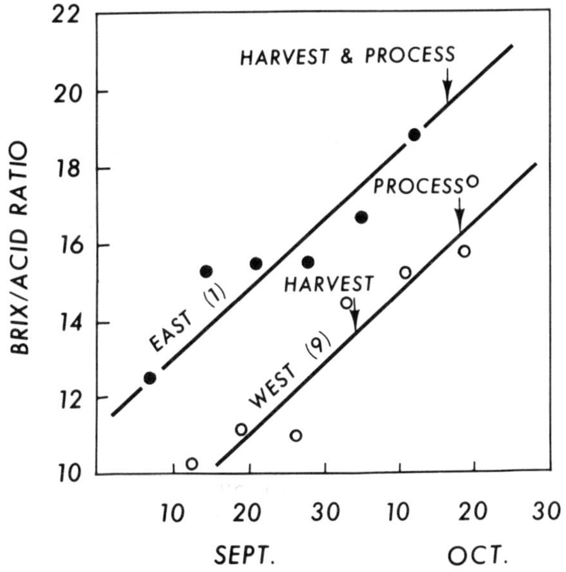

FIG. 6. Detailed information on the rate of maturation of Rhode Island Greening apples as measured by changing Brix/acid ratios for the East and West pilot orchards.

TABLE 1

CHANGE IN CROP AND SIZE GRADE ON RHODE ISLAND GREENING TREES WITH FULL CROPS (TAKEN FROM DATA IN REFERENCE 9)

	13 September	*23 September*	*4 October*
Average apple diameter, cm	6·78	7·01	7·21
Relative crop weight left on the tree	100	110	118
Distribution of above crop weight in size grades:			
Under 5·71 cm	1	0	0
5·71–6·35 cm	10	6	3
6·35–6·99 cm	47	37	22
Over 6·99 cm	42	67	93
Total	100	110	118
Relative value of apples	100	122	141

it was feared that any holding in common storage would detract from the finished product. The canned slices prepared from the apples in orchard No. 1 had superior colour and flavour, and the texture was firm.

More detailed data on changing Brix/acid ratios and suggestion to the growers and processors for the 4 pilot orchards are summarised in Figs 5 and 6. Actually, the decision to process the one orchard harvested early (No. 6) was made on the basis of changing pressure test in common storage rather than Brix/acid ratio.

In essence, all of the apples harvested on or after the minimum date suggested for harvesting yielded the Fancy grade for the processed product. This meant about one-quarter of a dollar more for each case of slices produced. The benefits to the growers are summarised in Table 1.

Needless to say, the entire New York apple industry benefited from this programme which was, in essence, monitored by a simple chemical expression of maturity and processing quality.

REFERENCES

1. Shallenberger, R. S. and Moyer, J. C. (1958). *J. Agric. Food Chem.*, **6**, 604–6.
2. Shallenberger, R. S., Pallesen, H. R. and Moyer, J. C. (1958). *Food Technol.*, **13**, 92–3.

3. SHALLENBERGER, R. S. and SAYRE, C. B. (1960). *Proc. Amer. Soc. Hort. Sci.*, **75**, 445–8.
4. ADKIN, J. D. and SHALLENBERGER, R. S. (1959). *Bitter Carrots and Apple Storages*, Farm Res. Reprint No. 263, N.Y. State Agric. Exp. Sta., Geneva.
5. SONDHEIMER, E. (1957). *Food Research*, **22**, 296–9.
6. SHALLENBERGER, R. S., ADKIN, J. D. and MOYER, J. C. (1960). *Food Res.*, **25**, 419–23.
7. LA BELLE, R. L., SHALLENBERGER, R. S., WAY, R. D., MATTICK, L. R. and MOYER, J. C. (1960). *Food Technol.*, **14**, 463–8.
8. SHALLENBERGER, R. S., LA BELLE, R. L. and MOYER, J. C. (1961). *Proc. N.Y. State Hort. Soc.*, 72–8.
9. CURTISS, JR., O. F. (1961). *Proc. N.Y. State Hort. Soc.*, 78–83.

Index

Acid detergent fibre method, 61
Advisory Committee on Pesticides, 86
Aflatoxin, 217
Agricultural policy, 33
Alcohol, 29
  insoluble solids, 75
American Dry Milk Institute (ADMI) Specifications, 234
American Society for Testing and Materials, 196
Analytical Methods Committee, 45–7
Animal husbandry, 265–6, 277
Antibodies, 119, 124, 127, 128
Antigens, 119, 124, 127
Apple
  harvesting, 316–17
  processing industry, 317
  slices, upgrading study, 316–22
Arsenic in milk, 216
Ascorbic acid, 25
Association of Official Analytical Chemists (AOAC), 42, 43
ATP, 144, 169
  bioluminescence, 167–70, 175

Bactec, 166
Bactometer-32, 164
Bactometer-120, 164
Beet purée, off-flavour, 312–14
BET monolayer water, 228, 229
Biological risks, 84
Bioluminescence, 167, 169
Bitterness in vegetables, 68
Bleeding effects, 271–2
Blood removal, 271
Botulism, 10, 143
British Standards Institution, 196
Brix/acid ratio, 318–20
Butter, 197, 222, 227, 229–31
Butter fat, 58–60
Butyric acid, 58, 59, 60

Cadmium in milk, 216
Calibration
  models, 68
  pitfalls and problems, 77–8
Campden Food Preservation Research Association, 192
Cancer, 26, 94
Canned foods, 143, 145
Canning process, 20, 23
  continuous process evaluation, 309–10
  dynamic system model, 303–4
  evaluation from external temperature history, 301–10
  model formulation, 304–7
  model performance, 306–7
  numerical integration, 304
Carbohydrate, 27, 32, 205, 267

Carcinogenicity, 88, 89, 93, 94
Carrots, off-flavour, 315–16
Caseinate, 240
Cell counting methods, 160
Cereal starches, 294
Cerebrovascular disease, 26
Cheese, 197, 218, 227, 231–4
Chemical/physical data and sensory variables, 72
Chemical residues as potential food contaminants, 90
Chemiluminescence, 167
Chicken rearing, 266
Chilling, 272
Chocolate, 191
Cholesterol, 26
Clostridium botulinum, 176, 227
Clostridium tyrobutyricum, 231
Codex Alimentarius, 43, 51
Coliform test, 137
Coliforms, 147
Colony counting methods, 160
Common Agricultural Policy, 51
Common Customs Tariff, 50
Community Bureau of Reference (BCR), 43
Computerised data analysis, 78
Confectionery, 191
Consumer
  complaints, 276
  education, 33, 35
  preferences, 276
Contamination, 78, 90, 137, 140, 150, 216
Cooking effects, 274
Copper in dairy products, 216
Cream, 222
Critical Control Points, 151, 152
Cryostat microtomy, 112
Cryostats, 110–12
Cured meat, 49–56

Dairy
  industry, 162
  products, 30, 213–56
    solubility of, 238
Degenerative diseases, 26
Descriptive profiles, 185–7
DFD (dark-firm-dry) meat, 257, 265, 267–8
Dietary goals, 27, 35
Dietary guidelines, 26–35
  implementation, 31–5
Difference tests, 184–5
Differential Interference Contrast (DIC) technique, 109
Direct epifluorescent filter technique (DEFT), 161, 175
Discrimination testing, 98
Drying process, 286–7
Duo-trio test, 184

Electrical stimulation, 272
Electrophoresis, 122–3
Emulsification, 241–6
Endothia parasitica, 231
Energy contents, 27, 29, 31, 32
Enrichment serology, 173
Enterobacteriaceae, 147
Enzyme
  digestion procedures, 61
  immunoassay (EIA), 124, 131
  inactivation, 21
  injection, 269
  preparation, 274
Enzyme-labelled immunosorbent assay (ELISA), 125–7, 129–32, 173
Enzyme multiplied immunoassay technique (EMIT), 124
Enzymic activity, 228
Epidemiology of food-borne disease, 142–3
Escherichia coli, 147, 159
European Economic Community, 33, 42, 43, 50, 51, 57, 58, 94, 260
Evaporation modelling, 286
Evisceration of poultry, 271
Extraction techniques, 169–70
Extrapolation process, 86
Extrinsic factors, 141
Extrusion-cooking, 285–6

Faecal coli, 147
Fat, 27, 30, 31, 32, 34, 35, 56, 215, 260
Fat-free protein, 52–5
Fat globule membrane, 219
Fatty acids, 60
Fibre
  consumption, 26
  contents, 18–19
  determination, 60–2
Fibre optic lamps, 106–7
Fish, 142, 192
Fish meals, 266
Flavour Profile, 186, 197
  Specification, 198
Fluorescence immunoassay (FIA), 124, 131
Fluorescence microscopy, 106, 109–10
Fluorescent antibody method, 172
Fluorescent reagents, 110
Foam stability, 246
Foamability, 246
Foaming capacity, 246
Folacin, 20, 22
Folate, 16, 21
Folic acid, 16
Food
  additives, 10, 86, 88, 89, 217
  analysis, 1–12, 41–4, 47, 117–18, 127–32
    direct and indirect method, 67–9
  chemicals, 87
  consumption, 39–64
  engineering system modelling, 285–8
  industry, 9, 10, 36
  processing, 17–26
  quality, 1–12
  quality analysis, 65–80
    trends in, 78–9
  regulation, 40
  specification, 40
  surveillance
    programme, 92
    studies, 91
    techniques, 93
Food Additives and Contaminants Committee, 86, 88
Food and Agriculture Organisation, 8
Food and Drugs Act 1955, 39, 87
Food-borne disease, 142–3
Food Standards Committee, 44, 45
Fractionation procedures, 61
Free fatty acid, 219
Freeze-drying process, 287–8
Freezing
  effects, 273
  loss of vitamins during, 20
Frozen foods, 7
Fruit, chemical basis, 311–23

Gas chromatography, 60, 176
Gastric cancer, 6, 7
Gelation, 240–1
Glucose syrups, 296
Glutamine, 314
L-Glutamine, 312
Goitre, 9
Grading of meat, 275, 278

Hazard
  analysis, 148–52
  characteristics, 150
Hazard Analysis Critical Control Points (HACCP) concept, 148, 151–3
Heat processing, 19
Heavy metals in dairy products, 216
Hemagglutination, 123
Hepatitis A, 143
Herbicides in dairy products, 216
Heterogeneous assays, 125
High-pressure liquid chromatography (HPLC), 21, 41
Histochemical staining, 112–14
Homogeneous assays, 124
Hydrolysis products of starch, 295

Hydrophobic grid membrane filter
(HGMF), 169–70
Hypertension, 217

Ice-cream, 138
Identification methods, 170–1
Immunoassays, 118
application to food analysis, 127–32
classical techniques, 120–3
design of, 120–7
labelled, 120, 123–7
non-proteinaceous components, 131–2
proteinaceous components, 129–31
sample preparation, 128–9
scope of, 127–8
Immunochemical interactions, 118
Immunodiffusion
characteristic patterns of precipitation, 122
single radial, 121
two-dimensional, 121
Immunological methods, 117–33
Immunological principles, 118–20
Impedimetric detection, 163–6
Implicit factors, 141
Infection, 140
Infective disease, 26
Information
feedback, 275
sources, 277
Infrared method for fat determination, 215
Inhibition/antiglobulin mode, 127
Institutional catering, 24–6, 31
Interference microscopy, 108
International Dairy Federation (IDF), 197
acetic acid/acetate method, 215
International Standards Organisation, 196, 197
Intrinsic factors, 141
In-vitro test systems, 89–90
Iodine levels in milk, 217
Iodine staining, 113
Irradiation effects, 23
Ischaemic heart disease, 26
Iso-Grid based methods, 170

Karl Fischer method, 229
Kinaesthesis, 186
Kjeldahl method, 47
Kraft Foods Ltd, 33

Label products, 266
Label system, 278
Lactobacillus, 166, 232
Leaching of nutrients during cooking, 19
Leatherhead Food RA, 288
Legislation, future prospects for, 81–95
Leuconostoc, 166
Light microscopy, 103–15
Limulus assay, 167
Lipid oxidation, 221–3
Lipids, 113–14
demonstration with osmium tetroxide vapour, 113–14
Lipolysis, 219
Lipoprotein lipase, 219
Lysinoalanine, 224

McGovern report, 27, 28, 29, 33
Maillard browning, 209, 223–5, 228
Maize yield determination, 297, 299
Malnutrition, 8
Market research in quality control, 97–101
Marketing system, 275
Mastership of Food Control (MFC), 11
Mathematical models, 78, 280
Meals-on-wheels, 25
Meat
colour, 261
content, 44–9

Meat—*contd.*
distribution, 273–4
fatness, 260
processing, 277
production, 259–60, 265
products, 45
regulations on, 44, 49
quality, 258–9
guidance as regards, 263
quality control, 257–78
crossbreeding effects, 264–5
feed effects, 266–7
influence of breed, 263–4
objective measurement, 259–61
selection effects, 264
subjective measurement, 261–3
transport to slaughter, 267–9
storage, 273–4
tenderisation, 273, 274
texture, 260
toughness, 268, 274, 275
Medicines Act 1964, 86
Mercury in milk, 216
Metachromasia, 112
Methyl butyrate procedure, 59
Methyl ester method, 59
Microbial activity, 227
Microbial ecology, 140–2
Microbiological examination, 143–8
Microbiological food poisoning, 139
Microbiological procedures, 143–8
Microbiological quality control, 135–55
future prospects, 175–6
need for good methods, 174–5
need for rapid methods, 159
new methods and their applications, 160–71
rapid methods for, 157–79
role of, 158
use of term, 136
Microbiological safety, 142
Microbiological specifications, 146–7
Microcalorimetry, 167
Microorganisms, 139, 140, 141, 147, 148, 150, 161, 162, 165, 168, 170, 214, 218, 227
Microscope
design, 104–8
illumination, 106
objectives, 105–6
stand, 104–5
Microwave cooking, 19, 22, 23
Mid-infrared transmission spectrum, 71–2
Milk, 7, 8, 137, 165, 214
composition of, 214
deterioration of, 218
enzymatic deterioration, 218–21
heat stability of, 225–6
hygiene and public health aspects, 216–18
iodine levels in, 217
microbiological deterioration, 218
pasteurisation, 7, 8, 216, 217, 220
production, 214–15
quality aspects, 215–16
quality control, 215
UHT, 218, 221, 225
Milk fat, 59
Milk powder, 222, 226, 234, 237
Milk products
deterioration of, 218–26
high-protein, 235
moisture in, 226–29
Milko-Tester method, 215
Minerals in milk, 214
Model building procedures, 280–3
Model classification, 283–5
Modelling applications, 279–89
Modelling research programme, 288
Monetary compensatory amounts, 51
Mucor meihei, 231
Mucor pusillus, 231
Multiple Linear Regression analysis, 70
Multivariate quantitative analysis, 69

Muscle sensations, 186
Mutagenicity, 88, 89

National Food Survey, 15
Near-infrared (NIR) reflectance spectrophotometers, 69–76
Neutral detergent fibre method, 61
Nicotinic acid, 23
Nitrate as a food additive, 217–18
Nitrite in foods, 10, 217
Nitrogen content, 46, 47
Nitrogen factor, 46, 47, 49, 52
Nitrosamines, 10, 218
No-effect-level, 94
Nomarski differential interference contrast, 109
Nutrient(s), 214
- activity, 21
- changes during processing, 17–26
- deficiencies, 17
- degradation, 21
- intakes, 15
- loss, 20, 21, 22, 25
- requirements, 14
- retention, 22, 24
- stability, 19

Nutrition, 8
- education, 33, 34
- information, 33, 34, 35
- teaching, 34

Nutritional adequacy, 14–26
Nutritional quality, 13–38
Nutritional sciences, 33
Nutritional value of household food, 14

Off-flavours
- beet purée, 312–13
- processed carrots, 315–16

Optical contrast methods, 108–10
Optical microscopy, 103–15
Optical probe, 275
Orange juice, 166
Organoleptic properties, 22
Osmium tetroxide, 113–14
Osmotic manipulation, 227
Ouchterlony, 121, 129

Packaging materials, 93, 95
Paired Comparisons test, 184
Partial Least Square regression methods, 72, 74
Pasteurisation, 7, 8, 216, 217, 220
Pathogens, 139, 146–7, 166, 216
Penicillium roqueforti, 217
Pesticides in dairy products, 216
Pesticides Safety Precautions Scheme, 86
pH effects of milk and heat stability, 220–1, 225, 236, 241, 267, 268
pH values, 225
Phase contrast microscopy, 108
Phosphatase test, 137
Pig
- meat, 267
- production, 275
- slaughter, 267

Polarising microscopy, 108
Politics of Health Group, 9
Polychlorinated biphenyls residues in milk, 216
Polychlorinated dibenzodioxins residues in milk, 216
Polycyclic aromatic hydrocarbons residues in milk, 216
Polyunsaturated fatty acids, 26
Poly(vinyl chloride), 93, 95
Potassium chloride to replace sodium chloride in milk, 217
Potato chips, 206–7
Potato tubers, 203, 204
- chemical composition of, 204–9
- dry matter and starch contents, 204
- flesh darkening, 209
- nitrogen compounds, 207–8
- organic acids, 208
- processing, 204
- specific gravity, 204
- storage and quality, 203–11

Potato tubers—*contd.*
  sugar content and composition, 206
  vitamin C content, 208
Poultry, 142, 273
  industry, 261
  raising, 266
  slaughtering, 275
  water content, 56–8
Principal Component Analysis, 72, 73
Process analysis, 279–83
Propionibacteria, 227
Protein(s), 27, 32, 214, 235–46
  emulsifying properties of, 241
  solubility, 236
  viscosity, 236
Proteinase, 220, 221
Proteolysis, 220–1
PSE (pale-soft-exudative) meat, 257, 265, 267–8, 270
Psychochemistry, 311
Psychophysical chemistry, 312
Pyrrolidonecarboxylic acid (PCA), 312–13

QC6, 192
Quality, definitions, 182
Quality control
  aspects of, 182–3
  contribution of, 277
  market research in, 97–101
  textbooks on, 194
  see also Microbiological quality control; Sensory quality control
Quantitative microscopy, 114
Quartz halogen illumination, 106, 109

Radioimmunoassay (RIA), 124, 125, 131, 132
Radiometric detection, 166–7
Raw meats, 168
Recipe Hazard Analysis, 149
Recommended daily amount (RDA), 14, 15, 16, 26
Reichert–Polenske–Kirchner procedure, 58
Relative Ability of Prediction, 74, 75, 76
Rennets, 232
Research and development in the meat industry, 276–7
Rhode Island Greening, 316–22
Riboflavin, 23
Rickets, 9
Risk-assessment, 82, 83, 93, 94
Risk–benefit decisions, 87
Risk-estimation, 82
Risk-evaluation, 82, 93
Risk-management, 81, 83, 85, 92, 93, 95
Risk-perception, 82
Risk-prediction, 85
Roquefortine, 217
Rose–Gottlieb method, 215
Rowett Research Institute, 8

Salads, 143
Salmonella, 159, 166, 171–4
Salmonellae, 142, 148, 149
Salmonellosis, 143, 149
Salt, 7, 26, 53, 55
Sample preparation, 110–12, 128
Sampling procedures, 146
Sandwich/antiglobulin mode, 127
Sausages, 44
Sensory quality control, 181–201
  aspects of, 183
  current practices, 187–8
  developments in UK, 191
  developments in USA, 189
  historical background, 188–9
  international symposium, 195
  international view, 193–4
  methods of, 183–7
  recent symposia, 196–8
  selected developments, 190–1
  senses involved, 183
  terminology, 183
Sensory quality prediction, 73–6

Sensory variables prediction, 72
Shellfish, 142
Slaughter
  conditions, 267–79
  effects, 270–1
  methods, 275
Specimen preparation, *See* Sample preparation
Standard error of estimation, 70, 75
Standard error of prediction, 70, 75
Standards organisations, 195–6
Starch and starch products, 31, 34, 40, 113, 114
  analytical methods, 296–8
  general directions for, 293–6
  quality analysis, 292
  quality control, 291–300
  quality criteria, 292
  quality standards, 292–5
Starch demonstration using iodine vapour, 113
Statistical control chart techniques, 152
Stereology, 114
Sterilising effect, evaluation of, 302
Strecker degradation, 223
Streptococcus cremoris, 232
Streptococcus diacetyllactis, 232
Streptococcus lactis, 232
Streptococcus thermophilus, 232
Strokes, incidence of, and salt intake, 6, 7
Stunning methods, 269–72
Sugar, 31, 268

Temperature history at can-centre, 302
Tetrachloroanisoles, 266
Tetrachlorophenols, 266
Thermal denaturation, 237
Thermal destruction of microorganisms, 302
Thermal processing, 19
Thiamin, 22, 23
Thiobarbituric acid (TBA) test, 222
Toluene distillation method, 229
Toluidine blue staining, 112–13
Total colony count, 147
Total plate count, 147
Total viable count, 147
Toxic metals in dairy products, 216
Toxic substances in foods, 139
Toxicity testing, 87, 88, 89, 92
Toxicological research, 87
Toxicological tests, 86
Toxins, 139, 146–7, 150
Triangular test, 184
Triglycerides, 219
Tuber and root starches, 295
Tuberculosis, 7, 8

Vacuum packing, 274
Vapour staining, 113–14
Vegetables, 20
  bitterness in, 68
  chemical basis, 311–23
Veterinary Products Committee, 87
Vinyl chloride, 93
Vitamin A, 19, 20
Vitamin B complex, 18, 23
Vitamin C, 18–20, 22–6, 35, 208
Vitamin D, 20
Vitamin(s), 214
  losses, 20
  water-soluble, 19

Water absorption, 237–40
Water activity, 228
Water/protein ratio, 51–6
Water sorption, 227
Whey protein concentrate, 240
Whippability, 246

Xanthine oxidase, 221

Youden Rank Sum Test, 59

Zeiss Micro Videomat, 114
Zero Tolerance concept, 147
Zinc intake, 16